A WORLD BANK COUNTRY STUDY

China
External Trade and Capital

The World Bank
Washington, D.C., U.S.A.

Manufactured in the United States of America
First printing September 1988

World Bank Country Studies are reports originally prepared for internal use as part of the continuing analysis by the Bank of the economic and related conditions of its developing member countries and of its dialogues with the governments. Some of the reports are published informally with the least possible delay for the use of governments and the academic, business and financial, and development communities. Thus, the typescript has not been prepared in accordance with the procedures appropriate to formal printed texts, and the World Bank accepts no responsibility for errors.

Any maps that accompany the text have been prepared solely for the convenience of readers. The designations and presentation of material in them do not imply the expression of any opinion whatsoever on the part of the World Bank, its affiliates, or its Board or member countries concerning the legal status of any country, territory, city, or area or of the authorities thereof or concerning the delimitation of its boundaries or its national affiliation.

The complete backlist of publications from the World Bank is shown in the annual *Index of Publications*, which contains an alphabetical title list and indexes of subjects, authors, and countries and regions; it is of value principally to libraries and institutional purchasers. The latest edition of each of these is available free of charge from the Publications Sales Unit, Department F, The World Bank, 1818 H Street, N.W., Washington, D.C. 20433, U.S.A., or from Publications, The World Bank, 66 avenue d'Iéna, 75116 Paris, France.

Library of Congress Cataloging-in-Publication Data

China : external trade and capital.
p. cm. -- (A World Bank country study)
ISBN 0-8213-1121-2
1. China--Commercial policy. 2. China--Foreign economic relations. 3. China--Commerce. I. World Bank. II. Series.
HF1604.C45 1988
382'.0951--dc19 88-20815
CIP

This report and its annexes are based on the findings of a mission that visited China during October 1986. In addition to interviews and discussions in Beijing, the mission visited Zhengzhou (Henan Province), Shanghai, Fuzhou and Xiamen Special Economic Zone (Fujian Province). The mission consisted of Gerhard Pohl (mission leader), Peter Harrold (deputy mission leader, trade policy) and Joel Bergsman (foreign direct investment), Basil Kavalsky (foreign exchange allocation), Margaret Kelly (IMF, foreign exchange policy and debt management) Hyung-Ki Kim (technology transfer), Wouter Tims (primary commodity trade), Mieko Nishimizu (import policies), Marko Voljc (export policies), Christine Wallich (external capital flows and debt management) and Candy Wong (mission secretary). Research assistance in Washington was provided by Nicola Favia, Yasheng Huang, Lili Liu, Min Zhu and Umnay Sae-Hau.

The mission was accompanied by a Chinese counterpart team from a number of government agencies, led by Zhu Ang, Deputy Director, International Trade Research Institute, Ministry of Foreign Economic Relations and Trade.

CHINA

EXTERNAL TRADE AND CAPITAL REFORM ISSUES AND OPTIONS

MAIN REPORT

Table of Contents

Page No.

TABLES IN TEXT

BOXES

ANNEXES

CHINA

EXTERNAL TRADE AND CAPITAL

Summary and Conclusions

1. As a central element of its overall strategy to improve allocative efficiency and promote the modernization and growth of the economy, the Chinese government introduced at the end of 1978 a process of reform aimed at decentralizing production and investment decisions and subjecting them increasingly to market influences. So far, the most far-reaching reforms have occurred in the rural sector with the introduction of the household responsibility system, under which households are the principal production and decision-making units in agriculture and related rural activities.

2. While reforms in the urban industrial and commercial sectors proceeded at a slower pace, the introduction of the "open door" policy in early 1979 was one of the earliest and most wide-ranging elements of the reform package, and a major departure from the preceding two decades of self-reliance and autarkic economic and technological development. Overall, the "open door" policy has been very successful, yielding dramatic increases in international trade and exchanges and contributing to higher efficiency and higher growth of the Chinese economy.

3. In October 1986, a World Bank mission visited China to analyze, in collaboration with a Chinese counterpart team from a number of government agencies, the present status of China's foreign trade and capital system and, on the basis of this analysis, make suggestions for further improvements. This summary provides a short overview of the missions findings and recommendations that are further detailed in the Main Report and a companion volume of Annexes that provides further analysis and detail.

The "Open Door" Policy in International Respective

4. Since the "open door" policy was adopted at the end of 1978, rapidly increasing exports of raw materials and manufactured goods, increased earnings from tourism and other services, and the use of foreign direct investment and other capital inflows have permitted a dramatic increase of imports of capital goods, machinery, technology and materials in short supply. This was clearly a major factor in the dramatic improvement in the efficiency of the Chinese economy, although other factors--such as the rural reforms and partial enterprise and price reforms so far introduced--were also important, and perhaps more important than the "open door" policy alone.

5. While initial results of the "open door" policy have thus been impressive, both in terms of the immediate objective to increase the capacity to import and the ultimate objective of raising economic efficiency through technology imports, present policies with respect to foreign trade and capital flows are far from optimal. Further policy changes could contribute to sustain recent rapid growth of external trade and thus to increase technology

transfer and economic efficiency. Without further changes it is quite possible that foreign trade growth will slow down, as the high rates of recent years reflect primarily the transitional effect in moving from almost complete insulation to a partly open, but by international standards still relatively inefficient foreign trade system.

6. Different economies have adopted different trade policies, ranging from the almost complete autarky adopted by China during the past two decades, to the extremely open "laissez faire" approach adopted, for example, by Hong Kong or (since 1967) by Singapore. In between these extremes are a great number of different policy regimes, characterized by different degrees (and different instruments) of government intervention designed mainly to protect certain sectors from foreign competition. In developing countries protection is usually extended to industry, while industrialized countries often protect agriculture or declining industrial activities.

7. International experience suggest that developing countries that have adopted more outward-oriented trade strategies have had better economic performances than countries that have adopted an inward-oriented economic strategy (paras. 1.12-1.19). Outward oriented trade policies involve no, or very little, use of administrative restrictions on foreign trade, promote exports through flexible exchange rate policies which maintain competitiveness, apply relatively low and uniform tariffs on imports, and provide import duty and indirect tax rebates for export production.

8. Under outward-oriented (or "neutral") trade policies, export and import-substituting activities are equally (or almost equally) favored. By contrast, a trade system that relies extensively on administrative import restrictions and high (and often highly variable) tariff rates inevitably creates a bias against exports, because the exchange rate tends to become overvalued (lower in terms of domestic currency units per unit of foreign exchange) as import demand is artificially lowered. This overvaluation of the exchange rate inevitably makes import-substituting activities more profitable than export activities. The effect of an administratively fixed (and often even more highly overvalued) exchange rate usually implies an even larger anti-export bias.

9. Developing countries that have moved to an outward-oriented (or "neutral") trade system have not only experienced far more rapid growth of exports and imports, they have also experienced faster growth of domestic economic activity, often considerably exceeding the direct impact of increased foreign trade on domestic economic activity (para. 1.14 and Table 1.1). These indirect benefits of an outward-oriented trade strategy are related to productivity increases made possible by more rapid technology transfer and diffusion into the domestic economy. Direct contacts with buyers and suppliers and transfer of technical personnel between enterprises are among the most important channels for enhanced technology transfer and diffusion.

10. Some costs as well as benefits may be associated with increased foreign trade and external economic relations. One potential disadvantage is that foreign competition could stifle infant industries--activities that could become internationally competitive, but only after some time. Other

disadvantages include the possible transmission of primary product price volatility into the domestic economy, and the possible emergence of large trade deficits or surpluses. But the skillful use of appropriate policy instruments can soften this tradeoff--minimizing the costs while securing the benefits. International experience also suggests that developing countries that have adopted an outward-oriented economic strategy have been able to adjust to external shocks more easily than inward-oriented countries (paras. 1.18-1.19 and Table 1.3).

11. By comparison to outward-oriented developing countries, China's "open door" policy today would have to be characterized as "inward-looking." It continues to place heavy reliance on administrative import and export decisions, including mandatory planning; it restricts imports and some exports through licensing and other quantitative restrictions; it imposes high (and highly variable) tariffs on imported goods to protect domestic industry from foreign competition; it limits direct contacts between domestic enterprises and foreign buyers and suppliers through the intermediation of monopolistic Foreign Trade Corporations; and it uses a cumbersome administrative foreign exchange allocation system, and is still somewhat inflexible in its use of the exchange rate as an economic lever.

12. The impressive record of countries applying outward-oriented trade and development strategies deserves China's consideration. But, is a switch to an outward-oriented development strategy possible and feasible for a large country like China in today's world of slow economic growth and protectionism? What would happen in international markets if other large countries such as India were to pursue the same strategy at the same time?

13. The most important reason for an outward-oriented trade policy is to reap the indirect benefits of a more open trading system, including the myriad of efficiency gains that enterprises can make when they are in direct contact with buyers, suppliers and competitors. China should not adopt an outward-oriented strategy merely, or even primarily, to maximize export revenues. Foreign competition provides a spur to the efficiency of domestic enterprises and provides strong incentives to keep up with progress in technology, organization and management practices made elsewhere. The present administratively intermediated foreign trade system, in contrast, creates an "air-lock", in which most of the indirect benefits of external trade are blocked from reaching the domestic economy.

Key Features of the Present Trade System

14. During the 1949-78 period, China's economic strategy was essentially one of self-reliance. Domestic needs were to be satisfied as much as possible by domestic production, and foreign trade was used to supplement shortfalls in such production--primarily in food, essential raw materials, and capital goods.

15. Trade flows were determined through a centralized planning system under the authority of the Ministry of Foreign Trade (MFT). The annual foreign trade planning process would identify the required imports, and exports would be selected to finance the desired level of imports, so as to

avoid any significant trade deficits that would require foreign borrowing. Once the plan was determined, it would be entrusted to the twelve main centralized foreign trade corporations (FTCs) for implementation. To ensure the insulation of the domestic market, the FTCs had monopoly powers within specified scopes of business, and they would procure all goods for export and sell all procured imports at the domestic prices for these goods.

16. From 1979 to 1985 the trade system evolved rapidly. The centralized FTCs lost some of their monopoly powers, and their branch offices began to operate as separate units. In addition, provincial authorities created their own FTCs to fulfill provincial export aspirations, and line ministries found it convenient to establish corporations to engage in external trade in their products directly. A formal system of foreign exchange retention [1/] at the provincial and enterprise level was also introduced, and, when combined with the introduction of import licensing and an initial decentralization of license-issuing authority, this period saw a rapid change in the locus of trade activity. From being a residual activity carried out in a highly centralized manner, trade became, during this period, a central focus of effort. These various reforms in trade practices over the period were summarized in the September 1984 document on the reform of the trade system adopted by the State Council (para. 2.15 and Box 2.2). Nevertheless, many trade practices, such as pricing and administrative allocation remained essentially unchanged.

The Impact of the Present Trade System

17. The "Air-Lock". The FTCs are the main point of contact between China and the world market, and Chinese enterprises are to a large extent insulated from world price developments and have only limited contact with foreign buyers and suppliers. This isolation was an explicit aim of the trade system as originally constructed, as world market forces were viewed as irrational and potentially harmful to national interests. Although much has changed since 1979, the air-lock still exists to a considerable extent. The air-lock creates four problems, which may not have been critical in the early years of export development, but which will become increasingly important as China seeks to expand exports of new, less homogeneous products:

(a) Inefficiency of Exporting. Under the current system, exports are not determined efficiently according to China's comparative cost advantage. The economic costs of earning foreign exchange vary widely among different export products with profits made on some, and losses on others.

(b) Inappropriate Export Patterns. Because world prices are not passed on to producers, the production of profitable exports is not encouraged nor is production of unprofitable exports discouraged, because the producers are not made aware of, and thus do not respond

---

1/ A foreign exchange retention quota is a right to purchase foreign exchange based on past export sales.

to, the profits and losses incurred. (Even if passed on, enterprises might not respond in a fully appropriate way, because they are not yet fully responsible for their profits and losses.)

(c) Lack of Information. The air-lock of the FTC between the producer and the market prevents enterprises from reacting in a timely fashion to market opportunities. At the same time, the absence of contacts between foreign buyers and sellers and Chinese enterprises means that these enterprises are foregoing much "free" technical assistance in such areas as product specifications and design, new product developments, capital equipment, factory design, quality control, etc. Experience elsewhere has shown such direct contacts between foreign buyers and suppliers and domestic enterprises to be one of the most important, most effective and cheapest sources of technology transfer and marketing know-how.

(d) Lack of Competition from Imports. Import controls and high tariffs prevent import competition from stimulating efficiency in domestic production.

18. Foreign Exchange Allocation. Foreign exchange allocation mechanisms have two essential, overlapping functions: they allocate foreign exchange among the various potential users, and they determine the price at which foreign exchange is traded. The importance of this latter function cannot be overemphasized, and has two major effects. Firstly, the exchange rate alters the relative attractiveness of producing a specific good or service for export markets vis-a-vis the domestic market and the ability of the domestic product to compete with imports. In addition, if changes in the exchange rate are permitted to have an impact on domestic prices, the relative prices of tradeable goods and nontradeables (such as power, domestic services, restaurants) will be altered, thus influencing the production and investment decisions of enterprises. It is partly because China does not permit the exchange rate to move in such a way as to equalize demand and supply of foreign exchange that it is necessary to allocate foreign exchange administratively, since at the present price of foreign exchange there is inadequate supply to meet demand.

19. Protection of Domestic Production. Protection of domestic production from imports acts automatically as a disincentive to exports, and limits the many indirect benefits of engaging in foreign trade (paras. 1.7 and 2.30). Protection in the Chinese trade system is provided through four mechanisms: trade planning, import pricing, licensing and tariffs. As trade decision-making is decentralized, and international prices are passed on to final users through wider application of the "agency system", import licensing and tariffs will become the predominant sources of protection.

Reforming Trade Institutions

20. With its enormous resource base and population, China could eventually produce and export a wide variety of goods and services. The question is what to produce and what to import and export, and how these decisions should be made. Such decisions become increasingly complex as an economy

develops, and international experience suggests that they can be made most efficiently by enterprise managers guided by market prices (modified, if necessary, by "economic levers"). In foreign trade, it will be important to establish a policy framework that promotes efficient decisions in trade and production. Such a trade reform will necessarily inter-relate with other areas of reform, notably enterprise reforms, pricing policies and macro-economic policies (para. 2.36 and Chapter IV).

21. International experience suggests that China could benefit substantially by removing the tight compartmentalization or "air-lock" between domestic and international markets that results from the present operating rights and procedures of the FTCs. However, if decentralized decision-making is to lead to efficient operations, competition needs to be introduced, and prices and other economic levers (in particular the exchange rate) have to reflect the true costs of resource use. Some of the specific measures that could be considered include:

(a) Eliminating, over time, the product-specific trading rights of FTCs, permitting them to engage in the trade of any commodity, thus becoming de facto general trading corporations (GTCs).

(b) Making FTCs fully responsible for profits and losses, and eliminating any plan exports that imply substantial losses to the FTCs. At the same time, subsidies for command plan imports that remain necessary because of large differentials between domestic and international prices which continue for domestic policy reasons (e.g. fertilizer) should be provided by specific product subsidies in the state budget, rather than from FTC revenues, or general subsidies to FTCs.

(c) Eliminating the exclusive right of Foreign Trade Corporations to engage in foreign trade and leaving the choice of whether or not to use an FTC, and which FTC to use, to enterprises. FTCs would then become service organizations that would have to justify their role by being more efficient than other foreign trade channels. The only exception would be "special" exports, for which China faces inelastic demand or has a very large market share (see paras. 2.53-2.56).

(d) Eliminating the strict separation of domestic and foreign trade, giving FTCs the right to engage in all types of domestic wholesale and retail trade and domestic commercial organizations the right to engage in foreign trade.

(e) The role of foreign buyers and foreign trade corporations in China's external trade could also be increased. Joint ventures between Chinese FTCs and foreign GTCs could, for example, bring benefits from the latter's extensive marketing networks, and facilitate the transfer of marketing know-how to China's FTCs.

22. These recommendations are quite consistent with the September 1984 report of the Ministry of Foreign Economic Relations and Trade on the future

reform of the trade system. However, in many key respects the reforms outlined in that report have not been implemented, and remain the key institutional reform issues. Once the decision to decentralize to enterprises has been taken, it will be necessary not only to make the institutional reforms described above, but also to adjust some of the economic levers affecting trade decisions.

Reforming the Trade Environment

23. Exchange Rate Policies and Foreign Exchange Allocation. If trade decision-making is decentralized to enterprises, and international prices are passed on to both exporters and importers, the exchange rate will become a more important factor in determining the volume and pattern of exports and imports. The exchange rate can only play this role efficiently if exchange rate policy is implemented flexibly and actively to ensure that Chinese exports remain competitive in world markets and, in combination with other policies, ensures a viable medium-term balance of payments.

24. At the present time, China maintains a managed floating exchange rate system, under which the exchange rate is based on developments in the balance of payments and movements in costs and exchange rates of China's major trading partners. However, the present exchange rate has only limited impact on trade decisions. Foreign trade and other external transactions are still largely determined by administrative interventions, including the trade plan, mandatory imports and exports, administrative restrictions on a substantial number of import and export transactions, and so on. These decisions, however, are being increasingly decentralized to local governments, and enterprises can use their foreign exchange retention quotas to import machinery and other unrestricted goods for modernization investments ("technical transformation").

25. Trade reforms of the type proposed in this report would make the exchange rate a more effective policy instrument by increasing links between foreign and domestic prices. While trade reforms will make the exchange rate a more effective policy instrument, it is also true that a more appropriate and flexible exchange rate policy would make trade reforms more effective. This objective could be achieved by a more active use of exchange rate policy within the context of the present exchange system. Alternatively, China may decide to allow market forces to play a more direct role in exchange rate determination and move to a system in which the exchange rate would be determined in the market by the supply and demand for foreign exchange. This could be particularly useful during the transition towards a more market-oriented foreign trade system. It would be appropriate and useful to discuss changes in foreign exchange allocation and exchange rate policy with the IMF.

26. If the present managed floating exchange rate system is maintained, exchange rate adjustments would be needed to compensate for the removal of administrative import restrictions or subsidies. Balance-of-payments developments, desired reserve levels and indicators of international competitiveness (see para 3.6 and Box 3.1) could be used to estimate the required adjustments. An advantage of this option is that it would not represent a major change from the present exchange rate system, but would introduce more

flexibility than at present. A disadvantage of this option is that it would take quite some time (several months or quarters) to ascertain whether any exchange rate adjustments made have been sufficient to compensate for the removal of trade restrictions or other changes in the domestic or international economy. This might make it difficult to phase out administrative allocation of foreign exchange rapidly.

27. An alternative approach that would permit a more rapid transition towards market determined allocation of foreign exchange would be to permit trading of foreign exchange retention rights among enterprises and other units at a freely negotiated price. This would be similar to the approach used in the domestic market where transactions at flexible prices have been introduced while maintaining fixed prices for the same goods allocated by the Plan.

28. While not desirable as a permanent solution, such a system would improve on current practice. Since the exchange rate for foreign exchange retention rights would be freely determined, it would permit rapid removal of administrative restrictions without running the danger of incurring large balance of payments deficits. The exchange rate established in the market for foreign exchange retention rights would give an indication of the direction and magnitude of the required adjustment of the official exchange rate to compensate for the removal of administrative restrictions.

29. The problems with such a system are similar to the use of dual (plan-market) prices in the domestic economy. Enterprises or individuals that have access to foreign exchange at the official rate will always be tempted to sell it at the market price for foreign exchange established in the market for foreign exchange retention rights. It would thus be desirable to move the official exchange rate as rapidly as possible towards the rate established in the market for foreign exchange retention rights, eliminating any gap between the two rates after a relatively brief transition period.

30. To ensure that the rate established in the market for foreign exchange retention rights is realistic, it would be important for the market in foreign exchange retention rights to cover a large proportion of foreign exchange transaction and to have a large number of enterprises participate, particularly those enterprises that are already responsible for profits and losses. It will also be desirable to increase the foreign exchange retention ratio for enterprises, ultimately to 100%.

31. The State will, of course, remain a major user of foreign exchange for key projects. The creation of such a market for foreign exchange does not mean that the State would have lower access to foreign exchange, but that it may be obtained in different ways. Indeed, creation of a market in foreign exchange can be expected to increase the supply of foreign exchange available to the economy as a whole--and thus potentially to the State--both by reducing the hoarding of foreign exchange, and by stimulating exports. If the increased retention ratios reduce the foreign exchange available directly to the State below the desired level, the State can always enter the foreign exchange market directly to purchase additional foreign exchange to fund key projects. In addition, however, the State could save itself considerable levels of foreign exchange by changing the ways it funds the inputs for key

projects. Instead of maintaining low prices for the command plan imports and subsidizing all such imports, it would be preferable to provide specific subsidies direct to the key projects, but adjust the prices of the strategic products, so that the subsidy is provided for the priority uses, but not for non-priority uses, as is the case at present.

32. It is also important to consider the relationship between the exchange rate and domestic prices. The exchange rate links international and domestic prices and determines the relative price between tradeable and non-tradeable goods and services. In general, changes in the exchange rate will affect the relative prices of different goods and services, and not the general level of prices. Inflation is primarily caused by excess money creation, and this will eventually necessitate an exchange rate change. Of course, a depreciation of the exchange rate will raise the prices of imports, but international experience has shown that such price effects have frequently been anticipated prior to such a depreciation. It is thus usually the case that rather than an exchange rate change causing inflation, it is inflation which causes the exchange rate change.

Import Licensing and Tariff Reform

33. Trade reforms will be more effective if a more flexible exchange rate policy is implemented. Appropriate fiscal and monetary policies would also need to be implemented. Additional enterprise and price reforms would also complement exchange reforms. At the same time, trade reforms would also make the exchange rate a more effective policy instrument. A flexible exchange rate policy would allow quantitative restrictions to be gradually phased out. However, there may remain valid industrial policy reasons to restrict certain imports to protect domestic enterprises[2/] for a limited period of time until they have become internationally competitive. Such protection should be provided mostly by tariffs rather than import licensing on other administrative import restrictions. Only in very exceptional cases are quantitative restrictions equivalent, or perhaps even superior, to price (tariff) interventions (para. 2.64). It would thus be desirable to replace licensing by tariffs as soon as possible.

34. The present tariff schedule, with rates ranging from 0-200%, results in a highly variable 'effective' protection of different industrial subsectors. International experience has shown that such highly variable protection can lead to substantial inefficiencies. Tariff rates should therefore be made more uniform, perhaps with a range of 10-50%. On the other hand, the widespread exemptions from import duties for machinery and capital goods imported for capital construction and technical transformation result in a penalty on domestic producers of such goods, which could, in many cases, achieve efficient production in China. Tariff exemptions for capital construction and technical renovation should thus be eliminated. Tariff exemptions or rebates would then be restricted to imported inputs for export production (see

---

2/ Ideally, production subsidies would be preferable to trade measures, but budgetary resources might not be sufficient.

below). Tariff reform would probably be best phased over several years. In the first stages it will be desirable to pre-announce planned tariff adjustments planned to occur over a period of several years so that domestic enterprises can adjust accordingly.

Export Incentives

35. The most important export incentive at present is the foreign exchange retention system for enterprises, which compensates to some extent for the anti-export bias of the present trade system. The retention system could be expanded by making access to foreign exchange more automatic, both for exports and for import-substituting enterprises, since a dollar saved through efficient import substitution is as good as a dollar earned through increased exports. However, as long as tariffs or other import restrictions are applied for reasons of industrial policy (e.g. infant industry protection), the system will continue to have an anti-export bias. One way to reduce this anti-export bias is to rebate to exporting enterprises the tariff duties collected on inputs used in the production of export goods. This is administratively challenging, but there is a large international experience which could help avoid some of the difficulties. In this way, any enterprise anywhere in China would reap the advantages that the Special Economic Zones now provide, and this would at the same time, provide the indirect advantages of greater export orientation (para. 2.67) throughout the economy.

36. A second measure that could be taken to reduce anti-export bias is to rebate domestic taxes on export production. An administratively efficient and internationally acceptable way of doing so would be to replace the present industrial and commercial tax with a value-added tax system. This would, of course, be a major undertaking and should await a more general reform of China's tax system. It may also be possible to link such rebate systems with a system for permitting access by indirect exporters to foreign exchange retention rights.

37. A third measure, and one that could perhaps be taken earlier, would be to provide improved access to domestic working capital financing to all exporters and, through a system of "domestic letters of credit", to all enterprises that provide inputs into production for exports. Such a credit facility would, of course, have to be consistent with the overall credit plan of the People's Bank of China. Such a system would also make it possible to extend rebates of tariffs on imported goods used in export production to indirect exporters (suppliers to export enterprises).

38. These export incentives would all require advance planning and administrative sophistication and should be considered for implementation only in the medium term--once substantial progress has been made in the reform of the foreign exchange allocation mechanism, the decentralization of foreign trade rights, the reduction of detailed administrative foreign trade planning and licensing, and a reduction and harmonization of tariff rates. An implementation of, say, five years would appear feasible.

Foreign Direct Investment

39. Foreign direct investment that brings in desired advanced technology and capital can be stimulated by a number of policy actions. These include, most importantly, measures that would make it less necessary to allocate foreign exchange. Recently, measures have been announced that would make it easier for foreign joint ventures to gain access to foreign exchange by becoming de facto foreign traders on behalf of domestic enterprises. While this is progress in the right direction, access to foreign exchange could be made even more automatic through implementing a more flexible exhange rate policy. Transport costs, slight quality differences, brand-name recognition and other similar factors often make import substitution easier than export promotion--particularly in new products using more advanced technology. Thus, there is a very useful role to be played by foreign joint ventures in producing for the domestic market, and in a number of sectors it may take ten years or more until production for exports will become competitive.

40. More important than preventing 'exploitation' by foreign investors (that might, in the worst case, involve a small fraction of production value in excessive royalties, overpricing of supplies or services) is to prevent economically inefficient foreign direct investment. Apart from domestic economic inefficiencies, the potentially most worrisome source of inefficiency is excessive protection from import competition. Fortunately, China has a very large domestic market that will justify numerous enterprises (and joint ventures) in nearly any line of business, thus permitting vigorous competition among domestic enterprises as well as joint ventures. But in some cases this will not be enough, and high levels of import protection could seriously reduce the incentives for efficiency.

Interrelations with Other Reform Measures

41. While the trade policy measures summarized in the preceding section are, as stated, closely related to other economic reforms, progress can be made in implementing these trade reforms independently of progress in other economic reform areas. The most crucial precondition is the maintenance of domestic macroeconomic balance and stability. All too many developing countries have in the past attempted to reform their trade systems in the face of large government budget deficits, permissive monetary and credit policies to finance these deficits, and resulting rapid inflation. Their task has often been rendered even more difficult by heavy external indebtedness that left little room to maneuver, as short-term reductions in exports or surges in imports could simply not be financed. But very often also, trade reform measures have failed because initial steps were too timid, particularly with respect to exchange rate system reforms.

42. Maintaining Macro-Economic Balance. Efficient decentralization of decision-making and introduction of further reforms would be much facilitated by stable aggregate demand and stable prices. Of particular importance in this regard are further steps to restrain government spending and to give the People's Bank full authority to limit the expansion of money and credit. Increased interest rates, particularly on enterprise deposits and capital construction loans, could help to dampen excess demand pressures and to

channel resources to the investments with the highest yield. Stable macroeconomic management is particularly important in managing the balance of payments and in limiting foreign borrowing to a viable level (Chapter III). Apart from prudent budgetary and credit policies, appropriate exchange rate adjustments as discussed above are essential to maintain macroeconomic balance.

43. China does not, at this moment, face extreme macroeconomic imbalances. However, the experience of the past two or three years shows that China's economic and political system is not immune to such dangers either. There are pressures for continued high government expenditures and easy bank credit, at the very time when the role of the central government is being redefined and revenues decentralized to enterprises and local governments. When combined with a low political tolerance for inflation, this leads to calls for renewed or continued administrative controls over prices, imports and so on. Macroeconomic balance is therefore crucial during a transition towards a more efficient trade system based on decentralization of decision-making and competition.

44. Domestic Economic Reforms. In other respects, trade reforms could begin to be implemented relatively independently of the progress of domestic reforms. This is so, because in many respects the decentralization to enterprises of foreign trade decisions is currently trailing behind the decentralization of domestic production and marketing decisions. Similarly, competition among enterprises in the domestic market is already reasonably advanced in those commodities where China's export prospects in the near term are brightest: relatively labor-intensive, diversified manufactures, including not only traditional exports such as handicraft, processed food, textiles and garments, but, more importantly, new products such as consumer electronics, standard electrical and mechanical machinery, fabricated metal products, and so on. The most important missing element to become internationally competitive in these products is better design and quality that can be acquired efficiently only under a more open system of foreign trade and international economic relations (para. 2.45 and Box 2.5).

45. This is not to say that trade reform can be carried out without regard to further progress on price reform. Further price reform is desirable and necessary both to increase the efficiency of resource allocation in the domestic economy--particularly for capital-intensive basic raw materials (steel, chemicals, power, etc.)--and also to ensure an efficient set of signals to govern trading decisions. A wide-ranging trade reform without price reform would lead to irrational exports of some goods, such as steel-products and energy intensive goods, and excessive imports of consumer goods. However, for many of the goods mentioned in the previous paragraph there has already been considerable progress in price reform, and it is our judgement that the proposed initial steps in trade reform do not have to wait for further progress in other areas.

46. These considerations suggest a phasing for the recommended trade reforms. By identifying those sectors and subsectors where price and enterprise reform have already made good progress, candidates for early trade reform could be selected. This could involve liberalization of trading rights

in those sectors, together with increased foreign exchange retention, elimination of plan allocation for imported inputs, and removal of import licensing. Once trade reforms had 'caught up' with price and enterprise reforms in these sectors, progress in extending the trade reforms to other sectors could be linked with further progress in price and enterprise reforms (paras. 4.32-4.37).

47. The creation of a more sophisticated 'neutral' environment for export enterprises (including duty and indirect tax rebating, automatic access to working capital finance, etc.) will of course require simultaneous movement in the areas of tax and financial systems reform. The primary constraint there is the administrative capacity required to prepare and implement these reforms. It will thus take at least 3-5 years to prepare and implement these measures.

48. Similarly, in the area of foreign direct investment there are not too many constraints arising from the domestic reform process. The most important constraint is the requirement to balance foreign exchange receipts and payments. Apart from this, progress will have to be made in eliminating differences in the legal and administrative environment between domestic enterprises and foreign joint ventures. This would in a first phase mostly involve giving domestic enterprises the same managerial autonomy and responsibility that joint venture enterprises already enjoy, except for the over-generous corporate income tax provisions that joint ventures now enjoy. However, enterprise reform should not stop there. Further steps are required, particularly to enhance factor mobility by creating markets for labor services, land use, and capital, or improving the efficiency of these markets.

49. Thus, foreign trade and other foreign economic relations play an essential role in the domestic economy. Foreign trade not only provides access to machinery, technology and goods in short supply, but also the multitude of contacts with buyers, suppliers and competitors that have proved to be an essential and low-cost source of technology transfers and information about market opportunities. To maximize these indirect benefits of foreign trade, it is essential that enterprises have direct contacts with buyers and suppliers and can make foreign trade decisions autonomously. The larger the number and types of enterprises that can engage in such contacts, the more rapid technology transfer and diffusion are likely to be. Foreign trade should thus not be regarded as a separate sector or activity, but as an integral part of enterprise decision-making on production and investment. However, if such decentralized decision-making is to lead to efficient resource allocation, prices will have to reflect economic costs, competition will have to be vigorous, and macro-economic stability has to prevail. Reforms will thus have to move simultaneously on these several fronts.

I. THE "OPEN DOOR" IN INTERNATIONAL PERSPECTIVE

1.1 As a central element of its overall strategy to improve allocative efficiency and promote the modernization and growth of the economy, the Chinese government introduced at the end of 1978 a process of reform aimed at decentralizing production and investment decisions and subjecting them increasingly to market influences. So far, the most far-reaching reforms have occurred in the rural sector with the introduction of the household responsibility system, under which households are the principal production and decision-making units in agriculture and related rural activities.

1.2 While reforms in the urban industrial and commercial sectors have proceeded at a slower pace, the introduction of the "open door" policy in early 1979 was one of the earliest and most wide-ranging elements of the reform package, and a major departure from the preceding two decades of self-reliance and autarkic economic and technological development. Overall, the "open door" policy has been very successful, yielding dramatic increases in international trade and contacts and contributing to greater efficiency and higher rates of growth of the Chinese economy.

1.3 In October 1986, a World Bank mission visited China to analyze, in collaboration with a Chinese counterpart team from a number of government agencies, the present status of China's foreign trade and capital system and, on the basis of this analysis, make suggestions for further improvements. The mission also benefitted from an earlier study of domestic enterprise and financial sector reform issues jointly undertaken by another Bank mission and Chinese counterpart team.[1/] This report summarizes the mission's findings and recommendations, and a companion volume of annexes provides more in-depth description and analysis. Chapter I first looks at the benefits and costs of increasing foreign trade and other external economic relations in the light of international experience and then briefly discusses trade policy measures adopted by successful exporters and how these compare to China's "open door" policy. Chapter II then discusses the present trade system and options for reform. Chapter III looks at macro-economic management issues relating to external trade and the balance of payments, and Chapter IV discusses the sequencing of trade reform and its interrelation with other elements of economic reform.

A. Recent Progress and a New Juncture

1.4 Since the "open door" policy was adopted at the end of 1978, increased exports of raw materials and manufactured goods (rising at 15% p.a. in terms of US$ during 1979-85), increased earnings from tourism and other services, and the use of foreign direct investment and other capital inflows

---

1/ World Bank: China--Finance and Investment, 1988.

have permitted a dramatic increase of imports of capital goods, machinery, technology and materials in short supply. Imports in 1985 were $38 billion, five times the level of 1975. This massive inflow of technology, capital goods, and intermediate goods was a major factor in the dramatic improvement in the efficiency of the Chinese economy,[2/] although other factors--such as the rural reforms and partial enterprise and price reforms so far introduced--were also important, and perhaps more important than the "open door" policy alone.

1.5 While initial results of the "open door" policy have thus been impressive, both in terms of the immediate objective to increase the capacity to import and the ultimate objective of raising economic efficiency through technology imports, many Chinese as well as foreign observers believe that present policies with respect to foreign trade and capital flows are far from optimal. The impressive gains of the past eight years reflect, to a large extent, the comparatively easy initial gains of opening up to external trade. Further improvements could not only raise the efficiency of foreign trade and therefore lower the domestic resource costs of importing foreign technology, they are essential for China to increase its exports (and capacity to import) at the rapid rate that is required if the high targets for economic growth and modernization are to be achieved.

1.6 A related issue arises from the fact that China is quickly becoming a major factor in world trade, at least in some product categories. While China's share in total world trade is still less than 2%, its share of world exports of textiles and clothing has doubled to 8% since the introduction of the "open door" policy, and it is now among the top five suppliers in both categories. Rapid growth in these and other products, where China has comparative advantage resulting from its low wages and skilled labor force, will require structural change--and possibly economic and social dislocations--in importing countries that might lead to increased protectionist pressures. China can, to some extent, reduce these pressures by adopting a trade system that is more transparent and less likely to attract countervailing actions by major trade partners.

B. The Role of Foreign Trade: International Experience

1.7 There are at least three reasons why countries engage in foreign trade. First, differences in natural resource endowments lead to differences in relative cost of production, and trade permits countries to specialize in the production of those commodities of which they are lower-cost producers. Second, trade permits less developed countries to overcome differences in human resources (technology, management skills, etc.) by acquiring goods and services embodying more advanced technologies, and thus avoiding "reinventing

---

2/ During 1981-85, the investment rate of 30% of GDP resulted in a rate of growth of 10% p.a. while an almost identical investment rate during the preceding 10 years resulted in a growth rate of only 6% p.a. Put differently, the incremental capital-output ratio declined from an average of 5 during the 1970s to 3 during 1981-85.

the wheel" and thereby speeding up the process of economic development. Third, external trade permits countries to expose their domestic enterprises to international competition and thus ensures that domestic industry will live up to the highest standards of efficiency.

1.8 While all three factors play a role, the second (technology transfer and development) is of particular importance for a large developing country, such as China. By contrast, the first is predominant for some resource abundant countries with small populations such as, for example, capital-surplus, oil-exporting countries. The third factor is particularly important for small countries where, without external trade, even modest economies of scale would lead either to sub-optimal and inefficient scale of plants, and/or to monopolistic industry structures and inefficiencies. This is not to say that the competitive impact of foreign trade is not relevant and beneficial for larger countries--quite to the contrary. Among the advanced industrialized countries, the competitive stimulus is often regarded as one of the most important benefits of external trade.

1.9 Increased external trade could also have disadvantages. One potential disadvantage is that foreign competition could stifle infant industries--activities which could become internationally competitive, but only after a period of time in which necessary experience and skills are developed. Other possible disadvantages include the transmission into the domestic economy of primary product price volatility, fluctuations in world demand for industrial products, and the possible emergence of undesirable large trade deficits or surpluses or unwanted inflows and outflows of capital. (These concerns are discussed in Chapter III and Annex V.) International experience suggests that these costs are usually outweighed by the benefits, as discussed in the following paragraphs.

1.10 While external trade is the most important component of international economic relations, there are other complementary means to increase external economic contacts, technology transfer and economic development. Tourism and exports of other labor services serve to augment the earnings from commodity exports and thus to increase the capacity to import; foreign borrowing permits increased imports today to be paid for by future export earnings, and can thus accelerate technology transfer; and foreign direct investment permits the import of capital goods, technology, management skills, foreign financing and risk-sharing in one bundle. Last, but not least, overseas education and training can be one of the most effective forms of technology transfer. Each of these special forms of foreign economic relations has its own advantages and disadvantages, but they are dwarfed by the far larger volume of commodity trade. Trade thus takes a special and dominant place in international economic policy-making.

1.11 Different economies have adopted different trade policies, ranging from the almost complete autarky adopted by China from 1960 to 1978, to the extremely open "laissez faire" approach adopted, for example, by Hong Kong or (since 1967) by Singapore. In between these extremes are a great number of different policy regimes, characterized by different degrees (and different instruments) of government intervention designed mainly to protect certain sectors from foreign competition. In developing countries, protection is usually extended to industry, while industrialized countries often protect agriculture or declining industrial activities, such as textiles, ship building or steel. These trade policy interventions are either of an administrative and quantitative nature (import restrictions, licensing, foreign exchange rationing, "voluntary" export restraints) or are effected through "economic levers" using the price mechanism (tariffs and other border levies). Box 1.1 classifies trade policy regimes into four different categories.

Box 1.1: CLASSIFICATION OF TRADE STRATEGIES

	Strategy	Examples
I.	Closing of economy with tight administrative restrictions on trade and foreign investments.	Burma from 1962 Sri Lanka to 1976 USSR to 1986 China to 1978
II.	High protection, using administative restrictions on imports and/or high tariffs (resulting in overvalued exchange rates).	South Korea to 1962 Brazil to 1967 and after 1979 India China from 1979
III.	Relative openness, emphasizing export promotion through realistic exchange rates and export incentives, but using selective import protection through tariffs and limited administrative import restrictions.	South Korea from 1962 Brazil from 1967 to 1973
IV.	Substantial openness with little protection against manufactured imports (but sometimes high protection for agriculture) and few restraints on investment and capital flows.	Singapore from 1967 Chile from 1976 South Korea from 1988 /a Industrialized countries

/a After completion of the five-year import liberalization program preannounced in 1983.

1.12 International experience suggests that developing countries that have adopted more outward-oriented trade strategies have had better economic performances than countries that have adopted an inward-oriented strategy. Outward-oriented trade policies (Categories III and IV in Box 1.1) involve no, or very little, use of administrative restrictions on foreign trade, promote exports largely through a market-related exchange rate, apply relatively low and uniform tariffs on imports, and provide import duty and indirect tax rebates for export production.[3/] In terms of the categories in Box 1.1, most developing countries since World War II have adopted policies that can be classified as belonging to either category II or III. Large improvements in export and national income growth can be observed between categories II and III (Table 1.1). The main difference between these two strategies is that category II relies extensively on administrative restrictions on trade combined with high tariffs, while category III places predominant reliance on a market-based exchange rate system, combined with lower and more uniform tariffs. A market-based exchange rate system implies the absence of administrative foreign exchange allocation, with the market itself ensuring adequate export revenues to meet foreign exchange needs, through automatic adjustment of the exchange rate to balance demand for and supply of foreign exchange.[4/] In terms of economic incentives, China's "open door" policy compares most closely to category II rather than III (export promotion), modified by a political commitment and some economic incentives towards export promotion (see Chapter II, paras. 2.16-2.18).

1.13 Under outward-oriented (or "neutral") trade policies, export and import-substituting activities are equally (or almost equally) favored. They should not be confused with "export-promoting" strategies under which some countries have adopted positive bias in favor of exports. Outward-oriented strategies involve the absence or near-absence of bias against exports, creating reasonable opportunities for exports, but not implying necessarily a reliance on exports as the major source of growth in the economy. By contrast, a trade system that relies extensively on administrative import restrictions and high (and often highly variable) tariff rates inevitably creates a bias against exports, because the exchange rate will become overvalued (lower in terms of domestic currency units per unit of foreign exchange), as import demand is artificially lowered. This overvaluation of the exchange rate, combined with high import protection, makes import-substituting activities more profitable than export activities. The overvaluation of the exchange rate is usually more extensive and serious if import protection is provided by administrative import restrictions (which could be seen as equivalent to a tariff with a rate of infinity).

1.14 The superior performance associated with an outward-oriented strategy not only holds across countries (where differences in culture, work ethic, savings pattern etc. could account for some of the difference), but has been equally true for a country that has changed policies over time. The countries shown in Table 1.1 all changed their trade strategies at some time from an import substitution to an outward-oriented strategy: South Korea around 1960, Brazil around 1967, Colombia and Tunisia between 1965 and 1970.

3/ Countries that have adopted outward-oriented trade policies also generally rely on decentralized production, marketing and investment decision-making by autonomous enterprises, influenced by market prices, for both domestic and foreign sales and purchases.

4/ See Chapter III for a fuller discussion.

All showed dramatic increases in exports and domestic economic growth after switching to a more outward-oriented economic policy. The effect of an outward-oriented strategy on economic growth appears to be largest for small countries, which tend to have a higher ratio of external trade to national income. But even in large developing countries, such as Brazil, the effects of an outward-oriented strategy on domestic growth and efficiency have been large. More recent evidence also suggests that the benefits of an import-substitution strategy tend to diminish over time, as the opportunities for efficient substitution are exhausted, and successive import-substituting investments become more costly.

Table 1.1: TRADE STRATEGY, EXPORT GROWTH AND ECONOMIC PERFORMANCE, SELECTED COUNTRIES

		Trade strategy (see Box 1.1)		Export earnings/a growth (% p.a.)	Real GDP growth (% p.a.)
Brazil	1955-65	II	(import substitution)	1.1	5.5
	1965-76	III	(neutral)	28.2	7.6
Colombia	1955-65	II	(import substitution)	-1.4	1.9
	1970-76	III	(neutral)	16.9	6.5
South Korea	1953-60	II	(import substitution)	-6.1	5.2
	1960-76	III	(neutral/export promotion)	41.6	9.2
Tunisia	1960-70	II	(import substitution)	6.8	4.8
	1970-76	II/III	(partial export prom.)	23.4	9.4
China	1960-78	I	(autarchy)	7.8	4.6
	1978-85	II	(modified import subst.)	15.7	8.8

/a At current prices in US$.

Source: A.O. Krueger: The Effects of Trade Strategies on Growth, Finance and Development, June 1983, World Bank staff estimates.

1.15 The four newly industrializing economies (or NICs) of East Asia--South Korea, Singapore, Hong Kong and Taiwan, China--have been particularly successful in their outward-looking strategy. Despite their relatively small size, their combined merchandise exports now amount to some $110 billion--equivalent to about one-half of Japanese or US exports and accounting for fully one-half of all exports of manufactured goods of developing countries. Their export performance has been largely based on manufactured goods, and they have tripled their combined share of world trade in manufactured goods over the past fifteen years (Table 1.2).

1.16 While China has made good progress in promoting exports of manufactured goods, its growth rate performance still remains slightly below that of the other developing economies of South-East Asia, although somewhat above that of Latin American countries (Table 1.2). Other developing countries have barely held their combined market share in world trade, with the gains in some countries offset by substantial losses in others.

Table 1.2: TRENDS IN MANUFACTURED EXPORTS

	Share of world trade (%)		Growth (% p.a.)	
	1970	1984	1970-80	1980-84
Industrial countries	88.1	80.1	18.2	-1.9
Developing countries	6.7	14.8	25.4	5.6
East Asian NICs	2.4	7.5	28.3	8.5
South East Asia	0.1	1.2	40.2	10.9
China	0.5	1.3	26.7	9.3
Latin America	1.0	2.4	25.4	7.4
Other LDCs	2.6	2.3	19.7	-5.7

Source: World Bank Trade Data Base.

1.17 Some costs as well as benefits may be associated with increased foreign trade and external economic relations. Two categories of potential economic costs of an outward-oriented economic strategy were identified above: the stifling of infant industry by foreign competition and greater vulnerability to fluctuations in international prices and world demand. The international evidence suggests that these costs have been outweighed by the benefits. Countries that have adopted outward-oriented policies have experienced far more rapid growth of manufactured exports, and have also experienced more rapid and more efficient industrial development generally. For example, some of the most successful outward-oriented NICs have recently shifted from earlier export successes in textiles, clothing and consumer electronics to machinery, automobiles, shipbuilding, and personal computers. They are not only gradually diversifying their industrial sectors but have also become internationally competitive in these new sectors that have received relatively little protection. Moreover, skillful use of appropriate policy instruments can soften the trade-off between the costs and benefits, such as selective import industry protection, and phased liberalization policies (see Chapter II).

1.18 International experience also suggests that outward-oriented developing countries have weathered external shocks much better than inward-oriented countries, even though external shocks have been larger for outward-oriented countries, since their external trade is larger relative to the size of the domestic economy. For example, a World Bank study 5/ of the adjustment of 28 developing countries to the oil price increases of the mid-1970s showed that the outward-oriented economies were able to maintain higher growth rate of national income than the inward-oriented economies, even though the increased cost of oil imports (or "shock") was far larger relative to the size of their economies.

1.19 A recent study undertaken for the World Development Report 1987 provides additional evidence from a larger sample of 41 developing countries and the recent years of slower growth and adjustment to renewed external shocks. While growth rates of national income have slowed down in 1973-85 compared to 1963-73, the differences between outward- and inward-oriented countries have been maintained. Table 1.3 also shows that the efficiency of investment, as measured by the incremental capital-output ratio (i.e. the investment required for a unit increase in net output) has remained far higher (i.e. a lower ICOR) in outward-oriented countries than in inward-oriented countries. Table 1.3 also provides some evidence about the long-term impact of different trade strategies: in outward-oriented countries the share of the labor force employed in manufacturing has nearly doubled over the past two decades, while it has increased only marginally in inward-oriented countries.

5/ B. Belassa: "Adjustment to External Shocks in Developing Economies", World Bank Staff Working Paper No.472, 1981.

Table 1.3: TRADE POLICY AND ADJUSTMENT TO EXTERNAL SHOCKS

	Outward-oriented countries /a	Inward-oriented countries /b
Real GDP Growth (% p.a.)		
1963-73	7.9	5.2
1973-85	5.0	3.7
Real GNP per capita Growth (% p.a.)		
1963-73	5.2	2.7
1973-85	2.5	1.0
Incremental Capital-Output Ratio		
1963-73	2.5	4.1
1973-85	4.9	7.0
Manufacturing Employment (% of total)		
1963	13.2	12.7
1980	23.0	14.1

/a 13 countries in 1963-73, 11 countries in 1973-85.

/b 28 countries in 1963-73, 30 countries in 1973.85.

Source: World Bank: World Development Report 1987, Chapter 5.

1.20 While the evidence provided above does not prove a causal link between different types of trade strategies and economic performance, the data are nevertheless quite significant. If the countries are further subdivided by different degrees of outward and inward orientation, the differences in economic performance are even more striking (see World Development Report 1987, Chapter 5).

C. Successful Trade Policies

1.21 By comparison to outward-oriented developing countries, China's "open door" policy today would have to be characterized as an "inward-looking" strategy. This might appear paradoxical, given China's success in export markets since the introduction of the "open door" policy. China has moved from an extreme position of nearly complete autarky during the past two decades to a policy regime that is partially open. China's impressive export performance over the past eight years may thus be largely a transitory phenomenon. If this supposition is correct--and more detailed corroborative analysis is provided in the following chapters and the Annexes--China will probably have to undertake substantial additional reforms of its trade system to maintain these gains.

1.22 What constitutes a successful "outward-oriented" strategy? Different countries have pursued somewhat different policies, but a number of common elements falling into three different categories can be cited: (a) decentralization of decision-making to enterprises; (b) a favorable incentive environment for exports; and (c) stable macro-economic management.

Decentralization of Decision-Making

1.23 International experience strongly suggests that decentralization of trade decisions to the enterprise level can be very important in helping to realize the potential benefits of increased external contacts. Direct exposure of exporting firms to foreign buyers and competitors has proved to be an extremely effective way not just of learning in the abstract about new and better products and production processes, but also of learning how to introduce them in practice. Decentralization of export and import decision-making to enterprises is consistent with the central thrust of China's economic reforms in the productive sectors of decentralizing production and investment decisions to enterprises and subjecting them increasingly to competition and market forces.

1.24 Decentralization of decision-making implies that enterprise managers would determine the details of external transactions. To ensure that their decisions were in accordance with China's overall economic interests and broadly consonant with government strategy, internal reforms to make enterprises more sensitive to costs, to customer requirements, and to profits and losses would be essential, as would be an appropriate system of prices. Of particular importance for the economic rationality of decentralized export and import decisions is the relationship between domestic and world prices. In many respects, the more direct the linkage the better, since world prices can provide appropriate signals to Chinese producers and consumers about the value or cost of particular goods to China in world markets. To a considerable degree, trade reform is thus an integral and essential part of enterprise reform, and there are close linkages between domestic price reforms and trade reform. (This subject is discussed further in Chapter IV.)

Export Incentives

1.25 A realistic exchange rate has probably been the most important element of the successful trade strategies of other countries. With the decentralization of export and import decisions to enterprises, the exchange rate will also become an increasingly important element of trade policy and export promotion in China. Indeed, it should become the most important instrument. In general, the exchange rate should tend toward that level for which the country's earnings from the exports of goods and services [6/] are sufficient to cover all its import needs, assuming that most import and export decisions are made by independent enterprises on the basis of profitability considerations.

6/ Plus policy-determined capital in flows (see Chapter III).

1.26 A market-based exchange rate can be modified by other policy instruments. For example, if a tariff is imposed to protect domestic enterprises from import competition, some enterprises or consumers will switch to domestically produced goods, because imports are now more expensive. The demand for imports will thus be less, and the market-clearing exchange rate (in terms of dollars per yuan) will be higher. Quantitative import restrictions have a similar affect. If, for example, imports of large numbers of commodities are restricted, there will be less total demand for imports, and the exchange rate will be market-clearing at a higher rate (in terms of dollars per yuan) than if there were no such restrictions. But this higher exchange rate also creates an anti-export bias. In many countries extensive quantitative import restrictions are the main reason for an overvalued exchange rate. Instead of letting their exchange rates depreciate to a level which would reestablish balance between demand for and supply of foreign exchange, many developing countries have adopted extensive licensing and other quantitative restrictions, resulting in import-substitution bias and poor export and economic performance, as discussed in the preceding section.

1.27 Of course, China does not have a market-determined exchange rate at present. As discussed in more detail in Chapter II, a significant share of exports and imports is still determined administratively. As in other developing countries, administrative import restrictions and high tariffs are bound to lead to an overvaluation [7/] of the exchange rate. Furthermore, the uncertainties inherent in administrative allocation lead enterprises to hoard imported goods, to hoard foreign exchange allocations and to pad import requests. This leads to apparent excess demand for imports, or "import hunger", quite similar to the more familiar phenomenon of "investment hunger" in China due to administrative allocation of low-cost investment funds. Thus, it becomes very difficult to determine at what level the exchange rate would settle once administrative restrictions on trade were eliminated or significantly reduced.

1.28 Some tentative steps in the direction of more decentralized foreign exchange allocation and partial market determination have been undertaken with the introduction and expansion of foreign exchange retention quotas for export enterprises (see Chapter II). But more systematic and wide-ranging measures are required. Some of the options for the transition toward a more efficient exchange rate regime are discussed in Chapter III. While decentralized import and export decisions by independent enterprises responsible for profit and losses, made on the basis of a unified exchange rate, are likely to lead to the most efficient allocation of resources, domestic prices also have to be rational to make decentralized foreign trade decisions efficient. The connection between reforms of foreign exchange allocation and domestic price reform is further pursued in Chapter IV.

7/ Thus, an exchange rate can be judged to be overvalued either when there is an excessive balance-of-payments deficit, or when restrictions on imports or exports subsidies are required to achieve balance in the market for foreign exchange (see para. 3.5).

1.29 Most countries impose <u>tariffs</u> on imports, either to protect domestic industry from foreign competition or to generate government revenues. In many ways, tariffs are preferable to quantitative import restrictions as a tool of protection. Successful exporting countries have tended to rely more on tariffs and less on quantitative import restrictions than countries that have adopted inward-looking (and generally less successful) policies. The reasons for preferring tariffs to quantitative restrictions as instruments of infant industry protection are quite similar to those that lead to preferring price determined rather than administrative allocation of foreign exchange. Price interventions--such as tariffs--are more transparent, create less uncertainties for enterprise managers and eliminate the pursuit of favors and windfall gains (such as, for example, obtaining restricted imports at the official exchange rate for resale at a higher price). Such pursuit of windfall gains or "economic rents" is a major source of inefficiency in many developing countries. With a tariff, such windfall gains are avoided, and, moreover, the revenues generated accrue to the government.

1.30 However, the imposition of tariffs or other import restrictions is likely to lead to an overvalued exchange rate, even if the exchange rate is market-determined. Protecting domestic industry--or, more precisely, import-substituting activities--imposes a burden on export industries. The higher the protection extended to import-substituting activities, the higher the penalty on exporters. One solution, adopted by a number of successful exporting countries, is to rebate tariffs on all inputs used in export production. While this reduces the anti-export bias of tariff protection, it does not fully eliminate it. Some successful exporting countries have provided additional subsidies to exporters to make up for the remaining anti-export bias. However, importing countries have become increasingly sensitive to export subsidies that put their own industries at a competitive disadvantage and have started to impose countervailing taxes.

1.31 The domestic tax system can also lead to an anti-export bias, particularly if turnover taxes are levied on several successive production stages. This occurs, for example, in the case of China's industrial and commercial tax. Many export-oriented countries have therefore reformed their tax systems to minimize anti-export bias. Tariff drawback and value-added tax systems are internationally accepted ways to minimize anti-export bias for exporters, by making imported inputs available at internationally competitive prices, and avoiding undue taxation of export production.

1.32 Some of the most successful outward-oriented economies have completely dispensed with infant industry protection by imposing no or very low import tariffs. Hong Kong and Singapore have followed this strategy very successfully. Others have used protective measures in the past and have recently phased out quantitative restrictions and substantially reduced tariff protection. South Korea has recently followed this path and will soon complete a ten-year program of trade reforms that includes a complete phasing-out of import restrictions for manufactured goods and a drastic reduction in tariffs. Only agricultural activities will remain protected by import restrictions, industrial activities only by tariffs. Korea's recent export success suggests that this is at least as good a policy as the mixed export promotion/import substitution policy pursued during much of the 1970s. The excellent performance of East Asian economies that have adopted a less restrictive import policy much earlier also attests to that.

Stable Macro-Economic Management

1.33 Another important element in the success of outward-oriented trade strategies has been prudent and stable macro-economic management. This is particularly important during the transition from an inward-looking to an outward-looking strategy. Many developing countries have failed in their efforts to shift towards a more outward-oriented strategy, because macro-economic imbalances led to unsustainable balance-of-payments deficits during the early stages of the transition. These deficits have often been followed by quantitative restrictions on imports and foreign exchange rationing and a return to an overvalued exchange rate, bias towards import substitution and so on.

1.34 The most frequent sources of macro-economic imbalances have been inappropriate fiscal and monetary policies. Governments have been unable or unwilling to finance ambitious expenditure programs with adequate taxation, or have promoted large "strategic" industrial development programs outside the government budget through directed credit and permissive monetary policies. If a major move towards a more effective outward-oriented strategy is to be successful in the future, appropriate fiscal and monetary restraint will be essential.

D. Foreign Trade Prospects

1.35 China's "open door" policy still entails a rather substantial import-substitution bias and many other elements usually associated with an inward-looking development strategy. The impressive record achieved by outward-oriented trade and development strategies deserves China's consideration. But, is a switch to an outward-oriented development strategy possible and feasible for a large country like China in today's world of slow economic growth and protectionism? What, for example, would happen in international markets if other large countries such as India were to pursue the same strategy at the same time?

1.36 The first point that can be made is that China should not adopt an outward-oriented strategy merely, or even primarily, to maximize export revenues. Internationally traded goods will necessarily represent a small portion of China's total output. The most important reason for an outward-oriented trade policy, therefore, is to reap the indirect benefits of a more open trading system, including the myriad of efficiency gains that enterprises can make when they are in direct contact with buyers, suppliers and competitors. Foreign competition provides a spur to the efficiency of domestic enterprises and provides strong incentives to keep up with the progress in technology, organization and management practices made elsewhere. The rate of growth of export earnings is far less important than the extent of contacts that production enterprises and commercial units have with the outside world and the effectiveness of the diffusion of the information thus gained to other domestic enterprises. In contrast, the present administratively intermediated foreign economic relations create an "air-lock", in which most of the indirect benefits of external trade are blocked from reaching the domestic economy.

1.37 A higher degree of diversification of exports and imports is also likely to carry with it more technology diffusion and higher productivity gains. In all successful outward-oriented economies, labor mobility (within and between enterprises), especially among technical personnel, has been an essential ingredient in this transmission. Overseas education and training have also been important.

1.38 The growth of world output and world trade has slowed down considerably in recent years, and it is reasonable to assume that the high growth rates of the 1950s and 1960s will not return in this or the next decade. The reduction in the responsiveness (or elasticity) of world trade with respect to world economic growth can be largely attributed to the slow growth in consumption and trade of primary goods (Table 1.4). This trend is likely to be lasting, as economic growth in advanced industrialized countries is becoming less and less material-intensive.

1.39 Exports of manufactured goods have held up much better, however, (Table 1.4) and East Asian exporters of manufacturers have continued to enjoy export growth rates of close to 10% p.a. in volume terms (Table 1.2).[8/] Worldwide, the responsiveness (or "elasticity") of growth of world trade in manufactures with respect to growth of production (and national income) has not markedly changed. During 1980-85 this elasticity [9/] was actually somewhat higher than in the 1960s (but slightly lower than in the 1970s). The relatively good export performance of developing country manufactures holds even for those manufactured goods for which producers in industrialized countries have been strongly affected by the increased competition, such as textiles, clothing, footwear, automobiles, steel and so on. While the required structural adjustment in industrial countries--displacement of workers, plant closures etc.--is undeniably resisted and has resulted in a mushrooming of import barriers, market penetration has continued to increase and has reached already very high levels in some product categories, such as garments (Table 1.5).

8/ Prices in dollar terms fell slightly during 1980-85.

9/ i.e., the rate of growth of world trade volume divided by the rate of growth of world production.

Table 1.4: GROWTH OF WORLD PRODUCTION AND TRADE VOLUME

	Production growth (% p.a.)			Export growth (% p.a.)		
	1960-70	1970-80	1980-85	1960-70	1970-80	1980-85
Agricultural products	2.5	2.2	2.6	3.9	3.5	1.2
Minerals and fuels	5.4	2.7	-2.6	7.2	1.7	-3.6
Manufactured goods	7.4	4.3	3.1	10.2	7.1	4.8

Source: GATT: International Trade 1985-86, Table A.1.

1.40 The share of primary commodities in China's exports has changed little in recent years, remaining at about 50%. But, within this 50%, there have occurred significant changes in composition. The share of non-oil primary commodity exports has fallen from 50% of total exports in the early 1970s to 26% in 1985, and the share of agricultural commodities fell somewhat more rapidly (to 14%) than the share of other primary commodities. The good performance of primary commodity exports in total can be entirely attributed to the rapid growth of petroleum exports, a trend already changing as a consequence of falling petroleum prices. In the future, it is quite possible that China's exportable surplus of domestic oil production will stagnate or even decline, given rapidly growing domestic demand and only moderate exploration results.

1.41 While China's export performance in manufactured goods was respectable during the past eight years (Table 1.2 and Annex 1), it was highly variable, with manufactured exports increasing rapidly between 1978 and 1981, then growing only modestly between 1981 and 1985. After the exchange rate adjustments vis-a-vis the US dollar and, even more importantly, the decline of the US dollar vis-a-vis other currencies, exports of manufactures improved again, increasing by about 30% (in terms of US$) in 1986 (see Annex 1). Textiles and clothing account for about 40% of manufactured exports, followed by miscellaneous exports (handicrafts, toys, etc.) with 25%. Machinery, electrical and electronics products are only 6% of manufactured exports (or less than 3% of total exports).

Table 1.5: MARKET PENETRATION OF MANUFACTURED IMPORTS IN SELECTED INDUSTRIALIZED COUNTRIES, 1975-83
(% of apparent consumption)

	Total Manufacturing		Clothing		Nonelectrical Machinery	
	1975	1983	1975	1983	1975	1983
All Imports						
US	7.0	10.3	9.8	20.3	7.3	11.8
Japan	4.9	5.3	8.3	13.0	5.5	4.3
West Germany	24.2	35.1	44.9	73.2	30.4	39.6
Imports From Developing Countries						
US	2.0	3.4	7.7	17.8	0.5	2.3
Japan	1.7	1.9	6.2	10.1	0.4	0.3
West Germany	2.4	4.0	14.7	28.7	0.9	1.2

Source: OECD Compatible Trade and Production Data Base.

1.42 One explanation for the continued market penetration in manufactured goods, despite nontariff barriers in industrialized countries, is that these trade barriers are far more porous than they appear. Inventive exporters often find ways around these restrictions, for example by shipping the goods in a form or with components not covered by the restrictions. Coats with removable sleeves that are imported as vests (which are not covered by the restrictions) come to mind, or woolen sweaters that are now made in silk/alpaca/angora blends that are not subject to restrictions. Decentralization of marketing decisions to enterprises appears to be essential, if such market opportunities are to be pursued effectively. At the same time, China will have to make strong efforts to shift to new and different export products, especially machinery. But to become successful in these more sophisticated products, quality and design are essential, and it is unlikely that China can become a successful exporter in these product categories, unless export decision-making is decentralized to enterprises, and the trading system becomes more open to permit more rapid technology acquisition and diffusion.

1.43 An important trend that could help to stave off increased protectionism in industrialized countries is the greater interest and more active involvement of developing countries in the General Agreement on Tariffs and Trade (GATT). While developing country interest was very limited during the 1960s and even 1970s, and largely focussed on obtaining special treatment and on limiting reciprocity under GATT, many developing countries now realize that they have a stake in the preservation of an open trading system and are very actively participating in the new Uruguay Round of multilateral trade negotiations. They also realize that they will have to accept more reciprocity if the trading system is to be kept open.

1.44 Recently, China formally indicated her intention to resume membership in GATT. Given the changed trading environment, it will probably become necessary for China to accept more reciprocity in GATT than other developing countries had to accept in the past, if China wants to have the better assured access to major export markets that participation in GATT provides. External trade reforms that would enable China to reap the many benefits of an outward-oriented economic strategy would also serve to make China's trade system more transparent and acceptable to other GATT members.

II. CHINA'S FOREIGN ECONOMIC RELATIONS: ISSUES AND POLICY OPTIONS

2.1 In light of the lessons of international experience outlined in Chapter I, this chapter presents a description and analysis of China's system of foreign economic relations. Part A outlines the key features of the trade regime, both historically and as of October 1986. Part B provides an analysis of the impact of the current regime. Based on this analysis, Part C recommends a set of institutional reforms and Part D a set of policy reforms that would have to be implemented concurrently if the institutional reforms are to succeed. Finally, in Part E we analyze other issues in China's foreign economic relations, notably the management of technology imports and foreign investment.

A. Key Features of the Chinese Trade Regime

The Historical Context

2.2 During the 1949-78 period, China's economic strategy was essentially one of self-reliance. This was reflected in the approach to trade and the trading system adopted. Domestic needs were to be satisfied as much as possible by domestic production, and foreign trade was to supplement shortfalls in such production--primarily in food, essential raw materials, and capital goods. Nevertheless, there was always a recognition that China could not be entirely self-sufficient, especially in capital goods, and that progress would be served by obtaining foreign technology either by purchase or through assistance from friendly countries. However, the enthusiasm for technology imports varied over the period, and the trends in such import activity are generally referred to as the "four waves" of imports (see Annex 1, paras. 1.4-1.7).

2.3 Although these "four waves" resulted in considerable levels of technology imports, they were generally characterized by the purchase of embodied technology: i.e., whole plants or production lines acquired on a turnkey basis.[1/] This was consistent with a general approach of isolating the domestic market from the "destabilizing" influence of world markets, which characterized trade policy during this period. The level and composition of trade were determined through a centralized planning system under the authority of the Ministry of Foreign Trade (MFT).[2/] The annual foreign trade

---

1/ The only significant exception to this was during the 1956-60 period, when significant numbers of plants were imported from the USSR. These imports were generally accompanied by blueprints and technical assistance and were replicable and more easily maintained. Many of these plants are still in operation.

2/ After a government reorganization in March 1982, the Ministry of Foreign Trade was combined with the Ministry of Foreign Relations, and was renamed the Ministry of Foreign Economic Relations and Trade (MOFERT).

planning process would identify the required imports, and exports would be selected to finance the desired level of imports, so as to avoid any significant trade deficits that would require foreign borrowing. Once the plan was determined, it would be entrusted to the twelve main centralized foreign trade corporations (FTCs) for implementation. To ensure the insulation of the domestic market, the FTCs were given monopoly powers within specified scopes of business, and they would procure all goods for exports and sell all procured imports at the domestic prices for these goods (Box 2.1). Trade plans were expressed in quantitative terms, and any resulting financial losses for the FTCs were covered by budgetary grants (see Annex 1, paras. 1.8-1.10).

Box 2.1: THE PRE-1978 TRADING ENVIRONMENT IN CHINA

Since 1978, China's trade volume has more than doubled and some US$8 billion in foreign investment has been made. These statistics are indicative of the remarkable change in attitude to trade and the role of the outside world since 1978. Before 1978, contacts were extremely limited, with virtually no trade business possible between the twice-yearly Canton Trade Fair. No officials carried business cards and would only identify themselves by surname and corporation. At the Trade Fairs, foreign businessmen would meet with the FTCs to do business. "Between the Spring and Autumn Canton Fair, foreign trade corporation managers were loath to answer letters or telexes, so the Fair assumed enormous importance. On the opening day crowds of visiting business people from all over the globe gathered at the steps of the trade fair complex, and once the opening ribbon was cut, a frenzied stampede took place."

Another key feature was the extreme 'airlock' imposed by the FTCs between the foreign supplier and the Chinese end-user. "Ultimate end-users were not only not present for commercial and technical negotiations, but were generally not even identified. Apart from the time factor, the potential for misunderstanding was enormous. Many companies that sold technical products during the early or mid-1970s found out in later years, when they were allowed access to their earlier sales' end-users, that huge waste had resulted, which sometimes reflected unfairly on their products' reliability and their reputations.

From: Thomas D. Gorman's "China's Changing Foreign Trade System, 1975-85," in Robert Delfs and Thomas Gorman and Owen Nee: "China", Euromoney Publications, London 1986.

2.4 The "open-door" policy was officially launched in December 1978 at the Third Plenary Session of the 11th Central Committee of the Chinese Communist Party, as one component of the overall economic reform program launched at that time. However, the first clear indication of the government's intent to "open the door" came in July 1979, with the adoption of the "Law of the People's Republic of China on Joint Ventures Using Chinese and Foreign Investment", which thus permitted foreign investment in China for the first time since 1949.

2.5 From 1979 to 1985, the trade system evolved rapidly. The centralized FTCs lost their monopoly powers, and their branch offices began to operate as separate units. In addition, provincial authorities created their own FTCs to fulfill provincial export aspirations, and line ministries found it convenient to establish corporations to engage in trade in their products directly. A system of foreign exchange retention at the provincial and enterprise level was also introduced,[3/] and, when combined with the introduction of import licensing and an initial decentralization of license-issuing authority, this period saw a rapid change in the locus of trade activity. From being a residual activity carried out in a highly centralized manner, trade became, during this period, a central focus of effort, with provincial authorities and institutions in the vanguard. These various reforms in trade practices over the period were summarized in the September 1984 document on the reform of the trade system adopted by the State Council (see Box 2.2).

2.6 Perhaps the most important changes during this period were in the scale of activities, as trade doubled, and in the general attitude towards trade. From being a slightly suspect activity (see Box 2.1), foreign trade became one of the most desired and respected occupations. Nevertheless, many trade practices, such as pricing and the role of planning, remained essentially unchanged.

The Trade Regime in October 1986 [4/]

(a) Foreign Trade Planning

2.7 The foreign trade plan remains central to the trade regime in China, albeit with three important changes from the pre-1979 system: it is now driven more by export possibilities than by import requirements; it was a top-down process until 1979, but has become more of a bottom-up process, with

---

3/ Foreign exchange retention was introduced in 1979, but was formalized in January 1984 with standard rates, and was subsequently modified in January 1985 such that the retention rights were shared equally between the enterprise exporting and provincial authorities.

4/ For readers not familiar with Chinese trade institutions and policies, a more detailed description is provided in Annex 1. It should also be noted that all figures quoted in this section are World bank estimates based on interviews at the enterprise level, and the foreign trade plan remains unpublished.

Box 2.2: MOFERT'S REPORT ON THE REFORM OF THE TRADE SYSTEM OF SEPTEMBER 1984

On August 14, 1984, MOFERT submitted a report to the State Council on Reform of the Foreign Trade System, which was approved by the State Council on September 15, 1984. The State Council urged all responsible units to "carry out these reforms vigorously ... step by step in a planned way." There were five key elements of reform identified by MOFERT:

(a) Separate Government Functions from Enterprise Management and Strengthen Administrative Management of Foreign Trade. Administrative departments were to leave all day-to-day functions related to trade to the foreign trade enterprises. This would leave MOFERT free to concentrate on such areas as drawing up regulations, formulating long term plans, advising on the appropriateness of economic levers related to trade, conducting negotiations with foreign countries, and conducting research and training.

(b) Simplify Administration and Transfer Power to Lower Administrative Levels and Bring into Full Play the Managing Initiative of Various Foreign Trade Enterprises. "Foreign trade enterprises of all types should become independent of their original administrative departments, whilst keeping their own accounts, assuming responsibility for their own profit and losses and developing in the direction of specialization and socialization. There must be a large number of small and medium sized companies and enterprises to participate in foreign trade. Big production enterprises may handle foreign trade business subject to approval."

(c) Adopt Import and Export Agency System and Improve Operations and Management of Foreign Trade. "By import and export agency system, we mean that foreign trade enterprises should provide diversified services, handle import and export business as entrusted by production units and order-placing departments and collect service charges, while profits and losses are to be borne by the entrusting unit." This would "facilitate the combination of foreign trade enterprises with production units" and "raise economic efficiency."

(d) Reform the Foreign Trade Planning System and Simplify the Contents. This was aimed at "transferring more decision-making power of management to the foreign trade enterprises and production units," so that they could be more flexible and responsive to changing market needs, and "fulfilling the state plan with the maximum economic return."

(e) Reform the Foreign Trade Financial System and Strengthen the Economic Means of Regulation. This required the elimination of the state's responsibility for profits and losses in trade. The foreign trade enterprise should pay taxes instead of turning over profits to the state.

Source: Almanac of China's Foreign Economic Relations and Trade, 1985, pp. 388-398.

estimates of export availability and import needs made at the local level; and we estimate that it now covers only about 70% of trade. The planning system is described in detail in Annex 1 (paras 1.32-1.57). One key feature of the planning process that has remained during this period of change is that it is essentially a negotiating process between the local and national levels of administration.

2.8 The export plan has two components: the command plan and the guidance plan. The command plan covers some 120 commodities (compared with 3,000 in 1978) and we estimate that it accounts for about 70% of the plan in value terms (or 50-60% of all exports). These include such commodities as oil, coal, agricultural products, handicrafts, textiles and garments. The guidance plan covers the remaining 30% of the plan, or about 20% of all exports. The command plans are mandatory, are stated in physical quantities and are very specific, and producers receive inputs for export production under the materials allocation system. In contrast, the guidance plans contain value targets assigned to provincial authorities and FTCs, which have considerable flexibility in determining how to achieve them.

2.9 The import plan has undergone much more reform than the export plan. The import command plan in general now covers only the seven key raw materials [5/] which are under "unified management" (albeit comprising an estimated 40% of all imports) and is closely related to the traditional role of filling shortfalls in domestic production for the materials allocation system. The guidance plan (covering about 30% of all imports) is essentially a foreign exchange allocation mechanism covering essential imports for investment projects and of raw materials, spare parts and capital goods. The balance of imports (30%) are financed either out of foreign exchange retention by provinces and enterprises or by foreign borrowing by noncentral authorities, and are controlled by the import licensing system (see paras. 2.13-2.15).

(b) Foreign Trade Corporations and Trade Pricing

2.10 It has already been noted that, prior to 1978, all trade was conducted through twelve centralized FTCs. In 1986, it remained the case that nearly all trade was conducted by FTCs, but by a much larger number of them. Only Sino-foreign joint ventures and a few Chinese corporations have been granted direct trading rights. In 1981, FTCs (and their branches) under MOFERT controlled 89% of trade, but by 1984 this share had fallen to 72%, as a result of the proliferation of FTCs created under ministries other than MOFERT and by provinces. The total number of FTCs is unknown but is at least 1,200. Moreover, provincial branches of national FTCs became separate financial and operational entities. Each FTC has a prescribed "scope of business," outside which it may not operate. Most FTCs continue to be specialized in particular commodities or commodity groups, except for new FTCs established by provincial authorities, whose scope of business is basically

---

5/ The "unified management" commodities are steel, chemical fertilizers, rubber, timber, tobacco, grain, and polyester and other synthetic fibers.

defined as "trading in anything for which there is no FTC with monopoly power."

2.11 The FTCs conduct all trading activities, from the identification of markets and negotiation of contracts to the procurement of goods and their shipment. For exports, the large part of procurement takes place at domestic prices, which can be either fixed, floating, or free-market. Because FTCs' primary concern is to achieve overall export targets, they are not concerned to ensure that each individual export activity is profitable, or that each branch is profitable, provided that export targets overall can be achieved with given budgets.

2.12 The import system is very different from that for exports. Command plan imports and imports for major investment projects are assigned to specific FTCs, but for all other imports end-users can select an appropriate FTC. However, the more significant distinction relates to pricing. Whereas exports continue to be procured in general at domestic prices, the agency system is used for all noncommand plan imports; i.e., the price to the end-user is the import price plus the FTCs' costs, unless this would be lower than the fixed domestic price, in which case the domestic price is charged. Of course, losses are incurred in importing certain "unified management" commodities--such as steel and fertilizers, where the domestic prices are lower than world prices--but FTCs are compensated directly for such losses.

(c) Import Licensing and Tariffs

2.13 As the trade reforms have progressed, the import licensing regime and the customs tariff have emerged as important economic levers, used both to control "excessive" import growth and to protect domestic industry. If a good is defined as restricted under the January 1984 regulations (see Annex 2, paras. 2.20-2.30), it requires an import license. As of October 1986, there were 45 goods in this category, which accounted for about 30% of all imports. The list has grown over time, in part as a reaction by the Government to actual import trends.

2.14 Major or sensitive imports (command plan goods, assembly lines, major consumer goods) are handled centrally by MOFERT, and other goods locally (see Annex 2, Table A2.1). For restricted imports not included in the Plan, an application must go through several layers of administration, and can be rejected or cancelled after approval for a variety of reasons. Even if approved, the State Administration for Exchange Control (SAEC) may not permit access to foreign exchange rights, as happened for several months in 1986 for computer imports.

2.15 Until the adoption of the open-door policy, the practical purpose of the customs tariff was to raise revenue, as the planning mechanism was the primary determinant of the level and structure of imports. Tariffs are now becoming important economic levers in influencing import decisions. The principal purpose of the tariff, in addition to its revenue-raising function, is to protect and promote domestic industry, as well as to discourage "wasteful" imports. Tariffs (including temporary surcharges called the "regulatory tariff") range from 0-200%, with the highest rate applying to motor vehicles, and the zero tariff to a limited number of essentials such as grain and live animals and plants. We estimate that the average rate is 38%, cascading in the usual way--27% on intermediate products/raw materials, 31% on capital goods and 63% on consumer goods. The actual average rate of collection is, however, only 12-16% of import value, because of various exemptions, mostly on capital goods for technical transformation, joint ventures, and for the special economic zones. The potential impact of the tariff structure in terms of effective protection is discussed in Annex 2, paras 2.69-2.81.

(d) Incentives for Exporters

2.16 The trade planning and import regime described above is one that offers considerable protection for domestic industry and, consequently, creates a high degree of anti-export bias within the economy. To counteract this bias, several forms of export incentives have been created. By far the most significant of these is the foreign exchange retention mechanism. Under this mechanism, 25% of all foreign exchange earned is retained at the provincial level, with equal shares going to the enterprise producing the export and to the provincial authorities. It is also reported that these retention rights can rise to as high as 70% for above-plan exports, and are also higher for certain provinces, such as Fujian, Guangdong and Inner Mongolia.

2.17 Other export incentives are offered through the FTC system. Firstly, there is a more or less formal system of performance bonuses in direct proportion to performance against plan targets. For each US$ earned, if the plan target is achieved, the bonus is 3 fen, and for each US$ earned above the target, 10 fen. (Although such bonuses are targeted for producing enterprises, they are paid through FTCs and it is not clear to what extent they are passed on.) In addition to these bonuses, FTCs--rather than enterprises--carry any losses on individual exports, balancing such losses with profits made on other exports. Thirdly, it is reported that some provincial authorities also provide subsidies to their provincial FTCs in order to generate higher local foreign exchange retention rights.

2.18 A third type of incentive is provided to so-called export production bases; i.e., production facilities geared exclusively to exports under the control of FTCs or ministries. Various incentives may be offered to such facilities, such as low interest or grant financing, tax rebates, and preferential access to foreign exchange and required inputs. FTCs often arrange "compensation trade" financing of capital equipment for such facilities (see Annex 4, para. 4.28). The Government is considering expanding the production base system. This would offer to Chinese enterprises similar incentives to those offered to foreign investors in joint ventures (see Annex 4, Table 4.8).

B. The Impact of the Current Trade System

2.19 The trade system has undergone considerable reform in recent years, which is reflected in the volume and structure of trade (see Annex 1) as well as in the dramatic increase in the number of participants in foreign trade. However, further expansion of trade may now be more difficult, unless steps are taken to improve the efficiency of the present trade system. This section assesses the main problems that remain to be addressed in the current trade regime. The four main issues identified are: (a) the "air-lock" that has been created between producers and the world market; (b) the limitations of the foreign exchange allocation mechanism; (c) the degree of protection given to domestic industry; and (d) the absence of automatic and effective export incentives.

(a) The "Air-Lock"

2.20 We use the term "air-lock" to describe the buffer that has been created between Chinese enterprises and world market forces. The FTCs are the main point of contact between China and the world market, and Chinese enterprises are to a large extent insulated from world price developments and have very limited contact with foreign buyers and suppliers. Indeed, this isolation was an explicit aim of the trade system as originally constructed, as world market forces were viewed as irrational and potentially harmful to national interests. Although much has changed since 1979, the air-lock still exists to a considerable extent.

2.21 Its existence derives from the rules for the operations of FTCs and from limited trade rights. Each FTC has a fixed scope of business, outside of which it may not trade. This severely limits the extent of competition in trading, although the degree of monopoly varies a great deal between subsectors.[6/] At the same time, producers have no choice but to export through one of the FTCs, as only a small number of enterprises (except Sino-foreign joint ventures) have been given direct trading rights. Thus, for most producers there is no choice about whether to export directly or through an agent, and very limited choice about which agent to use.

2.22 The FTC system also permits a procurement pricing system to exist which is affected by world prices to only a limited extent. Whilst noncommand plan imports do now reflect world prices, most export procurement prices offered by FTCs are the same as the prevailing domestic prices.

2.23 The air-lock creates four problems, which may not have been critical in the early years of export development, during which China rapidly expanded traditional exports such as oil and standard textiles in which it has an obvious comparative advantage, but which will become increasingly important as China seeks to expand exports of new, less homogeneous products.

(i) Inefficiency of Exporting. Under the current system, exports are made in an economically inefficient way. The domestic costs of earning foreign exchange through exports varies widely, either because FTCs are able to subsidize many exports,

---

6/ For example, only the China National Textiles Import and Export Company (Chinatex) is permitted to trade in textiles, and it rigidly allocates quotas to its provincial branches. In contrast, there can be considerable competition for procurement of processed foods.

by cross-subsidy from profitable exports or imports, or because of distorted domestic input prices. Thus, some exports may be financially profitable but economically inefficient. For example, low electricity and steel prices would tend to encourage steel products exports, which may not be viable if input prices reflected world market values.

(ii) Inappropriate Export Patterns. Because world prices are not passed on to producers, or used as the primary determinant of which products will be exported, the pattern of exports will probably not correspond to China's comparative advantage. The production of profitable exports will not rise, nor will production of unprofitable exports fall. Similarly, because changes in world prices are also not passed on, the Chinese economy is prevented from reacting to changing external market conditions. The essential problem is that the signals from the world market are generally blocked at the level of the FTC.

(iii) Lack of Information. The air-lock of the FTC between the producer and the market also has serious consequences for the flow of information. Firstly, there is the problem of reacting in a timely fashion to market opportunities. If all export opportunities must be processed by the FTC, it may take so long to pass the necessary information on to a producer, that, by the time there is a response, the opportunity has gone. There are examples of this in China (see Box 2.3). Secondly, the absence of contacts between foreign buyers and sellers and Chinese enterprises means that these enterprises are foregoing much "free" technical assistance concerning such areas as product specifications and design, new product development, capital equipment, factory design, quality control, etc. Experience elsewhere has shown such direct contacts between foreign buyers and suppliers and all kinds of domestic enterprises to be one of the most important, most effective, and cheapest sources of technology transfer and marketing know-how (See Box 2.5 and 2.8 below). Moreover, as China develops exports of more sophisticated manufactures, including capital goods, direct contacts with foreign purchasers will also be important for the development of such skills as after-sales services, and installation. While FTCs attempt to obtain such information and to pass it on to enterprises, this becomes increasingly difficult, as exporters become more numerous, and exports become more diversified.

(iv) Lack of Competition from Imports. The final problem is that the air-lock prevents imports from performing one of their most important functions (para. 1.7), that of stimulating efficiency in domestic production by ensuring the maintenance of competitiveness.

(b) The Foreign Exchange Allocation Mechanism

2.24 Foreign exchange allocation mechanisms have two essential, overlapping functions: they allocate foreign exchange among the various potential users, and they determine a price at which foreign exchange is traded. The importance of this latter function cannot be overemphasized and has two major effects. Firstly, the exchange rate alters the relative attractiveness of producing a particular product for export markets or for the domestic market as well as the ability of domestic production to compete with imports. In addition, if changes in the exchange rate are permitted to have an impact on domestic prices, the relative prices of tradeable goods and nontradeables (i.e. nontradeable services such as power, domestic services, restaurants) will be altered, thus influencing the production and investment decisions of enterprises. Thus, the exchange rate is of key importance in determining a country's balance-of-payments situation.

2.25 The pricing and allocation functions of the exchange rate are overlapping in those economies in which its determination is left to market forces of supply and demand, because then it is the price of foreign exchange that determines its allocation; i.e., potential users of foreign exchange will only choose to acquire it for uses whose value justifies the price paid for it. Many countries, including China, do not permit market forces to determine foreign exchange allocation, but instead allocate it administratively. As already noted, 25% of foreign exchange earnings are allocated in equal shares to the provinces and enterprises which generate them, with most of the balance being allocated directly by the state plan for imports, debt services, reserves accumulation, etc. Moreover the exchange rate is determined administratively (options for alternative ways of doing this are discussed in Chapter III). It is partly because China does not permit the exchange rate to move in such a way as to equalize demand and supply of foreign exchange that it is necessary to allocate foreign exchange administratively, since, at the present price of foreign exchange, there is inadequate supply to meet demand. In China, this is compounded by the absence of strict budget constraints on enterprises, which dampens further the impact of any rise in the exchange rate on the demand for imports.

2.26 The foreign exchange retention system for provinces and enterprises has been established as a means of offsetting, at least partially the anti-export bias in the trade system, and is used as an export incentive. In a situation in which the market clearing function of the exchange rate is suppressed, resulting in excess demand for foreign exchange, the ownership of and permission to use foreign exchange is highly valued. Moreover, the scheme provides exporters relatively more assured access to imported inputs and enables them to reduce, to some extent, the heavy administrative costs of applying for foreign exchange through the regular channels.

Box 2.3: THE EFFECT OF DIRECT TRADING RIGHTS ON A CHINESE ENTERPRISE

The No. 2 Abrasive Wheel Factory in Henan Province is a long-established producer in China, accounting for a large share of domestic market production. Some 30% of its output is exported to 69 different countries. Until March 1986, all its exports were arranged by the China National Machinery Import and Export Corporation (CMIEC). In March 1986, it obtained direct trading rights.

In our discussions, factory managers gave three reasons for seeking these rights: (a) they wanted direct contact with customers; (b) they wanted to avoid unnecessary intermediaries; and (c) they wanted more direct access to world market information. When asked about the effects of having direct foreign trading rights, factory managers gave a good example showing how important direct foreign trade rights and contacts are to export success in diversified manufactures. A Japanese customer recently telexed directly an inquiry regarding 100,000 tons of abrasive materials, involving 12 different specifications and different delivery dates. The factory was able to telex back a price quote the same day and was awarded the contracts within 24 hours.

When asked what would have happened if exports had still to be arranged by CMIEC, the factory manager said that CMIEC would not have had enough information about sourcing the order; it would have taken two weeks to one month to reply to the inquiry, and, by that time, the order would have probably been lost to a competitor in another country.

It should also be noted that the factory finds several of the contracts it inherited from CMIEC to be unprofitable. As soon as these are fulfilled, they will be terminated, and only profitable exports will be made. (The company's calculation of profit includes a premium that it attaches to retained foreign exchange.)

2.27 For provincial authorities, this incentive is very powerful, as the possession of foreign exchange increases provincial independence and enables them to carry out some projects without central approval and funding. This independence is so valued by provincial authorities that some have found it worthwhile to supplement national export incentives (see paras. 2.32-2.35 below) with incentives of their own. For example, as already noted, it is reported that some provincial and municipal authorities provide subsidies to their FTCs so as to encourage increased exports and augment provincially retained foreign exchange.

2.28 The retention scheme has undoubtedly encouraged the development of industries which can compete internationally, and it has permitted exporters to undertake technical transformation projects. It is also a welcome recognition on the part of the authorities that foreign exchange is important and merits policy consideration. However, there are severe limitations to the present foreign exchange allocation mechanism, and the retention scheme in particular, both in terms of promoting efficiency, and in encouraging exports and avoiding balance-of-payments deficits:

(i) Its most serious shortcoming is the same as that of the FTC system (para. 2.23(i) and (ii)) in that it does not provide signals as to where China's comparative advantages in foreign trade lie, because the "air-lock" insulates the effects of changes in exchange rates from enterprises. FTCs do find exporting more profitable when the exchange rate is devalued, but, even so, the effect of an exchange rate change is severely muted. Enterprises which can earn foreign exchange without difficulty, such as textile producers, but have relatively small foreign exchange needs, have little incentive to export more or to upgrade the quality of their export production, because they derive little benefit from additional foreign exchange earnings. On the other hand, producers who can make substantial profits on the protected domestic market are induced to export, even at a financial loss, in order to be able to finance import requirements.

(ii) The power of the incentive implied in foreign exchange retention quotas is seriously diminished by limitations on their tradeability. If retention rights were tradeable, this would create stronger export incentives for producers with surplus retention rights.

(iii) Another major drawback is that, whilst the retention system offers a major incentive to export under current conditions, its value cannot be measured and varies widely for different types of exporters, as noted above.

(iv) Given the scarcities of foreign exchange, the current retention system encourages provincial authorities to establish production facilities geared for export production, but, as the system is not giving signals about which facilities to establish, it may be encouraging the development of exports which are not justified from an economic point of view.

(v) The system as currently operated makes the control of foreign exchange usage more difficult, as was witnessed in 1985, when at least some part of the rapid import expansion can be attributed to the unforeseen usage by provincial authorities of retention rights accumulated in previous years, despite the import planning and licensing system.

(vi) The retention system only provides foreign exchange to the final exporter, and not directly to the indirect exporter who provides inputs to the final exporter. While some informal mechanisms exist to overcome this, there is no established foreign exchange incentive sharing procedure.

(vii) Finally, the incentive is also diminished by uncertainty over the availability of foreign exchange, and by the possibility of losses resulting from exchange rate changes between the date of the acquisition of the right and the date of usage.

(c) Protection of Domestic Production

2.29 Protection of domestic production from foreign competition (e.g., through a tax on imports) acts automatically as a disincentive to exports (i.e., like a tax on exports). Excessive protection usually leads to very substantial losses in economic efficiency (see Chapter I, para. 1.7). China has tended not to regard imports as a source of beneficial competition for domestic industry, but rather as a complement to domestic production, filling domestic shortfalls and supplying technical expertise (usually embodied in machines) not available domestically. Protection in the Chinese trade system is provided through four mechanisms: trade planning, import pricing, licensing and tariffs. For command plan commodities, the plan determines the level of imports and ensures that import prices will not undercut domestic prices. This is supplemented by a licensing system which provides highly variable levels of protection by quantitatively limiting specific imports. In addition to offering protection, the increasingly important licensing system also arbitrarily awards economic rents to license holders, carries high administrative costs, and offers inducements for corruption. The tariff system itself also offers a high (and variable) degree of protection, as was discussed earlier (para. 2.15).

2.30 All these elements of protection ensure that production of goods for the domestic market in China is more profitable than export production and considerably more so for some products than for others. Even a uniform level of protection (provided, for example by a uniform tariff rate on all imports) reduces the level of exports and imports and thus the rate of technology transfer from abroad compared with a zero tariff situation. The quantitative restrictions and highly variable tariff rates presently found in China imply, in addition, significant distortions in domestic resource allocation as a result of the variable (and almost unpredictable) protection provided to domestic industries. In many countries, such a variable pattern of protection has led to highly inefficient industries and monopolistic practices.

2.31 In China, distortions arising from protection may not have been a major problem in the past, since pricing and investment decisions have been made administratively. However, China's economic reform will make these issues more important, as enterprises are granted greater freedom in pricing, production and investment decisions. If the present trade regime is maintained as these reforms are introduced, resources will be drawn towards those more heavily protected sectors--consumer goods, light machinery--and away from less protected sectors--agriculture, mining, intermediate products, capital goods. These problems may not be as serious in China as in smaller countries, because China's large market for nearly every product could make competition among domestic enterprises a potent force in reducing the worst effects of variable import protection. Nevertheless, economic efficiency could be significantly reduced. In particular, resources would be attracted way from export-related production.

(d) The Encouragement of Exports

2.32 For many of today's exports from China, the decision to export is either administrative--in the command plan or by an FTC--or else it is taken by a producer or province in order to gain access to foreign exchange. Exporting is regarded essentially as the means of financing a desired level of imports without recourse to excessive external borrowing. This is, of course, the fundamental purpose of exports, but China has created a system in which the imports to be made and the individual exports to finance them are determined to a significant degree by administrative decision, rather than permitting the volume and composition of imports and exports to be determined by economic levers.

2.33 As explained in para. 2.23, this approach may lead to "inefficient" exporting. Moreover, as enterprises (including FTCs) become fully responsible for profits and losses, it may become increasingly difficult to achieve the desired level of exports, as unprofitable exports are redirected to the more profitable domestic markets. The current system of export inducements (including performance bonuses) help to compensate for the anti-export bias in the system, but carry a fiscal burden (see also Box 2.4).

2.34 The strongest export incentive offered in China is the foreign exchange retention system as discussed in paras. 2.24-2.28. Although problems associated with the retention system have been noted above, it is nevertheless a powerful incentive. This power, however, derives from the weakness of the foreign exchange allocation system. If that system were able to satisfy China's foreign exchange needs, there would be no need for an incentive, whose power lies in the fact that it avoids the pitfalls of the allocation mechanism. Under alternative foreign exchange allocation systems (see Chapter III), the power of the incentive provided by the retention scheme would disappear, especially if that system included a market-based exchange rate.

2.35 The third set of questions about the present incentive regime concerns the "export production bases." This is a more general issue in connection with export planning. Experience in many countries has proved the difficulty of "picking winners"; i.e., it is very hard to guess in advance what the sectors of most rapid export growth will be. Of course, it is easy simply to plan for further growth of existing exports, but if this is where all the incentives go--which seems to be happening at present in China--many potential exports will be missed. If there is no generalized mechanism available, whereby exporters--not just the pre-selected ones--can get the incentives, then the potential new exporters will be discriminated against and will not be able to fulfill this potential.

Box 2.4: EXPORT PROMOTING SUBSIDIES AND GATT

Ideally, shifting to an outward-oriented trade strategy can best be accomplished by removing existing trade barriers, accompanied by appropriate exchange rate adjustments. In practice, many developing countries have attempted to achieve a similar goal by introducing export incentives--including subsidies--without dismantling import barriers.

In justifying this second approach, it has been argued that import liberalization can take place only slowly because of vested interest groups; exchange rate adjustment may cause domestic inflationary pressures; import taxes constitute a major source of government revenues and cannot be reduced; and the use of export incentives without dismantling import barriers encourages both import substitution and export expansion.

Export subsidies, however, have in recent years increasingly come under the threat of countervailing actions by some industrialized countries. Even domestic subsidies not directly related to exports have become subject to scrutiny and retaliation. In the US alone, 117 subsidy-related countervailing duty actions were initiated during 1980-85, compared to 45 during 1975-79 and only 2 during 1970-74.

Since subsidy-related countervailing actions could possibly be abused and used as a protectionist device, a number of developing countries have dismantled export subsidies that are not acceptable under the GATT rules and have joined the GATT Subsidies Code and/or entered into bilateral agreements to obtain better protection against such actions. (Under the Subsidies Code and national legislation in the case of the US, material injury has to be proved before such actions can be taken).

Promoting exports by an export subsidies-cum-import barrier scheme--a policy option successfully implemented by some developing countries during their transition from inward to outward-oriented trade strategies is thus no longer a politically feasible second-best alternative to an import-liberalization cum currency devaluation scheme.

From: Nam, Chong-Hyun: "Export Promoting Policies Under Countervailing Threats: GATT Rules and Practice", World Bank, Discussion Paper. VPERS 9, 1986.

C. Reforming Trade Institutions

Introduction

2.36 With its enormous resource base and population, China could eventually produce and export a wide variety of goods and services. The question is what to produce, and what to import and export, and how these decisions should be made. Such decisions become increasingly complex as an economy develops, and international experience suggests that they can be made most efficiently by enterprise managers guided by market prices (modified, if necessary, by "economic levers"). In foreign trade, it will be important to establish a policy framework that will promote efficient decisions on trade and production. (Inevitably, such a trade regime will inter-relate with other areas of reform, notably enterprise reforms, pricing policies and credit policies, and these relationships and sequencing issues are discussed in Chapter IV.)

2.37 The recommendations that follow would move China towards a regime that has worked successfully for many of the world's most rapidly developing countries, although the recommendations have been adapted to the particular circumstances of China. Such a system could be compatible with a planned commodity economy and could be implemented without serious dislocation to domestic production activities, although careful phasing and monitoring would be needed. In this chapter, the discussion focusses on medium-term reform goals in the area of foreign trade, and discussion of phasing, immediate steps and links with other reform areas is left to Chapter IV. The recommendations are essentially an elaboration of MOFERT's recommendations on trade reform, adopted by the State Council in October 1984, and the principles for the reform of the Customs Tariff, as adopted in March 1985. They would also be consistent with other economic reforms being adopted in China that stress the role of economic levers in place of administrative allocation.

2.38 A reformed foreign trade system would operate essentially through economic levers, and these levers would in turn depend on appropriate macro-economic policies. In particular, exchange rate policies, domestic monetary policies, and foreign borrowing policies would need to work in a complementary way. The trade policy recommendations which follow fall into two types: (a) institutional reforms designed to bring about a true decentralization of decision-making in trade; and (b) economic policy reforms designed to change the economic environment within which the new decision-makers would operate. Institutional reforms are discussed in this section, and economic policy reforms in Section D below.

Decentralization of Trade Decision-Making

2.39 At the present time, there are many different persons and institutions involved in making decisions concerning foreign economic relations: central planning authorities, MOFERT, national FTCs, local FTCs, provincial authorities, enterprise managers. It is undoubtedly true that considerable decentralization has taken place already from the center to the provinces. However, the decision to trade has, in most cases, not passed down to the level of the enterprise. The analysis of this chapter (and Annexes) has focussed on the key issues of the problems created by the separation of the producing unit from world markets, and the absence of an appropriate environment to induce efficient exports.

2.40 Decentralization in this sense does not mean that provinces should take over decision-making for trading, but rather that enterprises should take such decisions in reaction to the prices and economic levers they face. To achieve this will ultimately require major reforms across the spectrum of economic policies, notably including enterprise reform and domestic price reform. However, major progress can be made in the meantime, although for the reasons stated earlier, it is likely that simultaneous action would be required on exchange rate management. Several steps would be required to achieve efficient decentralization to the enterprise level and, as has been done in other areas of economic reform, it would cause least disruption if changes were introduced over time.

2.41 International experience has shown that no single organizational form of foreign trade is "best" for every product and enterprise. Product characteristics and the organization of production and distribution for a particular product strongly influence the choice of international trade and distribution channels. For some products, particularly raw materials and other standard products, relatively little knowledge of product characteristics and user requirements is needed. For other products, for example high quality garments, detailed knowledge of (often rapidly changing) consumer tastes is required. For still other products, for example, specialized machinery, detailed knowledge of product characteristics and user requirements may be needed and some technical after-sales services might also be required. It is thus very unlikely that the same organizational structure would be appropriate for these rather different situations.

2.42 The appropriate marketing channel will also depend on the characteristics of the buyer. Consumer goods will almost always require the intermediation of a distributor (wholesaler, retail chain), while sales of producer goods might not require any intermediary and are often carried out through direct contacts between producer and user. The size of the market is also an important factor. For sales to large markets, direct marketing or the use of specialized (domestic or foreign) traders might be the most appropriate, while for small markets a (domestic or foreign) general trading corporation may be the most appropriate.

2.43 Finally, the stage of development is an important factor. Having a comparative advantage in the production of a particular product does not necessarily imply having a comparative advantage in marketing that product. Most of China's East Asian neighbors have concentrated in their development of export capabilities first on attaining proficiency in production and have relied primarily on foreign buyers to market their products, only gradually moving into export marketing themselves.

2.44 The role of foreign buyers is particularly important in those manufactured goods where familiarity with consumer requirements (e.g. product design, styling, packaging) is of utmost importance (Box 2.5). It is exactly in these types of products that China's export capabilities and competitiveness is most constrained, because of the still too limited contacts between domestic producers and foreign buyers and suppliers. (The importance of these contacts for technology transfer and acquisition is discussed in Box 2.8).

2.45 The international experience suggests that China could benefit very substantially by removing the tight compartmentalization or "air-lock" between domestic and international markets that results from the present operating rights and procedures of the FTCs. As for domestic enterprises, substantial efficiency gains could be made by decentralizing decision-making. However, if decentralized decision-making is to lead to efficient operations, competition needs to be introduced, and prices and other economic levers (in particular the exchange rate) have to reflect the true costs of resource use. Some of the specific measures that could be considered include:[7]

(i) Eliminating, over time, the product-specific trading rights of FTCs, permitting them to engage in the trade of any commodity, thus becoming de facto General Trading Corporations (GTCs).[8]

(ii) Making FTCs fully responsible for profits and losses, and eliminating any plan exports and imports that imply substantial losses to the FTCs. At the same time, subsidies for command plan imports that remain necessary because of large differentials between domestic and international prices which continue for domestic policy reasons (e.g. fertilizer) should be provided by specific product subsidies in the state budget, rather than from FTC revenues, or general subsidies to FTCs.

(iii) Eliminating the exclusive right of Foreign Trade Corporations to engage in foreign trade. If appropriate indirect levers (prices, exchange rate, tariffs etc.) are used, there is no reason to exclude any enterprise from engaging in foreign trade, unless that enterprise produces one of the "special" exports discussed in paras. 2.53-2.56 below. Alternatively, direct foreign trade rights might be given first to all production enterprises whose exports or imports exceed a certain amount, say, US$1 million.

7/ These recommendations are quite consistent with the September 1984 report of the Ministry of Foreign Economic Relations and Trade on the future reform of the trade system (see Box 2.2). However, in many key respects the reforms outlined in that report have not yet been implemented and remain the key institutional reform issues.

8/ Careful phasing of such a policy for different types of products would, of course, be necessary given different rates of progress of price reform in different areas (see paras. 4.31 - 4.36).

Box 2.5: WHAT FOREIGN BUYERS DO

The following excerpt from a study of 113 successful exporting enterprises in South Korea, undertaken by World Bank staff in 1976, highlights the importance of direct external trade contacts between production enterprises and foreign buyers:

"The relations between Korean firms and the foreign buyers went far beyond the negotiation and fulfillment of contracts. Almost half the firms said they had directly benefitted from the technical information foreign buyers provided: through visits to their plants by engineers or other technical staff of the foreign buyers, through the provision of blueprints and specifications, through information on production techniques and on the technical specifications of competing products, and through feedback on the design, quality, and technical performance of their products by letter and telex.

Three-quarters of the firms said that the requests and recommendations of foreign buyers influenced the design, style, packaging, or technical specifications of products exported. Most of the firms confirmed that some of their exported products were made directly in accord with designs, patterns, or other specifications supplied by foreign buyers.

Did the foreign buyers mainly affect the packaging? Did they affect the design or styling (as would be expected for garments, for example)? Or did they affect the basic technical specifications? Almost three-quarters of the firms mentioned product design and styling. Packaging was also frequently mentioned, but few firms mentioned packaging alone. About half the firms indicated that requests by foreign buyers affected the technical specifications.

In a more detailed evaluation of the advantages to firms of direct contacts with foreign buyers, more than half the firms surveyed considered those contacts to be important for the adaptation of product design and styling to market requirements--and for the development of new products or new product varieties. About two firms in five said that contacts with foreign buyers were important for improved techniques of quality control and for improved techniques of production; one in five for improved cost accounting and control. Because of the activities of foreign buyers in supervising and checking export shipments, the exporting firms had a strong motive to implement effective methods of quality control. Three-quarters of the firms confirmed that foreign buyers attempted some supervision over shipments, usually by preshipment inspections. Other methods included periodic visits to the factories and constant surveillance by inspectors that buyers had stationed in the factories. In addition, foreign buyers made suggestions about techniques of cost accounting and control."

From: Rhee, Ross-Larson and Pursell: "Korea's Competitive Edge - Managing the Entry into World Markets"; World Bank/Johns Hopkins University Press, 1984, p. 61-62.

(iv) Eliminating the strict separation of domestic and foreign trade. FTCs could be given the right to engage in all types of domestic wholesale and retail trade (and manufacturing too). This would help to bring increased competition and efficiency to domestic commerce. At the same time, domestic commercial organizations could be given foreign trade rights, perhaps with some minimum requirements first that might be eliminated later.

(v) Consideration could be given to permitting a larger role for foreign buyers and foreign trade corporations in China's external trade. Joint ventures between FTCs and foreign GTCs could bring benefits from the latter's extensive marketing networks, and facilitate the transfer of marketing know-how to China's FTCs.

2.46 It is not possible to predict with any certainty or precision what the results of such a trade reform would be on the level of exports. Since exports that were not profitable would decline or be eliminated, total exports would probably fall in the absence of other reform measures. It was thus argued earlier that exchange rate reform would also be necessary to induce the appropriate level of exports needed to finance imports without excessive borrowing. If this were done, there would be no net change in the value of trade, but the composition of trade would change, as unprofitable or inefficient exports were replaced by profitable ones.

The Foreign Trade Planning System

2.47 If trade decisions are to be decentralized to enterprises, it will not only be necessary to change the way in which FTCs operate but also the way trade planning is carried out. We estimate that command planning continues to cover about 50% of total trade. Thus, half of all trading decisions are taken administratively and not necessarily according to economic criteria. Of course, it is likely that many of these imports and exports would take place within a non-command framework, but the absence of choice leads to distortions within the trade system. MOFERT has clearly stated the intention of moving from command to guidance planning, and some progress has been made in this respect. It has not been possible to reduce the scope of command planning faster because of the absence of appropriate economic levers--tariffs, exchange rate, export rebates, etc. As these are developed, it will be both possible and necessary to reduce command planning; otherwise, the economic levers would not be fully effective.

2.48 This is not to say that there should be no trade planning. The nation's trade balance is crucial to macroeconomic stability and the nation's creditworthiness, and the government must be able to adjust its economic policy levers, as necessary. Trade planning should continue, therefore, in the form of projections of likely exports and imports, and the careful monitoring of developments to ensure that the projected pattern is being, at least in the macro sense, achieved. This will be particularly important during the period of adjustment from the present system to the recommended future system, since it is very difficult to project adjustment problems and to time the adjustment path correctly. This also requires that continued attention be given to the preparation and improvement of trade statistics, so that the situation can be monitored with the most timely information.

The Agency System

2.49 In its October 1984 policy statement, MOFERT identified the introduction of the agency system as a key step in trade reform. We would strongly endorse this proposal and urge its implementation at the earliest opportunity. The changes recommended in para 2.45 (i-iii) above would be equivalent to a full implementation of the agency system. Although MOFERT recommended the introduction of the agency system for all trade except in agricultural and handicraft products, it appears to have been introduced to only a very limited extent, probably covering less than 25% of total trade thus far.

2.50 One of the main problems of the present system is that some exports take place at a loss, and some imports have to be quantitatively controlled. To eliminate these two problems, producer and importer must be able to feel the full effect of world prices. The main reasons that the agency system has not yet been put in place appear to be threefold: (a) it is feared that exports would decline; (b) it is feared that increased imports of consumer goods would occur because of high domestic prices, resulting both in balance of payments problems and industrial dislocation; and (c) conversely, it is feared that there would be shortages of key raw materials, since these could not be imported profitably at low fixed domestic prices. These are legitimate fears, if no accompanying measures are taken. However, a package of reforms, such as those recommended in Part D below and in Chapter III, could help to avoid such results. Successful introduction of the agency system requires the simultaneous introduction or management of other economic levers and, at the same time, these economic levers require the agency system to be in place to function well.

2.51 As one example of this, it is interesting to note the effect that the absence of the agency system has on the impact of one of the main economic levers, the exchange rate. The exchange rate was devalued by 17% in July 1986. One of the purposes of the devaluation was to improve the profitability of exports, by raising the Renminbi equivalent of world market prices. Amongst all the enterprises (except joint ventures) that the mission visited, there was only one enterprise whose export price had changed since the devaluation, and this enterprise had direct trading rights. Not one of the enterprises which exported through an FTC had received any benefit from the devaluation. This is not to say that a devaluation would have no impact on exports at all, since it would increase FTCs' profits (or reduce their losses) and permit them to finance a higher level of exports with any given budget constraint. Nevertheless, the absence of any direct benefit to enterprises from the devaluation--and indeed some enterprises did suffer increased import costs--seriously reduces the impact of a devaluation on exports. An increase in exports was an explicit objective of the devaluation, but the absence of the agency system is undermining the impact of that action.

Competition and Entry Barriers

2.52 If the trade system is to become efficient, the present monopolies must be removed. The October 1984 statement foresaw this, and some considerable progress has been made, but there do remain some artificial barriers. These are in two forms: (a) monopoly controls over imports and exports of certain commodities are vested in particular FTCs; and (b) MOFERT continues to prescribe the 'scope of business' of all FTCs and has to approve the creation of new FTCs, and the granting of trading rights to producers. If producers decide to export through an FTC (which many will), they should be free to select the FTC that best meets their needs. This means not only that FTCs should not have monopolies over particular commodities, but also that provincial boundaries should be no hindrance either. If an FTC in Shanghai or Guangdong can export Sichuan's products more efficiently, they should be permitted to do so. Clearly, to overcome the barriers to inter-provincial trade in exportables would require reforms of the foreign exchange retention scheme, given current export incentives.

The "Special" Exports and Strategic Imports

2.53 There are special market considerations affecting exports of oil, textiles and garments, and fresh and live food to Hong Kong, and exports of certain metals and minerals in which China is a dominant world supplier. China may wish at times to constrain oil exports out of political solidarity with other developing countries; China is required to limit exports of textiles and garments to comply with its obligations under the Multi-Fibre Arrangement (MFA); and China supplies 95% of Hong Kong's fresh food market, and, in the past, excess competition for this lucrative market led to price declines and an overall reduction in export revenues. At the present time, these exports are controlled quantitatively through strict monopoly powers vested in national FTCs. These FTCs then allocate quotas to their provincial branches, which in turn allocate quotas between factories. In the case of food exports, these quotas are allocated as frequently as every month by the National Cereals, Oils and Foodstuffs Import and Export Corporation in Beijing.

2.54 The present arrangements for these special exports work quite well for China, and, although we would suggest that they eventually be dismantled, this should be done with care and in a well-planned way. There are two ways in which these exports can be limited in the future, which would eliminate the essential problem of the present system that it locks in the present export pattern and suppresses new, potentially more efficient exporters.

(i) Export Taxes. Especially for oil and food exports, the imposition of an export tax could both achieve the desired level of export restriction and would generate revenue for government, instead of excess profits for quota-holders. It would also permit the export shares of different producers to change over time in line with their efficiency. Economic research could determine the appropriate tax levels.

(ii) Quota Auctions. In a restricted environment, export quotas have a price. The more efficient the exporter, the higher the price the producer can offer to buy a quota. For textiles and garments, auctions could be a much better way of allocating available export quotas and would have the same merits as an export tax. Quota auctions would provide strong incentives for increased exports of higher quality varieties and thus increase export revenues. The same could be tried for food exports, even in conjunction with an export tax.

2.55 Similar considerations also apply to the imports of certain essentialy raw materials, which are generally the same as those of the import command plan. The fixed domestic prices of steel, fertilizer and grain, for example, are well below import parity levels. Consequently, large losses are incurred in carrying out these imports. Clearly, if all the reforms recommended were carried out, there could be conflicts in arranging for imports of these loss-making, command plan commodities. Conversely, there could be attempt to export some of these same items procured at the low domestic price. It must be recognized that pricing and allocation reforms may take longer in these areas than in, say, light manufactures, and the timing of reforms of trading arrangements in such products would have to be linked very closely to progress in price reform (see paras. 4.32-4.37).

2.56 However, this is not to say that current arrangements could not be improved upon, especially in the context of trade sector reforms. In particular, the current level of subsidies on these products are not accounted for separately or specifically, but rather are included within overall subsidy accounts. Whilst trading arrangements involving monopolies/monopsonies are likely to be required for these commodities for some time, it would be appropriate to develop specific subsidy accounts related to the imports of these commodities required for state purposes. Alternatively, instead of maintaining low prices and subsidies for all such imports, it would be preferable to provide strategic subsidies direct to the key projects, but adjust the prices of the strategic products, so that the subsidy is provided for the priority uses, but not for non-priority uses, as is the case at present. Not only would this avoid cross-subsidy practices, it would also reveal explicitly to policymakers the budgetary costs of current pricing policies for these products.

The New Role for the FTCs

2.57 The proposal that the exclusive foreign trading rights of FTCs be substantially or fully eliminated (para. 2.45 (iii)) does not mean that FTCs would lose their role and and go out of business. Most enterprises would still prefer to use FTCs for all or part of their exports or imports. However, they would have considerably more choice and would use the trading corporation that provided them with the most efficient services. Since there are some economies of scale involved in trading (e.g. maintenance of overseas offices, telecommunications facilities etc.), one could expect the most efficient FTCs to grow into very substantial general trade corporations (GTCs). But unless their managers have considerably more decision-making freedom on such questions as where to open foreign offices, how to staff them, how much to invest in telecommunications facilities, or how many trips salesmen make, they can hardly expect to provide services equivalent to and competitive with foreign trade corporations from other countries. The more China's comparative advantage shifts towards diversified manufactured goods, the more important will effective overseas marketing become in determining success or failure.

2.58 For independent and profit-oriented FTCs to operate efficiently, it is essential that they be exposed to competition from other FTCs. To promote competition, two measures appear essential:[9/]

(i) Independent FTCs responsible for profits and losses should not be unified under one owner. Otherwise, they are likely to operate in collusion rather than in competition, and their efficiency will suffer.

(ii) Government responsibility for ownership or control should be separated institutionally from its responsibility for regulating an enterprise's (FTC's) external environment. Otherwise, there will always be a tendency by the regulatory agency to protect the enterprises under its control from competition, e.g., by restricting the entry of other enterprises into that line of business.

2.59 Ownership Options. The above principles suggest that the FTCs should be separated from MOFERT. One possibility would be to make each provincial branch an independent profit-oriented enterprise that would compete with other FTCs from other provinces for export and import business. The danger of this proposal, especially under the present foreign exchange retention system, is that provincial authorities would be tempted to monopolize all foreign trade of their province through the provincial FTC in order to maximize foreign exchange retention within the province. An essential complementary measure would thus be to pass on all foreign exchange retention rights to production enterprises. Competition could be strengthened either by permitting free entry into foreign trade activities or, at least, by substantially lowering entry barriers. At the same time, these new exporters should be permitted to carry out foreign trade for any other enterprise on an agency basis. The recent decision to allow foreign joint ventures to engage in foreign trade is a very sensible step in this direction. However, the potential benefits are reduced by the present quantitative restriction on their export activities (i.e., limited to their foreign exchange requirements).

2.60 In order to limit provincial attempts to monopolize foreign trade under the provincial FTCs, it would also be desirable to permit FTCs to engage in domestic trade. With their considerable technical and commercial skills, they could prove a potent force toward promoting interprovincial and interregional trade in China. Joint ventures by several provinces to create such general trading corporations could be useful. Similarly, international trust

---

9/ For a discussion of enterprise ownership and management issues see: World Bank: China: Finance and Investment, 1988, Chapter 3.

and investment corporations at the national and provincial levels are well suited to extend their activities further into international and domestic trade and could provide trade and financial services to exports and importers at the same time.

D. Reforming the Trade Environment

2.61 Once the decision to decentralize has been taken, it will be necessary not only to make the institutional reforms described above, but also to adjust some of the economic levers directly affecting trading decisions. In particular, attention would need to be given to the three areas of foreign exchange allocation, the import regime, and export incentives, as these will critically affect enterprise trading decisions.

Foreign Exchange Allocation

2.62 As has already been stated several times, the key accompanying reform will be to ensure that there is a market-clearing exchange rate. Options for ways to ensure this are discussed in Chapter III. However, there are two questions in foreign exchange issues: the rate and allocation. Ideally, there will one day be a full-fledged market for foreign exchange, and anyone who needs foreign exchange would be able to enter that market to buy it. In line with the general approach of reforming in stages, it is important to consider how the current allocation system can be modified so as to improve its economic functioning and move the system towards greater reliance on the market.

2.63 The existing allocation mechanism, and in particular, the retention scheme, can be reformed in two directions, before a more comprehensive solution is adopted.[10/]

(i) Tradeability of exchange retention rights. At the present time, enterprises are permitted to transfer their foreign exchange retention rights to another enterprise, but only at the current official exchange rate. Consideration could be given to developing a market in which such rights could be traded at a negotiated exchange rate. Such an option would act as an inducement to efficient exporters and assist with the allocation of foreign exchange to the highest value uses.

(ii) Increased retention rates. If the first approach were adopted, it would then also make sense to raise gradually the proportion of foreign exchange retained by enterprises. As this occurred, two things would happen: the central government would have less foreign exchange available to allocate, and enterprises would have greater surpluses to trade. For the first problem, the government could either enter the market itself as a buyer, or it could cease providing foreign exchange to some users and send them instead to the market.

10/ China will also want to discuss the advantages and disadvantages of the approaches outlined with the International Monetary Fund.

A New Environment for Imports

2.64 The environment for imports will be governed to a large extent by progress in two other areas: reform of the FTCs as described above, and reform of the exchange rate regime. Many of the problems of the present import regime derive from the use of import licensing and other forms of quantitative restrictions. The key element in the reform of the import regime is, therefore, to introduce an exchange rate regime that eliminates the need for such restrictions. As progress is made on this front, it is strongly recommended that all quantitative restrictions be phased out, so that control of the level of imports is achieved solely by the exchange rate and the customs tariff.

2.65 One instrument is already at hand to assist in the transition from quantitative restrictions to tariffs: the regulatory tariff, which is a surcharge to the tariff schedule. This could be used to dampen overall demand for imports, so that the initial changes could be more gradual than otherwise, thus avoiding the need for "shock treatment" to the system. A similar mechanism in its impact could be the adoption of a system for auctioning import licenses. (This is discussed further in Annex 2, paras. 2.53 and 2.204).

2.66 The effective protection rates generated by the present tariff structure vary considerably from one product to another with results that are perhaps not really intended by policymakers. Thus, once it becomes the principal instrument of protection, the tariff structure would need to be revised, with the primary intention of introducing more equality of protection amongst different products. This is a time-consuming process, particularly in terms of planning a transition. Preparation should therefore begin at an early time, under a reconstituted Customs Tariff Committee. In the meantime, one of the most important initial steps that can be taken is to streamline the current exemptions to the tariff.

A New Environment for Exports

2.67 The major problem of the current export regime is that there is an inefficient system of compensation for the inherent anti-export bias of the present trade regime. In addition to the simple export incentive scheme suggested below, the most important export incentive will come from reform of the foreign exchange regime, both in terms of rate determination and allocation, as already discussed.

2.68 The success of many East Asian countries in promoting exports has rested on a trade and industrial strategy that stresses specialization based on comparative advantage. The export policy complementing such a strategy should focus on removing the disadvantages domestic firms may face vis-a-vis foreign competitors. As China move towards decentralization, it will be important to ensure that Chinese enterprises are also freed of any such disadvantages. This is generally referred to as creating a 'neutral status' for exporters, whereby exporters are permitted to compete on an equal footing with their foreign competitors. In addition to exchange rate issues, there are three key areas where reforms could be undertaken to achieve this "neutral status."

(i) Duty-free Inputs for Exports. In principle, Chinese exporters can obtain duty-free imported inputs for exports, but the system is not automatic, or even well-known, and its application seems to depend on an enterprise's relations with its FTC. Moreover, there seems to be no provision for the drawback of duties actually paid on such imports for exports (See Annex 2, para 2.146-2.162). Assuring exporters free access to imported raw materials and intermediate inputs at world prices is an important element of providing neutral status. The simplest way to do this is to permit exporters to import duty-free the imported components of exports, with licenses for such imports being granted automatically. Again, such a regime seems to apply already for sino-foreign joint ventures. The current arrangements which apply to larger exporters (duty-free entry plus export verification) seems reasonable, but should be made automatic and universal, and in particular, it should operate as well for small, less-well connected enterprises as for large ones. Provisions are also desirable for drawing-back duties actually paid or for exemption or drawback status for domestic suppliers of inputs for exporters, and for exempting domestic suppliers of their obligations for the consolidated industrial and commercial tax. Such provisions would both enable the Chinese exporter to compete on an equal footing, and eliminate any resulting discrimination against domestic suppliers. An automatic system for such exemptions or drawbacks should be introduced as soon as possible (see Box 2.6).

(ii) Financing of Exports. As with access to foreign exchange and duty-free imports, some ad hoc arrangements exist for pre- and post-shipment financing of exports from China, both in local currency and foreign exchange, through the Industrial and Commercial Bank and through the Bank of China. Experience from other countries has shown that export financing at uniform interest rates for all economic activities generating value added for exports has proved to be critical if a country is to exploit fully its export potential (see Box 2.6). In many countries, such facilities are frequently accompanied by guarantee and export credit insurance schemes. Much of the reason for the absence of such facilities in China is probably the present role of FTCs in foreign trade. As enterprises become increasingly responsible for their own trade, it will be most important for such facilities to be established by the banks with rediscounting at an institution such as the People's Bank of China.[11/] Alternatively, these exporters' credit facilities could be combined with export credit facilities, which China may wish to offer to overseas buyers, into an export-import bank. Although, such facilities would guarantee exporters

11/ For a fuller discussion of how all these export incentives operate, see Annex 2, and in particular, paras. 2.163 to 2.171 and Box 2.3.

access to credit, it should be stressed that there is no economic justification for subsidizing the interest rates charged on such credit. The guaranteed access to credit itself should help to compensate for any residual anti-export bias in the system, and should itself only be extended so long as the anti-export bias remains.

(iii) Access to Foreign Exchange. The limitations of the current foreign exchange retention scheme were discussed earlier. For exporters, it is critical to ensure that foreign exchange is readily available to finance the imported component of exports. Failure to do so can cause exporters to miss delivery dates or be unable to respond to order inquiries, which can seriously damage an exporter's reputation. There are many ways to arrange such access for exporters, including the current provisions in place for sino-foreign joint ventures. The final form would depend on any reforms that China decides to introduce in the foreign exchange allocation mechanism.

E. Technology and Foreign Investment

2.69 In the past, China has preferred to develop known technologies by copying imported equipment or through completely independent research and development, rather than by importing technological know-how. This strategy of creating, and often recreating, technology contrasts sharply with the absorptive strategies of Japan and, more recently, the newly industrializing countries of East Asia, which aimed to assimilate and adapt foreign technologies as fast as possible. International experience has shown that the absorptive strategy has many advantages for a technological latecomer, because selective importing of technologies generally involves lower risks, a shorter time lag, and a lower cost of acquisition. Indeed, even the most advanced industrialized countries rely extensively on the absorptive strategy--not to do so would soon mean falling behind in technology and productivity.

BOX 2.6: PRESHIPMENT EXPORT FINANCING

There are three types of financing needed by exporters: preshipment, postshipment and investment. Of these, experience has shown that it is the first which is most critical. It is also the one which is most difficult to organize. In particular, it has proved difficult to arrange such schemes to include indirect exporters (suppliers of inputs to final exporters) and those direct exporters which utilize general trading corporations. One innovation in several East Asian countries that seems to address this latter problem well is the domestic letter of credit (DL/C).

The principle of the DL/C is to provide credit to the indirect exporter on the basis of the direct exporter's creditworthiness. When the exporter receives an irrevocable letter of credit for his exports--or other firm evidence of an export order--his bank is able, on the basis of this to open a second similar credit account on his behalf, with the indirect exporter as the beneficiary. The DL/C states that the bank will pay the indirect exporter when the latter submits evidence of delivery of goods to the final exporter. Armed with this DL/C, the indirect exporter can obtain production financing for his output.

The second benefit of this scheme--as well as providing credit directly to the exporter and indirect exporter--is that it provides a firm basis on which to grant export incentives to the indirect exporter. The documentation provided to the exporter's bank as verification for payments against the DL/C is the very same verification needed to assure authorities about the amount of export incentives--usually in the form of indirect tax rebates--that the indirect exporter has earned. In some countries, the government has also taken the next logical step and has assigned responsibility for administration of the export incentives to the banking system.

Thus, the DL/C solves one of the major problems of administering export incentive schemes: involving and ensuring full benefits for the indirect and small exporters, who would otherwise find themselves discriminated against.

2.70 The issue is not whether China should upgrade its technological capability through its own research or through imports. Studies in other countries have shown that these two routes are complementary. Enterprises with strong research and development capabilities can make more productive use of imported technologies and can be selective in importing. Selectivity is the key to using imports in upgrading technology. In the past, China has tended to alternate between the extremes of importing turnkey plants or relying wholly on domestic research and development. But there are many intermediate options. Elements of unpackaged technologies that can be imported include licenses, designs, key equipment, and consultants to help solve management, marketing, or engineering problems. Recent Chinese policy has stressed the need to import "software" (know-how) in addition to, or instead of, "hardware" (equipment). This is an important advance in technology policy, because it recognizes that individual elements of technology can be traded, and that equipment is not necessarily the most important element. While these are steps in the right direction, they do not yet go far enough. In order to maximize the benefits from technology transfers, further changes are needed.

2.71 As the subject of technology transfer and development is beyond the scope of the present study, the present discussion is limited to those aspects of technology transfer and development that are most closely related to trade and external economic policies in general,[12/] focussing first on different types and channels of technology transfer, and then more extensively on one vehicle, foreign direct investment.

External Economic Policies and Technology Transfer

2.72 The Nature of Technology. The term 'technology' refers to a very broad concept that has many different aspects. Technology can be "embodied" in machinery or human beings, or it can be "disembodied"; e.g., in the form of manufacturing instructions, product specifications or computer codes. An important aspect of technological knowledge is that much of it is not explicit, but tacit; that is, it resides within human beings or organizations and cannot easily be transferred except by transferring people or a whole organization. Very often, technology is "organizational" technology; that is, the ability to produce something with greater efficiency or at higher quality without necessarily using different machinery or other 'hardware" (Box. 2.7).

12/ A more comprehensive treatment of technology policy issues is contained in: World Bank: "China, Long-term Development Issues and Options" (1985), Chapter 7: "Managing Industrial Technologies" and in Background Papers 5-8 to that report.

Box 2.7: ORGANIZATIONAL TECHNOLOGY - THE CASE OF THE AUTOMOBILE INDUSTRY

The success of Japanese automobile companies in world markets in recent years provides an interesting example of the importance of organization as an element of manufacturing technology and productivity. The success of Japanese automobile companies has been based on their much higher labor productivity compared to US or European producers.

This higher labor productivity has been brought about not so much by more or better machinery (such as assembly robots) but rather by organizational innovations, in particular the just-in-time (kan ban) inventory system that greatly reduces inventories and material handling, and a quality control system that emphasizes the role of assembly workers and largely eliminates the need for quality inspectors and supervisors.

These two organizational innovations have permitted Japanese automobile companies to produce the same volume of cars in technically nearly identical factories with far fewer employees. Most of the savings are in inventory handling, quality inspections, supervisors and other overhead personnel. Today, Japanese automobiles plants are generally also more automated than most other plants. Together, these organizational innovations and higher automatization have increased labor productivity to twice the level achieved by competitors in other industrialized countries.

2.73 What the example in Box 2.7 shows is that technical hardware is only one element in the acquisition and development of technology, and has to be complemented by other elements. While the importance of 'software' has recently been stressed by Chinese policymakers, particularly in the context of foreign direct investment, in practice most technology transfer is still hardware-focussed. The transfer of 'soft' elements of technology is impeded by the "airlock" of the FTCs and the limited authority of enterprise managers over the use of foreign exchange (except in the case of hardware imports from foreign exchange retention quotas).

2.74 Experience in other countries has shown that channels of technology transfer other than machinery or foreign direct investment can be very important and less expensive and more effective. Examples include not only overseas education and training of technical personnel, but also hiring of foreign technical specialists, retired managers and so on. The case of a foreign manager being hired to run an engine manufacturing plant in Wuhan has become well-known and celebrated. However, what is unusual about this is how little use has been made by Chinese enterprises of this possibility in comparison to other countries. Japan and many of China's neighbors have made extensive use of foreign managers and technical advisors, especially during the start-up phase of a new enterprise or industry. Many Chinese enterprises would probably use this channel much more, if they had greater authority over the use of their foreign exchange. While the salary of a foreign manager may be high by comparison to Chinese salaries, they are often cheaper than unnecessary imported equipment or inefficient use of imported equipment. Studies of successful exporting enterprises in other countries have shown the importance of these and other 'informal' channels of technology, such as the advice provided by buyers of products and suppliers of equipment (Box 2.8).

2.75 Equally important as more, and more efficient, technology transfer is better domestic diffusion of the technology acquired. Very often, technical and managerial competence varies widely among domestic enterprises. Allowing greater labor mobility, especially among technical and managerial personnel would perhaps be the most important measure. Technology diffusion can also be enhanced by the development of a domestic technical and management consulting industry.

2.76 The examples above show that there is no single best way of transferring technology. All possible avenues--direct foreign investment, licensing, turnkey projects, purchases of material and equipment, consulting services, employment of foreign managers and technical specialists etc.--should be used, and each has its own advantages. The question is not which channel to use, but how to make best use of each channel, and this will be different in every case, depending on capabilities within each enterprise, the availability of local sources of technology, the availability of alternative foreign sources of technology, and so on. Only the enterprise managers directly involved can really judge which channels will be most appropriate. One of the most effective ways to absorb foreign technology is the 'apprenticeship' pattern, in which foreign assistance is relatively extensive at the beginning, such as for a plant using new technology, but is gradually reduced as further capacity is added and engineering services are localized.

2.77 Some Chinese observers argue that the liberalization of technology transfer has already gone too far. They point to the negative side-effects of decentralized technology import decisions, such as the emergence of excess capacity in a number of fields, brought about by the indiscriminate duplication of productive capacity in many parts of the country, either through ignorance of each other's planned activities or because of unreasonably high demand estimates. The case of some 120 television assembly plants being established in the last several years under the aegis of provincial and local governments is an example. Another negative side-effect has been the preemption of potentially invaluable opportunities for local suppliers to fill some of the machinery and plant equipment requirements. Given the packaged nature of the transfer of complete production lines, the scope for local suppliers has tended to be limited.

Box 2.8: SOURCES OF TECHNOLOGY

A survey of 113 South Korean export enterprises undertaken by World Bank staff in 1976 (see also Box 2.5) provides an interesting account of how successful exporting enterprises have acquired technologies (see Table). Of the various sources of technology, contacts with buyers and suppliers was the most important source, followed by employment of technical staff with work experience in other domestic enterprises or abroad. By contrast, licenses and technical agreements were cited as important sources of technology in only 8% of all cases. Overall, local and foreign sources were about equally important, but many domestic sources of technology were initially foreign, having already been assimilated by other domestic enterprises. This study shows the overwhelming importance of informal channels of technology transfer and the crucial role of efficient domestic diffusion of technology acquired from abroad.

IMPORTANCE OF DIFFERENT SOURCES OF PRODUCTION TECHNOLOGY (%)

	Local	Foreign	Total
Buyers and suppliers	9	20	29
Transfer of labor	11	13	24
Local technical know-how	19	-	19
Technical assistance	3	8	11
Licenses and technical agreements	-	8	8
Government R&D and information support	9	-	9
Total	51	49	100

Source: Rhee, Ross-Larson and Pursell: "Korea's Competitive Edge - Managing the Entry into World Markets"; World Bank/Johns Hopkins University Press, 1984, Chapter 4.

2.78 However, the source of these difficulties does not lie in the recently reduced control over technology imports, but rather in the still only partly reformed enterprise environment, in particular the still limited decentralization of decision-making to enterprises, the limited responsibility and accountability of enterprise managers, and the limited extent of competition, profit orientation and performance incentives under which enterprises and their managers operate. One of the main advantages of foreign joint venture enterprises in China is that they can overcome these restrictions far more easily than domestic enterprises, and this is one reason for the popularity of joint ventures in China. While these joint ventures provide an important experiment and role model for domestic enterprises, changes need to be made to give similar rights to domestic enterprises.

2.79 Quality Control. China also needs to give greater emphasis to quality control and quality assurance in the introduction of foreign technology, since prospects for finding windows of opportunities for Chinese manufactured goods in foreign markets hinge critically on meeting international standards. Allowing foreign quality control and assurance entities to come into China, either on a wholly-owned basis or through joint ventures with Chinese counterparts, could lead to more rapid international acceptance of Chinese products. For example, the absence of internationally accepted certifications of quality, (such as United Laboratories, UL), removes many of China's electronics components factories (i.e. printed circuit boards) from their own local market, as end-users do not wish to procure components that lack such certification.

2.80 Technology Transfer Legislation. Some government agencies have pressed for legislation with respect to technology transfer in order to protect domestic enterprises against unfair and restrictive practices by foreign licensors. A more effective way to address 'unfair restrictive clauses' in technology transfer agreements might be through enacting an anti-monopoly and fair trade law that would cover both domestic and foreign contracts. What is needed is a "promotional" rather than a 'regulatory' approach to technology transfer, but with an ultimate safeguard mechanism against abuses by foreign suppliers of technology. As technology transfer becomes more an enterprise-initiated rather than a state-initiated matter, it is also crucially important to streamline administrative procedures for effecting technology transfer.

Foreign Direct Investment

2.81 Until 1979, China was essentially closed to foreign direct investment. Technology was imported, first through turnkey plants and technical assistance from the Soviet Union, and later through turnkey projects and machinery purchased from capitalist industrialized countries. Since 1979, as part of its policy of opening to the outside world, China has permitted and tried to attract foreign direct investment from private foreign companies, mostly in the form of joint venture enterprises.

2.82 Progress in this area since 1979 has been, in many ways, remarkable. Indeed, it can be said that the growth of foreign direct investment is the symbol of the policy of "opening to the outside world." China has rapidly adapted to the needs and methods of the foreign investor, and the accumulated level of actual foreign investment in place--about US$6.5 billion is the end of 1986--is a testament to the seriousness of this policy. Moreover, China has showed a clear and sensible willingness to experiment and to learn from experience.

2.83 Nevertheless, the Government is rightly concerned about the amount and composition of the ventures that have been established, which have fallen short of the goals set. Many have been in (a) exploitation of coal and offshore oil; (b) labor-intensive manufacturing, mostly by overseas Chinese; and (c) hotels and ancillary services for tourists and other foreigners. These investments are useful but have not brought as much advanced technology as desired. Furthermore, the total amount has been less than China had hoped to, and could, attract; and, recently, the level of new commitments has been falling. Among the many reasons behind the less than fully satisfactory record of foreign direct investment so far is an inconsistency between (i) China's foreign investment regulations, which have put a premium on joint ventures being able to export, right from the start of their existence; and (ii) China's natural attraction to foreign investors, which is mostly its domestic market.

2.84 Among the things that China wants from foreign investment, the most frequently emphasized is "advanced technology." In earlier periods, great emphasis was put on "hardware"--machinery and equipment, or the plans to build it. More recently, the importance of management skills, labor training, and ability to organize, administer, and continue to develop an enterprise has been recognized, as well as the ability to continue to develop and create new hardware. Having the supplier of the technology committed to the success of the enterprise that is to absorb it has come to be seen as something of value--an important reason why the managers of many Chinese enterprises want to enter into joint ventures with foreign partners instead of merely purchasing machinery. Production and marketing of exports has also been desired, while the capital that comes with foreign direct investment has been a less important goal. This is consistent with experience elsewhere, which shows that, while the capital flows associated with foreign direct investment are useful, the other aspects are its most important benefits.

2.85 Most countries permit several different kinds of cooperation between foreign and local enterprises. In China, six different forms have been included in statistics and discussions of foreign investment; these are described in Annex 4. Of these six kinds of activities, the ones that would normally be thought of elsewhere as foreign investment are: wholly foreign-owned ventures, equity joint ventures, some contractual joint ventures and some co-production agreements for development of coal and oil. Little or no actual investment is involved in the two other forms: compensation trade, and processing and assembling. The availability of all these varied forms of "absorbing foreign capital" is, in general, good for China, because it gives enterprises great flexibility in choosing the best way to associate with foreign companies. While equity joint ventures potentially offer a wider range of benefits, and for a longer time than do the other forms, they are also more difficult to negotiate and may be more complex to operate. The contractual joint venture has been very popular, in large part because of the flexibility it permits.

2.86 Excluding compensation trade, and processing and assembling (which in most countries would not be counted as investment), and also the small number (but significant amount) of joint oil production agreements, foreign investment in China, as of the end of 1985, in wholly foreign owned ventures, equity joining ventures and contractual joint ventures consisted of: 4,742 project agreements signed and approved, for $8.5 billion, of which only $2.4 billion were actually invested. To put these numbers in perspective, $8.5 billion would have been about 3% of China's GDP, while $2.4 billion was about 0.8 percent. A comparison with Brazil, whose economy is about two thirds as large as China's, but which has welcomed foreign investment for most of the twentieth century, might give a very approximate idea of how much foreign investment China could ultimately attract; Brazil has a stock of foreign investment estimated at something above $30 billion, or about 12% of its GDP.

The Role of Foreign Direct Investment

2.87 As one of the many forms of technology transfer, foreign direct investment in joint ventures or wholly foreign-owned subsidiaries provides a whole bundle of different things. What distinguishes it from other technology "bundles", such as turnkey plants, technology licensing, or management contracts, is that it provides for some degree of risk sharing, since the provision of equity funds entails a residual ownership claim on the earnings of an enterprise, and usually a direct participation in, or control over, management. This direct involvement and the claim on profits provides a strong incentive for the foreign partner to perform well. A foreign partner with a significant share in the ownership of a joint venture will be interested in continuing to upgrade the technology as the joint venture develops. He will also be interested in providing organizational, management and marketing skills, rather than just selling some machinery at a profit.

2.88 Multinational corporations possessing technology and management skills that give them an edge over competitors are often highly reluctant to sell this knowledge, but may transfer it to companies in which they have an ownership interest in order to gain access to other markets or to production sites where costs are lower. Another characteristic that makes some types of knowledge more profitable to exploit within a corporate group (as opposed to selling or licensing the knowledge to companies not associated with the parent company) is that the knowledge is difficult or impossible to embody in a set of machines, plans, etc. Examples of such knowledge include the organization skills needed for complex production processes, such as automobile production (see Box 2.7); or skills and organizational capabilities needed for marketing a product or service abroad. When these problems are most difficult, complex and long-lasting, foreign direct investment is most useful.

2.89 Foreign direct investment also has limitations. It tends to concentrate in certain sectors and in certain types of countries. For very large countries such as China, much of it, especially the high-tech varieties, tends to be motivated primarily by the domestic market. Like any capitalist corporation, foreign investors are motivated by profits and increased markets. However, foreign investment can be attracted if laws and practices are made consistent with both the attractions of the host country and the motivations of the foreign investors. Moreover, recent history in several developing countries, for example Brazil, has shown that joint venture enterprises can generate export surpluses, even if their original primary motivation was the domestic market. Box 2.9 describes some of the different approaches that different kinds of countries have taken towards foreign investment.

Policy Issues

2.90 A major policy weakness underlying China's problems in attracting foreign direct investment is that Chinese policy-makers tend to pursue too many objectives at the same time. The natural advantage of foreign direct investment and joint ventures is to introduce a complex bundle of technology, management and marketing skills that cannot be easily embodied in machinery or turnkey plants, and these activities are most likely to be found in import-substituting activities, where China's large market provides the major attraction, and its skilled and low-cost labor force provides the possibility to become internationally competitive in due course. Often, however, this will take a number of years. For example, it took 10-15 years until the automobile industries of Japan and South Korea became internationally competitive, and exports became a significant share of total production.

2.91 This time is needed for the enterprise to get established, train its work force, achieve an efficient scale of production, find or help create local sources of high quality and competitively priced inputs and components, and get its costs of production down to where it can compete in international markets. The Chinese pursuit of motivating exports from foreign investment ventures, which is admirable in itself, is applied too zealously to all ventures regardless of their particular needs and abilities, and the difficulties this causes deter other potential investors from coming to China. Both the foreign investors and the Chinese side need to be more realistic in their expectations of how long it takes some ventures to export, and the Chinese authorities need to provide ways for the enterprise to have access to the foreign exchange it needs in the interim.

2.92 Another problem facing China in dealing with foreign investment, common to many other countries as well, is that the implementation of policy directions often falls short of the laws, regulations, and intentions of the Government. For example, many high officials recognize the situation with respect to import substitution and the foreign exchange balance requirement. But, in practice, adequate solutions to the problem are not always implemented. Additional attention is needed to ensure that actual practice is consistent with the policy directions laid down.

Box 2.9: DIFFERENT STRATEGIES TOWARDS FOREIGN INVESTMENT

Different developing countries have adopted different approaches to foreign investment. There have been three different approaches: (a) some of the middle-income countries have been relatively open to foreign direct investment, such as Brazil, Mexico and the Philippines; (b) others have been more defensive, limiting foreign investment either moderately (India, Turkey until recently) or severely (Japan in the 1950s and 1960s, South Korea before 1980); (c) finally, a few countries have tried to attract foreign investment, but have failed to create an appropriate environment (Egypt, Yugoslavia).

Brazil, particularly in the late 1960s and early 1970s, has been more open to foreign investment than almost any other developing country--except a few small Asian economies such as Hong Kong and Singapore. There were no restrictions on profit remittances, no maximum or minimum restrictions on equity shares held by the foreign partner, and foreign investment was welcomed in most manufacturing subsectors. No special tax incentives were given to foreign investment per se, although substantial inducements were offered to export-oriented investments. Foreign investment first was largely attracted into import substitution activities. However, with a shift towards outward-oriented trade policies in the late 1960s, many joint ventures reoriented their production to profitable export sales.

South Korea, like India, has taken a less welcoming, more defensive approach. Until the 1980s, joint ventures were limited to a narrow list of sectors. Foreign direct investment was excluded from activities that competed with Korean firms in export markets or for local inputs. The foreign share of ownership was limited to 50%, except for firms that exported all their output or had particularly valued technology. Neither Korea nor India attracted much foreign direct investment, but have recently relaxed their restrictions on foreign investment. South Korea, of course, accomplished a remarkable record of growth and development without much help from foreign direct investment.

Yugoslavia and Egypt decided to open their economies to foreign investment in the 1960s and 1970s, respectively. Both were countries with substantial markets and therefore attractive to foreign investors. However, both involved themselves in a contradictory situation not unlike China's: their overall trade policy framework discriminated against exports and they also imposed an enterprise-level foreign exchange balance requirement on joint ventures. Both attracted very little foreign investment.

Source: Annex 4

2.93 The Foreign Exchange Balance Requirement. From a balance-of-payments point of view it really does not matter whether foreign exchange is earned by exporting or by substituting domestic production for what would otherwise have been imported. What does matter, however, is the efficiency of export or import-substituting activities. For activities that require advanced technology, management and marketing skills, it will often be more efficient to engage first, and perhaps for a considerable length of time, in import substitution. The present policies that require, with a few negotiated exceptions, foreign exchange balance for joint venture enterprises is the single-most important obstacle to attracting foreign direct investment into those activities where they could potentially make the greatest contribution. The fact that such activities would indirectly save foreign exchange (by reducing import requirements) is not given adequate recognition by the present policy environment.

2.94 The most important policy change needed to attract foreign direct investment into activities where it can make the best contribution is thus the elimination of the foreign exchange balance requirement. The most desirable way to do this would be by introducing a market for foreign exchange for all enterprises (not only foreign joint ventures), where foreign exchange could be freely bought and sold at a market clearing exchange rate. Alternative options for introducing such a foreign exchange market are discussed in Chapter III. The recent announcement that foreign joint ventures will be permitted to export Chinese commodities up to an amount equivalent to their foreign exchange requirements is a step in the right direction although the limitations placed on which products are eligible has severely restricted the usefulness of this arrangement. A better arrangement, introduced in the October 1986 "Regulations on Encouraging Foreign Investment," is allowing the ventures to buy and sell foreign exchange for RMB amongst each other, at rates they themselves are free to negotiate. This practice, so far restricted to intra-municipal or intra-provincial transactions, could be expanded to the national level. However, this is likely to be a far less efficient vehicle than a foreign exchange market that would also open these possibilities to domestic enterprises.

2.95 Screening, Approval Procedures and Incentives. Potential foreign investors have encountered serious difficulties in China in negotiating not only with potential partners but also with the government. One pervasive problem is the complexity and the many changes over time in the rules, procedures, incentive structure, etc. As Box A and Table 8 in Annex 4 show, joint ventures are subject to approval by many different authorities at the municipal, provincial or central level. Different ministries (or their municipal or provincial equivalents) enter the picture, depending on the sector of the proposed venture. Each Special Economic Zone has its own set of procedures and incentives. Municipal and provincial governments frequently issue new rules and permit new incentives, which of course differ from place to place. Moreover, these are often not collected in any one published document, and in some cases are not published at all. Steps need to be taken to simplify the process, to make all the relevant information more readily available, to aim for more stability in the rules of the game, and to assure that provincial and local authorities follow both the letter and the spirit of the basic laws and regulations.

2.96 Tax and Other Incentives. Investors usually ask for high protection, which in general should not be granted. Similarly, China should take care in accepting foreign investment in those sectors which currently benefit from high rates of effective protection (such as consumer goods industries), unless it can be shown that such investment can survive without such protection. Income tax exemptions and other incentives that may increase after-tax profits have little or no influence on investment decisions of domestic market-oriented ventures, and thus in most cases are needless giveaways from the government to the investors. Brazil, for example, has attracted a great amount of foreign direct investment without income tax exemptions. Export-oriented investment, on the other hand, requires conditions for competing with other countries, such as highly cost-effective labor, easy access to inputs at world market prices, excellent infrastructure, etc. For competitive reasons, income tax exemptions may be useful in attracting such investment, although they do not make up for deficiencies in other areas. In a country such as China, it may make sense to concentrate a package of fiscal and other incentives for export-oriented firms on certain geographic areas that have the transportation, labor, and infrastructure needed by such firms--as is the intention in the Special Economic Zones. However, a "neutral" trade environment, available throughout the country for any enterprise, is likely to be more effective, as discussed above (para. 2.66-2.67).

2.97 Independence of Management. Chinese regulations and other actions have restricted the ability of joint venture managers to implement and achieve the good management practices and efficient operation that are among the major benefits that foreign investment can bring. Among the major problem areas have been limitations on the ability to select workers, to reward them for good performance or penalize them for bad performance, and to fire them if necessary. These restrictions have included limitations on the organization of productive processes and of the size and composition of the work force. Other, more subtle modes of interference occur when Chinese managers or workers in joint ventures respond to the dictates of political officials (both inside and outside the enterprise), rather than to the appropriate official of the enterprise, on operational matters. The government has recognized the necessity of increasing the independence of enterprise management, and Articles 12 and 15 of the October 1986 regulations have guaranteed considerable freedom to managers.

2.98 Exploitative or Collaborative Behavior. Another pervasive problem is the habit of some Chinese partners and many officials of continually trying to extract the most short-run benefit in dealing with foreign investors, to the detriment of China's long-term gains from foreign investment.

2.99 In examining the experience of other countries, it is clear that the successful countries have treated the process as a positive sum game--i.e., they approached foreign investment as an activity that should leave all parties better off than they were before. They have treated the foreign investors as potential long-term allies in the development of the country. To insure a positive contribution, they have regulated foreign investment; they have directed it to where they wanted it; they have prohibited it from some activities and have given it incentives to engage in others. But they have done this in ways that have helped joint venture enterprises to prosper, thus attracting more reinvestment of profits from existing enterprises and more new investment from others. Some officials agree that China should adopt such an approach to aim at maximizing long-term benefits from all potential foreign investors, not just immediate benefits from those already there. Adopting this more far-sighted approach, as well as taking steps to assure its implementation throughout the country, are worth considerable effort.

2.100 Local Sources of Finance. It is normal practice in most countries to finance a certain part of a company's needs with debt. The appropriate debt/equity ratio varies with the riskiness of the venture, the expected variability in its cash flows, and other factors, but in most cases investors find it unnecessarily expensive and risky to finance companies completely with equity. In China, some progress has been made in providing institutions and channels through which joint ventures can borrow or obtain loan guarantees--either in RMB or in foreign currency. But more could be done. One problem is the legal ceilings placed on the debt/equity ratio of each foreign joint venture, which depend only on the size of the company. (Small companies must be financed 100% with equity). These restrictions make no sense from the point of view of the enterprise. There are two other problems--different but related--with the current state of affairs regarding sources of loans and guarantees. One is a problem for the enterprises: it may be difficult for them to borrow what they need. The other is a problem for China: almost every existing source of loans or loan guarantees in effect involves the Chinese State, ultimately, as the lender or the guarantor. This obligation may be in part responsible for the government's mixed feelings about foreign investment as a source of capital. What is needed, therefore, is the creation and strengthening of institutions and channels that can lend to joint venture enterprises and are not subsidized by the State, but responsible for their own profits and losses.

2.101 Policies for Export-Oriented FDI. To attract FDI that is focussed on producing manufactured goods primarily for exports, any country must compete with other countries that are also trying to attract the same investments. This competition is very keen. The characteristics that tend to attract such investment are: (a) disciplined, hardworking and skilled labor; (b) good transportation and communication facilities; and (c) freedom from government interference in the management of the enterprise. Other characteristics of some importance are low prices for other inputs such as land, utilities, etc.; political stability; and low taxes.

2.102 Geographically, China's location in the Far East places it in direct competition with the world's best performers in the competition for this kind of investment. Potential foreign investors in export-oriented ventures have found that labor in China is neither as cheap as they had expected nor as highly productive. Regulations or practices have often required some sort of parity of wages for local workers with workers in similar occupations in more advanced countries. Foreign investors have also encountered high rents for factory sites, high charges for electricity and water, and deficiencies in communication and transport systems. They have encountered bureaucratic difficulties in doing business.

2.103 Recognizing these problems, the Government has been taking steps to solve them. There has been progress on every one of the problems mentioned. The 22 Articles of October 11, 1986 promise better treatment in regard to surcharges on wages, site rentals, utility supply and charges, taxes, and the freedom to manage enterprises without interference, including the freedom to hire, fire, and set wages independently. Additionally, regulations issued on December 1, 1986, provide for importation of inputs without the need for licenses or the payment of duties or other taxes. Thus, although the results will depend on how well these regulations are implemented and how well other problems facing export-oriented enterprises are dealt with, policies for such enterprises are being improved significantly.

2.104 Technology Transfer. The authorities rightly stress that foreign investment is especially welcome when it brings advanced technology that China needs. The regulations of October 11 specifically provide for better treatment of such enterprises. However, past experience suggests that the criteria of what constitutes useful "advanced technology" may sometimes be too narrow. At times, there is excessive focus on "hardware"--machinery and equipment, or the plans, patents, or process description for making such equipment. As noted elsewhere in this report, the so-called "soft" aspects that increase efficiency--good management, labor training, efficient organization of production and of all other functions of the enterprise--are just as important.

2.105 The potential for technology transfer from foreign investment is by no means limited to the joint venture itself. Joint ventures can help to modernize the rest of a developing economy as well. Contacts with purely local enterprises can diffuse technology and good management practices throughout the economy. But such contacts must be permitted and indeed encouraged; joint venture enterprises should be encouraged (but not forced, without regard to price and quality) to purchase inputs from local sources, to sell products to local users, and to compete with Chinese enterprises. Of course, for the local institutions to benefit fully from this contact, they must themselves be motivated to improve and be free to improve. By moving in this direction, China's ongoing enterprise reform will enhance the usefulness of foreign investment in the modernization of the entire economy. However, to attract such foreign investment in significant amounts, China will have to make further progress on the problems discussed above, especially those associated with the foreign exchange balance requirement.

III. TRADE POLICY AND MACROECONOMIC MANAGEMENT

3.1 The second chapter of this report dealt with various issues relating to the efficiency of China's foreign economic relations: how to influence decisions on trade and exploit China's comparative advantage; how best to arrange for the utilization of technology and manage technology transfer; and how to promote appropriate foreign direct investment. The present chapter is concerned with the macroeconomic environment within which these decisions will be made. Whilst efficiency questions are critical, they can be overwhelmed if there is a failure to maintain macro-balance.

3.2 If macroeconomic policies are not appropriate, micro reforms can cause macroeconomic imbalances, which can result in a reversal of the micro-economic reforms, with adverse consequences for improvements in efficiency. Moreover, macroeconomic imbalances are likely to lead to large and unsustainable balance-of-payments deficits and an excessive amount of external debt, as illustrated by the experience of many countries, particularly the large Latin American states in the 1980s. Therefore, if China decides to decentralize foreign trade decisions to enterprises and independent foreign trade corporations, it will be vital to ensure that these are carried out in an appropriate macroeconomic environment. Of particular importance are the exchange rate, monetary and fiscal policies, and external debt management.

A. The Role of Macroeconomic Policies

The Exchange Rate

3.3 The exchange rate is one of the most important prices in an economy. It links international and domestic prices and determines the relative price between tradeable and nontradeable goods and services. If the exchange rate depreciates or is devalued, the price of tradeables--both exports and import substitutes--rises, and, in response, the supply of these products increases, and the balance of trade moves to the direction of a smaller deficit (or greater surplus). The size and speed of the supply response depends on the extent to which it results from (a) putting to use previously idle resources; (b) increased productivity through more intensive use of resources; (c) movement of resources from nontradeables, such as housing construction and services, to tradeables; or (d) movements of resources within the tradeables sector to more productive employment (e.g., from previously protected import substitutes to exports). The supply response will be quicker where the first two conditions prevail than in cases where a transfer of resources is required. If the exchange rate appreciates, the reverse of what happens in the case of a depreciation occurs, and the trade balance moves in the direction of a greater deficit (or smaller surplus).

3.4 Exchange rates can be determined by market forces or administratively. Where the rate is determined administratively, indicators are needed to signal whether the exchange rate is appropriate. These indicators may also be useful when the exchange rate is freely determined to assess the likely future path of the rate and to determine whether or not it is consistent with other policies and with short-term and medium-term economic policy objectives.

3.5 In assessing the appropriateness of an exchange rate, it is important to take into account the stance of other policy instruments. In particular, excessive administrative restrictions on external transactions, high import tariffs, and/or export subsidies result in an exchange rate (whether it is administered or freely floating) which is higher than would occur in their absence. While such an exchange rate may be consistent with external balance, it is not fully appropriate, in that it relies on restrictions that result in an inefficient pattern of foreign trade and a misallocation of domestic resources. If it becomes necessary to increase such restrictions to keep the balance of payments within sustainable limits, this is evidence that the exchange rate has become more overvalued. Alternatively, if restrictions are not increased, and an excessive balance-of-payments deficit emerges, this is also evidence that the exchange rate has become more overvalued.

3.6 Within the above context, there are a number of indicators for assessing the extent to which an exchange rate is inappropriate. The most often used indicators are elasticity analyses, various indicators of competitiveness, commodity-specific analysis, and exchange rates in legal or illegal parallel markets (see Box 3.1). While no one indicator is wholly reliable, if a number of indicators are used, and if proper account is taken of their statistical and methodological limitations and of the stance of other policies, an informed judgment can be made. Such a judgment must also take into account the objectives with regard to exports, debt and international reserves of the country concerned.

3.7 In cases where the exchange rate is administered, exchange rate policy must be implemented flexibly to ensure that the rate remains appropriate. For that reason, it is necessary to update exchange rate indicators frequently and to have the necessary political commitment to make exchange rate adjustments as required. Of course, an exchange rate adjustment can be avoided by an increase in administrative restrictions and tariffs. In terms of the aggregate demand for imports, administrative restrictions, tariffs, and an exchange rate devaluation can all have the same effect. However, economic theory and international experience strongly suggest that administrative restrictions tend to be less efficient than tariffs, and these are in turn less efficient than exchange rate adjustments. This is because an exchange rate devaluation discourages imports in a neutral fashion (i.e., does not distort relative prices among them as a selective tariff or administrative import restriction would do) and encourages exports at the same time. Consequently, the use of exchange rate adjustment is likely to lead to a more efficient pattern of foreign trade.

Box 3.1: INDICATORS FOR ASSESSING THE APPROPRIATENESS OF AN EXCHANGE RATE

The elasticities approach estimates the effect of exchange rate adjustments on export supply and import demand and uses such estimates in a simulation to arrive at an exchange rate adjustment that is consistent with medium-term balance of payments objectives. Unlike indicators of competitiveness (discussed below), this method has the advantage that it is not limited to comparison with a particular base period, and it allows other factors that influence the balance of payments to be taken into account. Like indicators of competitiveness, however, it is based on historical experience or econometric estimates and must be modified to take account of structural change. Data limitations make use of this method in its explicit form difficult.

The most frequently used index of changes in a country's overall competitiveness is the Real Effective Exchange Rate (REER). This is the nominal effective exchange rate index adjusted for relative price movements in the country concerned and abroad. The main difficulty with this index is that it requires choosing a base period when the country's external position was sustainable. If domestic and external policies and conditions are more adverse than in the base period, competitiveness would need to be improved beyond what it was in the base period. In addition, it needs to be modified to take into account structural or policy changes (e.g., a reduction in severe restrictions that have been used to keep the balance of payments deficit to a financeable level). Care is also required in interpreting the price indices used in this calculation, if extensive price and wage controls exist.

Commodity-specific analysis usually involves calculating the domestic cost of producing exports and import substitutes per unit of foreign exchange thereby earned, after correcting for all price distortions and netting out taxes and subsidies. This calculation provides an implicit exchange rate for each commodity and allows a ranking of activities according to comparative advantage and an assessment of the prevailing exchange rate. This method focuses directly on profitability and can be useful in countries where production of tradeables is concentrated in a few key commodities. Because of its data requirements, however, it is seldom used.

The existence of a parallel market where foreign exchange trades at a price different from the official rate is prima facie evidence that the official exchange rate is failing to reflect demand and supply fully. A legal parallel exchange rate is sometimes introduced as a transitional measure as a means of determining the appropriate level at which to reunify the exchange rate. The exchange rate in an illegal parallel market is a less reliable indicator of the equilibrium exchange rate, because the size of the market is limited by penalties for dealing in the market.

Source: Based on: "Formulation of Exchange Rate Policies in Adjustment Programs," IMF, Occasional Paper No. 36.

3.8 Rather than fixing the exchange rate, a number of developing countries have adopted floating rate systems in recent years. In some of these countries, dual or multiple exchange rates were maintained for short periods of time as transitional devices before unification of the exchange system. Most countries that adopted floating systems did so because of severe balance-of-payments difficulties, which previously had been addressed by extensive controls on foreign exchange transactions. This had led to disintermediation in official exchange systems, with large volumes of transactions going through unofficial exchange markets, making it difficult to predict the equilibrium exchange rate. At the same time, the lack of official foreign exchange resources had made it difficult to support the administered exchange rate. The floating of the exchange rate was intended to bring foreign exchange transactions back into legal channels and to permit a liberalization of exchange and trade restrictions. In other cases, it was believed that a floating exchange rate would lead to a more efficient allocation of resources than the previous administered system, while in still other cases there was a desire on the part of the authorities to reduce political responsibility for changes in the exchange rate. (Box 3.2).

3.9 As indicated above, some developing countries have maintained dual or multiple exchange rates for short periods as transitional devices to unified floating exchange systems (Box 3.3). Generally, multiple exchange rate systems are not encouraged, because they are likely to result in a misallocation of resources, are difficult to administer, provide incentives to seek illegal windfall gains, and are harmful to other countries which retaliate against such systems. Apart from these considerations, such systems often do not have their intended economic effects (e.g., to limit inflation or to influence the pattern of trade through their implicit taxes and subsidies). The lesson from experience is that if dual or multiple exchange rate systems are adopted as a means of determining the appropriate level for the exchange rate, they should be as part of a well-conceived plan that includes measures that will help eliminate the need for such a system, and brings about the unification of the exchange system during a specific and, preferably, brief period.

Box 3.2: RECENT EXPERIENCE OF DEVELOPING COUNTRIES WITH FLOATING EXCHANGE RATES

Until the early 1980s, the conventional wisdom was that the volume of currency transactions and the relatively underdeveloped state of financial markets in most developing countries ruled out the use of freely floating exchange rates for these countries. However, in the last few years, the number of developing countries with floating arrangements has risen to 15, from only one prior to 1983 (this was Lebanon which had little choice given its situation). There are two main forms of arrangement that have been developed: foreign exchange auctions (6 countries), and domestic interbank markets (9 countries).

In a foreign exchange auction (Bolivia, Ghana, Guinea, Jamaica, Uganda, Zambia), the general method of operation is for the central bank to put up a certain amount of foreign exchange for auction. There are rules to qualify for entry to the auction, and bidders submit written bids for the amount of domestic currency they are willing to pay for a certain amount of foreign exchange. The exchange rate is then determined as the price bid for the last unit of foreign exchange available at the auction. Auctions vary in frequency from daily to weekly, and the percentage of foreign exchange available to the central bank that is auctioned varies considerably from country to country.

Interbank markets permit commercial banks to determine the exchange rate, the rate is determined on an ongoing basis by negotiation between banks and clients, with the group of banks fixing the price so as to match available supply with their clients' demands.

It is clear from the list of countries that have adopted these schemes that most of them were in very serious economic difficulties, including low foreign exchange reserves, external arrears, and growing illegal transactions in foreign exchange.

The experience to date has been generally positive, although in general the interbank experience is 'happier' than that of auctions, three of which (Jamaica, Uganda, Zambia) are currently in difficulty. Not only have the arrangements permitted a correction of exchange rate disequilibria, they have also permitted countries to liberalize trade and capital arrangements. This, together with exchange rate changes, has frequently served to stem capital flight and has even encouraged reflow in some cases. Moreover, it has also been the case that fears that such arrangements would lead to a 'free fall' with unstable rates encouraging cost-push inflation, have been largely unfounded.

Source: Peter J. Quirk et al: "Floating Exchange Rates in Developing Countries:" IMF Occasional Paper #53, May 1987.

Box 3.3: THE TRANSITION TO A MARKET CLEARING EXCHANGE RATE - EXPERIENCES OF TWO ECONOMIES 1/

South Korea had extensive administrative restrictions on foreign trade in the late 1950s. Not only was the exchange rate overvalued and thus discriminated against exports, but the economy also had an inefficient multiple exchange rate system that applied different exchange rates for different types of imports and exports (e.g. government imports, other imports, different types of export goods). In its economic impact, the multiple exchange rate system was not very different from the present trade system in China, where export enterprises receive domestic, rather than international prices for their goods. The transition to a market clearing exchange rate in South Korea in 1964 was the initial and single most important element of trade reform.

During 1961-62, the government of South Korea pursued very expansionary fiscal and monetary policies. As a result, the official exchange rate became highly overvalued, and foreign exchange certificates (similar to China's foreign exchange retention rights, but with 100% retention) traded at an increasing premium (50% by April 1964) over the official exchange rate. In May 1964, the official exchange rate was devalued by 50%. However, the foreign exchange certificate continued to trade at a--albeit lower--premium. A year later, in March 1965, the official and the market-determined foreign exchange certificate rate were unified by setting the official rate on the basis of the certificate price quoted in the free exchange market. As fiscal and monetary policies remained expansionary, and inflation rates were consequently higher than those of trade partners, the nominal exchange rate continued to decline (in terms of dollars per won), but the real (inflation adjusted) exchange rate was very stable in subsequent years.

In 1982, the Ugandan economy was in a serious condition after a period of civil strife, and the exchange rate was seriously overvalued, but by an unknown amount. In July 1982, the Government established a two-tier exchange rate regime, with an official rate set by the Government, and a parallel rate determined by a foreign exchange auction. As one of the key purposes of using an auction was to ascertain the equilibrium exchange rate, this rate was used as the guide, and the official rate was gradually devalued so as to achieve convergence. This was done in stages over a period of 22 months, until convergence was achieved in early 1984. Initially, the parallel auction rate had been three times as high as the official rate, but, interestingly, the parallel rate did not depreciate any further over the dual rate period, and when unification of the rate was achieved, it was at a rate very similar to the opening parallel rate. It should, however, be noted that this successful transition was followed several months late by a surge of inflation as fiscal policies were relaxed, together with accommodating monetary policies to finance the rising public sector deficit.

1/ For a similar experience in another East Asian economy, see Liang and Liang in Hong: "Trade and Growth of Advanced Developing Countries in the Pacific Basin," KDJ Press, 1981.

Sources: For South Korea: Frank, Kim and Westphal: Foreign Trade Regimes: South Korea, NBER/Columbia University Press, 1975, Chapter 4;
For Uganda: as for Box 3.2.

Monetary and Fiscal Policies

3.10 A discussion of monetary and fiscal policies is beyond the scope of this report and has been dealt with in more depth in the Bank's recent 'Finance and Investment' report.[2/] However, it should be noted that monetary and fiscal policies impact on the external sector, and can either contribute to or help to alleviate balance of payments problems. Monetary policy should be formulated taking into account the objectives for the rate of national income growth and inflation and likely developments in money velocity.[3/]

3.11 What happens if money creation is higher than would be justified on the above grounds? Credit creation increases the buying power of individuals and enterprises, who use the credit to attempt to purchase goods and services. Rapid credit creation can lead to demand which cannot, in the short run, be satisfied domestically because of supply constraints, especially in an economy such as China's, which has been relatively slow to respond to changing market conditions. This excess demand results in domestic price pressures, or a deterioration in the balance of payments, or some combination of the two. In a situation of limited availability of foreign exchange, with fixed exchange rates and strict import controls, the increment in demand will be channelled entirely to the domestic market, and domestic prices will rise in line with the excess credit creation. The price increases will, in turn, bring about an overvaluation of the exchange rate, and exports will be less competitive (and fall), causing a deterioration in the current account of the balance of payments.

3.12 If there is foreign exchange available, and imports are less strictly controlled, part of the excess credit will be channelled into imports, limiting the impact on domestic price inflation. If a loss of international reserves is acceptable, this situation may not have harmful long-term effects, provided that the excess credit creation is quickly curbed. If foreign exchange reserves are scarce, a balance-of-payments deficit can only be avoided following excess credit creation if the exchange rate is permitted to depreciate. In this case, there will be domestic price changes, but compensated by exchange rate changes. This has been the typical situation of several Latin American countries in recent years, notably Brazil. This circular process of inflation and devaluation can only be stopped if the domestic sources of inflationary pressures are brought under control (e.g., budgetary deficits, excessive credit growth).

3.13 However, it is important to stress that a devaluation will not necessarily cause an increase in the general level of prices. The primary effect of an exchange rate change is to alter the relative prices of tradeable

---

2/ See: World Bank: 'China - Finance and Investment' 1988, Chapter 7.

3/ 'Velocity' refers to the ratio between national income and the stock of money. Velocity could decline as a result of increased complexity and monetization of the economy.

and nontradeable goods. Of course, prices of imported goods will rise, but experience has shown that such rises have frequently been anticipated prior to any devaluation, because the scarcity of foreign exchange to purchase such imports in a pre-devaluation period permits high prices to be charged for such imports on the domestic market. More frequently, it is the case that it is inflation due to excess money creation which leads to an eventual need for a devaluation. Indeed, in several of those countries which have recently adopted floating exchange rates, there has been a decline in inflation during the period following the floating of the exchange rate (see Box 3.4).

3.14 External borrowing may also facilitate an increase in imports. A rapid accumulation of external debt--particularly commercial debt and debt of short-term maturity--can quickly result in debt servicing problems. Firm control over the level and composition of external borrowing is necessary to avoid such problems (see paras. 3.30-3.35).

Box 3.4: INFLATION AND FLOATING EXCHANGE RATES

The impact on the rate of inflation of a switch to a floating exchange rate regime depends crucially on the stance of monetary and fiscal policies, as well as other policies adopted at the same time as exchange rate reform. In the case of many of the countries that have recently moved to floating rates (see Box 3.2) domestic price liberalization has been pursued simultaneously, not least because price repression had been necessary in order to maintain previously overvalued rates, with accompanying distortions in resource allocation. Therefore, in several of these countries--notably Bolivia, Philippines, the Gambia, Uganda, and Zaire--most price controls were removed at the same time as the change in exchange rate regime, and controlled prices were adjusted upwards in several other countries.

For four of the countries for which sufficient post-float data is available, there was a decline in the rate of inflation after an initial rise reflecting the exchange rate change (Dominican Republic, Jamaica, Philippines and Zaire), and indeed the rates fell to below the pre-float level. Most notably, in Zaire the pre-float rate of inflation had risen to 123% by end-1983, but had fallen to 10-15% p.a. by end-1985 after the float.

Source: As for Box. 3.2.

B. Macroeconomic Policies in Practice--Recent Developments in China's Balance of Payments

3.15 From 1980 to 1984, China ran a current account surplus. Both the trade and services balances were positive. The trade surplus peaked in 1982 at $4.6 billion (1.8% of GDP), before declining to a position of near balance in 1984 (see Table 3.1). Because of high levels of reserves and low outstanding debt, interest receipts exceeded payments. The services balance remained at about $2 billion in 1983 and 1984. In 1984, therefore, the current account still showed a surplus of $2.5 billion, or nearly 1% of GDP. The buoyant external situation over the period had resulted in a near tripling of reserves to $17.8 billion (equivalent to over 9 months of imports) in 1984. There was little external borrowing, and the recorded stock of medium and long-term debt was only 4.5% of GDP. A debt service ratio of only 3.9% (including substantial prepayment of debt) was extremely low in comparison to other developing countries.

3.16 Imports surged from $24 billion in 1984 to $38 billion in 1985--a 60% increase. Much of the increase occured in imports of raw materials in short supply domestically (steel, chemicals, fertilizer, timber) and capital goods with new technologies. As a result, the ratio of capital and intermediate goods imports to GDP was more than doubled in 1985. The current account moved to a deficit of $12 billion in 1985, with about 60% of this deficit financed by borrowing, and 40% by reserves drawdown.

3.17 Although some progress was made in reducing the deficit in 1986, reserves fell by about US$1 billion and there was external borrowing at almost the same rate as the previous year. The modest improvement in 1986 reflected improved export performance and a containment of imports, which nevertheless remained at a very high level by historical standards. Earnings from petroleum exports fell to about half the previous year's level, and the improved export performance was the result of an increase of about 30% in non-oil exports, mainly manufactures. The continued reserve drawdown and the cost of servicing the growing volume of foreign debt meant that the sizeable surplus on the services account disappeared in 1986. In future years, this can be expected to be negative factor of increasing significance, as debt continues to accumulate.

Table 3.1: CHINA - SELECTED ECONOMIC INDICATORS

	1982	1983	1984	1985p	1986e
	US$ billion				
Exports, fob	21.1	20.7	23.9	25.1	27.9
petroleum	4.9	4.3	5.6	6.8	3.4
manufacture	11.5	12.4	13.9	13.4	17.0
Imports, cif	18.4	20.4	26.0	41.7	39.9
Current account balance	5.8	4.9	2.5	-11.9	-9.5
Reserve changes (- = increase)	-6.3	-3.6	-2.4	4.6	1.3
	% change				
Real GDP	8.3	9.8	13.5	12.3	8.0
Money and quasi money	14.9	19.2	41.2	18.2	16.7
	% of GDP				
Overall fiscal balance	-1.5	-1.8	-1.6	-0.5	-0.4
Current account balance	2.2	1.6	0.9	-4.5	-3.7
Investment	30.3	30.9	29.4	38.4	38.6

Source: State Statistical Bureau, World Bank an IMF staff estimates.

3.18 Four main factors appear to be associated with the unusually rapid growth in imports:

(a) Credit expansion: during 1981-83, total credit, as measured by the net domestic assets of the specialized banks, grew relatively modestly. During 1984 and the first nine months of 1985, however, credit increased very sharply, by 45% in 1984 and by a further 25% during 1985. By June 1986, the rate of expansion had eased, although by this date net domestic assets were at double the level of December 1983. Figure 3.1 shows how credit expansion and the growth of imports and the balance-of-payments deficit compare. Much of the problem of excess credit creation during 1984-85 relates to the decentralization of credit decisions to the specialized banks, in advance of administrative or market instruments to control the overall quantity of such credit by those banks. Improved controls were established in April 1985, and the situation has since improved, although strains on the system seem to be emerging again, with a 30% credit expansion in 1986.

(b) Import liberalization: The easier access to imports described earlier (and in Annex 1) contributed to the problem. This was a two-part phenomenon. Firstly, the liberalization facilitated the spilling over of excess credit into imports, rather than domestic prices. Secondly, the liberalization may have sparked some of the demand for credit, since the availability of capital goods imports probably caused many enterprises to seek credit to finance such imports.

(c) Reduction of excessive foreign exchange reserves: The increase in domestic credit was translated into imports, partly because the Government decided that foreign reserves had risen to rather high levels (nine months of imports at end-84), and that some of these should be used to finance the modernization of the economy. Exchange and import controls were therefore liberalized, and enterprises and provinces were encouraged to use domestic credit to purchase foreign exchange up to the limit of foreign exchange retention rights built up in previous years.

(d) External debt. External borrowing increased sharply during 1985 and 1986. In 1985, this mainly reflected increased borrowing from foreign commercial banks--much of it at short-term maturity--by the Bank of China and other entities. The granting of foreign borrowing rights to provincial governments and enterprises without appropriate procedures for controlling debt also was instrumental in the rapid accumulation of external debt. External borrowing provided finance for imports in the context of more liberal import restrictions and, in some cases, boosted foreign exchange reserves to a level that permitted enterprises to use accumulated foreign exchange retention rights without running down foreign reserves to an inadequate level. The further significant accumulation of external debt in 1986 was partly responsible for the continued high level of imports in 1986, although, unlike 1985, a smaller proportion of such borrowing appears to have been of short-term maturity.

3.19 At the same time, exports did not grow much in 1985. There is no doubt that a major explanation of this is that FTCs had difficulties in procuring supplies for above-plan exports. This is because the partial liberalization of domestic prices for consumer goods, combined with overly rapid expansion of money and credit, led to price increases, which caused domestic markets to be much more attractive than export markets for above-plan production. A more depreciated exchange rate would have enabled FTCs to secure a greater proportion of above-plan production for export. At the same time, it would have limited the impact on import demand of import liberalization, increased external borrowing, and excess credit creation.

3.20 The deterioration in China's balance of payments reflects to a large extent a lack of coordination between macroeconomic and microeconomic policies and inappropriate use of macroeconomic policies, partly because of a lack of familiarity in using macroeconomic controls. In particular, the authorities were not able to control access to borrowed foreign resources, credit expansion was excessive, and exchange rate policy was not operated with sufficient flexibility. A more appropriate and coordinated use of macroeconomic policies would have helped to prevent import and exchange liberalization and economic reform measures from having adverse effects on the balance of payments. Two areas of policy are discussed in detail in the following section.

FIGURE 3.1: MONEY SUPPLY AND IMPORTS, 1983-86
(% change)

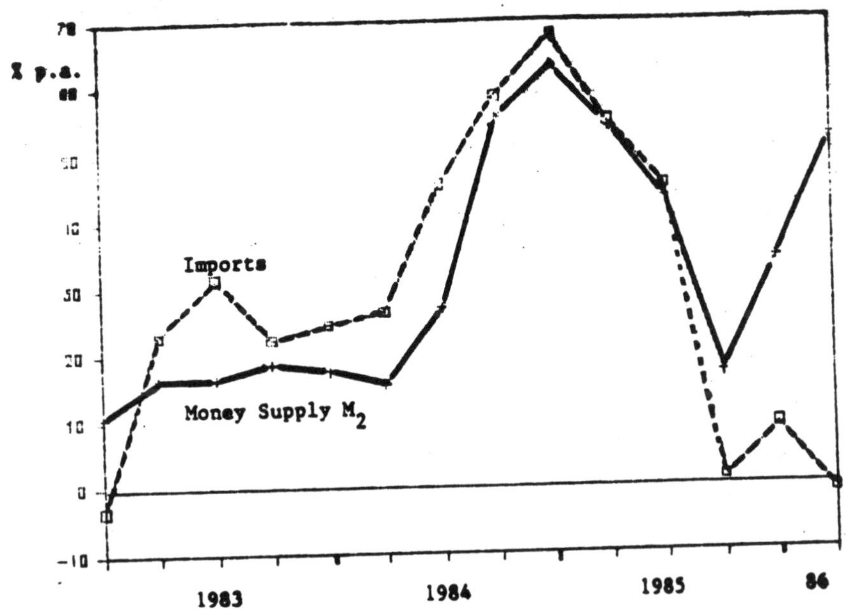

C. Macro-Policies and Trade Reform

Exchange Rate Policies and Foreign Exchange Allocation

3.21 In China, as explained in para. 2.23, the effect of the exchange rate is muted because of the "air lock" between world prices and domestic prices--especially producer prices of exported commodities. Administrative controls on domestic prices, production, income distribution, and factor mobility also dampen the potential effects of exchange rate policy. In particular, most enterprises are not fully responsible for their profits and losses and do not, at present, face the prospect of bankruptcy if they make substantial losses. Trade reforms of the type proposed in this report would make the exchange rate a more effective policy instrument by increasing links between foreign and domestic prices. However, the effectiveness of these reforms depend on their being complemented by further enterprise and price reforms.

3.22 While trade reforms will make the exchange rate a more effective policy instrument, it is also true that a more appropriate and flexible exchange rate policy would make trade reforms more effective. This objective could be achieved by a more active use of exchange rate policy within the context of the present exchange system. Alternatively, China may decide to allow market forces to play a more direct role in exchange rate determination and move to a system in which the exchange rate would be determined in the market by the supply and demand for foreign exchange. This could be particulary useful during the transition towards a more market-oriented foreign trade system. It would be appropriate and useful to discuss changes in the foreign exchange allocation and exchange rate policy with the IMF.[4/]

3.23 Currently, China maintains a managed floating exchange system, whereby the exchange rate for the renminbi is based on developments in the balance of payments and movements in costs and exchange rates in China's major trading partners. The U.S. dollar is the intervention currency. In practice, adjustments in the rate for the renminbi vis-a-vis the U.S. dollar tend to be made infrequently, with the result that over time the rate tends to move away from (or further away from) its equilibrium value. Infrequent adjustments provide some nominal stability in the cost of foreign goods. However, this advantage is outweighed by the resulting decline in competitiveness, which can occur, and the instability of the real (inflation-adjusted) exchange rate, and of expectations regarding the sustainability of the exchange rate.

3.24 If the present managed floating exchange rate system is maintained, exchange rate adjustments would be needed to compensate for the removal of administrative import restrictions or subsidies. Balance-of-payments developments, desired reserve levels and indicators of international competitiveness (see para. 3.6 and Box 3.1) could be used to estimate the required adjustments. An advantage of this option is that it would not represent a major change from the present exchange rate system, but would introduce more flexibility than at present. A disadvanage of this option is that it would take quite some time (several months or quarters) to ascertain whether any exchange rate adjustments made have been sufficient to compensate for the removal of trade restrictions or other changes in the domestic or international economy. This might make it difficult to phase out administrative allocation of foreign exchange rapidly.

3.25 An alternative approach that would permit a more rapid transition towards market determined allocation of foreign exchange would be to permit trading of foreign exchange retention rights among enterprises and other units at a freely negotiated price. This would be similar to the approach used in the domestic market where transactions at flexible prices have been introduced while maintaining fixed prices for the same goods allocated by the Plan.

3.26 While not desirable as a permanent solution, such a system would improve on current practice, not only because of the limitations of the current foreign exchange allocation system (see para. 2.28), but also because

---

4/ In formulating exchange rate policies, China has certain commitments as a member of the IMF under Articles VIII and XIV of its Articles of Agreement and its general role in the surveillance of members' exchange rate policies.

it could lead to an elimination of some of the present multiplicity of de facto exchange rates resulting from the current, highly variable levels of export incentives. Since the exchange rate for foreign exchange retention rights would be freely determined, it would permit rapid removal of administrative restrictions without running the danger of incurring large balance-of-payments deficits. The exchange rate established in the market for foreign exchange retention rights would give an indication of the direction and magnitude of the required adjustment of the official exchange rate to compensate for the removal of administrative restrictions.

3.27 The problems with such a system are similar to the use of dual (plan-market) prices in the domestic economy. Enterprises or individuals that have access to foreign exchange at the official rate will always be tempted to sell it at the price established in the market for foreign exchange retention rights. It would thus be desirable to move the official exchange rate as rapidly as possible towards the rate established in the market for foreign exchange retention rights, eliminating any gap between the two rates after a relatively brief transition period, measured in months, rather than years.

3.28 To ensure that the rate established in the market for foreign exchange retention rights is realistic, it would be important for the market in foreign exchange retention rights to cover a large proportion of foreign exchange transactions and to have a large number of enterprises participate, particularly those enterprises that are already responsible for profits and losses. It would thus be necessary to increase gradually the foreign exchange retention ratio for enterprises. The State would always be able to obtain foreign exchange for Plan requirements by entering the foreign exchange market.

3.29 Once the transition to a more market-oriented foreign exchange rate determination system has been completed by closing the gap between the official exchange rate and the market-determined rate for foreign exchange retention rights, it would be possible to opt either for a floating exchange rate system (no intervention by the central bank), or a managed floating exchange rate system where the central bank would intervene to stabilize the exchange rate to avoid undesirable short-term fluctuations in the real (inflation-adjusted) exchange rate.

External Debt Management

3.30 As already noted, the external imbalances of 1985 and 1986 resulted in a rapid accumulation of external debt, which rose from US$12 billion at end-1984 to an estimated US$27 billion at end-1986, with the ratio of debt to export earnings rising from 51% in 1984 to 97% in 1986. While the level of debt is by no means excessive in international creditworthiness terms, the trend needs to be monitored. If China were to continue to contract debt at the present rate, debt would be a serious economic issue by the 1990s. There are also questions related to the composition of debt with, at present, a high component of short-term debt. (See Annex V for a full description of China's external debt situation).

3.31 China's foreign borrowing in 1985 and 1986 was not simply a consequence of the large trade deficit, but a cause of it as well. The access of a number of actors to foreign borrowing and the inadequate controls over their actions, enabled a large volume of imports to be brought in. Insofar as creditors normally require a guarantee by the Bank of China or an other guarantor approved by the State Administration for Foreign Exchange Control (SAEC), there is a mechanism for controlling such borrowing through the approval limits of these guarantors. Insofar as approvals are not required (or not obtained), <u>and</u> guarantees are not asked by foreign banks, debt can be contracted by these enterprises and other units with relative ease. Indeed, in 1985 and 1986, foreign commercial banks were highly liquid and had become convinced that China was a profitable and secure market, and began to lend without guarantees. The understanding appears to have been that, since they were lending to provincial authorities or public bodies, these loans would in fact be guaranteed. Indeed, in the Latin American debtor countries, even private borrowing has effectively become sovereign risk with a blurring of the distinction between guaranteed and non-guaranteed private borrowing (see Annex 5, Box 5.3). Indeed, in Chile, private sector debt was taken over by the government as a condition of a debt rescheduling agreement. In the absence of effective control over foreign borrowing, there is serious risk that it could continue to increase inconsistent with a viable medium-term balance of payments.

3.32 There are essentially three steps involved in managing the external debt position: (a) assessing the size of external debt; (b) formulating a debt strategy; and (c) monitoring and supervising borrowing to ensure implementation of the strategy. Significant progress has been made with the appointment, in April 1986, of the State Administration for Exchange Control, (SAEC) within the People's Bank, as the sole agency responsible for the monitoring of external debt. SAEC conducted a debt survey in 1986, the first comprehensive debt survey in China. However, there continues to be a major discrepancy between the total public debt estimated by SAEC and that derived from creditor-reported statistics (see Annex V). This discrepancy appears to reflect short-term debt, particularly trade credits and borrowing by joint ventures. Efforts are underway to eliminate these discrepancies. Progress on this needs to be continued, as up-to-date information is essential for proper debt management.

3.33 Equally important is the need to extend the reporting system to include contingent liabilities and other debt-like flows. Contingent liabilities are guarantees of foreign obligations issued by government-affiliated institutions or enterprises in China, which are not presently reported centrally (although, in theory, the underlying borrowings are). If debt planning is going to be meaningful, it must be on the basis of as complete a coverage as possible. This means including debt-like flows such as obligations under leases, compensation trade or similar arrangements which are very similar to debt financing, but in China are often included in "foreign investment." Finally, there is a need to clarify the distinction between sovereign and other debt. Consider the example of a joint venture between a state enterprise and a foreign partner. If this joint venture borrows abroad--which it can do without any central permission--and is subsequently unable to repay, it may well be that the central government will feel compelled to assume the joint venture's foreign liabilities.

3.34 China's debt strategy has not yet been clearly formulated. A one-year plan for official borrowing is formulated at the same time as the trade and foreign exchange allocation plans, and there is also a long-term planning horizon with global targets for import and export growth and, consequently, an implicit debt strategy. However, there is no explicit medium-term debt strategy on which to base the one-year plans. Such a strategy needs to be concerned with both the volume and composition of debt.

3.35 The formulation of a strategy for the volume of debt should be based on the development of a medium-term (5-10 year) outlook for the balance of payments. The key issue is affordability. Contracting debt today permits a higher level of imports, investment and consequently--if investments are made wisely--higher economic growth and increased debt-servicing capacity. Chinese authorities have indicated a desire not to see debt-servicing (interest plus principal) exceed 15% of export earnings. As discussed below, these are conservative but appropriate targets. However, unless placed in a medium-term context, China could either end up exceeding such targets because of inadequate planning, or have to undergo sharp contractions in imports and borrowing at some future date to avoid exceeding them.

3.36 Having decided upon an appropriate volume of debt, it will be equally important to plan a debt composition strategy. This relates to maturity, interest rate risks, and exchange rate risks. Debt servicing could rapidly rise and become much higher than desired, if the planned volume of debt is contracted at variable rates in appreciating currencies, as was much of the 1985 commercial debt. Thus, these aspects of the borrowing plan should also be identified in advance, so that individual debt transactions can be judged in a framework. Of course, the appropriate volume of debt is determined, in part, by the expected composition of the debt, including cost (concessional vs. financial market debt) and maturity (short- vs. long-term debt). (See Annex 5 for a fuller discussion of these issues.)

3.37 The third and most difficult aspect of debt management is the control of debt. The conflicts here are several: balancing the need to decentralize micro-economic decision-making while maintaining overall macro-economic control; balancing the need to control non-sovereign debt with the desire to avoid accepting explicit or implicit sovereignty of the debt; and balancing provinces' and enterprises' desires to promote their own economic development with national economic management priorities. However, two issues are paramount: most foreign lenders do regard all lending to China as sovereign debt, given the public ownership status in China; and the sum of all potential borrowers' desires to contract external debt undoubtedly exceeds the level of debt which central authorities would consider prudent. Therefore, we would strongly recommend the maintenance, and strengthening of central control and approval procedures for external debt, but that subject to these procedures the conduct of debt operations should continue to be carried out by a variety of institutions. Detailed recommendations in this area are given in Annex V, but can be summarized as follows:

(a) Prior approval by a central government agency (such as the State Administration of Exchange Control, which we understand the Government has selected for this purpose) should continue to be required for all debt operations of the eight financial institutions with foreign borrowing rights. Extension of such rights to other institutions should be very gradual.

(b) Prior approval should be required of borrowing by joint ventures, direct overseas borrowing by subsidiaries of Chinese corporations, and the assumption of quasi-debt such as compensation trade. It is not suggested that detailed and difficult bureaucratic procedures be established for these forms of borrowing. Rather, they should be placed on a prior notification basis, with the right of objection by the central government debt agency. Certain minimum conditions (e.g., maturity) could be set for such borrowing.

(c) Contingent liabilities should come under the control of central authorities. These relate to guarantees issued by the 68 institutions so empowered.

D. Macro-Economic Outlook With and Without Reforms

3.38 The purpose of the reforms recommended in this report are to encourage efficient trade, which will permit technical transformation to take place and thus encourage economic growth, whilst avoiding debt crises. In the following paragraphs, these aims will be assessed in a simple quantitative framework. However, prior to presenting these analyses, it is important to stress that these are not projections for the Chinese economy, but rather indications of the direction and implications of changes of major macro-variables under different assumptions.

3.39 Given the focus of the report, the scenarios have been constructed using variations in two main variables: the rate of growth of exports and the level of external debt. The case was made in Chapters I and II that with the external constraints China is facing, future export growth will rely heavily on the growth of manufactured exports, and that the latter will be determined to a significant degree by the pace of trade policy reforms. Therefore, scenarios are worked out using two different assumptions for export growth rates of manufactures (5% and 10%). Similarly, the implications of different rates of growth of debt are examined. The assumptions made reflect the actual experience of developing economies pursuing different trade policies (Chapter I, Table 1.1).[5/]

5/ These scenarios are not constructed to be projections of the Chinese economy over the next eight years, but rather they are intended to illustrate the magnitude of the implications of alternative economic policy strategies.

3.40 The other two parameters which differ between the alternative scenarios are GDP growth and the level of consumption and domestic savings. The higher level of imports in Scenarios 3 and 4 permits a higher level of investment and thus GDP than in Scenarios 1 and 2.[6/] GDP grows at 8% p.a. in Scenarios 3 and 4, and at 6% p.a. in Scenarios 1 and 2. Similarly, the two high debt scenarios permit a higher level of consumption and lower level of domestic savings--at least in the first 6-7 years--than in the low debt scenarios. These scenarios have all been constructed using a macro-economic consistency model. Although there are limits on the extent that such models can simulate long-term structural changes, the assumptions have been chosen so as to reflect the actual experience of developing economies pursuing such different strategies.

3.41 Putting together these two sets of assumptions gives four scenarios, which can be typified by reference to particular country examples:

	Export Growth	Debt Growth	Example
Scenario 1	Low	Low	China pre-79, India
Scenario 2	Low	High	Poland
Scenario 3	High	Low	Taiwan, China
Scenario 4	High	High	South Korea

3.42 The results of these scenarios are shown in Table 3.2. It is instructive to compare the results in two sets of pairs. Consider first Scenarios 3 and 4 in comparison with Scenarios 1 and 2. By 1995, import levels are 38-46% higher in the first pair than in the second. The difference is less marked in 1990, showing the impact of sustained export promotion efforts. It is also interesting to note, however, that the early (1990) difference between Scenarios 3 and 4 in terms of import levels tends to narrow over time. In 1990, imports are 7% higher in Scenario 4 than in Scenario 3, but by 1995 the difference is down to 2.4%. This is because the higher debt service burden in Scenario 4 begins to absorb an increasing share of foreign exchange earnings.

6/ It is assumed that concessional funds available to China--at 0-2% interest rates--are the same under all scenarios, at about US$1.3 billion per annum. Other funds carry an average interest rate of 8% per annum, and consequently average rates of interest are somewhat higher in the high debt scenarios.

Table 3.2: MACROECONOMIC SCENARIOS
(Current US$ billion, unless stated)

	1986	1990	1995
Scenario 1 (low exports, low debt)			
Exports	27.9	36.4	55.4
Imports	37.6	40.1	59.4
Current Account Balance	-9.6	-4.1	-4.2
Debt Service/Exports of Goods and Service (%)	8.5	12.9	9.6
Scenario 2 (low exports, high debt)			
Exports	27.9	36.4	55.4
Imports	37.6	43.2	60.8
Current Account Balance	-9.6	-8.0	-8.0
Debt Service/Exports of Goods and Service (%)	8.5	16.5	17.8
Scenario 3 (high exports, low debt)			
Exports	27.9	42.9	80.8
Imports	37.6	46.4	84.0
Current Account Balance	-9.6	-4.0	-3.8
Debt Service/Exports of Goods and Service (%)	8.5	11.5	7.8
Scenario 4 (high exports, high debt)			
Exports	27.9	42.9	80.8
Imports	37.6	49.7	86.0
Current Account Balance	-9.6	-8.2	-8.3
Debt Service/Exports of Goods and Service (%)	8.5	14.6	13.9

Source: Mission estimates.

3.43 The other two pairs to examine are Scenarios 1 and 3 in comparison with Scenarios 2 and 4, that is, lower or higher debt. The debt service ratios of each country within a pair are similar, but in each pair the country with the higher export level can afford 45% more imports.

3.44 These are admittedly simple scenarios, but they bear strong resemblance to the recent experience of many countries. They demonstrate very clearly that over the medium-term, trade strategy is far more important than debt in increasing import levels. A debt accumulating policy is only sustainable for a short period, and should only be undertaken <u>in conjunction with</u> and <u>not as a substitute for</u> export promoting policies. Scenario 4 includes debt accumulation of US$9 billion per annum, but because of high export growth rates, debt servicing remain tolerable. Scenario 2, however, shows the results of using debt instead of export promotion, and demonstrates how a country can end up with high debt servicing but without high exports and domestic economic growth. The scenarios therefore emphasize the urgency for China to formulate appropriate trade policies and to develop both a debt strategy and the means to implement it.

E. Conclusions for Macroeconomic Strategy

3.45 The foregoing analysis suggests the need for a reorientation of economic planning, but with fundamentally similar objectives as past planning activities. China has already moved in such a direction. While trade planning and annual foreign exchange and debt plans continue to have a central function, there is already an 'above-plan' level of trade and debt, being influenced by economic levers.

3.46 The preceding analysis has focussed on the importance of defining a debt strategy and putting mechanisms in place to ensure that it can be achieved, as well as the critical role of the exchange rate in ensuring macro-balance. These two areas come together in macroeconomic planning. In carrying out such planning--to put it very simplistically--there are four key steps:

(a) based on a medium-term framework for the balance of payments, the government should identify a target for the current account of the balance of payments in the current planning year;

(b) the government should decide how this deficit (if any) is to be financed, thus establishing the debt ceiling, as well as targets for concessional and official lending, foreign direct investment, and private capital;

(c) the government should then adjust economic levers and other macro-economic policies to achieve the export and import targets. This notably includes exchange rate policy but also fiscal and monetary policies; and

(d) since events are unlikely to be fully predictable and controllable, the situation needs to be monitored during the course of the year--especially the level of foreign reserves and the accumulation of debt, which give early signals--so that economic levers can be adjusted as needed. It is in this context that a flexible exchange rate policy can be critical, for as noted it can act as the safety valve, so that if, say, the debt ceiling is enforced, the exchange rate can adjust for any inappropriateness in fiscal or monetary policy.

IV. INTERRELATIONS AND SEQUENCING OF REFORMS

4.1 As outlined in the preceding chapters, substantial measures would be required to make China's external trade system more efficient and maximize the benefits to the domestic economy from further opening to foreign trade and investment. Such changes would necessarily take a number of years. At the same time, China is also implementing other economic reforms leading, in particular, to greater decentralization of production and investment decisions to enterprises. Not only are the various trade policy measures discussed here closely interrelated, there are also important interrelations between trade policy reforms and other areas of economic reform. Indeed, trade policy reforms can be seen as an integral part of enterprise reforms. The question then arises what the appropriate sequencing and pace of trade and other policy measures should be.

4.2 Economic theory and international experience offer little help in deciding upon the sequencing and pace of trade reforms. In China the question is made even more difficult by the complex interrelations between trade and domestic economic reforms. There appears to be no alternative, therefore, to the cautious, experimental approach that the Government has adopted, acknowledging that some mistakes will be made, and that mid-term corrections will often be required in order to limit the costs of mistakes. Nevertheless, some observations about priorities and sequencing of reform measures can be made, and these are outlined below.[1/] Section A will discuss fundamental preconditions of efficient decentralization of economic decision-making to enterprises, followed by an application of these principles to external economic policies in Section B. Finally, Section C will analyze some of the interrelations between domestic and external economic reforms.

A. Fundamental Preconditions for Efficient Decentralization

4.3 As already noted, reforms of the trade system can be seen as one aspect of the ongoing enterprise reforms. By the late 1970s, China's leaders had concluded that improved economic efficiency and sustained growth required the decentralization of production decisions to the line managers of production enterprises. But decentralization alone does not assure efficient production. Enterprise managers may have the technical know-how and hands-on familiarity with their respective enterprise's operations and markets that central planners lack, but what is to lead them to produce those goods in greatest demand and to do so in the most efficient manner? Two further conditions appear essential: first, enterprises must also be subjected to competition, so if one fails to satisfy the needs of buyers at the lowest possible costs, another more efficient enterprise will capture the business. Second, there must be a direct link between the results of an enterprise and the rewards to owners, managers and workers. Most important in forging this

---

1/ The recent companion volume to this report: "China - Finance and Investment," 1988 provides a more detailed discussion of domestic economic reform measures and their phasing and sequencing.

link is to make enterprises separate accounting units responsible for profits and losses.

4.4 These principles are well understood in China, and although the reform measures implemented over the past few years have brought enterprises and other economic units closer in line with these principles, progress so far has been variable, depending on the type of enterprise (state, collective, private), the sector in which it operates (heavy industry, light industry, commerce), and the type of decision involved (production, investment, domestic and foreign trade, etc). In general, competition is strongest among the smaller private and collective enterprises, but state enterprises in some sectors (e.g. textiles) now also face substantial competition. Competition is still virtually absent in many heavy industry sectors, where most or all output continues to be allocated by the Plan. Also, while production and domestic marketing decision are now mostly in the hands of enterprise managers, they have far less autonomy in investment and foreign trade decisions. The former are still mostly subject to review by supervisory agencies and planning and economic commissions at the relevant levels, while the latter are controlled through administrative decisions on foreign trade and foreign exchange allocation. As discussed further below, there are good reasons to treat foreign trade decisions exactly like domestic production and marketing decisions.

4.5 Price Reform. Decisions made by enterprise managers in the pursuit of profit will only be consistent with efficient production if the prices of goods and the resources used in their production reflect the scarcities of, and the demand for, these resources. Substantial progress has, in fact, been made over the past several years in deregulating the prices of a large number of consumer goods. Some progress has also been made in adjusting prices of those commodities (largely heavy industry products) whose prices continue to be administratively set. Equally important has been the marketing of above-quota or outside plan production of these commodities at market-related prices, which has helped to ease shortages appearing under administrative allocation. The underpricing of financial capital (interest rates) is one of the most important sources of remaining price distortions, leading to excess demand for investment in the same way that an overvalued exchange rate (i.e. too low a price of foreign goods in terms of renminbi) leads to excess demand for imports. The interest rate and the foreign exchange rate are the two most important prices in a decentralized economy open to foreign trade, given the impact they have on resource allocation across the entire economy.

4.6 Other price distortions also influence foreign trade decisions. In particular, the underpricing of raw materials and other capital-intensive goods could lead to excessive exports of these goods and too little export of labor-intensive goods (such as light industry products), in which China's comparative advantage likely to be the is largest. This is because of the high explicit and implicit tax burden on labor-intensive manufactures that is used to provide the financial resources required to subsidize heavy industry production. Consequently, China's export pattern remains suboptimal, with exports using more domestic resources than necessary. Further progress in domestic price reform is thus desirable. Chinese enterprises have proven quite resilient to the relative price adjustments already introduced, and price reform (adjustment and decontrol of prices) could probably be accelerated, if the authority of the People's Bank in restraining the growth of money and credit is strengthened, and inflationary pressures are thus minimized.

4.7 Competition. Markets only function efficiently if enterprises are exposed to vigorous competition. The gradual decontrol of prices is the most important element in promoting competition and compelling enterprises to seek progressive improvements in quality and reductions in production costs. However, competition is not always a naturally self-sustaining state of affairs. Enterprise owners and managers will always have the incentive to try to monopolize markets and to reduce the threat of competition from other enterprises. The situation is particularly vulnerable where ownership is vested in government agencies that also have the power to regulate important elements of the enterprise environment and can, for example, restrict entry of other enterprises into a particular product line. As discussed in paras. 2.10-2.11, this does not only apply to domestic production and commerce, but also applies to foreign trade. In China, the benefits of restricting competition among domestic enterprises in export activities have often been overestimated, while the costs of such restrictions have not been sufficiently recognized (see paras. 2.20-2.23 and Box 2.3).

4.8 Enterprise Ownership and Responsibility. The assumption that enterprise owners will be motivated by profits in evaluating managerial performance in production and investment decisions requires that ownership rights, including those of state enterprises, are clearly defined, and that owners' interest are linked to profits and the long-term prospects of the enterprise. In China, state enterprises often are led to pursue noneconomic objectives which conflict with economic objectives, and government agencies have used their regulatory power to protect enterprises under their control from competitive pressures. Efficient decentralization will require some clarification of the nature and locus of enterprise ownership rights and responsibilities. As discussed elsewhere [2/] diversification of ownership and competition can help to reduce the temptation to promote noneconomic objectives. Further tax reform and the gradual phasing-out of adjustment taxes and other negotiated subsidies or levies would also be desirable; otherwise, prices will remain distorted. Finally, the legal rights and responsibilities of enterprises and their owners, creditors and workers need to be clarified (e.g., in an enterprise law and by implementing the bankruptcy code), and the rights and obligations of contracting parties need to be elucidated (e.g., in a commercial code).

4.9 Factor Mobility. As discussed in Chapter II (paras. 2.73-2.77), technology transfer and diffusion could be considerably accelerated if labor mobility, particularly among technical personnel, were to be increased. A number of changes could be made to facilitate greater labor mobility, in particular, freeing enterprises from the direct responsibility for social

---

2/ World Bank: "China - Finance and Investment," 1988, Chapter 3.

services such as retirement, unemployment, health care and housing, by establishing appropriate social insurance schemes and housing finance institutions.

4.10 Aggregate Demand Management. Efficient decentralization of decision-making and introduction of further reforms would be much facilitated by stable aggregate demand and prices. Of particular importance in this regard are further steps to restrain government spending and to give the People's Bank full authority to limit the expansion of money and credit. Increased interest rates, particularly on enterprise deposits and capital construction loans, could help to dampen excess demand pressures and to channel resources to the investments with the highest yield. Stable macroeconomic management is particularly important in managing the balance of payments and in limiting foreign borrowing to a viable level (Chapter III).

B. Priorities and Sequencing of Trade Policy Reforms

4.11 Among the many policy changes discussed in Chapters II and III, not all are equally important and urgent. Also, some measures could be implemented relatively quickly, while others should be phased-in over a number of years.

Foreign Exchange Allocation

4.12 One of the most important and urgent measures is the introduction of greater decentralization and market determination in foreign exchange allocation. As discussed in Chapter III, several options are available to manage this transition. While China has adopted a managed, floating exchange rate system, it is not market determined and consists, in effect, of a large number of different exchange rates, as Foreign Trade Corporations continue to cross-subsidize different exports by purchasing goods at domestic prices and selling at (often significantly different) international prices. This also applies to some extent to imports (see Annex 1). Even more important than the inefficiencies implied in these cross-subsidies are efficiency losses resulting from the administrative allocation of foreign exchange. International experience suggests that decentralized, market-intermediated allocation is more efficient, especially as the complexity of an economy increases.

4.13 Two main options are available for moving towards a foreign exchange allocation system in which the exchange rate, rather than administrative import restrictions or export subsidies, becomes the principal instrument in maintaining a sustainable balance of payments. In the first option, administrative exchange rate adjustments would be made to compensate for the removal of administrative import restrictions or subsidies. Balance of payments developments, desired reserve levels and indicators of international competitiveness (see para. 3.6 and Box 3.1) would be used to estimate the required adjustments. The advantage of this option is that it would be essentially a continuation of the present exchange rate system, but introducing more flexibility and more frequent adjustments than at present. The disadvantage of this option is that it might take several months or quarters to ascertain whether exchange rate adjustments have been sufficient to compensate for the removal of trade restrictions, and this uncertainty might make it difficult to phase out administrative allocation of foreign exchange rapidly.

4.14 The alternative approach would be to permit trading of foreign exchange or foreign exchange retention rights among enterprises and other units at freely negotiated prices. During a, preferably, short transition period, this approach would result in a dual exchange rate system, but the approach would call for the gradual adjustment of the official rate towards the parallel rate so as to eliminate the differential over the course of the transition period. However, there are certain dangers in this option which would need to be guarded against:

(a) If the market is too small, it could be very volatile, or have distorted results. Therefore, care should be taken to ensure a reasonable level of supply to such a market. The best way to do this is to increase the foreign exchange retention ratio for enterprises, whilst simultaneously drawing up rules governing who would enter such a market to buy foreign exchange and for what purpose.

(b) There is also a risk that differentials in exchange rates could emerge between provinces, because provincial authorities may attempt to prevent inter-provincial transfers of foreign exchange. Two measures could be taken in this regard. Firstly, care should be taken to ensure that any increased retention ratios are assigned to enterprises--including indirect exporters (as noted in para. 2.28 (vi))--and not to provincial authorities, and the People's Bank, through its provincial branches, should oversee and guard for any attempts by provincial authorities to prevent inter-provincial transfers of foreign exchange. Secondly, there is the organizational question. Clearly, in a country such as China, a large number of market locations would be necessary, but there are no established interbank mechanisms to ensure arbitrage between these locations. In this situation, it would make sense for the People's Bank itself, to operate such markets directly, possibly in the form of a variant on the auction mechanism, moving supply from one location to another to equilibrate marginal bids.

(c) The third danger is that such a market may overshoot because of excess demand for foreign exchange by enterprises which are not yet fully responsible for profits and losses. To ease this problem, initial access to the market could be limited to enterprises and other units that are responsible for their own profits and losses. Such access could be linked to other areas of reform, such as trade reform itself, reduction of central planning and allocation, and price reform. (See paras. 4.32-4.37 for further suggestions in this regard). Access to the market could be expanded over time in line with increased retention and further progress in trade and price reform.

4.15 The introduction of a foreign exchange market would be compatible with a requirement that all foreign exchange be turned over to the People's Bank, the Bank of China, or other licensed foreign exchange depositories. In this case, a foreign exchange market becomes a market in foreign exchange rights, quite similar to the existing foreign exchange retention rights.

However, the development of such a market could be facilitated by the issuance of transferable financial instruments ensuring access of the holder to the retention rights. Such instruments would thus replace the present practice of retention accounts.

4.16 The State will, of course, remain a major user of foreign exchange for key projects. The creation of such a market for foreign exchange does not mean that the State would have lower access to foreign exchange, but that it may be obtained in different ways. Indeed, creation of a market in foreign exchange can be expected to increase the supply of foreign exchange available to the economy as a whole--and thus potentially to the State--both by reducing the hoarding of foreign exchange, and by stimulating exports. If the increased retention ratios reduce the foreign exchange available directly to the State below the desired level, the State can always enter the foreign exchange market directly to purchase additional foreign exchange to fund key projects. In addition, however, the State could save itself considerable levels of foreign exchange by changing the ways it funds the inputs for key projects. Instead of maintaining low prices for the command plan imports and subsidizing all such imports, it would be preferable to provide specific subsidies direct to the key projects, but adjust the prices of the strategic products, so that the subsidy is provided for the priority uses, but not for non-priority uses, as is the case at present.

Decentralization of Trade Decisions

4.17 The decentralization of foreign trade decision-making and the simultaneous introduction of more competition among foreign trade corporations would be complementary to changes in the foreign exchange allocation system and is of equal priority. Among the many measures discussed in Chapter II (para. 2.45), eliminating product-specific trading rights (monopolies) of FTCs and making FTCs fully responsible for profits and losses (i.e., full application of the "agency system") are the most important measures. At the same time, consideration should be given to further removal of entry barriers into foreign trading. Chinese enterprises are currently losing many export opportunities because of the time-consuming and sometimes cumbersome intermediation of FTCs that have trade monopolies. But further progress in this direction depends on progress made in reforming the foreign exchange allocation system. The introduction of a full-fledged "agency system" for imports and exports would, in any case, require compensatory foreign exchange rate adjustments. While the commodity pattern of exports and imports would remain broadly the same under an "agency system," some unprofitable exports would cease, and incentives would therefore be required to stimulate additional exports of other commodities through exchange rate adjustments and a reform of the foreign exchange retention system, as outlined above.

4.18 However, the timing and phasing of these reforms would need to be linked to other areas of reform, and could be done on the basis of sectors. As in the case of reforms in foreign exchange allocation and rate determination, there are dangers in granting trading rights to enterprises that are not fully responsible for profits and losses, and it was noted earlier (para. 2.55) that trade liberalization in the case of products with heavily distorted prices could be harmful, both in terms of ensuring supplies of essential imports, and in encouraging non-economic exports, which could have the secondary danger of having an adverse impact on world commodity markets. (See paras. 4.32-4.37 for further suggestions in this area.)

4.19 Introducing competition among FTC's and giving foreign trade rights directly to production enterprises does not mean that the government will lose control over foreign trade. But that control would be primarily affected through macro-economic levers: chiefly, the exchange rate, control over the expansion of domestic money and credit, and control over the size of the budget deficit. Trade planning and policymaking would primarily operate through such indirect levers.

Import Licensing and Tariff Reform

4.20 The key element in the reform of the import regime is the introduction of an exchange rate system that eliminates the need for administrative restrictions to maintain the desired macro-balance of exports and imports. Once this were achieved, most quantitative restrictions would become redundant and could be phased out. Indeed, it would again be possible and desirable to link such reform to other reform areas. As the foreign exchange market is developed, the administrative restrictions on imports of certain commodities could be lifted in line with the shift of the financing of such commodities from the foreign exchange plan to the foreign exchange markets. For example, the retention ratio for garment exporters could be increased, and, simultaneously, they could be required to obtain all imported imports via foreign exchange either retained or purchased on the market. This could permit restrictions to be lifted on inputs for this sector. However, there may remain valid industrial policy reasons to restrict certain imports to protect domestic enterprises [3/] for a limited period of time, until they have become internationally competitive. Such protection should be provided mostly by tariffs rather than import licensing or other administrative import restrictions.

4.21 The present tariff schedule, ranging from 0-200%, results in highly variable 'effective' protection of different industrial subsectors. International experience has shown that such highly variable protection can lead to substantial inefficiencies. Tariff rates should therefore be made more uniform, perhaps with a range of 10-50%. On the other hand, widespread exemptions from import duties for machinery and capital goods imported for capital construction and technical transformation result in penalty on domestic producers of such goods, which could, in many cases, achieve efficient production in China. Tariff exemptions for imports for capital construction and technical renovation should thus be eliminated. Tariff exemptions or rebates would then be restricted to inputs into export production (see below). Tariff reform would probably be best phased over several years. In

---

3/ Ideally, production subsidies would be preferable to trade measures, but budgetary resources might not be sufficient.

the first stages, it would be desirable to pre-announce the tariff adjustments planned to occur over a period of several years, so that domestic enterprises can adjust accordingly.

Export Incentives

4.22 The most important export incentive at present is the foreign exchange retention system for enterprises, which compensates to a substantial extent for the anti-export bias of the present trade system. The retention system could be expanded by making access to foreign exchange more automatic, both for exports and for import-substituting enterprises, since a dollar saved through efficient import substitution is as good as a dollar earned through increased exports. However, as long as tariffs or other import restrictions are applied for reasons of industrial policy (e.g. infant industry protection), the system will continue to have an anti-export bias. One way to reduce this anti-export bias is to rebate to exporting enterprises the duties collected on inputs used in the production of export goods, or arrange for exemption for exporters. This is administratively challenging, but there is a large international experience which could help avoid some of the difficulties. In this way, any enterprise anywhere in China would reap the advantages that the Special Economic Zones now provide, and this would at the same time, provide the indirect advantages of greater export orientation throughout the economy.

4.23 A second step that could be taken to reduce anti-export bias is to rebate domestic taxes on export production. One internationally acceptable way of doing so would be to replace the present industrial and commercial tax with a value-added tax system. This would, of course, be a major undertaking and should await a more general reform of China's tax system. It may also be possible to link such rebate systems with a system for permitting access by indirect exporters to foreign exchange retention rights.

4.24 A third step, and one that could perhaps be taken earlier, would be to provide automatic access to domestic working capital financing to all exporters and, through a system of "domestic letters of credit", to all enterprises that provide inputs into production for exports. Such a credit facility would of course have to consistent with the overall credit plan of the People's Bank of China. Such a system would also make it possible to extend rebates of tariffs on imported goods used in export production to indirect exporters (suppliers to export enterprises).

4.25 These export incentives would all require advance planning and administrative sophistication and should be considered for implementation only in the medium term--once substantial progress has been made in the reform of the foreign exchange allocation system, the decentralization of foreign trade rights, the reduction of detailed administrative foreign trade planning and licensing, and a reduction and harmonization of tariff rates. An implementation period of, say, five years would appear feasible.

Foreign Direct Investment

4.26 Reform of the foreign exchange allocation mechanism would also be the most important policy measure to stimulate foreign direct investment that would bring in the desired advanced technology and investment. Recently, measures have been announced that would make it easier for foreign joint ventures to gain access to foreign exchange by becoming de facto foreign traders on behalf of domestic enterprises. While this is progress in the right direction, access to foreign exchange could be made even more automatic through the reform of the foreign exchange allocation system described earlier. In this context, it is again important to remember that a dollar saved through import substitution is as good as a dollar earned through export promotion. Transport costs, slight quality differences, brand-name recognition and other similar factors often make import substitution easier than export promotion--particularly in new products using more advanced technology. Thus, there is a very useful role to be played by foreign joint ventures in producing for the domestic market, and in a number of sectors it may take ten years or more until production for exports will become internationally competitive.

4.27 More important than preventing 'exploitation' by foreign investors (that might, in the worst case, involve a small fraction of production value in excessive royalties or overpricing of supplies and services) is to prevent inefficient foreign direct investment. Apart from domestic economic inefficiencies, the potentially most worrisome source of inefficiency is excessive protection from import competition. Fortunately, China has a very large domestic market that will justify many enterprises (and joint ventures) in nearly any line of business, thus permitting vigorous competition among domestic enterprises or joint ventures. But in some cases this will not be enough, and high levels of import protection could seriously reduce the incentives for efficiency.

C. Interrelations With Other Reform Measures

4.28 While the trade policy measures summarized in the preceding section are, as stated, closely related to other economic reforms outlined in Section A, progress can be made in implementing these trade reforms independently of progress in other economic areas. The most crucial precondition is the maintenance of domestic macroeconomic balance and stability. A number of developing countries have attempted to reform their trade systems in the face of very large domestic imbalances, characterized by large government budget deficits and permissive monetary and credit policies to finance these deficits, resulting in rapid inflation. Their tasks have often been rendered even more difficult by heavy external indebtedness that left little room to maneuver, as short-term reductions in exports or surges in imports could simply not be financed. But very often also, trade reform measures have failed because initial steps were too timid, particularly with respect to exchange rate system reforms.

4.29 China does not, at this moment, face extreme macroeconomic imbalances. However, the experience of the past two-and-a-half years shows that China's economic and political system is not immune to such dangers. There are pressures for continued high government expenditures and easy bank credit, at the very time when the role of the central government is being redefined and revenues decentralized to enterprises and local governments. When combined with a low political tolerance for inflation, this leads to calls for renewed or continued administrative controls over prices, imports and so on. Macroeconomic balance is therefore crucial during a transition towards a more efficient trade system based on decentralization of decision-making and competition.

4.30 In other respects, trade reforms could begin to be implemented relatively independently of the progress of domestic reforms. This is so, because in many respects the decentralization to enterprises of foreign trade decisions is currently trailing behind the decentralization of domestic production and marketing decisions. Similarly, competition among enterprises in domestic markets is already reasonably advanced in those commodities where China's export prospects in the near term are brightest: relatively labor-intensive, diversified manufactures, including not only traditional exports such as handicrafts, processed food, textiles and garments, but more importantly new products such as consumer electronics, standard electrical and mechanical machinery, fabricated metal products and so on. The most important missing element to become internationally competitive in these products is better design and quality that can be acquired more efficiently under a more open system of foreign trade and international economic relations (para. 2.45 and Box 2.5).

4.31 This is not to say that trade reform can be carried out without regard to further progress on price reform. Further price reform is desirable and necessary both to increase the efficiency of resource allocation in the domestic economy--particularly for capital-intensive basic raw materials (steel, chemicals, power, etc.)--and also to ensure an efficient set of signals to govern trading decisions. A wide-ranging trade reform without price reform would lead to irrational exports of some goods, such as steel products and energy intensive goods, and excessive imports of consumer goods. However, for many of the goods mentioned in the previous paragraph there has already been considerable progress in price reform, and it is our judgement that the proposed initial steps in trade reform do not have to wait for further progress in other areas.

4.32 These considerations suggest a way to proceed with the recommended trade policy reforms. Firstly, based on a examination of those sectors where price reform has been substantive, and where enterprises are generally responsible for their profits and losses, a list of candidate sectors/subsectors for early trade reform could be drawn up. For these sectors, there could be an immediate opening up of competition in trade, through the abolition of business scopes for FTCs and the effective monopoly powers of the relevant FTC for that sector/subsector. Any FTC or other trading organization would then have the right to trade in these products. Similarly, for these sectors/subsectors there could be a widespread granting of direct trading rights to enterprises in these sectors/subsectors, perhaps with the initial safeguard of only granting direct trading rights to enterprises that achieved a specified level of exports in the previous year, say US$1 million. At the same time, it would be necessary to ensure that the FTCs concerned become fully responsible for profits and losses.

4.33 This same classification could then be used to make progress on foreign exchange allocation and import licensing restrictions. For those sectors/subsectors where trade is to be liberalized, the foreign exchange retention ratio for the enterprises could be raised, perhaps substantially. Simultaneously, there would be a cessation of any foreign exchange allocations from the plan for these sectors/subsectors, with foreign exchange-deficient enterprises having to purchase foreign exchange from the foreign exchange market, which could be launched formally at the same time. Of course, such a market would not be limited to these enterprises, but would be open to any enterprise with surplus foreign exchange, or in need of foreign exchange. The higher retention ratios would provide the surplus foreign exchange to seed the market.

4.34 Again, a link could be made with import licensing. For these same sectors/subsectors, there could be a simultaneous removal of most quantitative restrictions on trade, including not only competing imports, but also freer access by enterprises in these sectors to imported inputs for their own use. In some cases, such as certain consumer goods, it may be necessary to facilitate the adjustment process by raising customs tariffs for a period of time, and the regulatory tariff could be used for this purpose. In general, however, the foreign exchange market should be relied upon to control the level of liberalized imports.

4.35 It is beyond the scope of this study to identify those sectors or subsectors where advances could be made rapidly. However, it would seem that textiles, most light industry sectors, and some capital goods sectors would be candidates. The concept could also apply to above-plan production of some heavy industry sectors, perhaps including coal.

4.36 Such an approach would be in line with the Chinese practice of experimenting with reforms in certain areas prior to full implementation. While such experimentation has usually been limited by geographic area, the proposal in this case is simply to use the same approach, but with limits in a sector/subsector basis. To avoid the problems of regional differentials in exchange rates and inter-provincial conflicts on trade flows, it is strongly recommended that trade reform experiments are <u>not</u> conducted in geographically limited areas.

4.37 Once a period of initial trial has been conducted with trade reforms, and the unavoidable errors that will occur have been corrected, the reforms could then be gradually expanded. It is recognized that progress in other reforms will act as a constraint to the speed with which such an expansion could take place. For example, trade in the seven command plan commodities may have to continue on present lines until progress on price reform has made much more progress. However, the point to be stressed is the coordination of these policy reforms in the future. Institutional trade reforms, trade planning, import licensing, foreign exchange allocation, price reform, and enterprise responsibility should in future be seen to make progress simultaneously. The trade reforms suggested for immediate implementation can thus be seen as 'catching up' with the progress already made in price reform and enterprise reform. Thereafter, they can move forward simultaneously.

4.38 The creation of a more sophisticated 'neutral' environment for export enterprises (including duty and indirect tax rebating, automatic access to working capital finance, etc.) will of course require simultaneous movement in the areas of tax and financial system reform. The primary constraint is the administrative capacity required to prepare and implement these reforms, which will consequently take at least 3-5 years to prepare and implement.

4.39 Similarly, in the area of foreign direct investment there are not too many constraints arising from the domestic reform process. The most important constraint is the reform of the foreign exchange allocation system, and this could be carried out relatively quickly. Otherwise, progress will mainly involve the elimination of differences in the legal and administrative environment between domestic enterprises and foreign joint ventures. This would, in a first phase, mostly involve giving domestic enterprises the same managerial autonomy and responsibility that joint venture enterprises already enjoy, except for the over-generous corporate income tax provisions that joint ventures now enjoy. However, enterprise reform should not stop there. Further steps are required, particularly to enhance factor mobility by creating markets for labor services, land use and capital, or improving the efficiency in these markets.

4.40 Thus, foreign trade and other foreign economic relations play an essential role in the domestic economy. Foreign trade not only provides access to machinery, technology and goods in short supply, but also the multitude of contacts with buyers, suppliers and competitors that have proved to be an essential and low-cost source of technology transfer and information about market opportunities. To maximize these indirect benefits of foreign trade, it is essential that enterprises have direct contacts with buyers and suppliers, and can make foreign trade decisions autonomously. The larger the number and types of enterprises that can engage in such contacts, the more rapid technology transfer and diffusion are likely to be. Foreign trade should thus be regarded not as a separate sector or activity, but as an integral part of enterprise decision-making on production and investment. However, if such decentralized decision-making is to lead to efficient resource allocation, prices will have to reflect economic costs, competition will have to be vigorous, and macro-economic stability has to prevail. Reforms will thus have to move simultaneously on these several fronts.

CHINA

CHINA'S TRADE SYSTEM AND INSTITUTIONS AND RECENT TRADE TRENDS

Table of Contents

CHINA'S TRADE SYSTEM AND INSTITUTIONS AND RECENT TRADE TRENDS

A. The Historical Context

Thirty Years of "Closed Door" Policies, 1949-78

1.1 From the founding of the People's Republic of China in 1949 until 1978, external economic relations were rather limited, both by design and in practice. Indeed, much of the emphasis of economic strategy during this period was placed on 'self-reliance' (zili gengsheng). This meant that China should rely essentially on its own resources--and savings--to bring about economic development, and should not rely excessively on foreign trade or capital. Indeed, not only were there strategic objections to developing external relations, but there were serious theoretical objections to trading with or borrowing from nonsocialist countries at that time (see paras. 1.12-1.17).

1.2 The system that was in place to conduct foreign economic relations during this period was designed with the concept of self-reliance in mind. It was a highly centralized system, with trading rights reserved for a relatively small number of central, highly controlled institutions. A large number of administrative procedures were erected to ensure both what trade would be minimized, and, equally important, that the domestic markets would be protected from the vicissitudes of world markets. These latter markets were regarded as sending irrational signals, since they were controlled by imperalistic and capitalistic forces, and consequently such signals should not be permitted to have negative influences on rational domestic planning procedures.

1.3 Nevertheless, it was always recognized that China was not totally self-sufficient, and that it would be better for the country to obtain technology by purchasing it or receiving it from friendly countries than to attempt to develop it. However, the extent to which such a recognition was translated into actual trading decisions varied a great deal over the period, and, in particular, the period of the Cultural Revolution saw a major decline in the role of the external sector. The trends in the level of trading activity during the 1949-78 period are generally referred to as the 'four waves' of imports. It is instructive to note that the moving force throughout this period was the decision on the level of imports. After such decisions were made, the level of exports would be adjusted accordingly so as to minimize any trade deficits, and it was only after 1978 that debt came to be regarded as an acceptable way to finance imports.

1.4 The first 'wave' occurred in 1956-60, when imports averaged US$720 million per annum, compared with only US$315 million in the four previous years, and only US$160 million in the four following years. These imports were essentially related to turnkey investment projects (as many as 260) implemented with the assistance of the USSR and Eastern Europe. Not only did these plants come as complete projects with financial assistance, but also there was a major technical assistance program, and the USSR provided full blueprints and specifications. This 'wave' was significant as an initial injection of capital and technology, and also permitted the replication and manufacture of spare parts. As a consequence, many Soviet-constructed factories or their replicas continue to function today.

1.5 After a few years of low import activity, the second, brief wave of imports took place in 1964-66, with imports of complete plants from Japan and Western Europe. However, this was at a significantly lower level than the first wave, and was not accompanied by technical assistance or blueprints, and, with the coming of the Cultural Revolution, the wave ended, and its potential impact was diminished. The third wave covered the period 1973-77 and occurred just as the Cultural Revolution was ending. It was labelled the "Four-Three Programme," a name describing the plan to spend US$4.3 billion on imported equipment over a four year period. Again, the program was essentially comprised of imports of whole plants, and is generally considered to have been a less than successful program, both because of inadequate planning of individual projects, and because of a repeated absence of accompanying software.

1.6 The fourth wave was equally short-lived. It occurred in 1978, accompanying the launching of Chairman Hua's ten-year plan (1976-85). This plan continued the strategy of favoring unbalanced growth--that is, an emphasis on a high level of capital investment in basic industries--yet differed from previous plans in proposing an increased reliance on imports of advanced technology and assistance from Western developed countries to achieve the Plan's objectives. In 1978 alone, contracts valued at US$6.4 billion were signed. However, with the launching of the economic reform program in late 1978, and the adoption of an intensive growth strategy--that is, one that stressed policy reform to increase the efficient utilization of existing capital assets--many of these contracts were cancelled.

1.7 It can therefore be seen that, apart from the first 'wave' of imports from other socialist countries, the various periods of opening up to imports were both short-lived and largely ineffective. Moreover, in all but the first wave, the imports were generally of whole plants, unaccompanied by software, and increased imports did not signify a real opening up to the outside world. Thus, although the level of imports varied over the period, the attitude towards imports remained essentially the same; imports were a necessary evil, only to be resorted to when failure to do so would threaten domestic growth, and when such imports were made, they were to be done in such a way as to isolate their impact on the economy as much as possible.

1.8 The institutional arrangements for conducting trade during this period reflected this attitude. For the first few years of the People's Republic, trade was controlled by a strict licensing system. However, from about 1952 onwards, this was replaced by a centralized planning system under the Ministry of Foreign Trade (MFT), the predecessor to the present Ministry of Foreign Economic Relations and Trade (MOFERT). All trade was conducted by centralized foreign trade corporations (FTCs), organized along product lines. Although other corporations were involved in aspects of trade--such as the China National Foreign Trade Warehousing Corporation--there were in effect only 12 FTCs at this time, all labelled "China National (Product) Import and

Export Corporation."[1/] These FTCs had (and still have) their head offices in Beijing, with branch offices in the main provinces producing or utilizing their products. Also at the local level were Foreign Trade Bureaus (FTBs), which were, in effect, provincial offices of the MFT. There were, therefore, two parallel organizations, both of which reported directly or indirectly to the MFT.

1.9 At this time, the annual foreign trade plan dominated all trading activity. This was compiled by the MFT in cooperation with the State Planning Commission (SPC). SPC would have its primary influence on the aggregate levels of imports and exports, while the MFT would determine the composition of imports and exports based on information supplied by FTCs and FTBs. Once the plan was formulated, it was up to the FTCs to implement the plan. This was a highly centralized activity at this time, and only head offices of FTCs had the right to sign contracts for imports or exports, although, once signed, the head offices would frequently assign responsibility for fulfilling a contract to a particular provincial branch. All exports were procured by FTCs at the fixed state procurement prices and formed a part of the overall production plan of individual enterprises. Thus, at this time, enterprises were entirely indifferent between exporting and production for the domestic market, and, indeed, many enterprises may not have been aware of the ultimate destination of their products. On the import side, FTCs would be provided with a foreign exchange allocation according to trade plan amounts, and the imported products they procured would then be sold on the domestic market at the fixed domestic price. As the RMB was overvalued during most of the period, most domestic prices for traded goods were above world market levels, and consequently most FTCs made profits on imports, which they appear to have used to cover losses on exports. However, the accounts of individual FTCs were aggregated within the overall MFT budget, so it is not possible to quantify the level of the subsidy.

1.10 This system did serve three essential purposes during this period: (a) it usually enabled China to avoid balance-of-payments deficits; (b) it permitted China to isolate the domestic market from any instability in the world market, reflected in close to zero inflation during this period; and (c) it enabled China to control very carefully the level and composition of imports and exports, and thus to protect infant industries in China. However, the shortcomings of such a centralized system, and four problems in particular, became increasingly apparent to Chinese policymakers.

(a) The system was very slow to respond to changes in local conditions, and to new export opportunities.

(b) No local initiative or 'enthusiasm' was stimulated.

1/ The product lines covered by these 12 corporations were technology, machinery, minerals and metals, chemicals, instruments, cereals, oils and foodstuffs, textiles, light industrial products, arts and crafts, native products and animal by-products, medicines and health-care products, and packaging.

(c) It reduced the effectiveness of the technology transfer effects of trade, by preventing contacts between buyers, sellers and enterprises.

(d) The system was in conflict with other reforms which the policymakers wished to institute, such as increased use of market forces and greater enterprise autonomy.

1.11 In Part B below, the changes that were introduced to the system are described, but prior to that it is important to see how trade theory has changed in China in recent years.

The Evolution of Chinese Trade Theory

1.12 Prior to 1978, there was virtually no theoretical debate on the role of foreign trade. It was considered that trade between rich, capitalistic countries and poor, socialist (or otherwise) countries generally involved exploitation by the former of the latter. As already noted, self-reliance was the basic maxim, with a concept that the maintenance of political independence required the achievement of economic independence. It is this long-running belief in the exploitative nature of trade that has led now to the oft-quoted Chinese approach to trade based on 'equality and mutual benefit.'

1.13 It must be recognized, however, that it was not, fundamentally, a change in theory which led to the development of the 'open-door' policy, but rather the reverse. That is to say, the development by senior leaders of the open-door policy spawned a theoretical debate among academics, many of whom sought to identify a theoretical justification for, or to question the theoretical soundness of the new policy.

1.14 The debate began with a reassessment of Ricardo's theory of comparative advantage in the framework of the Marxian labor theory of value. Although it rapidly became accepted that in theory there could be gains from trade (and in the debate, the gains that were referred to were generally the static gains from trade), the major debate that took place concerned whether such trade could be done on the basis of equality.

1.15 The main proponents argued that with large world markets having been in operation for many years, it was reasonable to suppose that world market prices were an adequate proxy for an 'average unit of universal labor,' and thus that trade according to world market prices was equal.[2/] Many Chinese economists strongly opposed this view, however, arguing that distortions in world markets were severe, resulting from imperfect competition and immobility

---

2/ It is interesting to note that Eastern European economists had settled this question to their satisfaction in the 1950s, and had concentrated their attentions subsequently on questions of trade optimization. One result of this debate was that trade between CMEA countries is indeed valued at world market prices measured in Swiss Francs.

of labor, land and capital, as well as the existence of monopolistic capitalists. These economists cited the rising prices of manufactures and declining (in real terms) prices of primary products. Moreover, many economists, citing the work of Emmanuel and Amin, went on to argue that even without such distortions, trade would be unequal because of different labor productivity among different trading nations, reflected in the higher wage rates of developed countries.

1.16 This argument was effectively rejected by the open-door supporters, who demonstrated that the only exploitation that such trade entailed was the exploitation of workers in advanced countries, who were not fully compensated for their higher productivity. Moreover, the work of Emmanuel, in particular, became discredited in China, because his contention that it was (partially) the existence of trade unions in developed countries that led to exploitation of poor countries in unequal trade was unacceptable to the Chinese, because it undermined the international solidarity of workers.

1.17 In the end, the debate was resolved by a general acceptance that trade could be beneficial, but that China would have to be careful in its trade dealings to ensure equality, and avoid those products (or make appropriate adjustments in trading) where exploitation would be likely to occur.

The Launching of the 'Open-Door' Policy

1.18 The turning point for the introduction of economic reforms, including the open-door policy, came in December 1978 at the conclusion of the Third Plenary Session of the 11th Central Committee of the Party. The adoption of a new economic strategy at that time should be seen in both its political and economic context. From the political viewpoint, it must be recalled that China had recently emerged from three traumatic political events in 1976; the death of Mao Zedong, the purge of the Gang of Four, and the end of the ten-year Cultural Revolution. It is very clear that in political terms, China was ready for changes. The chaos and upheaval of the Cultural Revolution had caused much distress and personal hardship as well as serious economic and social problems.

1.19 Since the launching of the first Five-Year Plan in 1953, China had followed a typical growth strategy for a centrally planned economy. Emphasis was placed on "extensive" growth, meaning an expansion of the means of production. This involved a suppression of personal consumption, both through pricing and rationing, and the consequent mobilization of high levels of savings. These savings were largely directed by the state into the capital goods and heavy industry sectors. This unbalanced growth strategy was considered necessary because of a belief that it was the development of the capital goods sector that determined a country's long-term growth rate.

1.20 As already noted in paragraph 1.6, this basic strategy was continued in 1977, with the adoption of the ten-year plan (1976-85), and, in fact, the capital funds budget under this plan was equal to the total investment of the previous 28 years. At the same time, China adopted the "Four Modernizations" policy, calling for the modernization of agriculture, industry, science and technology, and defense. While the strategy for achieving the Four

Modernizations has now changed, they remain a fundamental component of overall economic strategy.

1.21 It was at the CCP meeting in December 1978 that this strategy of extensive growth was firmly rejected--together with Hua's ten-year plan--in favor of a program of "readjustment, restructuring, consolidation and improvement." In particular, the new strategy stressed improved utilization of existing capacity, with an emphasis on productivity improvements, and thus on the technical transformation of existing enterprises rather than the creation of new enterprises. Other factors were also considered important: the old extensive growth strategy had required the suppression of people's living standards, even though a measure of the success of socialism should be improvements in the material welfare of the people; the heavy central control necessary to effect the extensive strategy was considered to have suppressed enterprise incentives; and the system of individual rewards was considered to have suppressed individual efforts--the "iron-rice-bowl" guaranteeing minimum welfare conditions and "eating from one big pot," meaning that the efforts of one individual were shared by all. This latter factor led Premier Zhao to remark in 1982 that the struggle to enforce the principle of "more pay for more work, less pay for less work, and no pay for no work is no less significant than the socialist transformation of private industry and commerce in the 1950s."

1.22 Thus, the context in which the open-door policy was launched was one of general reform of economic policies. The overall direction of reforms was to reduce the role of the central government and, thus, of directive planning and to place increasing reliance on the role of the enterprises and individuals, both reacting to appropriate incentives. Growth was to come through efficiency improvements, which meant technical transformation and modernization. In such an overall macro context, reform of the trade system in the way it has been pursued under the open-door policy is entirely natural. A crucial question, however, is whether the subsequent reforms of the trade system proceded too fast relative to reforms in other areas of the economy, and how future reforms of the system should be timed to coincide with other aspects of the reform program yet to be undertaken.

The Trade System in Transition, 1979-85

1.23 While the launching of the open-door policy can be traced to December 1978, the Third Plenary Session itself gave little direct guidance for reform, calling only for "expanding economic cooperation on terms of equality and mutual benefit with other countries on the basis of self-reliance, striving to adopt the world's advanced technologies and equipment." The next major turning point came in July 1979, with the adoption of the "Law of the People's Republic of China on Joint Ventures Using Chinese and Foreign Investment." For the first time, this meant that foreign investment was to be welcomed as well as foreign technology. From 1979 to 1985, the trade system evolved rapidly. The centralized FTCs lost their monopoly powers, and their branch offices began to operate as separate units. In addition, provincial authorities created their own FTCs to fulfill provincial export aspirations, and line ministries found it convenient to establish corporations to engage in trade in their products directly. A system of foreign exchange retention at the provincial and enterprise level was also introduced, and, when combined with the introduction of import licensing and an initial decentralization of license-issuing authority, this period saw a rapid change in the locus of trade activity. From being a residual activity carried out in a highly centralized manner, trade became, during this period, a central focus of effort, with provincial authorities and institutions in the vanguard. These various reforms in trade practices over the period were summarized in the September 1984 document on the reform of the trade system adopted by the State Council (see Main Report Box 2.2).

1.24 Several new institutions were created, although some were short-lived. The major new institutions were: (a) the Foreign Investment Control Commission (FICC), which was established to regulate all foreign investments in China; (b) the State Import and Export Commission (SIEC) which was charged with making policies on new trading arrangements and technology imports policy; (c) the General Administration of Customs, with particular responsibility for formulating policies for preferential customs treatment; and (d) the China International Trust and Investment Corporation (CITIC), primarily designed to bring together foreign and local partners in joint ventures. In March 1982, the FICC and SIEC were combined with the MFT and the old Ministry of Foreign Relations to form the new Ministry of Foreign Economic Relations and Trade (MOFERT). CITIC and GAC continue to report directly to the State Council.

1.25 During this period, several experiments were undertaken, but central control remained paramount. Ministries other than MOFERT were permitted to create their own trading corporations, and the FTCs under MOFERT were permitted to decentralize executive authority to branch offices. Provinces were also permitted to create their own foreign trade corporations under the provincial foreign trade bureaus. However, while many new FTCs were created during this period, and personnel in provincial branches and provincial FTCs began to gain experience, MOFERT maintained centralized control by requiring most imports to be approved centrally. By the end of 1983, it was believed that sufficient experience had been gained to permit a major decentralization to take place.

1.26 Three events in 1984 came together to create a major experiment in decentralization. Firstly, from January 1984 onwards, the informal arrangements for sharing foreign exchange between central government and other provincial authorities were formalized, with most provincial authorities given the right to retain 25% of their foreign exchange earnings for their own use. (Several provinces were provided with higher retention ratios--Fujian, Guangdong, Inner Mongolia and Tibet.) From January 1985 onwards, enterprises were allowed to use half of the retained foreign exchange for their own account. Secondly, provisional regulations for issuing import licenses were issued in January 1984, and the rules for implementing these regulations were published in May 1984. These regulations defined import rights, and were a blueprint for decentralization. Imports were classified as restricted or unrestricted. At that time, there were only 28 categories of restricted imports, and all imports of these commodities needed MOFERT approval. More importantly, the regulations permitted a group of institutions to import unrestricted items without reference to MOFERT. These institutions included all FTCs and branches under MOFERT, FTCs under other ministries, and FTCs run by provincial authorities. With the publication of these regulations, about 35% of imports were effectively liberalized from quantitative control.

1.27 The third event of 1984 was, as already noted, the adoption of the decision on reform of the economic structure adopted at the Third Plenary Session of the Twelfth Central Committee of the Communist Party of China. This was on the basis of a report on the reform of the trade system by MOFERT, which was approved in the State Council on September 15, 1984. There were five basic elements of reform of the trade system, which were designed to strengthen the implementation of the policy of opening up to the outside world, and the general economic reform program of removing government from day-to-day operation of enterprises:

(a) "Separating central policy for trade from its day-to-day management." This meant that "the foreign trade enterprises will conduct independently the import and export business, keeping their own accounts and assuming responsibility for their own profits and losses".

(b) "Transferring power to lower administrative levels and bringing into play the managing initiative of various foreign trade enterprises." This involved the abolition of the monopoly powers of the national FTCs, and the granting of trading rights to certain enterprises. It also envisaged the effective decentralization of power to individual branches of national FTCs, which would become separate accounting units.

(c) "Adopting the agency system for conducting foreign trade." The new system was to be adopted immediately with respect to imports, with "end-users taking responsibility for their own profits and losses." For export commodities, its application would vary from commodity to commodity, with the agency system being adopted for manufactured exports, but direct purchase to be continued for agricultural and handicraft products. The extent to which this most crucial of trade reforms has actually been adopted is discussed further in part B below.

(d) "Reforming the foreign trade planning system," by relying more on guidance plans and less on command plans.

(e) "Reforming the financial management of the foreign trade system." This step follows from the other reforms, as FTCs avoid "imposed" losses with the introduction of the agency system and the adoption of decentralized accounting. The individual FTCs were to begin paying taxes rather than handing over all profits to the state.

1.28 When these three elements were combined, it became a clear blueprint for the expansion of trading activities at the provincial level and for the proliferation of trading companies. Although statistics are not available, MOFERT data (which exclude trade under "special" arrangements such as joint ventures and compensation trade) indicate that in 1981 FTCs under MOFERT accounted for 91% of exports and 87% of imports, but that by 1984 those ratios had declined to 79%, and 65% respectively. These statistics also reveal that the main area for growth outside of the MOFERT FTCs was in technical imports. In 1981, imports by Techimport accounted for 16.5% of all imports; by 1984, this share had declined to 4.1% despite a rapid increase in the total volume of such imports. (Imports in SITC category 7 were US$4.6 billion in 1981 US$7.6 billion in 1984, and US$16.4 billion in 1985). Therefore the decentralization of 1984-85 was used at the provincial level particularly for increasing the levels of imports of machinery and equipment. In 1978, as already noted, there were only 12 FTCs, albeit with branch offices. By the end of 1984, there were over 1000 separate entities directly conducting foreign trade business.

1.29 This decentralization of trade management coincided with an acceleration of economic growth to 12% p.a.; a decentralization of banking, which led to very rapid credit creation; and a conscious decision on the part of the central government to reduce the level of foreign exchange reserves by increasing technology imports. The combination of these factors led to a rapid increase in the trade deficit. Because of this, the authorities felt compelled to tighten controls beginning in mid-1985. (See Main Report, para. 3.15-3.20).

1.30 It was not feasible to reverse fully the decentralization of trading authority that had already occurred. The approach taken was to increase the number of commodities on the list of restricted imports, and to introduce widespread export licensing. At the same time, the State Administration for Exchange Control (SAEC) attempted to restrict access to foreign exchange retention rights, in conjunction with apparently slower procedures for approving import licenses. In some cases, such as production lines for TV sets and automobiles, MOFERT introduced an outright import ban. The current status of import and export licensing is discussed in Annex 2.

1.31 Overall, therefore, during the 1979-85 period, there was some initial experimentation, followed by rapid decentralization, and when this had some perceived adverse consequences, some recentralization through an overlay of additional central controls. Nevertheless, from the point of view of day-to-day business, a major change in practices took place over the period, with the function of the center slowly changing to one of making policy and exercising overall controls.

B. The Trade System in October 1986: A Snapshot

The Role of the Foreign Trade Plan 3/

1.32 The Foreign Trade Plan remains at the center of the trade regime in China, as it has since the mid-50s. In the following sections, we will discuss the formulation and implementation of the Plan. However, it is also important to consider the overall role of the Plan, and its function with the macroeconomic framework. There are three key roles of the Plan in this regard.

(a) It acts as an instrument of protection, in that it attempts to exclude requests for imports when there is a local substitute available, regardless of price or quality. In this sense, the Plan acts as a part of the import quota regime.

(b) Similarly, on the export side, it attempts to overcome the anti-export bias in the trade system by mandating certain exports. A question to be addressed later is whether this is a more costly way for the economy to earn foreign exchange than the use of improved incentives.

(c) From the point of view of the central planners, the Plan has the critical role of attempting to balance imports and exports, domestic supply of and demand for critical commodities (such as steel where there remain domestic production shortfalls), and domestic and foreign demand for scarce consumer goods.

1.33 As noted in paragraph 1.27 above, one of the stated aims of the reform program is gradually to change the role of the plan, in particular reducing the role of mandatory or command plans. These were to be replaced over time by guidance plans, which would rely more for their implementation on the use of economic levers. To a significant extent, this process--which has been initiated at the level of Central Government--is being undermined at the provincial or municipal level by provincial authorities, who convert guidance plans received from the center into command plans at the provincial level.

1.34 However, there is no doubt that the role of the Plan has changed in two important ways in recent years. Firstly, before 1978, imports were the driving force. The list of necessary imports would be drawn up, and exports identified to generate the required foreign exchange or pay for them. In terms of process, this is now different, and an export target is first drawn up, which is then used to determine the affordable level of plan imports. Secondly, since 1979 the Plan has covered a smaller proportion of trade. Whereas before 1979 all trade was included in the Plan, which covered some 3,000 commodities, and very few imports or exports were made that were not

---

3/ It should be noted that all figures quoted in this section are World Bank estimates based on interviews at the enterprise level, and the foreign trade plan remains unpublished.

covered by the Plan, this is no longer the case. We estimate that about 70-80% of all exports are still within the Plan, but the level of above-Plan exports--which permit above-Plan imports--appears to be rising steadily, and, as we shall see (paragraph 1.45), the current incentives are geared to encouraging this trend.

Formulating the Foreign Trade Plan: Exports

1.35 The procedures for formulating the export and import plans are quite different, although the two processes occur simultaneously. Both commence in June-July of the year preceding the Plan year and are finalized at the National Foreign Trade Planning Conference, which is held in October each year, following which the Plan is submitted by the State Planning Commission for approval by the State Council. One essential feature of the general planning process in China that is hard to capture in a brief description is the iterative negotiations that take place. It is not the case that local organizations collect information and submit it to central planners who than produce a coordinated plan, but rather that a repeated set of interactions occur between the local and national levels, until the final result is obtained of a Plan which local officials feel able to implement (or, more usually, one whose targets they know they can meet and usually exceed with ease), and with which central officials are content.

1.36 The process for the export plan begins with branch offices of FTCs and other trading organizations, which are requested by MOFERT to provide quantitative estimates of goods available for procurement in the following year. These estimates are fed upwards to MOFERT and SPC. Of course, for most commodities, export production remains a small percentage of total production. It appears to be only in isolated cases--such as in the garment sector--that factories produce primarily for the export market. In such a situation, how should branch FTCs estimate export supply? Two factors are relevant: firstly, as described below (paragraph 1.45), incentives are provided for exceeding plan targets, so rational behavior on the part of FTCs suggests that they should attempt to minimize the planned level of exports; and secondly, they are aware of national targets for export growth over a particular Five-Year Plan Period.

1.37 Therefore, the logical behavior for an FTC is to take the present year's export target--assuming that it is a reasonable one--and increase it by the average rate of growth of exports for the plan period. For example, it is reported that the Plan level of exports for Fujian Province in 1985 was US$340 million. However, the actual outcome showed exports of US$490 million. Nevertheless, the Plan target for exports in Fujian Province in 1986 was reportedly raised to only US$380 million, while the province itself was targeting US$500-550 million. The Province thus succeeded in satisfying central targets with ease, and also benefitted from above-plan rewards.

1.38 When all estimates of export supply are assembled, MOFERT and SPC go through an elaborate procedure, in combination with the import plan, and derive a final export plan. It is at this point that a crucial step is made: the separation of the export plan into command and guidance plans. This is something that varies from year to year. It had clearly been the intention of MOFERT in October 1984 that command planning would be associated with products that would still be purchased directly--notably agricultural and handicraft products--whereas guidance planning would apply to agency procurement. However, command planning continues to apply to about 70% of Plan exports. Unlike import planning, in which there is a short list of command plan commodities (see paragraph 1.48), the coverage of the export command plans seems to vary from province to province. However, there are certain key commodities that are common to the export command plans of each province: agricultural products, handicrafts, oil, coal, textiles, garments, other metal and metallic product exports and machinery--a total of about 120 commodity items.

1.39 There are four essential elements that differentiate command plan exports from guidance plan exports.

(a) All producers of command plan exports are provided with production inputs through the materials allocation system (see footnote 3) at fixed state prices. Depending on the province, guidance plan commodities may or may not be so covered.

(b) Command plan exports are specified in quantities, as would be expected with products included in the materials allocation system. Guidance plans are specified in values, expressed in US dollars. Expected values of command plan exports and expected quantities of guidance plan exports are specified, but provinces are expected to achieve the quantity targets of command plan exports and the value target of guidance plan exports.

(c) The command plan targets are very specific, and for several commodities--such as textiles and coal--the provincial targets are for procurement to fill centrally-negotiated contracts, as in the pre-1978 system. For guidance plans, provinces are at liberty to change the planned composition of exports provided they fulfill the overall target.

(d) To accompany element (a) producers have no choice over supplying command plan commodities to specified FTCs. For guidance plan commodities, it varies from province to province, but there is nothing in the system to compel producers to supply FTCs. In some provinces, it is reported that guidance plans become translated into command plans, including materials allocation and compulsory export supply at fixed prices. In other provinces, FTCs compete with domestic purchasers for supply. For commodities where above production plan output can be sold on the free market, producers have to weigh the relative benefits of higher domestic prices or of access to foreign exchange retention rights (see Main Report, Chapter 3).

Implementing the Export Plan

1.40 At the present time, in stark contrast to pre-1978, the responsibility for implementation of the export plan for most commodities rests firmly with the provinces. Once the export plans have been agreed and distributed, it is up to the provincial MOFERTs and provincial branches of FTCs to go out and find export markets and contracts to fulfill the plan, except for a few selected commodities. Particularly in the early period of the decentralization in 1984, this led to some considerable competition among provinces. The current foreign exchange retention scheme (see Main Report Chapter 3), while giving relatively limited export incentives to producers, gives major incentives to provincial governments to increase exports. The higher the level of exports, the higher can be the level of imports approved directly at the provincial level, and thus the larger can be the number of modernization and expansion projects carried out in the province concerned.

1.41 The products in which China was able to increase its exports rapidly in 1984-85 were relatively homogeneous: agricultural commodities, textiles, handicrafts. As markets were relatively poorly developed at that time, it seems that provinces began to compete with each other to supply a relatively fixed demand. This were particularly the case for agricultural exports to Hong Kong, where large profits were originally being made. As a consequence, prices fell in the Hong Kong market, and total revenue fell. Similarly, with competition to fill fixed quotas for textile exports, a less than optimal composition of small exports arose. For these two groups of exports in particular, therefore, the central authorities felt compelled to recentralize export decision-making. It is now the case that provinces are given rigid quotas for specific commodities that they may export in these two commodity groups. In the case of agricultural exports to Hong Kong, the National Cereals, Oils and Foodstuffs Import and Export Corporation has a monopoly over such exports, which it exercises by giving monthly quotas for such exports to its provincial branches, with instructions that such quotas are to be spread evenly over the month. They also maintain offices in Hong Kong and watch market prices on a daily basis, so that supply can be regulated to maintain optimum prices. In these cases in which China is a dominant exporter, and in which demand is relatively inelastic, it is appropriate that some form of constraint should be operated on the level of exports so as to maximize revenue. However, there may be more efficient ways to organize these constraints then heavy central control (see Main Report, paragraphs 2.55-2.56).

1.42 As already noted, it is the provincial FTCs that implement the plan. For command plan exports, this is a straightforward process. These are mandatory, and FTCs arrange for the delivery and marketing of these goods, for which the producers are paid at fixed state prices. For guidance plan exports, there are five different modes of plan implementation.

(a) At the provincial level, guidance plans are converted to command plan, and the command plan procedure is followed. This appears to happen rarely in progressive provinces such as Fujian or Guangdong, but may be quite common elsewhere.

(b) Supply contracts are negotiated with producers at fixed state prices. This is easier to achieve the higher is the foreign exchange requirement of the producer.

(c) Supply contracts are negotiated at higher than fixed prices, where the producer has the alternative of supplying to the free domestic market. (FTCs cite competition from domestic purchasers as the single most important constraint to increasing exports.)

(d) FTCs negotiate contracts with producers on an agency basis, deducting their fees and passing on the international price to the producer.

(e) Supplies are procured from "captive" producers, which have been financed by the FTC. This practice was cited frequently in the lucrative seafood export business, and is often the case for the new FTCs set up by industrial ministries.

1.43 For the vast majority of producers, the FTC remains the sole outlet to the outside world. Furthermore, it appears that for most producers the FTC procures at the fixed state price. In many cases, this means that the FTC will suffer a loss, but in those cases where exporting is highly profitable, this is not passed on to the producer. Most FTCs procure a fairly wide range of commodities, and they cover losses on some lines with profits on others. It seems that the MOFERT policy of instituting export procurement on an agency basis has been implemented to only a very limited extent, and that most goods are procured by FTCs for their own account, in contrast to the situation with respect to imports (see paragraph 1.58). Indeed, of the five reforms announced in October 1984 (see paragraph 1.27), it is this reform which is most conspicuously not being implemented. One of the main reasons for this is probably that it became apparent in 1985 that full implementation of this policy would have resulted in a decline in the level of exports, unless there were a large devaluation of the Rmb.

1.44 There are, of course, other factors to be taken into account. Firstly, the FTCs had been in operation for many years when the reforms took place, and even branch offices had many contacts with overseas buyers. So far as the producers were concerned, the FTC would, as in the past, handle all such contacts and negotiations, including specifications, quality control, packaging, procurement of inputs etc. It was difficult for producers to break out of this pattern, in terms of acquiring new expertise, and incentives were not provided to encourage them to take on new, demanding tasks.

1.45 FTCs, on the other hand, remain strongly motivated towards achieving high levels of exports, and in particular to exceed export targets. FTCs seek to increase profitable exports, and they will frequently use these profits to finance loss-making exports, since the rewards for achieving high levels of exports and exceeding export plans are much greater than the rewards for making profits. FTC's profits are all handed over to their parent organizations, and while there may have been some stricter imposition of budget constraints on FTCs in recent years, there remain five very strong motivations for FTCs to expand the level of exports and to resist pressures from producers who wish to engage directly on export business.

(a) There is a more or less formal system of incentives provided by the central government to FTCs in direct proportion to the extent to which they fulfill or exceed export targets. These incentives take two forms: bonuses to individual employees of FTCs which may exceed the national limits on such bonuses; and bonus incentive payments to FTCs. These latter vary from province to province, but seem to be of the order of 3 fen per US dollar earned if the target is achieved, and 10 fen per US dollar for each dollar earned above the plan target.

(b) Pressure--and in some cases, it is reported, incentive payments--from provincial authorities to provincial FTCs increase exports in order to increase the level of foreign exchange retained at the provincial level, since 12.5% of all foreign exchange earned is available to provincial authorities to finance desired imports. Moreover, it is reported that: there can be higher rates of foreign exchange retention for above plan exports, presumably by negotiation.

(c) The greater flexibility in importing under the current regime permits FTCs to operate in profitable import activities and use the proceeds to cover any export losses. While this was always possible before, it is now much easier for FTCs to make their own choices in selecting imports.

(d) In the generally freer environment, there are attractive opportunities offered to the staff of FTCs, if they can achieve high levels of exports. In particular, staff of FTCs have opportunities to travel and, increasingly, they have opportunities to live and work in overseas offices of the FTCs. These are powerful incentives in China.

(e) Finally, there is the natural tendency of workers in an administered system to seek to expand or maintain bureaucratic size and power, since this is to a considerable extent the measure of success in such a system.

1.46 Overall, therefore, despite the apparently wide-ranging reforms that have been announced and implemented in the trade sector, we find an export system that retains many of the features of the pre-1978 system, albeit at a much less centralized level. We would summarize this in four distinct characteristics of the export system as it stood at end-1986.

(a) The foreign trade corporations continue to dominate export activity, and direct contacts between producers and export markets remain very limited.

(b) International market prices continue to have only a moderate impact on procurement prices and patterns, and domestic market prices continue to be the main determinant of export procurement prices.

(c) While command plans are less important than in the pre-1978 system, quantitative export targets remain of critical importance in the system.

(d) Related to (c), the quantity of exports continues to be much more important than the efficiency with which such exports are made.

The Import Plan

1.47 It has already been noted that there have been some substantial changes in the nature of the foreign trade plan since 1978. In line with general commodity planning, individual trade plans were drawn up at that time for some 3,000 commodities, whilst this has now been reduced to about 120 commodities. Moreover, the reform has been most far-reaching in the area of import planning. From a system in which all imports were carefully planned, in very close harmony with the production plan and the materials allocation system,[4/] there is now a much looser system, with four essential components:

(a) A command plan system for seven key raw materials, a steady supply of which is considered essential;

(b) A system of foreign exchange allocation for the import component of priority investment projects;

(c) A system of foreign exchange allocation for other priority imports of raw materials, spare parts and equipment; and

(d) An import licensing system to control noncentrally funded imports.

1.48 The import licensing system is discussed in Part II below. However, it should be noted that this aspect of overall control is growing in importance, not least because of the formalization of the foreign exchange retention system in January 1984, together with the decentralization of external borrowing authority and the growing numbers of foreign joint ventures. These three factors have resulted in a growing capacity to finance imports at the local level--i.e. without recourse to centrally controlled foreign exchange--and, in order to attempt to maintain macro-balance, the central authorities have rein-

---

4/ The materials allocation system was, until the recent economic reform, the basic tool for managing the economy in China. Even today, it remains of vital importance. Under the system, production of major commodities is planned, to the level of the production unit, and both raw materials and final outputs are allocated to users. Thus, a truck production factory would be required to produce, say, 100,000 trucks per annum, and the necessary amount of steel would be allocated to the truck factory. The trucks would, in turn, be allocated to end-users, to whom the truck factory would make deliveries. This system removes marketing from the sphere of influence of producers, and the sales occur at fixed state prices. It is through this system that the necessary level of imports of particular commodities could be planned; since there would be a determined quantity both of production and consumption of a particular commodity, imports would be planned to fill any gaps.

troduced and strengthened import licensing.[5/] Imports financed at the local and enterprise level without central foreign exchange now account for 30-40% of total imports.

1.49 The Command Plan. As noted above, command planning for imports is now reduced to covering only the seven key raw materials which are under "unified management": steel, chemical fertilizer, rubber, timber, tobacco, grain, and polyester and other synthetic fibers. Nevertheless, these commodities accounted for about 40% of imports in the 1982-84 period, although somewhat less in 1985-86 because of higher technology and equipment imports. The imports of these products are closely tied in with the materials allocation system, and the import requirements for these commodities are estimated by the State Planning Commission (SPC) in cooperation with various ministries responsible for production. As in the old trade planning system, the import requirement is calculated as the difference between the volume of the raw material required by the materials allocation system, less available domestic production.[6/] Since these commodities are considered national priorities, they are the first to receive a foreign exchange allocation.

1.50 Once imports have been determined and a foreign exchange allocation made, import responsibility is assigned to a particular FTC. Mostly, these are the national FTCs under MOFERT, such as the National Cereals Oils and Foodstuffs Import and Export Corporation, but some are assigned now to FTCs established under production ministries, such as the Ministry of Chemical Industry for fertilizers. The ministerial FTCs are generally better able to time imports into the domestic production cycle. Apart from these small recent changes, this segment of the import plan closely resembles the pre-1978 system.

1.51 Priority Investment Projects. This category covers two types of projects: imports of complete plants for industrial expansion, and centrally funded general investment projects, such as those funded by the proceeds of World Bank loans and credits. The former are of much greater importance. For these imports, the SPC is again the principal institution, since it must review and approve each project in the annual investment program. It appears to be only rarely the case that major projects are funded entirely locally. Issues related to the approval of major projects were discussed in the Bank's Finance and Investment report, and will not be repeated here. Suffice it to

---

5/ Foreign exchange retention rights do not have an expiry date. Thus, for example, an enterprise may accumulate a retention right in 1985 and use it in 1987. This would result in an "unplanned" import and demand for foreign exchange. The SAEC may not have taken foreign exchange retention rights fully into account in annual foreign exchange allocation planning (and, indeed, they may not have maintained full records of such rights at the national level).

6/ In 1985, in particular, there were quite high levels of steel imports financed at the local level as part of locally financed investment projects.

say that such projects require a full feasibility study, including estimated foreign exchange requirements. Any such projects including foreign exchange expenditures of US$100 million or more require State Council approval, while projects over Y 30 million require the approval of SPC. The detailed import requirements and technical specifications of modernization projects must also obtain State Economic Commission approval.

1.52 When all these steps have been taken, the project automatically receives a foreign exchange allocation. The nature of the project and its financing determine whether the foreign exchange is provided in the form of a grant, an RMB-denominated loan, a foreign exchange (usually US$) denominated loan, or simply an allocation of foreign exchange for which the sponsoring enterprise, ministry or province must provide the counterpart RMB to purchase the foreign exchange. Such imports are then incorporated into MOFERT's annual technology import plan, and since these large projects are generally implemented over a number of years, probably 60-70% of this part of the technology import plan is determined by decisions taken in previous years. This component probably accounts for about 15-20% of total annual imports, although such a breakdown of import statistics is not available.

1.53 <u>Other Priority Imports</u>. Once the command plan imports and priority investments projects have been provided for, SPC and SAEC will determine how much foreign exchange can be allocated for other uses. If an enterprise or a province wishes to import noncommand plan raw materials, spare parts or individual pieces of equipment, it will attempt to obtain a central foreign exchange allocation for these rather than use foreign exchange retention rights. Although, to a large extent, the imports that get included in this part of the program are determined on an ad hoc basis, priority is given to import components of command plan exports.

1.54 If the required import is an item of equipment, or a sets of items, it also requires SEC approval if it is above a certain limit. This limit varies from province to province (i.e. it is higher for the SEZs, 14 open cities, Fujian and Guangdong) but is generally US$50,000 per individual item and US$500,000 in total. Below this level, it is for the approval of the user's department in charge. It appears that SPC and SAEC essentially divide this part of the foreign exchange budget between departments according to historical shares, leaving final allocation up to those departments.

1.55 <u>Other Imports</u>. The process as just described leaves 30-40% of imports to be determined and financed by other means. While some attempt is made to plan these--for example by the requirement that all equipment imports above the levels mentioned in paragraph 54 are given SEC approval--the basic method of control is through import licensing. This is discussed in detail in Annex 2. However, it is important to note two features of planning in this area. Firstly, there are certain imports which central planners believe to have been imported in sufficient quantities already, or which they regard as "wasteful." In these cases, either an import ban will be introduced, such as for motor-cars or production lines for television, or else a zero or very low quota will be introduced.

1.56 Secondly, MOFERT, in conjunction with SPC, draws up a "plan" for imports of commodities not covered elsewhere in the plan, such as consumer durables, food, and other equipment. These "plans" are essentially guidelines for granting import licenses. Moreover, MOFERT probably also develops ceilings for licenses for individual provinces. Any such guidelines are retained within MOFERT, and are not made available to users. Therefore, enterprises and provincial authorities do not know whether their proposals for locally financed imports will be approved. Most provinces tend to submit requests for such licenses 2-4 times a year. However, whilst there are isolated cases of such applications being refused, and they may frequently be subject to delay, it seems that provided a requested import has financing available and there is no readily available domestically produced substitute, it is approved eventually. Finally, it should be noted that for all these imports, as well as for most imports in the third category (paragraphs 53-54), it is up to the end-user to decide on the best import channel. At one time, little choice was available, but now there is a choice between a national FTC, a branch of a national FTC, a provincial trade bureau, a provincial FTC, or an enterprise with trading rights.

Import Pricing

1.57 Just as the reforms of import planning have progressed further than export planning, so have reforms of the pricing system for imports. Whereas it seems that most procurement for exports continues to be made by FTCs on their own account at domestic prices, the agency system is well established in the import sector. Overall, however, there are three pricing systems for imports.

(a) Command plan imports are sold on the domestic market for the regular domestic price. This frequently results in losses for the FTCs because of lower domestic prices, and they are directly compensated for these losses.

(b) Imports of other items made by FTCs, by the state, or other import agents of goods where there is price control cannot be sold at less than the domestic price. Frequently, the State Price Bureau will determine a price for the imported equivalent to account for quality differentials, e.g. the domestic price for Japanese color televisions is some 25% above the price of domestic color televisions. Commodities in this group tend to be consumer goods, which are on the restricted imports list. However, it is on these imports that FTCs are able to make substantial profits.

(c) All other imports are made on an agency basis; i.e., the FTC requires payment of the full imported cost plus all taxes and its costs. The FTC's costs are generally only in the 1-5% range, as they do not aim to make profits on such imports. The only exception is for imports for foreign enterprises--such as hotels--for which quite large margins may be charged. In particular, it seems that virtually all imports of capital goods are now made on an agency basis, and as much as 50% of all imports.

C. Recent Trade Trends

Data Sources

1.58 The data used in the following analysis are drawn from four main sources: Chinese Customs Statistics (CCS); IMF - Direction of Trade Statistics (DOT); IMF - "People's Republic of China - Recent Economic Developments"; and the World Bank Trade Data System. Our primary source is the CCS, which reports on a quarterly basis imports and exports at the two digit level of the Standard Industrial and Trade Classification (SITC), starting from 1981. However, since these are in yuan, they had to be converted into US dollars and suitable quarterly exchange rates had to be found. Using the same lag structure as Chinese authorities, who work from monthly data, we simply lagged monthly averages given in the IMF's International Financial Statistics (IFS) by two months for periods through 1984, and by one month from the first quarter of 1985. The estimated quarterly exchange rates were then applied to the quarterly import and export values reported in the CCS and the results summed to form annual totals for each commodity group at the two-digit SITC level.[7/] For data before 1981 with similar commodity-group breakdowns, we draw on the World Bank Trade Data System, which aggregates exports and imports reported to the UN by China's trading partners. Information on import sources and export destinations is from DOT. Trade balances are also from IMF but from different documents: "People's Republic of China - Recent Economic Developments", in which imports are given on an fob basis, and in which adjustments in both imports and exports were made from 1982 onwards for re-exports.[8/] Because the mentioned sources may have used different accounting systems or estimating methods, some variation in the data is inevitable, but the overall trends that each displays are consistent with one another.

Overall Trends

1.59 Since the adoption of the "open-door" trade policy in 1979, China's merchandise exports and imports have been growing rapidly, though not at an even pace. (Growth between 1970 and 1978 was also high but from a much smal-

---

7/ Where comparison could be made, the results were found to be quite close to official government estimates, by commodity breakdown where available and in the aggregate. For example, except for 1982 total exports, in which our estimate is 3.3% lower than the official estimate, and for 1985 total imports, in which our estimate is 1.7% higher, the difference is less than 1%.

8/ The adjustment for re-exports was made on data on the basis of information provided by Chinese authorities. Imports intended for re-exports, identified mainly by non-change of ownership across the border, are subtracted from total imports reported by the Customs, and when these are finally re-exported their values are not counted, except for their value added which is recorded in the invisible accounts.

ler base and was therefore less significant in terms of the national economy and world trade.) Between 1978 and 1985, both exports and imports grew faster than GDP and also grew faster than world trade. As Table 1 indicates, during this period exports grew at an annual rate of about 14%, rising from US$10 billion in 1978 to US$25.6 billion in 1985, while imports grew at annual rate of about 19% from US$11 billion in 1978 to US$38 billion in 1985.

1.60 With this growth in the overall level of imports and exports, trade has become much more important in the economy as a whole. As Table 2 shows, both imports and exports more than doubled as a share of GDP, indicating that trade growth rates were well above GDP growth in the same period.

Table 1: CHINA'S MERCHANDISE EXPORTS AND IMPORTS, 1978-85
(in current US$ million)

	1978	1981	1982	1983	1984	1985	Annual growth 1978-85
Exports, fob /a	9,955	22,027	21,125	20,707	23,905	25,108	14.1
Imports, fob /a	11,131	21,047	16,876	18,717	23,891	38,231	19.3
Balance of trade	-1,176	980	4,249	1,990	14	-13,123	

/a Excluding re-exports.

Source: See para. 1.58.

Table 2: CHINA'S MERCHANDISE EXPORTS AND IMPORTS, 1978-85
(as % of GDP)

	1978	1981	1982	1983	1984	1985
Exports, fob	4.8	6.1	8.2	8.0	8.9	10.4
Imports, cif	5.4	8.0	7.2	7.7	9.5	13.5
Total trade	10.2	14.1	15.4	15.7	18.4	23.9

1.61 The same is true for China's share of world trade. As can be seen from Table 3, between 1978 and 1985, China's share of world exports doubled, while its import share rose from 0.9% to 2.3%. With a total trade at 24% of its GDP in 1985, China is no longer the isolated economy that it once was. In fact, with its significant and rising shares of world trade, it has now become an important member of the world community, and, coupled with its concentration in certain products and markets, could have a great impact on world trade, far beyond what its trade volumes would suggest.

Table 3: CHINA'S MERCHANDISE EXPORTS AND IMPORTS, 1978-85
(As % of World Trade)

	1978	1981	1982	1983	1984	1985
Exports, fob	0.81	1.17	1.28	1.32	1.40	1.52
Imports, fob	0.87	1.13	1.06	1.23	1.41	2.25

Source: IMF, Direction of Trade.

1.62 Average annual growth rates conceal wide fluctuations that have often characterized year-by-year trends in China's exports and imports. After a favorable performance from 1978 through 1981, exports fell successively in 1982 and 1983, rose again in 1984, and then slowed down in 1985, reflecting mainly the volatility of oil prices. In 1985, oil accounted for 24.7% of the country's exports. On the supply side, some difficulties were experienced in procuring goods for exports as many producers found it more profitable to sell their products in the domestic market in the face of rising demands for both consumer and investment goods. During the same period, imports fluctuated even more widely. This phenomenon stemmed largely from administrative decisions rather than market forces. Alarmed by what were then regarded as big trade deficits in 1979 and 1980--around US$2 billion in each year--and reflecting the changed economic strategy (see paras. 1.19-1.21), the authorities sharply cut back on imports in the ensuing three years, targetting action mainly on large industrial projects with heavy foreign inputs. Many of those were suspended or scrapped at that time. Subsequently, with the more liberal trade regime that was introduced in 1984, imports rose 27.6% in that year and 60.0% in the following. While in 1984 trade virtually balanced an account of a good export performance, in 1985 an unprecendented trade-account deficit of over thirteen billion dollars was incurred. In this year, exports rose about 5% in nominal terms.

1.63 The surge in imports in 1985 was caused by a coincidence of several factors, mostly associated with the urban reform started in 1984. In 1984, the economy was growing rapidly at about 14% in real terms. There were widespread shortages of industrial raw materials and strong demands for capital goods and consumer durables. Money supply and credit (mostly from domestic sources) rose sharply in the last quarter of 1984. Total credit as measured by the net domestic assets of the specialized banks and rural credit cooperatives rose by 45% during 1984. Two thirds of this expansion occurred in the final quarter largely due to difficulties in credit control in the face of strong credit demands from enterprises enjoying greater financial autonomy under the reforms. Strong credit expansion continued during the early part of 1985. On the supply side, it seems possible that the monetary and credit expansion may have been touched off by speculation that the People's Bank of China was about to replace the rigid lending practices with a new system of credit quotas, based on the volume handled by individual bank's in the past 12 months. As a result, with easy access to credit from the People's Bank of China which had not quite completed its restructuring started earlier in the year, banks rushed to issue more currency and to make loans to boost their credit volume, so as to secure a larger allocation in the coming year. Bank loans rose 48.4% in the month of December 1984 alone.

1.64 In the meantime, import and foreign exchange controls were eased as the foreign exchange situation had improved. By 1984 China's foreign reserve totalled US$17.8 billion or the equivalent of nine months of imports in that year. Against this macroeconomic background a more liberal trade policy was launched, designed primarily to decentralize foreign trade to the local level. To this end, as noted in Part A, a large number of new foreign trade bureaus and related agencies were set up across the country; local governments and some large enterprises were empowered to engage in foreign trade directly. Consequently, given the huge pent-up demand for imported consumer durables and for industrial goods, coupled with the profitability of such transactions, imports soared in the last quarter of 1984 and continued unabated through the first quarter of the following year, until the central authorities stepped in to restore many of the restrictions that it had earlier lifted. In 1985, iron and steel imports rose 65%, and imports of motor vehicles and chassis rose 200%. As a significant departure from the past practice, the authorities had on this occasion refrained from cancelling most of the import contracts signed with foreign firms, and import controls imposed on commodities were more selective than hitherto. This may mark a serious recognition of foreign trade as an integral part of the Four Modernizations Program and, more significantly, the necessity of utilizing foreign resources to supplement domestic resources if the program was to proceed unimpeded.

Commodity and Market Concentration

1.65 Despite rapid growth in recent years, China's patterns of trade have changed very little in terms of commodity composition and trading partners. Exports continue to be largely based on a few traditional products, namely, food, oil and textiles, while the large share of exports to the top four countries combined--Hong Kong, Japan, the US and West Germany--has stayed virtually unchanged. China's import pattern, on the other hand, seems to have changed radically with respect to end uses, although import sources have remained similar.

1.66 Selected exports are presented in Tables 1.1 and 1.2. Between 1978 and 1985, the combined share of the six most important commodity groups,[9] changed very little, accounting for just over half the total. However, the degree of concentration rose, as measured by the Gini-Hirshman Index, which is particularly sensitive to changes in individual shares.[10] This index went up from 23.9 in 1978 to 29.3 in 1985, largely because of the rapid growth of oil exports. China raised its oil export tonnage substantially in 1984 and 1985, and oil accounted for 24.7% of total exports that year, twice the 1978 share.

1.67 Imports by end use are presented in Tables 1.3 and 1.4. In contrast to exports, import composition in terms of end-use changed dramatically during this period. The share of capital goods went up from 18.7% in 1978 to 41.4% in 1985, while consumer goods halved, largely on account of a sharp decline in food imports. The share of raw materials also fell, although these imports increased substantially in absolute values. Within the consumer goods category it is interesting to note that the share of consumer durables--notably motor vehicles--actually rose from negligible levels in 1978 to 3.4% of total imports in 1985. The dramatic change in the import composition clearly mirrors the effects of the recent and on-going economic reforms. As a result of the rural reforms in which communal production was replaced by a household contractual system, agricultural output rose sharply in recent years, thus reducing food and agriculture-based raw material imports, particularly grain and cotton (see Annex 3 for a fuller discussion of this phenomenon). The increase in the share of capital goods imports was clearly driven by high investment demand, coupled with a desire to "modernize". Within the category of capital goods, most of the increase was attributable to machinery and equipment imports.

9/ Animals and meat, cereals, fruits and vegetables, petroleum, textiles, and garments.

10/ Gini-Hirshman Coefficient = 100 x $(Xjt/Xt)^2$

where j = commodity
n = number of commodities
xjt = exports of commodity j in period t
xt = total exports of goods in period t

1.68 China's exports and imports are heavily concentrated in a few markets, and import market concentration is still rising. As Table 1.5 indicates, the combined share of exports to the top four markets--Hong Kong, Japan, the US and West Germany--was 57.1% in 1985--almost the same as in 1981, but much greater than in 1978.

1.69 As can be seen in Table 1.6, the combined share of the same four trading partners was 64.9% in 1985, rising from only 45.1% in 1978.[11/] The increase shown between 1981 and 1985 actually took place largely in 1985, due mainly to a sharp rise in imports from Japan, which now accounts for one-third of the total. As a matter of fact, about three-quarters of China's trade deficit in 1985 was with Japan, around US$10 billion.

Trade with Developed and Less-Developed Countries

1.70 China's trade is heavily geared towards developed countries (DC's). This is hardly surprising, given China's abundance of cheap unskilled labor and relative scarcity of capital, both physical and human. In 1985, 41.8% of exports went to DCs compared with 27.2% to LDCs, not including Hong Kong (see Table 1.7). The share of DCs is, however, understated to the extent that the majority of Hong Kong's re-exports of Chinese goods is also destined for these countries (see para. 1.72).

1.71 The share of the LDCs went up dramatically between 1978 and 1981 but stagnated in more recent years. The share of DCs also peaked in 1981 and the increases of both groups between 1978 and 1981 were at the expense of the share of the COMECOM, (marked "others" in the table), whose share dropped dramatically in the same period. Shares of imports were more skewed and have become even more so in recent times. Over two-thirds of China's imports are from DCs, compared with 15.1% from LDCs.[12/]

Hong Kong Trade

1.72 Chinese published data do not show final destinations of China's exports to Hong Kong, but seem to record imports originating outside Hong Kong but transhipped through there according to their points of origin. On the basis of Chinese data, Hong Kong is China's largest export market and one of its major sources of imports, accounting in 1984 for 26.5 and 10.8% of China's exports and imports, respectively. (See Tables 1.5 and 1.6). However, if an adjustment were made for re-exports, Hong Kong's share of China's exports

---

11/ The increasing trend of import market concentration is confirmed by calculations of the Gini-Hirshman coefficients for import market shares: 30.6 (1978), 36.8 (1981) and 39.8 (1985).

12/ In 1985, for instance, there was a trade deficit of US$18.4 billion with DCs but a surplus of US$1.0 billion with LDCs, again not counting Hong Kong, which, if included, would change China's directional pattern somewhat, i.e., if Hong Kong's re-exports to DCs of Chinese goods were taken into account (see paragraph 1.72).

would be about half of the level shown, while shares of other countries, mostly industrialized, would rise correspondingly. Hong Kong would then be China's second largest export market, next to Japan. With reference to Table 1.8, according to Hong Kong's official statistics, in 1984 some 55% or US$3.6 billion of China's exports to Hong Kong were in fact reconsigned to other markets. One third of those is identified to have gone to the US alone.

1.73 The same table shows that in 1984 the value of Hong Kong's re-exports to China (or China's imports through Hong Kong) was US$3.6 billion. Given that recorded imports from Hong Kong are only US$2.9 billion it is clear that China correctly records the majority of Hong Kong's re-exports to China according to the initial country of origin, with Hong Kong serving at an entrepot. Given the large volumes of Chinese trade it handles, Hong Kong is a key player in China's foreign trade.

Conclusions

1.74 With imports and exports combined amounting to well over 20% of its GDP, China is no longer the isolated economy that it once was. Moreover, with around two percent of world trade, it has indeed become an important member of the world trading community. China's potential impact on world trade can be more fully appreciated if one considers that its imports and exports are relatively concentrated both in commodity composition and directional pattern. If this degree of concentration were to continue, China's exports, as their volumes grow, would be likely to run into growing foreign protectionism, as is already being experienced in textile and garment exports. As a long-term strategy, it is, therefore, important that diversification of export markets and, with some reservation, diversification of export goods be given serious consideration. To minimize the risk of foreign protectionism and to pave the way for increased volumes and wider range of its exports, it is necessary that China broaden the now heavily concentrated market base and be less dependent on individual markets. The case for product diversification, however, is not so clear-cut, and must be based on China's dynamic comparative advantage, as stressed in the Main Report.

1.75 The relatively wide fluctuations that have characterized China's trade, particularly in recent years, strongly support the case that has been made in this report that better coordination is needed between trade policy and other economic policies and, specifically, of price reform, monetary policy, and enterprise management. The unsustainably large trade deficit of 1985 appears to have occurred primarily because trade liberalization was carried out at a time when other macroeconomic policies were not in balance. Trade liberalization, per se, therefore, should not be blamed for the trade deficit that resulted.

Table 1.1: China - Selected Exports, 1978-85

COMMODITY	1978	1981	1982	1983	1984	1985	Annual Growth % 1981-85
Live animals, meat & meat preparations	552	743	850	784	777	764	0.7
Cereals & cereal preparations	398	293	222	214	442	1083	38.7
Fruits & vegetables	572	838	812	804	817	834	-0.1
Textile fibres	433	452	586	671	921	1158	26.5
Coal, coke & briquets	48	363	384	336	316	352	-0.8
Petroleum & petroleum products	1214	4803	4894	4319	5637	6805	9.1
Chemicals	492	1327	1191	1248	1356	1373	0.8
Textile, yarn & fabric	1585	2660	1973	2899	3655	3271	5.3
Machines & transport equipment	410	1082	1279	1217	1478	774	-8.0
Articles of apparel	658	1842	1930	2055	2634	2078	3.1
Footwear	98	225	229	222	251	260	3.7
Others	3289	7161	7290	7405	7624	8804	5.3
Total Exports	9750	21788	21639	22175	25908	27554	6.0

Sources: 1981-85: Chinese Customs Statistics; 1978: Staff's estimates based on Statistical Yearbook of China (total exports) & World Bank Trading System Data.

Table 1.2: China - Selected Exports, 1978-85

COMMODITY	1978	1981	1982	1983	1984	1985
Live animals, meat & meat preparations	5.7	3.4	3.9	3.5	3.0	2.8
Cereals & cereal preparations	4.1	1.3	1.0	1.0	1.7	3.9
Fruits & vegetables	5.9	3.8	3.8	3.6	3.2	3.0
Textile fibres	4.4	2.1	2.7	3.0	3.6	4.2
Coal, coke & briquets	0.5	1.7	1.8	1.5	1.2	1.3
Petroleum & petroleum products	12.5	22.0	22.6	19.5	21.8	24.7
Chemicals	5.1	6.1	5.5	5.6	5.2	5.0
Textile, yarn & fabric	16.3	12.2	9.1	13.1	14.1	11.9
Machines & transport equipment	4.2	5.0	5.9	5.5	5.7	2.8
Articles of apparel	6.8	8.5	8.9	9.3	10.2	7.5
Footwear	1.0	1.0	1.1	1.0	1.0	0.9
Others	33.7	32.9	33.7	33.4	29.4	32.0
Total Exports	100.0	100.0	100.0	100.0	100.0	100.0

Sources: 1981-85: Chinese Customs Statistics; 1978: Staff s estimates based on Statistical Yearbook of China (total exports) & World Bank Trading System Data.

Table 1.3: China - Imports by End Use, 1978-85
(in current US$ million)

	1978	1981	1982	1983	1984	1985	Annual Growth % 1981-85
Consumer Goods	1721	4003	4486	3515	3086	3373	-4.2
Food	1642	3608	4166	3119	2312	1566	-18.8
Durables	30	144	135	285	558	1456	78.2
Non-durables	48	251	184	111	217	350	8.7
Raw Materials	7046	10709	9833	11729	13759	19355	15.9
Fuel	65	82	187	111	139	171	20.3
Others	6980	10627	9646	11619	13620	19184	15.9
Capital Goods	2034	6427	3726	4764	8271	17780	29.0
Machinery & equipment	1122	5652	2967	3271	6227	13155	23.5
Construction	185	150	202	298	403	719	48.0
Transport	727	626	557	1195	1641	3906	58.1
Unclassified Commodities	89	900	1109	1337	2212	2455	28.5
TOTAL IMPORTS, c.i.f.	10890	22039	19154	21346	27328	42963	18.2

Sources: 1981-85 data: Chinese Customs Statistics; 1978: Staff's estimates based on Statistical Yearbook of China (total imports) & World Bank Trading System Data.

Table 1.4: China - Import Composition by End Use, 1978-85
(as % of total imports)

	1978	1981	1982	1983	1984	1985
Consumer Goods	15.8	18.2	23.4	16.5	11.3	7.8
Food	15.1	16.4	21.8	14.6	8.5	3.6
Durables	0.3	0.7	0.7	1.3	2.0	3.4
Non-durables	0.4	1.1	1.0	0.5	0.8	0.8
Raw Materials	64.7	48.6	51.3	54.9	50.3	45.1
Fuel	0.6	0.4	1.0	0.5	0.5	0.4
Others	64.1	48.2	50.4	54.4	49.8	44.7
Capital Goods	18.7	29.2	19.5	22.3	30.3	41.4
Machinery & equipment	10.3	25.6	15.5	15.3	22.8	30.6
Construction	1.7	0.7	1.1	1.4	1.5	1.7
Transport	6.7	2.8	2.9	5.6	6.0	9.1
Unclassified Commodities	0.8	4.1	5.8	6.3	8.1	5.7
TOTAL IMPORTS, c.i.f.	100.0	100.0	100.0	100.0	100.0	100.0

Sources: 1981-85 data: Chinese Customs Statistics; 1978: Staff's estimates based on Statistical Yearbook of China (total imports) & World Bank Trading System Data.

Table 1.5: China - Exports to Selected Countries, 1978-85
(As % of Total Exports)

	HK	JAPAN	USA	W GER	UK	FRANCE	ITALY	CANADA	AUSTRA	NETHER	OTHERS
1978	26.0	17.6	2.8	3.4	3.8	1.8	1.7	1.0	1.2	9.0	31.7
1981	24.5	22.1	7.0	3.9	1.9	1.3	1.2	0.8	0.8	2.1	34.4
1982	23.7	22.0	8.1	3.5	1.3	1.3	1.1	0.8	1.0	1.3	35.9
1983	26.2	20.0	7.7	3.9	2.7	1.0	1.0	0.9	0.8	1.5	34.3
1984	26.5	20.7	9.3	3.1	1.3	0.9	1.2	1.0	0.9	1.3	33.8
1985	23.6	22.3	8.5	2.7	1.3	0.8	1.1	0.9	0.7	1.2	36.9

Source: IMF, Direction of Trade Statistics.

Table 1.6: China - Imports from Selected Countries, 1978-85
(As % of Total Imports)

	HK	JAPAN	USA	W GER	UK	FRANCE	ITALY	CANADA	AUSTRA	NETHER	OTHERS
1978	0.7	28.4	6.6	9.4	2.7	2.3	1.7	5.3	6.6	1.2	35.1
1981	5.7	28.6	21.6	6.2	1.1	1.8	1.6	5.4	2.6	0.6	24.8
1982	6.9	20.6	22.8	5.1	1.4	1.2	1.7	6.5	4.8	0.5	28.5
1983	8.0	25.8	12.9	5.7	2.6	3.0	1.4	7.5	2.9	0.5	29.7
1984	10.8	31.1	14.8	4.8	2.0	1.4	1.7	4.1	3.5	0.6	25.2
1985	11.2	35.7	12.2	5.8	1.8	1.7	2.1	2.7	2.6	0.6	23.6

Source: IMF, Direction of Trade Statistics.

Table 1.7: China - Direction of Trade by Economic Region, 1978-85

	SHARE WITH DC'S		SHARE WITH LDC'S		SHARE WITH HK		SHARE WITH OTHERS	
	Exports	Imports	Exports	Imports	Exports	Imports	Exports	Imports
1978	36.4	68.8	18.3	15.1	25.4	0.7	19.9	15.4
1981	44.0	74.4	27.9	13.7	24.5	5.7	3.6	6.2
1982	42.9	68.9	29.4	15.6	23.7	6.9	4.0	8.6
1983	42.1	68.1	26.9	16.2	26.2	8.0	4.8	7.7
1984	41.9	69.0	26.5	13.4	26.5	10.8	5.1	6.8
1985	41.8	70.1	27.2	13.5	23.6	11.2	7.4	5.2

Source: IMF, Direction of Trade Statistics.
Remarks: LDC's does not include HK; this is included in "others".

Table 1.8: China-Hong Kong Trade, 1984
(in current US$ million)

	Imports from Hong Kong	HK Re-exports To China	Exports to HK	Of which : Re-exports
TOTAL	2854.9	3586.7	6592.9	3595.2
Food & Live Animals	29.9	47.5	1140.7	
Bev & Tobacco	26.9	81.0	62.3	USA 1122.8
Crude Materials	25.5	150.0	454.5	JAP 273.2
Mineral Fuels	33.1	32.3	291.2	INDONE 195.1
Animal, veg oils	1.6	2.9	24.3	SKOREA 184.8
Chemicals	44.9	210.2	208.1	S'PORE 151.2
Basic Manufactures	300.9	1179.0	2048.6	TAIWAN 127.8
Machinery, Transport	567.9	1331.6	532.9	
Misc. Manufactures	157.3	532.4	1826.0	
Not Classified	1666.9	21.8	4.3	

Sources: World Bank Trade System Data - based on Chinese official reporting to the UN;
Hong Kong s Census of Statistics Department.

CHINA

THE EMERGING TRADE POLICY ENVIRONMENT

Table of Contents

THE EMERGING TRADE POLICY ENVIRONMENT

2.1 Annex 1 reviewed the set of policy instruments and institutions that the government has traditionally employed to guide China's foreign trade. These instruments and institutions have been changed in recent years to make them more effective in implementing the country's Open Door Policy. In this context of continuing change, Annex 1 offered critical analyses of these instruments and institutions.

2.2 As part of the Open Door policy, the Government has also been developing other trade policy instruments. Although most are not new to China, these instruments take on economic functions in guiding foreign trade that are quite different from those in the past--functions that will become stronger as China proceeds with the reform of its economic system, and particularly more flexible prices that reflect relative scarcities and greater scope for producers to respond to those prices. Collectively, these instruments will play an important role in defining the new trade policy environment of China and will significantly affect the economic benefits the country can derive from foreign trade.

2.3 The economic benefits of international trade are many. They can be broadly classified into two groups, "static" and "dynamic". Both sets correspond to one of the most important functions of international trade: that is, the transmission of information about costs, efficiency, quality and technology in the rest of the world to domestic markets.

2.4 The <u>static</u> benefits are those associated with the more efficient allocation of domestic resources that results when a country engages in trade. At any point in time, a country can avoid using its resources to produce goods and services that can be purchased relatively more cheaply from abroad. Instead, it can employ these resources for goods and services that it can produce more cheaply, efficiently, at better quality, etc., and which therefore are competitive in export markets as well as in the domestic markets. Such a pattern of resource allocation is consistent with the country's international competitiveness and makes possible a higher level of national income than that without trade.

2.5 Over time, a country's international competitiveness does change. That change will be significantly affected by external changes such as technological progress. Controlling the course of changing international competitiveness--that is, maintaining or creating it over time--requires that domestic activities improve their efficiency, cost, quality and technology in production at rates equal to or greater than those of competing countries. International trade will transmit information about what is happening abroad to domestic producers, and will cause them to make competitive improvements on a continuous basis. These are the <u>dynamic</u> benefits of trade.

2.6 The present annex is concerned mainly with the effectiveness of China's "emerging" trade policy and instruments in realizing the two sets of benefits from foreign trade. It reviews the policies and instruments in two parts: first with respect to the import policy and second in relation to the export policy environment. It should be noted, however, that for a large country such as China, whose exposure to the world economy relative to GDP is necessarily less than that of small countries, the rules governing its domestic economy are at least as important as those governing its foreign trade in realizing the above benefits. This maxim is particularly important at the present juncture in China's economic modernization.

A. The Emerging Import Policy Environment

2.7 One objective most countries attach to import policies is the protection of domestic producers. Protection is accorded by any policy that prevents the entry of competing imports or makes them more expensive. Protective measures can be quite general, affecting different activities similarly, or highly selective, favoring specific activities over others. The most important policy instruments that determine the level and structure of protection are the exchange rate, tariffs, and quantitative restrictions. When these instruments are influenced by objectives other than protection, or when the instruments and objectives are not coordinated, import policies can result in an unintended level or structure of protection. Protection is also affected by sales, excise and other taxes, pricing regulations, or various measures to promote investment.

2.8 The exchange rate affects protection in a general manner. An undervalued exchange rate raises the local currency equivalent of both import and export prices and favors the domestic production of tradable goods relative to non-tradable goods and services. Some countries have used this approach as a key element of a trade policy environment aimed at promoting rapid development of industries for export. An overvalued exchange rate, on the other hand, provides "negative protection" for domestic production of tradables by lowering the cost of competing imports.

2.9 Quantitative restrictions, such as import licensing or prohibitions provide protection by restricting the supply of competing imports directly. By creating scarcity, however, the restrictions cause the domestic price to rise above the foreign supply price in the open market - or in the unofficial market if prices or distribution are controlled. This situation creates an opportunity for a windfall gain, or "rent", to those who can obtain the restricted imports at the official exchange rate and sell them at the market price. The same opportunity applies to those who can produce the restricted goods. In many countries, the severity of quantitative restrictions escalates, or "cascades", upwards from inessentials to essentials. When it is easier to obtain licenses for inputs than for final goods, the system creates incentives that favor production of the more restricted goods. If the opposite is the case, however, the system can discriminate against those final goods producers who are the users of restricted intermediate goods. The net effects of all these incentives in the economy are difficult to calculate. Usually, the protection provided under quantitative restrictions is highly discriminatory and variable, because the level of protection depends on the relative scarcity of each individual good.

2.10 Tariffs provide protection by directly raising the domestic price of imports. The tariff protection can be general. When tariff rates are uniform, they affect different producers of import substitutes similarly. Since exports do not enjoy tariff protection, a general uniform tariff favors production of import substitutes as a whole relative to exports. In practice, the tariff systems of most countries tax different products at different rates, often cascading upwards through the stages of production or from essentials to inessentials. Such a system creates incentives that discourage domestic production of raw materials, capital goods, or agricultural commodities that are imported at low duties, and encourage production of consumer goods or luxury goods. When combined with an overvalued exchange rate and/or with quantitative restrictions that also cascade, these incentives are further distorted.

2.11 Many countries have exaggerated or moderated the effects of the above measures by sales, excise or other taxes that are levied differentially between imports and domestic production or across different products. Excise taxes on luxuries are used by many to offset some of the protection afforded by high duties or severe restrictions. Sales taxes that are higher on certain imports than on their domestic substitutes have also been used to provide additional protection to the latter. Taxes and price controls on domestically produced raw materials affect the degree of protection given to both these activities and the industries that use them.

2.12 Whatever the combination of measures, protection creates a gap between the domestic price of a product and the cost of importing it and this permits the continued operation of enterprises with higher production costs than those of competing imports. In this way, protection results in costs to the economy by forcing consumers to pay higher prices for goods and by diverting resources out of activities where they could be used more efficiently and productively.

2.13 These extra costs may be temporary when incurred to assist new activities that will become competitive in the future. They may also be temporary when associated with industries that can be expected to disappear over time, as production techniques, organization, management, and worker skills improve and become more productive elsewhere. But, these costs may also be excessively high if they involve inefficient resource use over a long period of time, and permit the country's technological capacity, the basis for improving competitiveness over time, to lag.

2.14 Based on the experience of other countries, this section reviews two sets of policy instruments that are intended to play a key role in defining China's import policy for the future: the new import licensing system and taxes on imports. The most important of the latter is the recently reformed customs tariff system.

Import Licensing: An Emerging Administrative Lever

2.15 In moving toward a socialist economic system, where economic decisions regarding foreign trade are to be made by consumers and producers, there is necessarily a period of transition during which measures based on price incentives are introduced but are not yet fully effective, while the role played by traditional physical planning measures are being reduced but continue to influence the economy. At the beginning of that transition, there is a real risk that still distorted, albeit increasingly flexible, prices will guide the decisions of producers, workers, and consumers in a way that contradicts national objectives and harms the well-being of the population as a whole. The issue confronting the Government today is how to navigate China through that transition period without major economic imbalances, including balance-of-payments problems.

2.16 Partly for that purpose, the Government has chosen licensing as the administrative instrument to regulate imports. As prices are made more flexible and the scope for decision-making by economic agents is increased during the transition, import licensing will have two important effects. First, as the price controls are gradually lifted, the limits or bans on imports will affect the domestic prices of importable goods. Second, licensing controls the availability of imports to individual enterprises directly, and alters their revenues and costs depending on the level of licenses issued. Therefore, the degree of protection across different enterprises will be variable, and will also vary over time for each enterprise individually.

A Historical Perspective and the Policy Objective in Principle

2.17 Licensing was used to control all imports into China from 1951 to 1957. The purpose was to insure that imports remained within budget and were utilized to further the national objective of constructing a new socialist China. In 1957, the year in which China completed the transformation from private to social ownership, foreign trade became the monopoly of the state, and the import planning system (see Annex 1) replaced the import licensing system.

2.18 Import licensing was re-introduced for a small number of products in 1980. The first step in initiating the current system came on January 10, 1984, when the State Council issued the "Provisional Regulations on the Issuing of Import Licenses of the People's Republic of China". Following that declaration, on May 15, 1984, the Ministry of Foreign Economic Relations and Trade (MOFERT) and the General Administration of Customs (GAC) jointly issued the "Rules for the Implementation of the Interim Regulations on Licensing

System for Import Commodities of the People's Republic of China", which formally established the new system.

2.19 According to the provisional regulations, the objective of the new import licensing system is "to strengthen the planned management of imports, so that its economic results are enhanced and the development needs of the country's socialist modernization are better served". Underlying this stated objective is, as discussed above, the serious concern of the Government regarding the effectiveness of the trade policy instruments at its disposal during the initial reform period. In principle, the new system is to control those imports that take place outside the plan (see Annex 1). It is commonly understood, therefore, that the Government intends to increase the coverage of licensed imports along with the reduction in the plan-controlled imports.

The Licensing System

2.20 All imports into China are classified in two categories: restricted and unrestricted, with the import licensing applying to restricted goods. As of October 1986, there were 45 goods on the restricted list (Table 2.1). In principle, the restricted list can be changed monthly. A number of the restricted goods overlap with those in the annual import plan, whose coverage can also change. Thus, the overlap also changes over time. Since the annual import plan by itself does not prohibit imports of planned products, licensing serves to prohibit non-planned imports of restricted goods included in the plan (see para. 2.25 below).

2.21 The restricted imports include a substantial portion of China's total imports. Although comprehensive data on the value of imports for every product on the restricted list are not available, Table 2.2 presents information on a sufficient number of the restricted goods to indicate the coverage. (Information on the coverage in terms of domestic production was not made available to the mission.) In both 1984 and 1985, at least 30 percent of the total imports into China were on the restricted list. The value of restricted imports in 1985, more than half of which were steel, was at least $10 billion.

Table 2.1: RESTRICTED IMPORT LIST

	Restriction Date a/	Subject to Approval by: b/ SC	SEC	Other
A. Licenses Issued by Ministry of Foreign Economic Relations and Trade				
1. All motor vehicles, chassis and components		X		
2. Television sets and components		X		
3. Computers (including central processing units) and components		X		
4. Assembly lines for television sets	9/85		X	
5. Assembly lines for household refrigerators	9/85		X	
6. Assembly lines for household washing machines	9/85		X	
7. Assembly lines for radio-cassetts recorders	9/85		X	
8. Assembly lines for room air conditioners	9/85		X	
9. Assembly lines for motorcyles	9/85		X	
10. Assembly lines for light motor vehicles	9/85		X	
11. All synthetic fibers				X
12. Synthetic fiber monomers:				X
(a) Polyester slice				
(b) Caprolactam				
(c) Telephthalic acid dimethylesther				
(d) Pure telephthalic acid				
(e) Nylon 66 salt				
(f) Polyproplylene resin				
13. Synthetic fabric products:				
(a) Cloth				
(b) Garments				
(c) Knitted synthetic shirts				
(d) Skirts				
(e) Hosiery				
(f) Mosquito netting				
14. Rubber				
15. Timber				
16. Steel (rolled steel, scrap, scrapped ships)	1/86			X
17. Medicinal herbs and materials				X
(a) Antelope horn				
(b) Rhinoceros horn				
(c) Broad rhino horn				
(d) Tiger bones				
(e) Leopard bones				
(f) Musk				
(g) Cow oar				
(h) Hippocampus				
(i) Armadillo scale				
(j) Ginseng				
(k) Bentaron Seed				
(l) Cardamon inferior				
(m) Cardamon superior				
(n) Dragon's blood				
(o) Aloe wood				
(p) Saffron				
18. Pesticide/insecticide	1/86			X
19. Tobacco (cigarettes, cigars, pipe tobacco)				X
20. Duplicating machines and components		X		
B. Licenses Issued by Ministry of Foreign Economic Relations and Trade or Regional Commissions on Foreign Economic Relations and Trade				
21. Motorcycles (including motor-bicycles) and components		X		
22. Hydraulic truck lifts	11/85	X		
23. Electronic microscopes	11/85	X		
24. Electronic color scanners	11/85	X		
25. X-ray fault detectors	11/85	X		
26. Air conditioners	11/85	X		
27. Air-jet spinning machines	11/85	X		
28. Video tape recorders, associated equipment, and components		X		
29. Video tape duplicating equipment and components		X		
30. Radio-cassetts recorders		X		
31. Refrigerators and components		X		
32. Washing machines and components		X		
33. Cameras and components		X		
34. Wrist watches and components		X		
35. Kinescopes for television sets		X		
36. Electronic calculators and components				X
37. Radios and components				X
38. Electric fans and components				X
39. Bicycles and components				X
40. Components for radio-cassetts recorders				X
41. ABS resin				X
42. Sulfuric acid				X
43. Polycarbonate resin				X
44. Motor vehicle tires (new and used)	1/86			X
45. Demolition equipments for civil use				X
In addition:				
o Motor vehicles imported by joint ventures				
o Motor vehicles imported as gifts				
o All synthetic fibers other than tetron and acrylic fibers				
o Duplicating machines imported in small numbers for household use				
C. Licenses Issued by MOFERT Special Commission Offices at Major Ports				
o Part of imports into the 14 coastal open cities				
o Imports by regional branches of the central government agencies				
o Steel imports by joint ventures				
o As authorised temporarily by MOFERT				

a/ Dates when products are added to the restricted list since May 1984. Otherwise, the products were restricted on or before May 1984.

b/ SC: the State Council. SEC: the State Economic Commission. Others include the State Planning Commission and relevant ministerial authorities. For steel, this includes the Port Administration Office for transportation license.

Table 2.2: IMPORTS OF SELECTED RESTRICTED COMMODITIES
(In million yuan)

	1984	(%)	1985	(%)
Motor vehicles	2,092.77	11.25%	1,193.35	3.32%
Motor vehicle parts	374.66	2.01	884.74	2.46
Television sets	613.28	3.30	3,013.01	8.39
All synthetic fibers	1,804.67	9.70	4,172.99	11.62
Synthetic fiber monomers:				
Caprolactam	97.63	0.52	177.74	0.50
Polyproplylene resin	522.78	2.81	894.50	2.49
Rubber	704.20	3.78	649.57	1.81
Timber	1,527.97	8.21	2,406.41	6.70
Steel	9,773.17	52.52	21,019.11	58.55
Medicinal herbs and materials	65.18	0.35	115.78	0.32
Pesticides/insecticides	542.73	2.92	295.86	0.82
Tobacco	248.18	1.33	547.90	1.53
Radio cassette recorders	117.53	0.63	279.21	0.78
Wrist watches	36.33	0.20	78.02	0.22
Electronic calculators	87.53	0.47	173.63	0.48
(1) Total	18,608.43	100.00	35,901.82	100.00
(2) Total imports into China	62,046.80		125,783.46	
(1)/(2)		29.99		28.54

Source: China's Customs Statistics (1985.1), (1986.1), General Customs Administration, The People's Republic of China.

2.22 The licensing system is supposed to work as follows. An import license is valid for one year from the date of issue. If the order has been placed within the year, but the import has not cleared customs by the expiration date, an application must be filed for an extension. If the order was not placed within the year, the license expires. The license is issued to the users of the imports and is not transferrable.

2.23 The import licensing system is centrally administered by the Foreign Trade Administration Department of MOFERT. It issues the licenses for some restricted goods and delegates that authority for the remaining items to its special commission offices at major ports and to its regional counterparts--the Foreign Economic Relations and Trade Commissions (FERTCs). The commodities for which the special commission offices and the FERTCs can issue licenses differ somewhat across regions and over time. (The basic division of authority is given in Table 2.1.)

2.24 The application procedure for import licenses differs between items under the import plan and those outside the plan. The procedure for a planned commodity is much simpler. A potential importer must apply for a license using the annual import plan document issued by the State Planning Commission (SPC). The document specifies the commodity, the quantities to be imported, and the name of the potential importer. Since planned imports are entitled to an official foreign exchange allocation, the Bank of China releases the foreign exchange automatically once the license is issued. The potential importer then places an order with a trading company.

2.25 The application procedure for goods restricted outside the plan involves several layers of approval before a letter of credit can be issued. A potential importer must first obtain an import approval from its supervisory authority in the government--the central ministries or regional departments/bureaus. For many restricted imports, additional approval is required from the State Council (SC) or State Economic Commission (SEC). (See Table 2.1.) Once approved, an import certificate and signed application letter are issued. The latter must include the commodity to be imported, its specifications, quantity, unit price, total value, country of origin, sources of foreign exchange, form of trade, port of delivery, and contracting party that negotiated the proposed transaction(s) with the foreign party, etc. Armed with these documents, the potential importer can then apply for the license. Once the license is issued, the user must apply to the Bank of China for the foreign exchange to guarantee the letter of credit. Finally, the potential importer places an order with a foreign trade company.

2.26 An application for an import license can be rejected on various grounds. In addition, licenses already issued can be cancelled at any time. The official criteria for either of these actions are:

(a) The banning or temporary suspension of the import;

(b) Inconsistency with the foreign policy of China;

(c) Inconsistency with bilateral trade or payment agreements;

(d) Inconsistency with the hygienic and quarantine standards of the Ministry of Public Health or Ministry of Agriculture, Animal Husbandry and Fishery; and

(e) Conflict with the interests of the state, procurement through illegal channels (including violation of the foreign exchange control regulations), or irregular invoicing.

2.27 MOFERT allocates substantial manpower to check the prices quoted on license applications. The need for this procedure arises, because there is an incentive to over-invoice imports in the system, and because the foreign trade corporations currently lack the discipline to source the "best" price for their customers. Over-invoicing is a practice commonly observed in countries that use quantitative allocation of foreign exchange, and inefficient sourcing is a problem faced by many socialist countries that utilize foreign trade corporations like China. MOFERT checks the prices selectively for most products, although more comprehensive checking is carried out for major import items. For example, the prices of almost all automobiles and television sets are checked, and a coordination committee under MOFERT checks the prices of all computers. It is reported that more than US$5.7 million was saved through this procedure from the second half of 1984 to the end of 1985.

2.28 MOFERT is responsible for monitoring all licenses issued and used. It establishes an annual foreign exchange budget for each restricted good not included in the import plan. The budget, which is not made public, is said to have a notional regional allocation for each product. It appears, however, that the budget is "fungible" across different products and/or regions.

Import Licensing and Import Prohibition

2.29 It is important to note here that the import licensing system has been used to ban imports into China. There are now two types of prohibited imports outside the licensing system: all second-hand garments (since April 1985) and all motor vehicles (in place since November 1985, but scheduled to be lifted in November 1987). In addition, imports of the seven assembly lines on the restricted list (television sets, household refrigerators, household washing machines, radio-cassette recorders, room airconditioners, motorcycles, and light motor vehicles) are effectively banned, as the SEC no longer approves the required license applications. For assembly lines other than those for motorcyles and light motor vehicles, the prohibition will be in effect for the entire Seventh Five-Year Plan period (1986-1990).

Policy Objectives in Practice and Their Implications

2.30 So far, the licensing system has been used to control the growth of selected imports resulting from the administrative decentralization of import rights and accumulated foreign exchange retention, coupled with expansionary macroeconomic and inappropriate exchange rate policies. The list of restricted imports features nonessentials, as well as commodities that compete significantly with domestic production. Thus, in practice, the restricted list reveals two mixed objectives: control of the balance of payments directly through quantitative restrictions and protection for domestic producers.

2.31 Prominent among the products on the restricted list are luxury consumer durables and their parts and components. Here, the objective of the government appears to be balance-of-payments control rather than of protection--that is, control over the rapid growth of these imports. Regardless of the objective, licensing appears to have created rents in the system. These were reflected in the infamous "Hainan incident" of autumn 1984, in which the

Hainan government financed capital construction projects with the profits from imported motor vehicles and other consumer durables, using retained foreign exchange. In general, the supply response of consumer durables and other nonessentials is quite sensitive to price changes. Indeed, there are signs that licensing is beginning to generate extra incentives for both Chinese and foreign producers to invest in the production of the restricted consumer goods. A number of foreign investments have been attracted to these activities, some of which have begun production in the last two years.

2.32 One striking aspect of China's licensing structure is that, unlike that of many other countries, it is not cascading, but instead tends to be "integrated" along lines of activity. For example, as a result of the investment boom in consumer durables, imports of assembly lines for these consumer durables grew quickly. In response, seven assembly lines for restricted durables (items 4 to 10 on Table 2.1) were added to the list in September 1985 and, as mentioned, imports of these capital goods are effectively banned. The import prohibition works against the earlier incentives and indicates that the Government does not intend to use licensing to protect domestic production of these durables. The ban, however, may promote production of the assembly lines in China. The incentives may therefore begin to pull investments into these activities.

2.33 A similar pattern of integrated restrictions can be observed for synthetic textile products. With these activities, however, the objective of the Government appears to be more protection than control of the balance of payments. It is reported that consumers in China have developed a strong preference for synthetic over natural fiber products, as revealed for instance in the rapid growth of "used" garments imports, now banned. While the Government may regard synthetic textile products as inessential imports, China has been building the domestic capacity to produce them. This effort is based on an integrated strategy that includes developing the capacity in China's chemical industry to supply inputs to the textile industry.

2.34 The restricted import list includes all synthetic cloth and garments, as well as the chemical intermediates needed to produce these products. The list of restricted chemical intermediates covers all synthetic fibers and all important chemical materials needed to produce them. In addition, it includes some basic chemicals used by the textile industry--such as the ABC resin that is added to increase the crease resistance of textile products. Also included is a potentially important capital good for the textile industry, air-jet spinning machines, which are at the frontier of the spinning technology for natural and synthetic-blend fibers and are rapidly replacing the old generation of machines based on the open-ended rotary technology in the rest of the world. China does not have the capacity to produce the air-jet spinning machines but has a large domestic capacity to produce the open-ended rotary machines.

2.35 The restrictions on consumer goods provide protection to synthetic textile producers, while the restrictions on chemical intermediates provide protection to the chemical industry. However, textile producers using the restricted intermediates may be negatively affected, if they have trouble getting needed imports or when they must pay higher prices for domestic substitutes in the open market. Similarly, while the restriction on air-jet spinning machines protects the producers of domestic substitutes, it may affect textile producers negatively. The net results are complex and impossible to sort out for economists and enterprise managers alike, and for the Government. It is likely that the protection provided under these restrictions varies greatly across different enterprises and can lead to results quite unintended by policy-makers.

2.36 Recent additions to the restricted list point to the conflict the Government continues to face between administrative decentralization of imports and national development objectives and priorities. In addition to consumer goods, capital goods have been the main source of rapid import growth outside the plan. In November 1985, a group of capital goods (items 22 to 27 of Table 2.1) was added to the list.

2.37 Most recently (January 1986), three goods were added to the list: steel, agricultural pesticides and insecticides, and motor vehicle tires. Restrictions were imposed on these products in reaction to actual imports. In the case of steel, for example, "chaotic steel buying" was reported in 1985, with imports of basic steel products apparently exceeding the plan allocation by as much as 80 percent in mid-1985 and causing serious port congestion. The application for import licenses on steel products must now be accompanied by a transportation license from the Port Administration Office. The prices of some steel products in China's open market have risen to as much as double those of imported equivalents (including tariffs at the current exchange rate), while the administered prices associated with the plan quota allocation remain significantly below the import prices. (See CHINA: Cement Machinery Manufacturing Subsector Study, Report No. 6551-CHA, for price comparisons on pig iron, steel sections, coils, plates, sheets, and scraps.)

Some Practical Difficulties

2.38 Some enterprises have no difficulty importing, while others seem to face long delays and great uncertainty. The problems appear to be associated with the import licensing system. A well-functioning system should issue licenses quickly and regularly to efficient users of foreign exchange, and ensure that the licenses are actually covered by foreign exchange, so that letters of credit can be opened soon after they are issued. In this respect, there are several problems with China's licensing system.

2.39 The first problem involves difficulties in obtaining the approvals needed to apply for the license. The criteria for approval are not transparent to enterprises, appearing to differ from one authority to another, over time, and even from one official to another within the same authority. The one criterion of which enterprises are certain is the availability of domestically produced substitutes. But, there are many others, and there seems to be great room for administrative discretion. In addition, enterprises attach great importance to good personal relationships with officials. These relationships assure, at least, quick access to officials to explain the technical specifications for imports, why suitable domestic substitutes are not available, or why they need the import, etc. One middle-level manager in charge of foreign trade at a large and reputable enterprise reported that he devotes three days a week to visiting or telephoning officials in order to obtain approvals or to cultivate good personal relationships. While it is impossible to document in general, the real costs in time and manpower of diverting managers' attention in this way--and the corresponding losses in output--may be substantial to the enterprises.

2.40 A second problem is that possession of an import license does not necessarily guarantee a foreign exchange authorization for letters of credit. Consequently, all the application steps can be wasted, as the binding constraint is the final authorization by the Bank of China for release of the foreign exchange. For several months beginning in April 1985, for example, the Bank of China froze foreign exchange authorization for all imports of computers in order to investigate all licenses and pending letters of credit. Among the reasons for this kind of action are the problem of over-invoicing, detected after licenses have been issued, and gaps or inefficiencies in monitoring the volume of licenses issued and coordinating them with the foreign exchange budget. Whatever the reason, the incidents add to delay and uncertainty in obtaining imports and impose real costs on the economy. Anecdotal evidence indicates, for instance, that enterprises try to maintain uneconomically large inventories of imported intermediates or machinery parts whenever possible, because they are not sure when they will be able to restock.

2.41 These two problems lead to a third, and most important, difficulty with the system: it fails to allocate import licenses rationally and efficiently. Although it is not possible to document the impact of misallocations of foreign exchange on the economy as a whole, examples of arbitrary or irrational allocations at the micro level are beginning to appear, such as the dismantling of a relatively new imported vehicle because it is difficult to obtain licenses for parts or tires. An enterprise that is efficient, competitive, and able to save foreign exchange for China was denied a license for an essential import and runs at less than full capacity because it is not an exporter, while, at the same time, luxury items are available for those who can pay the price. As the coverage of import restrictions increases, so does the danger of misallocations.

A Fundamental Shortcoming of Any Quantitative Restrictions

2.42 Experience in other countries suggests that the most pernicious aspects of a licensing system are the effects it has on income distribution and social behavior. As long as excess demand for foreign exchange persists, those who are able to obtain it can earn large rents. Some of the anecdotes mentioned earlier suggest that such a situation may already have arisen in China. The rent amounts to a transfer of wealth from the government to a selected group of individuals. At the same time, the excess demand for foreign exchange can lead to the emergence of black markets and other forms of corruption. Albeit limited thus far, these difficulties have also been observed in China. While these problems can be and have been regulated and curbed, the incentive to take advantage of the system in this way will not disappear, until official prices are brought into line with market forces. Even with tight controls and good will, the existence of high potential rents from quantitative restrictions can lead to misdirection of people's efforts, misallocation of resources, and loss of potential output for the economy as a whole.

2.43 Another real economic cost associated with the import licensing system is its administration--in terms of skills, time, and money--by the government, trading companies, and enterprises. The larger the country is, or the more complicated the system, the greater is this cost.

2.44 At the same time, the current concern of the Government--to use licensing to regulate imports during the period of transition--is understandable. The questions of what can be done to assist that transition and the role of the licensing system are considered later in this annex and also in the main report. In the long term, however, any form of quantitative restrictions is likely to be antithetical to the functioning of competitive markets and the benefits they offer.

Taxes on Imports: Emerging Economic Levers

2.45 Economic levers such as taxes on imports will increase their effectiveness in parallel with the progress in China's reform and socialist modernization. While maintaining direct control over imports through import licensing, the Government has therefore also been strengthening the tariffs on imports. This section reviews the taxes China levies on imports and their potential effects on price incentives when the latter begin to influence the economic decisions of producers and consumers significantly.

A Historical Perspective

2.46 The first customs tariff system of the People's Republic of China was established in May 1951. The initial policy objective was to protect domestic industry from foreign competition. The tariff became irrelevant for this purpose, however, when the planning system took over control of China's foreign trade in the late 1950s. Since then, the practical role of these duties has been to raise revenue. From 1951 to 1983, 22 revisions were made to the original tariff schedule, mostly to increase the average rates of import duties and raise revenue.

2.47 With the launching of the Open Door policy and the administrative decentralization of trade, the Government began to use taxes on foreign trade as economic levers. Import duty orders issued in 1980, for example, reduced the tariff rates on light industrial equipment (particularly for the textile industry), some machine parts, industrial inputs used for export processing, and some primary products with domestic shortages (such as timber and rubber). The 1980 orders also began to raise the duties on commodities with adequate domestic production capacity.

2.48 Very quickly, the need emerged to streamline the use of these taxes as economic levers. Starting in 1984, the Government undertook a major reform of the tariff system in order to facilitate the open door policy. The reform addressed both the customs tariff on imports and the export tax. (The export tax is discussed in Section B below.) The new system went into effect on March 10, 1985, when two tariff laws were approved by the State Council: "Regulations for Import and Export Tariffs of the People's Republic of China" and "Import and Export Customs Tariff of the People's Republic of China". The former established the rules and regulations governing the formulation of tax policy and tax rates as well as the administration of the system. The latter established the new schedule for import tariffs (and export taxes.)

Policy Objectives: Customs Tariff and "Regulatory Tariff"

2.49 Today, all imports into China are subject to customs tariffs. In addition, selected imports are also subject to what is called a "regulatory tariff".[1/]

2.50 The principal policy objective underlying the new customs tariff is to protect and promote domestic production. As discussed at the outset of this annex, tariffs raise the domestic price of imports directly and provide protection to domestic producers allowing them to raise their price above the duty-free foreign supply price. As the reform of the pricing system and of enterprises progresses, the function of the tariffs as economic levers will increase. The recent reform of the tariff system by the Government is therefore to be highly commended.

2.51 As discussed earlier, when quantitative restrictions are imposed, the domestic price can rise to clear the market in which supply is determined by domestic production plus the permitted quantity of imports. If the gap between the demand and supply prices that result from the quantitiative restriction is less than the customs tariff, then the tariff sets the market-clearing price. Otherwise, the linkage between domestic prices and the tariff-inclusive price of imports is broken. In this case, the quantitative restriction determines

---

1/ Some imports are also subject to an indirect tax, the consolidated industrial and commercial tax (CICT), which applies to both imports and their domestically produced substitutes, and the rate of taxation is supposed to be the same between them. The CICT is discussed in China: Finance and Investment (Report No. 6445-CHA).

the internal price. Taxes on imports then serve the objective of transferring part of the rent from traders to the government.

2.52 It is precisely this objective that led the Government to introduce the regulatory tariff as a temporary import surcharge in July 1985. When time is needed to phase out quantitative restrictions, temporary measures such as the regulatory tariff of China are useful ways to eliminate large rents (a point discussed further at the end of this annex).

Nominal Tariff Protection

(a) Nominal tariff protection in a large country

2.53 For a small economy, the chance of affecting the foreign prices of imports is slight. For a large country such as China, the opportunity is likely to be greater. In the case of a number of imports, such as certain types of fertilizer, China can obtain extra quantities only by paying higher prices, while a reduction in its import demand lowers the foreign supply price. In this context, it is important to discuss here the meaning of protection, and in particular the meaning of the nominal rate of protection that a tariff provides to Chinese producers.

2.54 There are several possible meanings for "nominal" rate. However, for our purposes we need only consider the simplest definition: the nominal rate of protection is the proportional divergence between the domestic supply price and the foreign supply price. This may be a simplification for some products in the case of China, since China's imports obviously affect world prices. For example, the increased production of cotton in China in recent years has contributed to a fall in world prices. Similarly, a high tariff can lead to falling world prices when it is a large country such as China that imposes the tariff. The above discussion applies to taxes on imports other than customs tariff, such as the regulatory tariff.

(b) The structure of nominal tariff protection

2.55 The customs tariff of China has two schedules: a "minimum" and a "general" one. The minimum tariff schedule applies to imports originating in countries with which China has signed trade treaties (or agreements) with reciprocal favorable tariff clauses. As of December 1, 1986, there were 99 such countries, which included all China's major trading partners. Because imports originating in these countries accounted for over 90 percent of China's total imports in both 1984 and 1985, only the minimum tariff schedule is discussed here.

2.56 Fourteen tariff codes are currently subject to the import surcharge. Table 2.3 presents the list of these commodities, their corresponding surcharge rates, and customs tariff rates. Unless otherwise noted, the discussion below concerns import duties including the surcharges for relevant codes.

Table 2.3: IMPORT SURCHARGES ("REGULATORY TARIFFS")
(In percent)

Commodities	Surcharge	Tariff
1. Polyester textured filaments (yarn)	40	70
2. Woven fabrics, other than tire cord, of synthetic fibers	40	100
3. Woven fabrics, other than tire cord, of regenerated fibers	40	100
4. Woven fabrics, of manmade fibers (discontinuous or waste)	40	100
5. Electronic calculators	80	60
6. Digital data processing machines of a word length less than 32 bits	40	50
7. Peripheral equipment for digital data processing machines of a word length less than 32 bits	30	30
8. Color video projectors	70	80
9. Television pictures turbes	50	30
10. Sedan cars, jeeps and passenger vehicles with less than 30 seats	80	120
11. Motor trucks with a loading capacity less than 8 tons	50	50
12 Motorcycles, autocycles, and cycles fitted with an auxiliary motor, with or without sidecars; sidecars of all kinds	20	120
13. Photo-copying and thermo-copying apparatus	80	50
14. Television image and sound records or reproducers	70	80

Source: General Customs Administration, The People's Republic of China.

2.57 Figure 2.1 summarizes the distribution of China's import duties. The customs tariff schedule has a range of zero to 150 percent (the general schedule a range of zero to 180 percent). The tariff rates and import surcharges combined result in import duties of 0-200 percent. The maximum import duty applies to motor vehicles (sedan cars, jeeps and passenger vehicles with less than 30 seats), which are subject to a surcharge of 80 percent. Zero duties apply to essential imports, such as live animals and plants, grains, pharmaceutical products, salts, printed matter, a few precision instruments, and some precious metals (silver, gold and platinum).

Figure 2.1

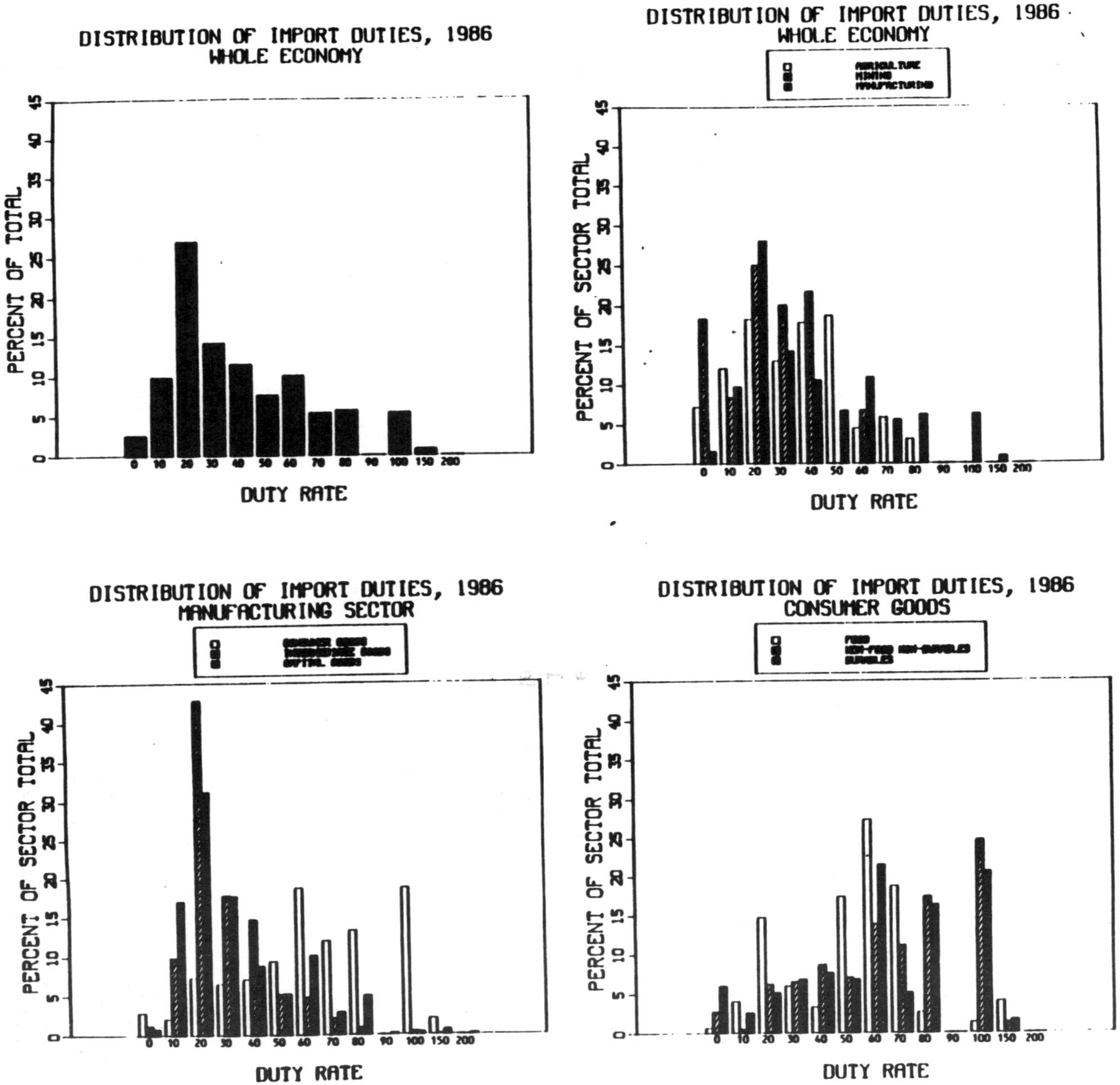

Note: The numbers labeling the horizontal axis are the upper bounds of each range, except for zero. (For example, 10 means duties greater than 0 but less than or equal to 10 percent.)

2.58 Figure 2.1 also summarizes the structure of China's import duties by depicting the frequency distributions of duties by major category. In general, the manufacturing sector has higher duties than the agricultural and mining sectors. Manufacturing also has the widest range of duties. Within this sector, the duties are lower for intermediate and capital goods. For a large proportion of them -- well over two-thirds -- the rates fall between 0-40 percent. Within the intermediate goods category, heavy intermediates or goods at the lower stages of processing tend to have lower rates. Within the capital goods category, parts and components tend to have lower rates. In contrast, duties for consumer goods are generally higher--about two-thirds of consumer goods have duty rates above 50 percent--and are more widely dispersed. Among consumer goods, essentials such as cereals, flour, and vegetable oils enter at low duty rates, while nonessentials or items viewed as luxuries, such as some processed foods, textile articles, and household articles, carry substantially higher rates. Luxury consumer durables, such as household appliances, carry the highest rates.

2.59 Table 2.4 presents the average (unweighted) rates of import duties for China and 12 developing countries, chosen on the basis of the ready availability of comparable data on tariffs and other import duties. The table shows that China's structure of import duties is not unusual. Many developing countries exhibit a similar cascading of import duties, from high rates on consumer goods to low rates on raw materials, intermediates, and capital goods--reflecting the objective of protecting domestic activities. In China, the cascading structure is stated concretely in a set of guidelines established for the 1985 tariff reform. They also provide the framework the Customs Tariff Committee has used in adjusting the tariff rates since then.[2/]

(a) Tariff exemptions or low tariff rates should be applied to goods needed for national development or to consumer essentials that are either not produced domestically or are in short supply.

(b) Tariff rates for raw materials should be lower than those for manufactured goods and even lower for those materials that cannot be developed quickly in the short term because of natural constraints.

(c) Tariff rates should be low for parts and components of machinery and equipment that are neither produced domestically nor produced at

---

2/ The Customs Tariff Committee has the authority to set tariff policy and tariff rates. The Committee consists of representatives from the General Customs Administration, MOFERT, Ministry of Finance, State Planning Commission, State Economic Commission, relevant line ministries, and enterprises (on invitation). The Committee is chaired by the Director-General of the General Customs Administration, and co-chaired by a Vice-Minister of Finance. The Committee meets quarterly, except when an urgent matter arises. Requests for adjustments in tariff rates can be initiated by either the authorities supervising the line of production in question or by the enterprises themselves.

acceptable standards of quality, and these rates should be lower than the rates for the corresponding complete machinery and equipment.

(d) Relatively high tariff rates should be applied to goods that can be supplied domestically and to consumer nonessentials.

(e) Even higher tariff rates should be applied to goods whose domestic production requires protection.

Table 2.4: NOMINAL PROTECTION RATES--AN INTERNATIONAL COMPARISON
(Unweighted mean in percent ad valorem)

Country	Year	Intermediate Goods	Capital Goods	Consumer Goods	Whole Economy	(Coeff. of Variation)
CHINA	1986	27.2%	31.1%	62.6%	38.4%	(0.73)
Argentina	1986	21.2	25.0	21.9	31.8	(0.43)
Bangladesh	1985	97.9	80.5	116.1	96.5	(0.70)
Costa Rica	1985	17.7	16.7	33.7	30.5	(0.91)
Ecuador	1986	30.6	29.5	66.4	37.8	(0.99)
Hungary	1987	14.2	14.0	22.6	16.9	(0.37)
India	1986	151.3	124.9	135.4	137.6	(0.50)
Kenya	1985	47.6	49.7	69.3	53.6	(0.65)
Mexico	1985	23.5	23.5	32.2	24.7	(0.77)
Morocco	1985	21.6	18.1	43.0	26.6	(0.77)
Thailand	1985	27.8	24.8	48.5	37.8	(0.72)
Turkey	1985	29.4	34.9	55.3	36.0	(0.86)
Yugoslavia	1985	18.0	20.7	20.0	18.5	(0.30)

Source: SINTIA country files, Industry Department

2.60 Based on these guidelines, the 1985 tariff reform accomplished a major reduction in tariffs for a large number of commodities. As shown in Table 2.4, the average (unweighted) rate of import duty for the entire Chinese economy in 1986 was 38.4 percent. The result of this reform can be seen in the international comparison. The mean duty rate of China is significantly below that of India, Bangladesh, and Kenya--countries that, among all developing countries, are considered to have erected exceptionally high tariff barriers to trade. China's mean duty rate is comparable to that in lower middle-income countries such as Ecuador, Thailand, and Turkey.

2.61 At the same time, the guidelines generated relatively large differences in nominal tariff protection across activities. In addition to the mean, Table 2.4 presents the "coefficient of variation" for each country (the ratio of the standard deviation of the distribution of import duties to its mean). This summary statistic indicates the degree of dispersion of import duties. The higher the ratio, the greater is the difference in the nominal tariff protection accorded different producers. Among the countries presented in Table 2.4, three--Argentina, Hungary, and Yugoslavia--stand out as those having relatively uniform duty rates across different commodities. All three have conducted tariff reforms with the explicit objective of reducing and minimizing the difference in the rates of nominal tariff protection economy-wide.

2.62 In 1985, the ratio of import duty actually collected (Y 20.5 billion) to total imports (Y 125.8 billion) in China was 16.3 percent. This ratio is substantially lower than the mean duty rates discussed above. This difference is partly attributable to the cascading structure of import duties.[3/] It is also attributable to a set of duty exemptions permitted in the system. The principal exemptions apply to:

(a) Imports used in the production of exports;

(b) Capital goods imported to further the national objective of the "technical transformation" of industry; and

(c) Imports (mostly unrestricted capital and intermediate goods needed for productive activities) for 4 special economic zones, for economic and technical development zones in the 14 open coastal cities, for Sino-foreign joint ventures, and for Sino-foreign cooperative enterprises.

Although exact information was not made available, it is likely that exemptions under (b) and (c) explain most of the difference observed in 1985.[4/]

2.63 The present structure of import duties, therefore, plays a relatively small role in the generation of government revenue in China, compared with most countries. Although the share of import duties in total government revenue has been increasing since 1980, it amounts to less than 10 percent. (See Chapter 6, China: Finance and Investment, Report No. 6445-CHA.)

3/ Import values according to the customs tariff codes were not made available to the mission. Therefore, trade-weighted measures of average duty rates could not be calculated.

4/ The values of imports exempted from import duties for these purposes were not made available to the mission. Assuming that all capital goods imports entered duty-free, and that the import content of the total value of exports is 15 percent, the imputed ratio of duty collection to the remaining imports in 1985 is about 37 percent--in contrast with the mean duty rate of 38 percent.

Effective Tariff Protection

2.64 The role of tariffs in promoting development depends on their effectiveness in providing incentives to domestic producers. In the trade policy reform to date, the Government has been replacing one set of quantitative restrictions with another, while at the same time preparing for tariffs and flexible domestic prices to play a more effective role. Under these transitory circumstances, it is difficult and also misleading to assess the structure of incentives conferred by the tariff alone. However, the structure of tariff protection still establishes what should become the base line of incentives. It indicates the incentive structure that would prevail if quantitative restrictions were phased out, and the economic role of prices were enhanced.

2.65 The discussion of the nominal rate of tariff protection thus far has focused on the incentives affecting the output of producers, and not on inputs. This does not present a complete picture of the incentives conferred by tariffs. It is widely recognized that tariffs on inputs negatively affect protection for the using industry--just as quantitative restrictions have a negative impact on the using industry. The cascading structure of nominal protection and tariff policy guidelines discussed earlier shows clearly that the Chinese authorities recognize this effect as well.

2.66 The concept of the effective rate of tariff protection is useful in assessing the net impact of the taxes on imports on the structure of incentives. (See Box 2.1 for an illustrative explanation of the effective rate of tariff protection.) This concept of protection involves two considerations that differ from that of nominal protection. The first was discussed above: tariffs on inputs reduce protection for the using industry. The second consideration follows from the first: the appropriate price in assessing incentives is the effective price of the activity of a producer--that is, the price of the value added produced--and not the price of the product itself. As explained in Box 2.1, the effective rate of protection measures the degree to which domestic value added in an activity diverges from the value added at international prices; i.e., the value added that would prevail under free trade.

2.67 When the effective rate of protection is positive, the resources available under protection to compensate factors of production exceed those available at international prices. This condition can encourage more resources to enter that activity than would be the case in the absence of the tariff protection. Negative effective rates indicate that fewer resources are available under protection than at international prices, a condition that tends to discourage resources from entering that activity. A relatively high effective rate indicates that an activity is subsidized compared to others in the economy, so that there is an incentive to expand. A relatively low rate implies that an activity is taxed vis-a-vis others, so that there is an incentive to contract. Whether or not, and to what extent, the potential incentives result in an expansion of domestic activity depends not just on the effective rate but also on the responsiveness of domestic supply to prices.

BOX 2.1: THE EFFECTIVE RATE OF TARIFF PROTECTION--AN ILLUSTRATION

A simple hypothetical example can illustrate the concept of the effective rate of protection. Consider an importable product, cotton yarn. Suppose that the only intermediate input used for cotton yarn is cotton, also an importable product. In the first instance, there are no restrictions on trade, including tariffs, and both products are freely imported. The price received by the domestic cotton yarn industry is 10,000 yuan per unit, which is also the foreign supply price, including transportation cost and foreign tariffs, if any. For the unit of cotton needed to produce 10,000 yuan worth of yarn, the industry pays a price of 5,000 yuan. The "effective price" per unit of yarn that the industry realizes after payment for the cotton is therefore 5,000 yuan (Y 10,000-Y 5,000).

Now, suppose that tariffs of 30 percent for cotton yarn and 3 percent for cotton are imposed. (In fact, these are the minimum tariff rates in China for cotton yarn sold for further processing and for raw, carded, and combed cotton.) The effective price of yarn is therefore increased to 7,850 yuan--the duty-inclusive price of yarn (13,000 yuan) minus the duty-inclusive price of cotton (5,150 yuan). That is, with the tariff, the effective price is 57 percent higher relative to the effective price of 5,000 yuan under free trade. Therefore, the industry has 57 percent more resources available to compensate the factors employed in producing its value added, i.e., workers and investment. Thus, the effective rate of protection conferred by the tariffs to the domestic cotton yarn industry is 27 percent wage points above the nominal rate of protection. Although the prices used in this illustration are fictitious, the tariff rates are not, and it could characterize the status of effective protection for cotton yarn in China. Let us consider two other cases in which the tariff rates are changed.

<u>Case 1</u>: The tariff on cotton yarn is reduced to zero, but the tariff on cotton remains at 3 percent. The effective price of yarn falls below the free-trade price to 4,850 yuan--the free-trade price of yarn (10,000 yuan) minus the tariff-inclusive price of cotton (5,150 yuan). The result is negative protection for cotton yarn at -3 percent. The cotton yarn producers are worse off, compared with the free-trade situation. Exporters in many countries often find themselves in a similar situation, since their sales in the world market do not enjoy the tariff protection accorded domestic producers of import substitutes.

<u>Case 2</u>: The tariff on cotton yarn remains at 30 percent, and the tariff on cotton is raised to 30 percent. The effective price of yarn is 6,500 yuan--the difference between the duty-inclusive prices of yarn (13,000 yuan) and of cotton (6,500 yuan). The effective rate of protection is now 30 percent. This case illustrates the principle that the effective rate equals the nominal rate of protection when tariffs on outputs and inputs are the same (as long as no inputs are obtained at free-trade prices.) The effective rate, otherwise difficult to observe directly, becomes visible to policy-makers.

2.68 The effective rates of protection commonly differ from activity to activity, in part because the nominal rates of protection on inputs and outputs usually differ. Given the structure of nominal protection in China, it might be expected that the effective rates would differ across activities. In addition, the effective rates differ among activities, because the input-output structure--the share of input costs in the total cost of production--varies among them. As noted earlier, quantitative restrictions and domestic policies have significantly affected the degree of protection and structure of production in China. Under these circumstances, it is misleading to use the current production data for China to estimate the effective rates of tariff protection.

2.69 Nevertheless, the effective rates can provide some insight into the structure of incentives implied by the present tariffs, which could turn out to guide China's development as the reform moves forward. That understanding can also assist in evaluating whether the implied incentive structure is consistent with China's policy objectives, or whether it differs significantly from what is intended by policy-makers. A simulation of the effective rates, based on a hypothetical input-output structure, can be used to provide--very roughly and tentatively--some of these insights. To see how robust the simulated results are, two production structures that are very different from each other have been chosen for the simulation. One is based on the 1970 input-output coefficients of a large industrialized economy (Japan), the other on the 1980 coefficients of a small lower-middle income economy (Thailand). The result of the simulations, can be interpreted as the effective protection that would prevail under the present tariff structure, in the absence of quantitative restrictions and price controls, if these coefficients represented the input-output relationships of China under free trade. Put another way, the simulations generate the effective protection that would have prevailed in these economies if they had adopted China's current tariff schedule as the only means of regulating trade.

2.70 Table 2.5 summarizes the results of the simulations on the effective rates of tariff protection. The "large country" and "small country" cases generate similar results, with both showing high and extremely variable effective rates. The average rate of protection for the economy as a whole is about 67 percent for the large country case and 54 percent for the small country case. The simulated effective rates for individual activities range between -211 percent and 914 percent in the large country case, and between -206 percent and 262 percent in the small country case. Distributions of the simulated effective rates of tariff protection are given in Figure 2.2 (for the large country case) and Figure 2.3 (for the small country one).

2.71 The simulated rates of effective protection cascade in ways that closely follow the nominal tariff rates. (This cascading structure is summarized in Table 2.5 and depicted in Figures 2.2 and 2.3.) In both simulations, the manufacturing sector has the highest average rate of effective protection,

Table 2.5: SUMMARY OF SIMULATIONS ON EFFECTIVE RATES OF TARIFF PROTECTION
(In percent)

	Effective Rates of Protection			Average
	Average	Minimum	Maximum	Nominal Rates
"LARGE COUNTRY" SIMULATION				
Agriculture	36.41	3.13	60.38	29.06
Mining	15.66	-4.61	37.68	16.66
Manufacturing	76.60	-210.68	914.48	42.16
Consumer goods	81.48	-210.68	208.82	61.15
(a) Food products	57.26	-210.68	208.82	61.86
(b) Non-food non-durables	102.42	10.06	194.42	61.83
(c) Durables	89.37	61.95	158.01	57.84
Light intermediates	138.91	-20.05	914.48	44.57
Heavy intermediates	21.72	-15.80	76.96	19.67
Capital goods	36.80	-1.75	120.81	32.12
WHOLE ECONOMY	67.45	-210.68	914.48	38.75
"SMALL COUNTRY" SIMULATION				
Agriculture	30.71	-2.30	112.70	26.63
Mining	17.74	-6.60	62.21	17.33
Manufacturing	65.34	-205.77	261.94	42.90
Consumer goods	86.62	-205.77	261.94	55.61
(a) Food products	73.34	-205.77	261.94	53.92
(b) Non-food non-durables	82.11	-2.26	199.86	54.06
(c) Durables	133.60	69.46	236.67	64.19
Light intermediates	66.14	24.31	167.79	39.46
Heavy intermediates	36.73	1.46	111.63	24.93
Capital goods	34.41	-6.91	109.38	27.62
WHOLE ECONOMY	53.76	-205.77	261.94	37.22

Source: SINTIA Country Files, Industry Department

Note: The simulations are based on the input-output coefficients of Japan, 1970, for the "large country" case and of Thailand, 1980, for the "small country" case.

Figure 2.2

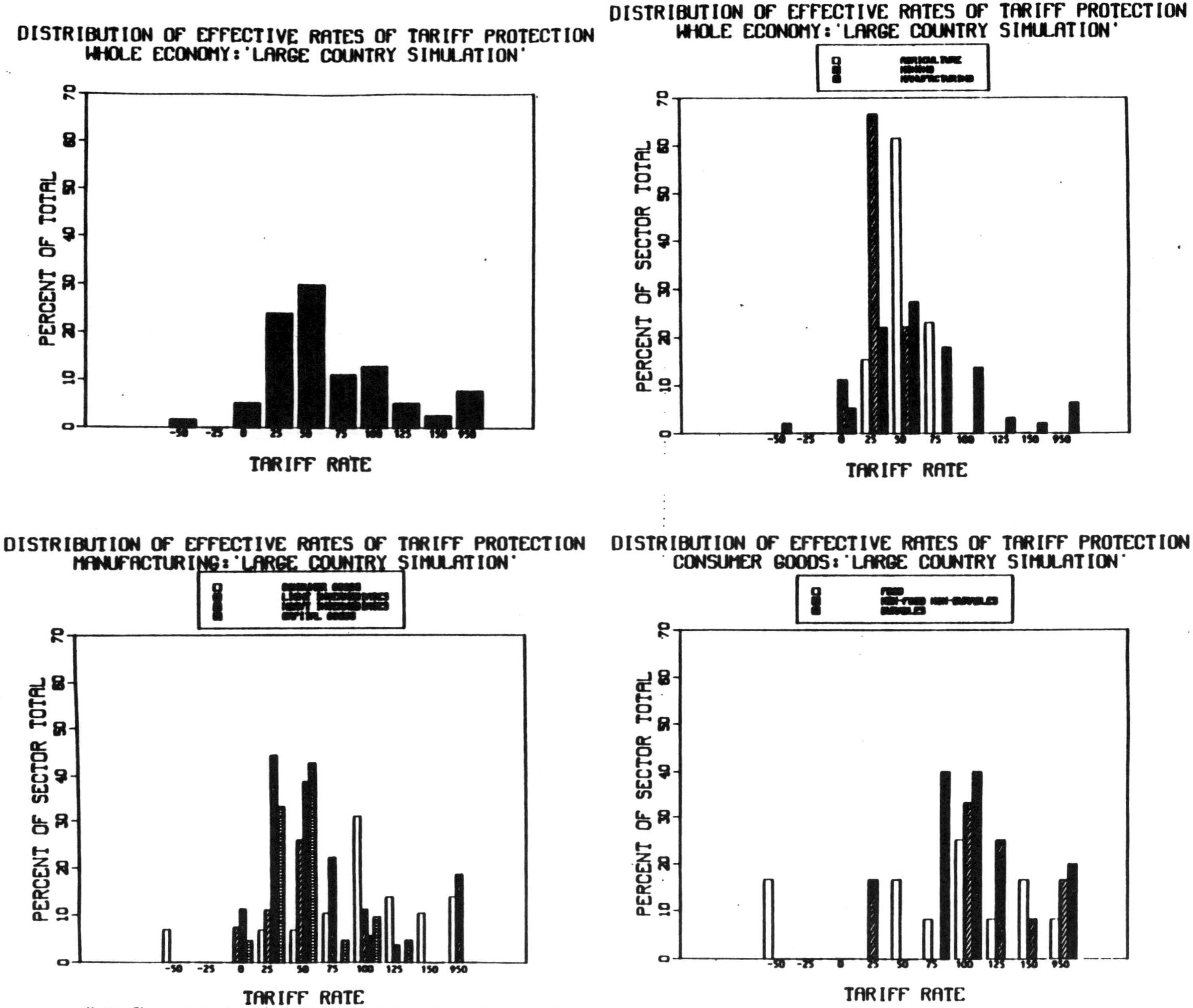

Note: The numbers labeling the horizontal axis are the upper bounds of each range, except for zero. (For example, 10 means effective rates of tariff protection greater than 0 but less than or equal to 10 percent.)

Figure 2.3

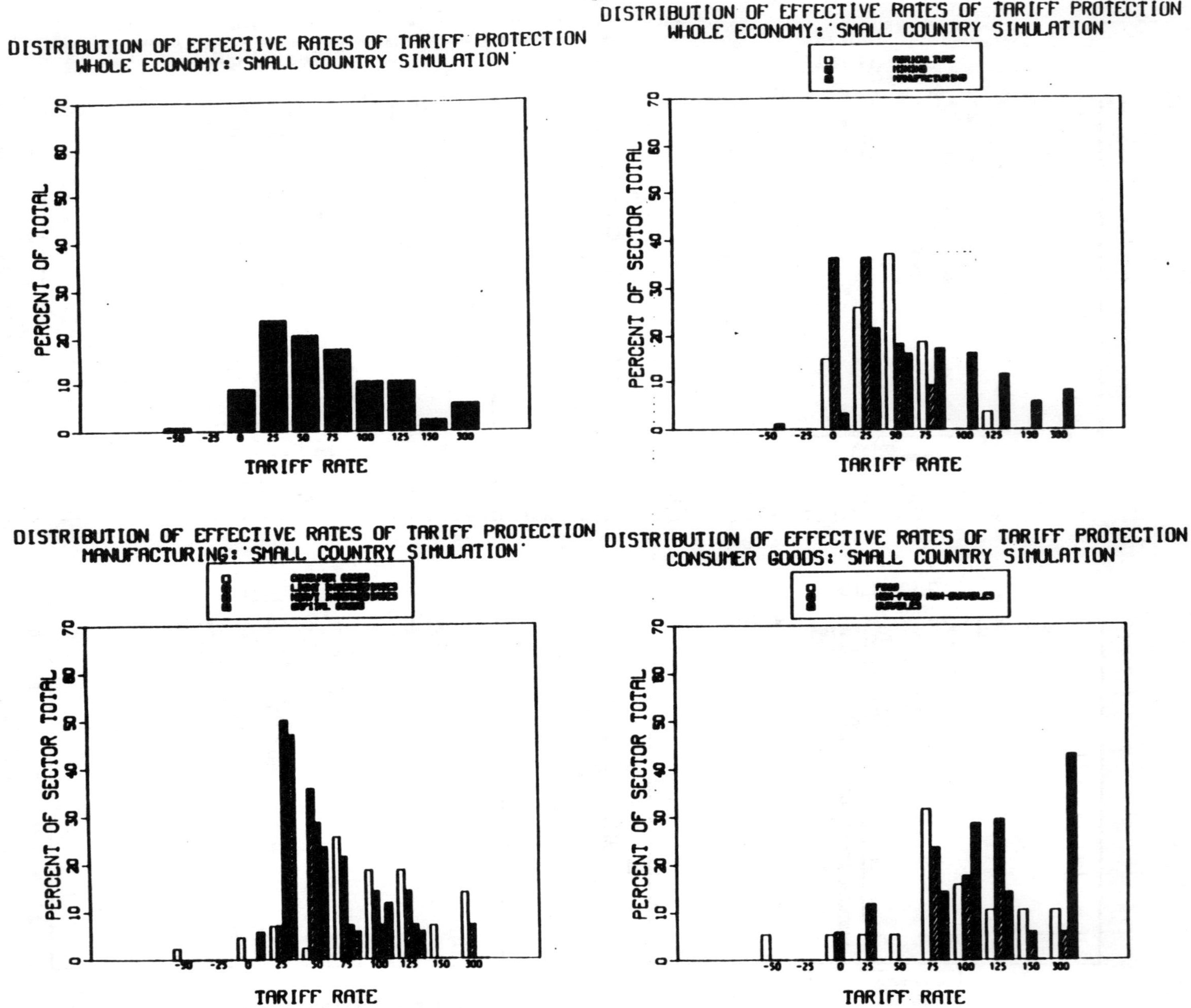

Note: The numbers labeling the horizontal axis are the upper bounds of each range, except for zero. (For example, 10 means effective rates of tariff protection greater than 0 but less than or equal to 10 percent.)

as well as the widest range of effective rates. Both the average level and the variation in effective rates are significantly lower for agriculture and mining.

2.72 Within manufacturing, consumer goods and light intermediate goods are provided with higher levels of effective protection, with greater variations in these rates across activities. Heavy intermediates and capital goods show similar levels and ranges of effective protection. Within the consumer goods category, food products receive the lowest average level of protection but have the most diverse range of protective rates. In both simulations, non-food consumer goods and consumer durables have much higher average rates of effective protection than food products.

2.73 Negative protection is indicated in such food manufacturing activities as edible oils, various grain milling, and prepared meats, and in a number of mining activities such as iron, tin, and tungsten ores. Agricultural and industrial machinery activities are among those showing distinctly low effective rates. In the small country simulation, rates in excess of 200 percent are seen in such activities as slaughtering and metal furniture. In the large country simulation, rates in excess of 200 percent are encountered mostly in textile activities. They include silk reeling, rayon spinning, silk weaving, woolen weaving, rayon weaving, and synthetic fiber weaving (which has the highest effective rate, at 914 percent).

2.74 Thus, the simulations indicate that China's tariffs would have three main incentive effects in the context of the hypothetical market-oriented economies. First, with respect to import-substitution activities in the economy, the incentive environment would induce resources to move toward manufacturing and would discriminate against agriculture and mining. This tendency may be consistent with the Government's objective to modernize Chinese industry. However, the simulations imply that this resource shift would be accomplished by "taxing" agriculture and mining relative to manufacturing at rates of about 30-60 percent.

2.75 Second, within the manufacturing sector, the simulated incentive environment would induce resources to move toward the production of consumer and light intermediate goods rather than toward heavy intermediates or capital goods. These movements would be achieved by implicitly taxing the latter relative to the former, with the "tax" ranging from 30 percent to as much as 100 percent.

2.76 Finally, for the economy as a whole, the simulations indicate that there would be a bias against export activities and in favor of import-substitution activities. This result is not surprising, since any protection for domestic producers means subsidizing them against activities undertaken at international prices--that is, foreign producers and Chinese exporters. The simulations point out, however, that this bias might be quite large. If an exporter could purchase all its inputs at world prices, it would receive a zero effective rate of protection (since it sells at world prices and receives no tariff protection on its products). In this case, the implicit tax on export activities relative to import-substituting activities would be roughly 50-60 percent on average for the economy as a whole. If an exporter could not purchase all inputs at world prices--e.g., if it had to pay duties on imported inputs--then it would receive negative protection in effective terms. In this case, the incentive environment's discrimination against exports would be even larger. (See Case 1 of Box 2.1.) The interesting feature of these simulations is the extent of bias they display against certain high-priority activities, such as agriculture, the capital goods sector and exports. It is not at all clear that this is what the policy-makers intended when designing the tariff.

Protection and Efficiency

2.77 The Government sees the emerging instruments of trade policy described and analyzed above as means of controlling foreign exchange expenditures during the early period of transition to a market-oriented planned system, and as a means of promoting development--in part by shielding Chinese producers from import competition. These are policy goals that China shares in common with other socialist economies in the process of reform, as well as with many other developing countries. However, the experience of many of these countries indicates that, if the period of protection of domestic industry lasts too long, and if the incentives offered to producers are too high and open-ended, the costs to the economy can be very high in terms of the misallocation of resources and lack of technological dynamism.

2.78 In China, particularly at its present crossroads in economic modernization, the costs--as well as the benefits--of protection depend critically on conditions in the domestic economy, particularly as regards the mobility of domestic resources, the structure of market prices, the degree of competition in markets, and the autonomy of producers responsible for their own business decisions. Improvements in these conditions are necessary in order to realize the full benefits from trade. However, the same improvements may raise the costs of protection flowing from the emerging trade policy instruments.

2.79 Regardless of the policy objectives, quantitative restrictions on competing imports results in a commitment to open-ended protection for domestic industry no matter what the cost. The analysis of this annex has noted signs that this problem could be emerging in China--particularly in those segments of the economy where price flexibility has been introduced through open markets (such as in the case of steel products) or where investment resources are more mobile (such as foreign investments).

2.80 The preceding analysis has also indicated that the current structure of tariffs can imply potentially high and varying levels of incentives for producers of tradable goods in China. The estimated structure of effective tariff protection suggests the likelihood of a bias towards the production of final consumer goods rather than towards intermediate or capital goods. It also suggests the possibility of an overall bias in favor of industrial production and against agriculture and mining. Last but not least is the discriminatory incentives against exports, unless accompanied by compensating assistance.

2.81 Countries that have long exposed their economies to a structure of incentives similar to the one that appears to be emerging in China have experienced at least one common problem: they have ended up with an economic structure that by and large is not internationally competitive. In extreme instances, these countries have promoted activities that earn less foreign exchange in exports or save less foreign exchange through import susbtitution, compared to the foreign exchange costs of their intermediate inputs. In other words, these economies could have saved foreign exchange by shutting down these activities. More frequently, they have developed activities that generate insufficient amounts of net foreign exchange earnings or savings. Opportunities were missed whereby the employed workers and investments tied up could have earned or saved more net foreign exchange for the economy in other activities.

2.82 There are essentially two reasons for this impact on international competitiveness. The first is the misallocation of resources, as a result of interventions in trade that reduce the static benefits discussed at the outset of this annex. When prices reflect full economic costs and benefits, financial incentives help ensure that autonomous producers will make efficient decisions. With varying levels of protection, product and input prices are imperfect guides to economic costs and benefits. If the emerging incentive environment is maintained as the reform moves forward and production and investment decisions are decentralized to enterprises, it may have serious implications for the efficiency of investments and productive employment of workers.

2.83 The second reason is the way in which protection influences the effort of enterprises with respect to technological progress and productivity growth. It corresponds to the dynamic benefits of trade discussed at the beginning of this annex. Many countries have provided protection for an excessively long time and afforded incentives that turned out to be quite open-ended. Often these conditions were combined with weak competitive conditions in domestic markets. Shielded from both external and internal competition, producers had little incentive to find ways to reduce costs, improve product quality, develop new product lines, find and invest in new technology, and raise their capacities to improve or modify foreign technology in a way suited to market conditions at home. In short, a sufficient number of dynamic business enterprises and equally dynamic workers and business managers failed to emerge. Such consequences are particularly evident among countries that have employed quantitative restrictions to protect domestic producers for a long time. In this regard, tariff protection is superior, in that it can transmit changes in foreign prices over time, communicating to domestic producers the effects of cost-saving technologies and innovations abroad and inducing them to reduce costs and to improve the profitability of their operations. With quantitative restrictions, this important linkage is broken.

2.84 The variations that emerged in effective protection and in the resource costs to generate net foreign exchange were not the intended consequence of policy in these countries. Rather, they arose from the complexity of their trade policy regimes and, in most countries, from the use of quantitative restrictions as opposed to tariff protection. Nevertheless, the problem lasted too long undetected or unresolved. In the long run, the wasteful misallocation of resources, low productivity performance, and weak or inappropriate technological bases have imposed substantial costs on their development. Today, in the face of acute scarcities of foreign exchange, many countries are having to bear the additional costs of undoing past mistakes.

2.85 China has two important advantages. First, it is in a position to learn from the experience of other countries. Its future trade policy can aim at enhancing the role of prices as guides to economic costs and benefits, and not at distorting them; and it can aim at enhancing the role of competition in forcing producers to innovate and upgrade their technologies. The second advantage of China relates to competition: unlike most developing countries, China can seek and increase competition internally among Chinese producers, as well as externally through import competition or export rivalry.

B. The Emerging Export Policy Environment

2.86 Promoting exports is one objective many countries set for their trade policies. There are various reasons for this. In particular, since all countries protect domestic producers in one way or another, they find it necessary to provide promotional incentives that compensate for the implicit "tax" on exports, as discussed earlier.

2.87 At the same time that they promote exports in general, many countries also restrict exports of selected commodities by limiting their quantity (embargo, quota, or licensing) or by altering the export prices (export tax or price controls). The objective varies depending on the commodity, the country, and over time. Often, however, it is to raise the foreign prices of exports to the country's own advantage. The reason is that these countries have a position on the export side that is quite different from that on the import side; they may -- at least in the short term -- be one of the key suppliers of a commodity in the world market.

2.88 Based on lessons derived from the experience of other countries, this section reviews China's two export policies -- restriction of exports and promotion of exports -- which are beginning to shape the country's export policy for the future.

Export Restriction: Policy of a Large Country and of Adjustment

2.89 China is placing increasing reliance on two instruments to restrict its exports: export taxes and export licensing. In general, both measures create a divergence between domestic and world prices, the export tax directly and licensing indirectly. Correspondingly, both measures alter the distribution of domestic production between domestic demand and exports, the export tax indirectly and licensing directly.

2.90 Export taxes introduce a wedge between the foreign demand price and the domestic price. The lower price offered to domestic producers as a result of the tax induces them to reduce export supply. In the exceptional case that the exporting country has a large share of the world market, this strategy can, however, shift the terms of trade in favor of the exporter, and increase total revenue. In general, however, the result is reduced exports and export earnings.

2.91 Quantitative restrictions on exports, such as those administered by export licensing, have the same effects as those of the export tax, but they restrict the supply of exports directly. However, there are several important differences between these two approaches to export restriction. First, under export taxes, the divergence between the domestic and the foreign price accrues as revenue to the government. In contrast, export licensing provides a possibility of windfall gains (legal or illegal) to those who can secure the licenses and sell the restricted quantities at the higher world prices--unless the licenses are auctioned or sold by tender. Second, export taxes provide a predetermined rate of assistance to domestic users, while the amount of output diverted to the domestic market, and away from exports varies according to the changes in world prices. In contrast, licensing provides users with the security of a predetermined level of production for domestic markets. The rate of assistance given to them increases or decreases depending on the rise or fall in world prices.

Policy Objectives of China

2.92 Today in China, export restrictions have two objectives. On the one hand, China is a major world supplier of a number of commodities, particularly primary products. Because a larger volume of these exports means lower prices, the Government is concerned about managing them to ensure that the country as a whole gains. Strictly from China's point of view, that concern is legitimate. Given that the Government wishes to take advantage of China's influence in the world market, restricting exports "wisely" is a policy that can improve the country's economic well-being.

2.93 On the other hand, there is an objective associated with the irrational divergences that continue to exist between domestic and world prices. When external market prices are more attractive than domestic prices, exporters are eager to sell abroad. But, because domestic prices are not permitted to rise to the levels of world prices, the Government is concerned that domestic shortages will result and so restricts exports. Thus, export restriction is used to prevent major domestic disruptions during a period of adjustment, while domestic prices are becoming realigned. Both export licensing and the export taxes are used to achieve the above two objectives in China. As will be seen below, however, there are important differences in the character of these objectives as served by the two instruments.

Export Licensing

2.94 Export licensing as now practiced in China, began in 1980, with the "Interim Procedures of the State Import-Export Commission and the Ministry of Foreign Trade of the People's Republic of China Concerning the System of Export Licensing (June 3, 1980)". The administration of export licensing was decentralized in 1985, in a manner similar to that of import licensing, as discussed earlier. Most of the licenses are issued by the regional Foreign Economic Relations and Trade Commissions, while the administration of the rest is split between MOFERT and its Special Commission Offices at the major ports. Unlike import licensing, the export licensing system apparently functions with a high degree of administrative efficiency.

2.95 The export license is issued to exporters and is not transferrable. The expiration date of a license depends on the stipulation of each export contract (e.g., the delivery date) and can run up to a maximum of six months from the date of issue. A one-time extension of up to two months is permitted on application. After that, a new license must be obtained.

2.96 Since 1980, the number of commodities subject to licensing has increased steadily. As of November 1986, there were 235 items, mostly primary products. (The list of commodities subject to export licenses is given in the Attachment to this annex.) These commodities amounted to roughly half of the total exports of China (or about a quarter, if crude and refined oil products are excluded). The licensing list is reviewed monthly and amended frequently. For example, there were 152 items on the list in January 1986; a recent (unofficial) report lists 212 items for January 1987.

2.97 The large number of items subject to licensing reflects the principal objective of the system--to assure favorable prices for primary exports to the Hong Kong and Macao markets, where China has established a dominant market presence. It has been reported that around 200 items are licensed specifically for this purpose. Because the Hong Kong and Macao markets function as daily auctions, and because of their proximity, the Government considers licensing as the most effective instrument for meeting the objective. The MOFERT office in Hong Kong employs more than 1,000 workers, who monitor price developments at the daily auctions. It reports the market trends back to Beijing, where the volume of exports is controlled directly through licensing on a continuous basis. Indeed, given the circumstances of these markets, export taxes may not give the same degree of precision to take advantage of China's market power.

2.98 There is another reason why the Government controls exports to Hong Kong and Macao. The price distortions in the economy, coupled with the excess demand for foreign exchange, have generated a strong incentive to participate in "parallel exports" and smuggling. Those with foreign trade rights (mainly the trading companies) have begun to export beyond their business scope or plan quota; even those without such rights have started to export. By the end of 1983, for example, the problem of "parallel exports" to Hong Kong had swelled to such proportions that the Hong Kong Chinese Chamber of Commerce began to press China for corrective measures.

2.99 Outside the Hong Kong and Macao markets, the Government is pursuing two further objectives through export licensing. One is the "distortion adjustment" objective discussed above, with the Government using licensing to ensure that the planned supply is available to domestic users. Commodities such as coal, pig iron, rolled steel, steel ingots, and phosphorous fertilizer are probably restricted for this purpose (see the Attachment). The other objective has to do with the quantitative restrictions that Chinese exports face in foreign markets. In particular, China has controlled exports of textiles and garments since 1985 in order to comply with its obligations under the Multi-Fiber Arrangement. About 25 items are subject to licensing for this purpose (see the Attachment). Although less formally, a similar objective underlies the export control of crude oil and refined oil products.

Export Tax

2.100 The export tax, which was reformed as part of the 1985 tariff reform discussed earlier, applies to a limited number of commodities. The tax is used to restrict exports in keeping with the "terms of trade" objective as well as the "distortion adjustment" objective. The taxable items cover roughly 5-7 percent of the total value of Chinese exports. Officially, the stated purpose of the tax is to prevent the export of relevant commodities in "excessively large quantities, disrupting the world market or causing bottlenecks at home". The guidelines established in the 1985 reform also specify that the tax should be applied on the following basis:

(a) When China's export is highly competitive, while the world market demand is limited relative to China's export capacity; or

(b) When there is a domestic shortage (for raw materials and semi-finished goods).

2.101 The list of taxable commodities and associated export tax rates are given in Table 2.6. The taxable items fall essentially into two groups. The first consists of primary products in which China is a major supplier in the world market. It includes minerals such as antimony, tin and tungsten, as well as agricultural and fishery products in which China has a substantial presence, particularly in the Japanese market. The "terms of trade" objective applies to most of the commodities in this group. The second includes basic metal products (a variety of ferro- alloys, pig iron, cast iron) and coal, with the "distortion adjustment" objective probably the more important one.

2.102 At the same time, the list seems to reveal a third objective of the export tax. As noted in Table 2.6, more than half the taxable items are commodities that are also subject to export licensing. Regardless of the objective of the licensing, the export tax for these items serves to transfer the exporters' rent to the Government as revenue.

Some Pitfalls in Restricting Exports

2.103 China's policy of restricting exports enhances the country's influence in the world market. The policy may be sound strictly from the point of view of China, but not necessarily from a global perspective. A large country such as China affects the relative prices of goods in the world when it changes its policy and domestic economic conditions. As such, China must be judicious in pursuing its export restriction policy. As pointed out earlier, China should ultimately eliminate the need to restrict exports because of domestic distortions. There is little to be gained and much to be lost by restricting them for this reason. The best policy is to correct the domestic price distortions.

2.104 Although using an export tax for the "terms of trade" objective is to China's advantage, there are some potential pitfalls. One has to do with the tax rates themselves. When the rate of the export tax is increased, two opposing tendencies result. The first is a shift in the terms of trade in favor of China. The second is a curtailment in the volume of exports, so that China tends to lose some of the advantages associated with the international division of labor through trade. The export tax rate at which the gain from

Table 2.6: EXPORT TAXES

Export Tax Rate	Commodities
10%	*Chestnuts Edible kernels of apricot, fresh or chilled *Ferro-manganese *Ferro-chrome Ferro-titanium Ferro-alloys other than manganese, tungsten, chrome, silicon, vanadium, molybdenum, & titanium
20%	*Jelly fish Fresh water fish, frozen Goat skins *Crude antimony ores and concentrates *Antimony and articles of antimony *Tungsten ores and concentrates *Ferro-tungsten *Ferro-molybdenum *Pig iron and cast iron
30%	*Prawns, fresh, chilled or frozen *Crude laquer *Ferro-silicon
40%	Herring roe, fresh or chilled Herring roe, frozen Herring roe, dried salted or in brine *Coal Lignite whether or not agglomerated Peat (including peat litter), whether or not agglomerated *Ingots and slabs of unwrought tin
50%	Cinnamon, cassia, lignea Dang gui (crytotaenia canadensis)
60%	*Eel, fried Hoantchy (astragalus membranaceus bge.)

Source: General Customs Administration, The Peoples Republic of China

Note: Asterisks indicate those commodities that are subject to export licensing.

the first tendency exceeds the loss from the second by the largest possible margin, so that the country is reaping the maximum benefits, is called the optimum export tax.

2.105 The optimum export tax rate depends heavily on the sensitivities of foreign demand to prices and therefore varies across different commodities. The lower that sensitivity, the smaller is the proportionate decline in the export volume relative to the increase in the export price that results from the tax, and therefore the higher should be the rate of the optimum tax. Although it is not easy to estimate such sensitivities, if the rates of 40-60 percent that pertain in China's tax schedule are to be "optimal" (see Table 2.6), the sensitivity of foreign demand must be exceptionally low. An optimal tax at 50 percent implies, for example, that the volume demanded would decline by only about 1 percent for 2-percent increase in the export price. The possibility exists that China may be over-taxing some exports from this point of view.

2.106 The sensitivities of foreign demand can, however, change over time: alternative supplies of the same commodity may emerge; close substitutes may appear; research and innovation may develop synthetic substitutes in response to higher world prices. These possibilities comprise another pitfall that needs to be taken into account in formulating China's export policy. China has already faced some of these eventualities in the Hong Kong, Macao, and Japanese markets. A policy to restrict exports is a decision to balance the gains from export restrictions in the short term against potential losses in the long term.

2.107 Finally, there is the issue of foreign restrictions or retaliation. The history of international trade shows, sadly, that increased exports may provoke import restrictions abroad, the long-standing case of textiles being just one example. If foreign restrictions are real or can be expected with some certainty, then it may be wise for China to restrict some of its exports. Several countries have pursued that policy -- Japan's voluntary export restraints on passenger cars being the most recent and highly publicized example. It must be stressed once again, however, that such policies are "wise" strictly from the point of view of China and are justified only when foreign retaliation is certain. Even then, export restriction can be dangerous, depending on the ramifications in terms of the political economy of trading partners.

Export Promotion: Policies Instruments and Institutions

The Current Export Promotion Policy

2.108 The export incentive environment, which is discussed later, reflects, to a large extent, the Government's basic policy objective regarding exports: to raise the volume of exports in order to enable the country to import the technology, machinery and equipment, raw materials and other inputs needed for economic development. In pursuing this objective, less than adequate consideration has typically been given to the cost and efficiency of generating foreign exchange through exports.

2.109 The export incentive environment that has emerged over the years, in particular since the initiation of the "Open Door" policy, is somewhat of a hybrid. On the one hand, it incorporates the remnants of the old, centrally planned foreign trade system, heavily influenced on the other hand by the initial effects of the economic reforms.

2.110 The incentive framework also attempts to compensate producers and foreign trade corporations partially for the bias against exports. As was argued earlier, the current policy and institutional set-up of China's external trade sector discourages trade in general and exports in particular. The high level of overall protection afforded domestic producers makes domestic sales in general more profitable than exports. Resources are thus being pulled into sectors catering to domestic markets. Exporting under such circumstances becomes increasingly unattractive unless offset by explicit subsidies and incentives. These subsidies may prove costly and will be ineffective, unless the overall trade policy environment moves toward a more reasonable structure and level of protection for domestic producers.

2.111 It has been pointed out elsewhere that, in addition to the trade policy environment, China's institutional organization and business practices in the external trade sector most likely also discriminate against efficient exports. Frequently, products that are not internationally competitive get exported, while many export opportunities (particularly by smaller firms) most likely go untapped. Thus, China may not be benefitting from exports to the extent it could. It is the mission's impression that many firms (producers and foreign trade corporations alike) are exporting not because doing so is financially attractive, but because they are obligated to fulfill their export plan targets and because they need the foreign exchange for their imports.

2.112 As firms become responsible for their profits and losses, it will be increasingly difficult for China to increase or even sustain the level of its exports. With export plans becoming increasingly indicative and less binding in nature, there is a real danger that more and more firms that are currently exporting will shift their sales to the more lucrative domestic market, which is generally characterized by excess demand. Similarly, foreign trade corporations, conscious about and responsible for any losses they may incur from exports, will lose interest in exporting.

2.113 The export incentive system is likely to become inadequate for a continued export drive and for improvements in value added and the composition of exports. What follows is a critical assessment of the incentive environment and a description of the more automatic export incentive system deemed necessary for export promotion policies in the context of the reformed foreign trade policy.

2.114 In order to compensate partially for the anti-export bias of the trade policy, whose existence policy-makers recognize, China has developed a set of specific instruments and institutions designed to encourage the production and marketing of exports. Most of these instruments reflect the nature of the centrally planned economy that characterized China during the more than three decades following the revolution. The principal incentive mechanisms affecting exports involve the use of foreign exchange by exporters, financial incentives and bonuses, and export procurement prices. These instruments, which have recently undergone changes, are complemented by other, more widely known incentive mechanisms, such as import duty and domestic tax exemptions and production and investment financing for exports.

2.115 Foreign exchange retention rights. The right to retain a certain portion of export earnings is currently viewed by both exporters and government authorities as an important incentive to export. Producing firms obtain a retention right that in most cases is equivalent to 12.5 percent of their export earnings. In addition, if their exports exceed the planned annual target, producers may get an additional quota of up to 70 percent of their above-plan export earnings. A firm can use these foreign exchange rights to pay for its imports of raw materials, spare parts and equipment needed for production or to buy consumer durables (presumably for its own use). In either case, the availability of foreign exchange is a prerequisite for permission to import and thus enjoys a considerable premium.

2.116 The mission found that the incentive for a firm or foreign trade corporation to exceed planned export targets is particularly strong: it leads many exporters to seek low plan quotas for their exports. Although not officially permitted, foreign exchange retention rights are occasionally also traded at a premium of perhaps one yuan per each US dollar generated by exports.

2.117 There are, however, limits to the use of retained foreign exchange earnings. Given the overall shortage of foreign exchange in China, the authorities have made the foreign exchange retention a de facto "entitlement quota" as opposed to a "cash retention." That is, a firm with foreign exchange rights has to apply to the authorities to be allowed to buy back what it requires for imports. In addition, the authorities can deny the importation of certain goods.

2.118 Bonuses under the export plans. As mentioned in the section on export plans (see Annex 1, paras. 1.40-1.46), targets are expressed both in physical units and value in foreign currency. In the case of a divergence between the two sets of targets during implementation of the plan, the value of the foreign exchange generated becomes the binding target. To increase the incentive to fulfill the export targets, exporters -- foreign trade corporations -- are entitled to bonuses when they fulfill their targets, over and above the bonus ceilings established for enterprises catering to the domestic market. (The mission was unable to obtain details about the extent and importance of this type of bonus on export performance). In addition, the trade companies receive 3 fen for each dollar earned within the plan target and 10 fen for each dollar exceeding the target value.

2.119 Export procurement prices. Currently there are three types of procurement of export commodities in China: (1) a centralized system that operates through the MOFERT foreign trade corporations; (2) the "agency system," which uses various types of trade organizations that act as exporters' agents; and (3) the system of integrating production and trade with exports carried out by the ministries' foreign trade corporations.

2.120 Under the first system, the State Price Bureau sets the procurement prices, which in principle are in line with domestic prices. However, producers are often reluctant to sell at such prices because of competitive bidding from domestic distributors and other trade corporations. In such cases, foreign trade corporations are allowed to offer negotiated prices, which are usually higher than the fixed domestic prices, thus providing firms some extra incentive to produce for exports.

2.121 The export procurement prices under the agency system should be consistent with world market prices. In many cases, however, the conversion of export earnings at the official exchange rate still leaves exports less profitable than domestic sales. Export prices under the agency system could be increased to encourage the enterprises producing exports. In a bargaining process between the firm and the trading corporation, the latter usually agrees to increase the export procurement price by an amount equivalent to the consolidated industrial and commercial tax (see China: Finance and Investment, Report No. 6445-CHA) and other fees that are levied on domestic sales.

2.122 Finally, the prices for exports carried out by the industrial ministries' trading corporations are determined internally at the ministry level. The pricing principle is that production enterprises should not assume any losses from exports.

2.123 Export production base system. The export incentives are aimed above all at export producers, some of which may be exporting only a small part of their output. An exception to this rule is the joint-venture export enterprise that has been set up primarily to engage in exports. In addition, some Chinese enterprises in the manufacturing and agricultural sectors have for a long time been producing exclusively for exports. These enterprises are usually known as export production bases or centers. In 1981, for example, there were 114 export production centers and almost 100 individual enterprises producing exclusively for the overseas markets, accounting for more than 20 percent of China's exports that year.

2.124 The rationale for an export production base has traditionally been to select products and enterprises that would enable China to produce a stable supply of acceptable quality commodities in which the country has a comparative advantage. The selection is usually made and the production base set up by MOFERT, the provincial authorities or an industrial ministry. Little detail is known about the selection criteria, beyond the type and quality of the commodity and volume of existing exports.

2.125 With the economic reforms, the intention of policy-makers is to use the "export commodity production system," as the export production base system is now called, to increase and diversify the composition and to improve the quality of China's exports. This objective is to be achieved by giving selected exporting firms more autonomy in decision-making, by linking exporters closer to the international markets and by offering them additional export incentives. The main additional incentives currently being considered by the authorities include: (1) preferential access to, and additional availability of, funds for export-oriented investments and export production and sales financing; (2) improved supplies of raw materials and other inputs needed for exports; and (3) higher foreign exchange retention rights.

2.126 China's commodity export production system can be viewed as a set of extra incentives that policy-makers are willing to offer a select group of enterprises producing for export. However, little detail was made available to the mission about the rationale for the policy, the basic selection criteria, and the institutional arrangements for the export commodity system. Limited information was obtained on how the commodity production system is working or is expected to work in practice, but it does appear to have some flaws.

2.127 First, the system is likely to be biased in favor of existing exporters/producers and traditional export products. It is easier for the authorities to work with established exporting firms producing traditional goods, since they are likely to yield quicker results at lower risk. However, this approach also prevents or at least reduces the access to incentives by other (perhaps more efficient) producers and hampers the emergence of new products in which China may have a comparative advantage.

2.128 Second, it appears that several layers of authority (MOFERT, the production ministries and the provincial/municipal governments) offer different basic and additional incentives to the producers under their supervision. The result is a multiple effective incentive environment and possibly greater distortions and perhaps less than optimal allocation of scarce financial, fiscal and foreign exchange resources for promoting exports.

2.129 In sum, it seems that the export commodity production system may be a rather costly way to promote China's exports, as opposed to the more neutral export promotion policy discussed below. This observation is particularly true, given that the authorities' objective is to increase the level of the country's exports and improve their efficiency, composition and degree of transformation. It is the mission's view that the well-functioning, basic export incentive system outlined below would be more adequate and cost-effective. Based on the experience of other countries, it can also be expected that such an incentive framework would also encourage smaller firms and indirect exporters to enter the export production chain.

2.130 Exporting firms operating under the foreign investment incentives enjoy an additional set of incentives. If an exporting joint-venture enterprise sells at least 70 percent of its production abroad, it is entitled to lower income taxes (one-half the rate charged other enterprises) even after the initial period of the tax holidays and reductions after the investment has expired. A potentially powerful incentive for exports, this could also be a self-defeating one, since it is not in accordance with internationally accepted practices. Here again, offering joint-venture exporters an automatic and administratively well-functioning basic incentive environment may prove to be a more viable, longer-term solution.

Issues and Options for a New Export Policy

(a) The neutrality concept in an export promotion policy

2.131 The following description and analysis of an export incentive framework is based largely on the experience of a number of East Asian economies that have had remarkable success in expanding their exports in the past two decades. This success rests, above all, on a trade and industrial strategy that stresses specialization based on comparative advantage, rather than on a simple effort to increase foreign exchange earnings via higher exports. The export policy complementing such a strategy, which is now being emulated by a number of other developing countries, focuses on removing the disadvantages domestic firms may face vis-a-vis foreign competitors in world markets.

2.132 A country cannot exploit its comparative advantages in the world market through specialization unless its enterprises are able to compete with foreign producers on equal terms and conditions. As such, domestic firms must operate in a "neutral" environment where prices evolve in undistorted fashion. Specifically, domestic firms need a realistic exchange rate, free trade with respect to inputs and outputs, competitive financial and primary input markets, and non-discriminatory domestic taxes.

2.133 If a country's trade and other policies provide positive protection for import-substituting activities, the basic neutral status for exporters reduces the anti-export bias, but it does not eliminate it. Exporters will be competing abroad under similar conditions as those faced by other competitors, but they will not enjoy incentives equivalent to producers selling domestically. The anti-export bias will be eliminated only if exporters are given additional incentives, so that the effective level of incentives to exporters equals that afforded to import-substituting activities.

2.134 Several elements are crucial for a neutral status to function efficiently and thus for an export promotion framework to be successful. First, the incentives reducing or offsetting the anti-export bias need to be given at the firm level, in a non-discriminatory way, to any enterprise participating in exports. Second, administrative arrangements, that ensure automaticity and equal treatment of all activities generating export value added, and that prevent abuse of the incentives and offer administrative convenience, need to be put in place.

BOX 2.2: THE MODIFIED TRADITIONAL INCENTIVE ENVIRONMENT
--A HYPOTHETICAL EXAMPLE--

Assume a hypothetical example, in which a firm exceeds its export target by 30 percent, at say US$130 as opposed to the planned amount of US$100. In this case, the effective retention right enjoyed by the firm would be 25.8 percent (12.5 yuan, i.e. the retention on the US$100 planned exports, plus 21.0 yuan, i.e. 70 percent of the export amount exceeding the planned level: (12.5 + 21.0)/130 = 25.8 percent).

Although not officially permitted, foreign exchange retention rights are occasionally traded at a premium. Often mentioned is a premium of one yuan per each US$ generated by exports. In our example, such an explicit premium on foreign exchange would represent 7 percent of the yuan equivalent of the firm's total exports.

In addition, FTCs receive 3 fen for each dollar earned within the plan target and 10 fen for each dollar exceeding the target value. In our hypothetical case, the exporting FTC would receive six yuan in bonuses, equivalent to 1.2 percent of the value of exports.

As regards export procurement prices, for an export worth US$130 valued at the official exchange rate (US$1 = RMB3.7), the yuan equivalent the producer receives would be approximately 480 yuan. The firm could sell the same product domestically for, say, 650 yuan. It would therefore lose 170 yuan if it exported at the official exchange rate. By deducting the accounting losses stemming from domestic taxes and fees and assuming a 12 percent consolidated industrial and commercial tax rate and other fees, the firm would get 560 yuan for its exports (implying an effective exchange rate of RMB 4.3 to a dollar, exceeding the official rate by 16.2 percent), and the trading corporation would assume a loss of 90 yuan, which is the difference between the firm's cost of production and the price in the international market.

Since the "foreign exchange entitlement quota" in practice means that the firm has to repurchase the foreign exchange needed from the Bank of China, the exporter bears the foreign exchange risk. In the case of the July 1986 devaluation (from yuan 3.2 to 3.7 for a dollar), exporters whose pre-devaluation dollar earnings were converted into local currency at 3.2 yuan for one dollar subsequently had to "buy back" the foreign exchange at 3.7 yuan for a dollar. In our hypothetical example, in which a firm exports US$130 and receives an effective retention rate of 25.8 percent, the effective loss to the enterprise in such a case would be about 13 percent.

In sum, the effective incentives for Chinese exporters resulting from phe existing export promotion regime depend on several factors: the degree of effective retention, the export target bonuses, the effective premium obtained in the informal foreign exchange market (or on imports the firm can undertake as a result of its export earnings) and the degree of foreign exchange risk borne by the exporter. The resulting incentives are, however, non-transparent, they vary in a discretional manner from firm to firm (depending on how individual firms make use of them), and they may lead to outcomes unintended by policy-makers, such as under-targetting of exports, imports of consumer goods, and illegal foreign exchange transactions.

(b) Basic export incentives - A critical assessment

2.135 Conceptually, the basic export incentive system is aimed at achieving a neutral status for exporters defined earlier. China's exporters often have to compete with producers from developed countries that operate under a system of flexible and realistic exchange rates, virtual free trade in inputs and outputs, prices that normally reflect scarcity values, competitive financial and primary input markets, and non-discriminatory domestic taxes. To put Chinese exporters on an equal footing with such competitors, those policy conditions have to be "simulated" to approximate the neutral status for export activities.

2.136 Access to foreign exchange. Experience in a number of successful exporting developing countries has shown that maintaining a realistic exchange rate for exporters, irrespective of the kind of trade policy a country employs, is key to export development. In addition, guaranteeing exporters automatic and easy access to the foreign exchange needed for imports is vital if producers are to seize the opportunities to export.

2.137 The current practice of foreign exchange retention rights has undoubtedly been an important incentive for Chinese enterprises to engage in exports. Most enterprises interviewed by the mission considered the right to retain and subsequently use their foreign exchange earnings as the most important incentive to export. Nevertheless, many firms also noted that there are serious limitations on the use of foreign exchange.

2.138 First, the exporter's retention is not in the form of "cash" or a foreign exchange deposit that allows automatic use of foreign currency. Rather, it is an entitlement right that requires sometimes lengthy procedures before the exporter can use his foreign exchange. Firms interviewed said that it takes at least one week to get an authorization to use foreign exchange.

2.139 Second, the "entitlement quota" de facto allows the exporter to "buy back" the required foreign exchange, with the firm bearing the foreign exchange risk. According to some exporters interviewed by the mission, firms that had exported before the July 1986 devaluation, for example, had to redeem their foreign exchange rights at the higher rate (yuan 3.7 to US$1) than the one at which their export proceeds were converted into yuan (yuan 3.2 to US$1).

2.140 Third, the trade authorities have the right to deny the import of certain goods, either because there is comparable domestic production or because the good in question is a luxury item. This authority to deny imports has limited the use of foreign exchange rights on the part of exporters, in particular since no formal mechanism to trade these rights exists. On the other hand, exporters whose import requirements are met via the foreign exchange budget (e.g., exports under the command plan) prefer to purchase the foreign exchange needed for export production from the central foreign currency pool and to save their foreign exchange rights for general imports (or perhaps trade them informally at a premium).

2.141 Clearly, the current arrangements do not permit Chinese exporters (producers and foreign trade corporations) automatic access to foreign exchange to meet their import needs. Regardless of the type of foreign exchange retention and/or allocation system China adopts in the future, all producers of exports should have automatic, ready and administratively easy access to foreign exchange to purchase the imported inputs needed for exports. A quasi-automatic system of foreign exchange use appears to be available to export enterprises with foreign investors (various types of joint ventures). Provided adequate control mechanisms are introduced regarding the use of foreign exchange, there is no reason why such a system should not also be extended to Chinese exporters.

2.142 Duty-free imports for exports. Chinese exporters can, in principle, get exemptions from import duties on imported inputs required for exports. The system, however, is not automatic. Whether and under what arrangements a duty exemption for the enterprise's exports is granted depends above all on the firm's connections with its trading corporation and with the government. The mission found that larger, well-established exporters have no difficulty getting duty-free imports, often via an apparently well-functioning bonded warehouse system or through their foreign trade corporations' import facilities. Smaller exporters and firms that export only occasionally, on the other hand, often end up paying import duties. A duty draw-back system, whereby firms get reimbursed for the duty paid on imports once the products have been exported, exists in principle but is not well-known to exporters and seems to be used only rarely.

2.143 The duty exemption is administered by the General Customs Administration. Upon a firm's request, usually through the foreign trade corporation, the Customs Administration physically checks the imported goods needed for export production and subsequently authorizes their duty-free entrance. Prior to the shipment of the export goods, the Administration inspects the final product and ascertains that the imported components were indeed used. A 3-5 percent wastage allowance is normally permitted. In the case of irregularities, the import duty and a fine are levied on the firm. Abuse on the part of producers and/or foreign trade corporations is reportedly very rare.

2.144 Enterprises operating under various joint-venture arrangements seem to have more automatic and administratively simpler duty and domestic indirect tax exemptions. All imports, including machinery and spare parts, can be brought into the country duty-free, as long as the joint venture produces for export. Most joint-venture firms are operating through a bonded warehouse system. In addition, the recently published provisions for foreign investment give exporting joint-venture enterprises additional incentives, such as an exemption from the consolidated industrial and commercial tax, a temporary exemption and subsequent reduction in the enterprise income tax, priority in obtaining short-term loans from domestic banks, and preferential treatment in export/import procedures.

2.145 Domestic suppliers to joint-venture firms, as well as suppliers to Chinese exporters (so-called indirect exporters), are generally not entitled to duty and tax exemptions. However, the mission came across some instances (mostly involving well-established exporters with longer-term relationships with their suppliers) in which an exception was made, and indirect exporters were exempted from the import duties.

2.146 Assuring exporters free access to imported raw materials and intermediate inputs at world prices is an important element of the basic neutral status. Experience in many developing countries has shown that this condition can be achieved, even if the country's trade policy offers relatively high protection to domestic industries. To reach a free trade status for a country's exporting sector, all producers of goods that generate export value added should be freed from or given automatic import licenses for raw materials and other inputs (in cases where import licenses are required). They should also be exempt from or reimbursed for import duties and indirect taxes on imports. Allowing exporters access to duty-free inputs is perhaps the single most important step in reducing the anti-export bias.

2.147 As pointed out, China's duty exemption scheme does not offer all exporters automatic free trade status. Access to imported inputs with tariffs and other taxes is not automatic and is often administered subjectively. Exporters who apply for imports needed for their production have to put up with the lengthy administrative procedure that requires a foreign exchange authorization and often the issuance of import licenses for each import transaction individually (see section A).

2.148 Further, as mentioned above, approval of requests for imports is not automatic. In cases where similar domestic production exists, the applying firm has to prove to the authorities that the product proposed for import is of superior quality and/or has other characteristics that make it indispensable for exports. The mission found out from the enterprises interviewed that frequently their import requests were turned down because of the existence of domestic production. That practice discourages exporters and their foreign trade corporations from even applying for the imports needed for exports. In some cases, the mission discovered that the trading companies themselves discouraged the producing firm from attempting to import goods that were produced domestically. This "self-censorship" in import decisions can be potentially detrimental to China's export efforts, particularly as industry attempts to move into higher value-added products requiring more sophisticated transformation processes and inputs.

2.149 In the area of import duty exemptions, just as in the case of the access to foreign exchange, the experience of the joint-venture export companies could be a useful guide. Under the new provisions for foreign investments, export companies can bring inputs, spare parts and components needed for export production into China free of duties, other import taxes and import licenses. Provided this environment proves satisfactory, the authorities should consider extending it to Chinese exporters. Again, there appears to be little justification for discriminating against wholly Chinese-owned export facilities so long as they are internationally competitive. Otherwise, the difference in incentives between the two systems is likely to encourage the establishment of "artificial" ventures with fictitious foreign partners, so that the Chinese company can benefit from the generous incentive scheme available to joint-venture exports.

2.150 Because of its discretionary nature, China's duty exemption is biased against smaller firms and occasional exporters and indirect exporters. As pointed out in earlier, larger, established exporters have set up arrangements directly with the Customs Adminstration or through their foreign trade corporations, whereby their imports can be brought in free of the duties and other domestic taxes levied on imports. In the case of Shanghai, for example, one of the largest points of entry and exit of merchandise in China, the Customs Administration operates imports for over 300 firms (20 of which are foreign trade corporations and 200 of which are joint ventures). Over 100 of the exporting firms in Shanghai operate through a bonded warehouse system. The Customs Administration has developed a system of import coefficients that serve as the basis for control of the larger exporters.

2.151 Smaller exporters visited by the mission fell broadly into two groups: they were unaware of their entitlement to duty-free imports for their exports and were paying all the duties levied; or they had to go through a lengthy procedure to obtain an exemption.

2.152 In addition to the duty exemption scheme (or the temporary import scheme, as it is known in some countries), most countries also have a duty draw-back system that allows reimbursement of the import duties once exports have taken place. A duty draw-back scheme can be particularly useful for occasional exporters, who at the time of importation do not know if they will sell domestically or abroad. As pointed out earlier, reimbursement of import duties is apparently less well-known in China and is very rarely used.

2.153 Finally, it should be pointed out that China does not allow domestic suppliers of exporters (so-called indirect exporters) duty- and tax-free importation of the inputs needed for production sold to final exporters. The only important exception are production enterprises directly supplying the trading corporations. The mission encountered several cases in which the final exporter was importing inputs that were being produced in China (at competitive costs and of international quality), but because no duty/tax exemption was granted the Chinese products were more expensive than the imports. These examples illustrate how the creation of a free trade status for all firms contributing to export value added can increase the domestic content of Chinese exports and bring benefits from exports to a larger number of Chinese enterprises.

2.154 Tax-free domestic inputs for exports. Similar to the import duty, in principle, Chinese exporters are also entitled to the exemption (or reimbursement) of the consolidated industrial and commercial tax on exported goods. However, this tax is an important source of revenue for the provincial and local governments, which have been reluctant to give it up. The mission found that only in isolated cases were exporters either exempted from or reimbursed for the industrial and commercial tax.

2.155 It was argued before that competitors in the international markets normally operate in an environment in which inputs are purchased at world market prices free of domestic taxes. This environment is a precondition for a free trade system and implies that exporters have to be exempt from all the indirect domestic taxes that are normally levied on local inputs. Based on the experience of several exporting developing countries, an indirect domestic tax exemption is an important step toward neutrality and is an internationally accepted practice.

2.156 China's consolidated industrial and commercial tax is levied on all domestically produced input including those used for exports. The tax ranges between 5 and 35 percent for the bulk of the products (see China: Finance and Investment, Report No. 6445-CHA) and can thus increase exporters' costs significantly. Unless the exporter gets reimbursed or exempted from this tax, he will be at a disadvantage vis-a-vis foreign competitors.

2.157 The mission's interviews indicated that firms frequently are unaware that they can get an indirect tax exemption or reimbursement. Further, the consolidated industrial and commercial tax is collected by the provincial and municipal governments and forms an important source of their revenue. Despite their desire to promote exports from their territory, local authorities have been reluctant to forfeit or pay back the consolidated tax levied on exports.

2.158 In sum, the domestic indirect tax exemption system for China's exports suffers from deficiencies similar to those in the import duty exemption scheme. The system is not automatic, it discriminates against smaller firms and occasional or first-time exporters, it is administratively costly and it excludes indirect exporters. Many potential exporters may never consider selling abroad, and many potential suppliers to final exporters never get included in the export production chain. As regards existing exporting firms, their profits (or losses) are affected by indirect taxes or by the costly procedures to get a tax exemption or rebate.

2.159 Financing of exports. There seems to be no specific facility in China to finance the production and sale of exports. Producing firms that desire working capital financing for production destined for exports can obtain bank loans for up to 70 percent of the value of production. In some cases (e.g., Fujian Province), all production can be financed by banking sources. The loan terms and conditions for pre-shipment export financing are identical to those for domestic production. Normally, the annual interest rate is between 7-8 percent, with a maturity of up to one year.

2.160 Local currency financing for domestic inputs in the industrial and agricultural sectors is provided by the Industrial and Commercial Bank and the Agricultural Bank, respectively, whereas the Bank of China offers foreign currency loans for imported inputs needed for export production. According to firms interviewed by the mission, the only difference between financing for local sales and exports is that the applications for the latter are processed faster, a fact that can occasionally be a considerable incentive to exporters. No pre- or post-shipment guarantee and credit insurance schemes seem to be available to the exporters and the banks. In many cases, however, the FTC procuring the goods has to guarantee the firm's foreign currency loan.

2.161 Traditionally, the FTC obtained the funds to finance export procurement through budgetary appropriations, based on their export plans. Lately, however, they have had to rely increasingly on bank loans and their own funds to finance the purchase of export goods from producers. These two sources now account for the bulk of their pre-shipment financing. Post-shipment (sales) financing is provided to the trading companies in local currency at 7.2 percent a year. Most sales financing is provided for a period not exceeding one year, although lately there have been some cases where the Bank of China has financed exports of heavy machinery and equipment with medium-term loans.

2.162 The experience of successful exporting developing countries has shown that one of the most important export incentives is assurance of automatic and equal access to export financing for all firms that generate export value added. Export financing at uniform interest rates for all economic activities generating value added for exports is critical, if a country is to exploit its export potential fully. In industrialized countries with highly developed money and capital markets, such access is ensured by the financial markets themselves. In most developing countries, however, the financial markets are shallow and segmented, and the government usually has to intervene to ensure adequate working capital financing for exporting.

2.163 Underdeveloped financial markets and other distortions in developing countries' markets normally lead to smaller and medium-size firms having great difficulty obtaining adequate financing for export production and sales. To alleviate this situation, many developing countries have, over the past two-and-a-half decades, established export financing facilities in their central banks or foreign trade banks, where pre- and post-shipment working capital loans given by commercial banks, usually for non-traditional exports, are rediscounted. Export financing schemes have been particularly important in the export success of some developing countries in East Asia but are also in use in a number of Latin American countries, e.g., Mexico (see Box 2.3).

2.164 In many countries, export financing facilities are complemented by pre- and post-shipment guarantee and export credit insurance schemes that encourage commercial bank financing of small and medium-size exporters and provide some coverage against the risks of international trade. Such risk-pooling schemes, set up by governments, have been crucial in offering a neutral status to all firms contributing value added for exports, particularly small enterprises and indirect exporters.

2.165 In China, it appears that large exporters and foreign trade corporations have no difficulty obtaining working capital financing for their production and sales. However, even for those exporters, access to bank funds is not automatic, the financing does not cover the entire value of exports, and

BOX 2.3: MEXICO'S EXPERIENCE IN PROMOTING EXPORTS

The case for a neutral incentive framework for exporters is based above all on the experience of several East Asian economies, including South Korea. Over the past two decades, these economies have been improving the policies, instruments and institutions needed to further promote and develop their exports. In addition, several other developing countries have also embarked upon more outward-oriented growth strategies and have developed incentives to promote exports.

Mexico has, since the 1982 financial crisis and in particular after the sharp fall in world oil prices, developed a comprehensive export development strategy to promote non-oil exports. The country's main objectives regarding overall trade reform and the focus of its export development strategy were spelled out in an Export Development Program published in the second quarter of 1985. The program establishes concrete growth targets for non-oil exports for the four-year period and emphasizes that the export strategy objective is a considerable increase and diversification of Mexican non-oil exports over the next four years. This objective will be achieved by further liberalizing the economy, encouraging efficiency, sharpening the policy focus and improving the measures and instruments supporting export development.

Mexico's export program includes the following specific policy measures and actions considered necessary for the execution of the export development strategy: (a) promotion (through financial and technical assistance) of investment projects aimed at increasing export-oriented production; (b) institutional support offered to exporters and streamlining and decentralization of administrative procedures; (c) financial and non-financial assistance to exporters; (d) international negotiations and non-conventional forms of foreign trade; and (e) improvements in the infrastructure necessary for exports.

The program's principal contribution to the promotion of Mexico's non-oil exports will be the creation of a "neutral status" for exporters. This status will be achieved by automatic access to financial and non-financial incentives for all producers generating value added for exports. Specifically, the program introduces duty- and indirect tax-free imports not only for final exporters but also for their suppliers (so-called indirect exporters), as well as access to official lines of credit for indirect exporters' and trading companies' pre- and post-shipment financing. In addition, foreign trade and customs procedures for exports/imports are being simplified and modernized; export financing, credit insurance and guarantee schemes have been amplified and streamlined; and the creation and development of trading companies have been encouraged.

Mexico recognizes that successful execution of such an ambitious program requires considerable strengthening of the institutions responsible for carrying out the export strategy (e.g., the Ministry of Commerce and Industrial Development and the National Bank for Foreign Trade). Moreover, individual agencies' responsibilities and arrangements for inter-institutional coordination are being addressed in detail. A high level Ad Hoc Committee for export promotion was appinted in late 1985 by the President, with a mandate to prepare specific proposals designed to carry out Mexico's medium-term non-oil export development strategy. As a result of the committee's work, a series of specific policy instruments was announced in early 1986 aimed at enabling Mexico to increase significantly its export effort and exploit fully the considerable export potential of first-time exporters and small and medium-size manufacturers.

Perhaps the most important innovation in the 1986 export promotion policy package is the introduction of the domestic letter of credit (DLC). The DLC is a commercial document issued by the final exporter stating that it will pay for the merchandise procured by the supplier under the terms and conditions specified in the document itself. Since this document is a negotiable commercial paper, commercial banks are willing to use it to rediscount with the government foreign trade bank the working capital financing they provide to indirect exporters. This characteristic of the DLC, namely, its acceptance as a commercial document by local banks, not only allows indirect exporters access to export financing, but also gives them access to the foreign exchange needed for imports, duty-free imports for export production, and exemption of indirect domestic taxes.

The introduction of the DLC has been complemented by an improved and expanded temporary admission scheme that allows established exporters, who sign a multi-year export contract with the authorities, to import inputs, machinery and equipment used for export production duty-free. In addition, trading companies now enjoy automatic access to export financing and exemption from the value-added tax and other domestic indirect taxes. Under the new incentive package, the guarantee requirements for temporary imports have been reduced, exporters have the right to retain up to 100 percent of their foreign exchange earnings (in foreign exchange accounts with domestic banks) for future imports and their suppliers' import needs, the various export financing credit lines have been consolidated, and the export insurance and guarantee schemes have been simplified.

the approval process is lengthy on the part of the banks. There seems to be no allocation of credit to finance the production and sale of China's exports. According to the firms interviewed by the mission, the speed and ease of access to export financing depends on how tight or easy the overall credit policy is. When credit is tight, it is more difficult and time-consuming to get export financing regardless of the volume and growth in export orders.

2.166 In the case of smaller firms, production for exports is often financed as part of general working capital financing. In a few cases, the mission found that the foreign trade corporations provided some financing to the supplying production enterprises. Indirect exporters other than output-supplying producers working with the foreign trade corporations have no access to export financing.

2.167 Not surprisingly, in the absence of an export financing framework, there are no pre- and post-shipment finance guarantee and no explicit export credit insurance schemes in China. Of course, the bulk of China's trade is still carried out by a limited number of monopoly foreign trade corporations. In contrast, export insurance and guarantee schemes, combined with export financing, have proved vital in the export success of many developing countries. As China reforms its enterprises and banks, the provision of pre- and post-shipment guarantees and assurance of bank export financing will become increasingly important for the future success of the country's exports, perhaps under the leadership and coordination of the Bank of China.

(c) Additional export incentives

2.168 The four basic elements, described above form the so-called basic export incentive framework needed to attain neutral status for a country's export sector. In many cases, however, offering these incentives to exporters is not enough to offset the anti-export bias of the trade policy environment. Even when exporters enjoy an environment approximating the conditions under which their foreign competitors operate, the protection enjoyed by domestic industries may still make exports less profitable than domestic sales, particularly under conditions of excess domestic demand.

2.169 This anti-export bias can be eliminated by "extending" neutral status for exporting activities, so that they are not discriminated against in favor of import-substituting activities. The level of export incentives in such a situation would equal that of import substitution. However, offering all exporters extra incentives (e.g., in the form of cash grants provided by the government) to eliminate that bias can be very costly and is not in accordance with internationally accepted norms. Most developing country governments, therefore, opt for a strategy, whereby basic export incentives are complemented by a temporary system of additional export incentives and, more importantly, by a gradual reduction in the country's protection for import-substituting industries.

2.170 The set of policy measures under China's export commodity production system can be considered a special form of additional export incentives designed to encourage investments in export-oriented production. Another set of incentives Chinese authorities are considering in the context of the export commodity production system and for exporters under the foreign investment incentives is longer-term credit for export-oriented projects.

2.171 An adequate supply of medium- and long-term investment funds for export-oriented projects is often critical to the success of a country's export efforts, particularly where it is trying to diversify its productive capacity and develop and promote new exports. In many developing countries, smaller firms (both existing and potential exporters) often have difficulty borrowing development capital and this constrains the expansion of their productive capacity and thus deprives the country of additional exports. A shortage of domestic medium- and long-term funds for project financing and the commercial banks' growing preference for lending to well-established, usually large-size, firms has been worsened by the developing countries' increasingly difficult access to external borrowing.

2.172 With the growing role of demand management policies and enterprises' increased reliance on bank credit, the situation regarding exporters' longer-term financing in China will not differ significantly from that in many other developing countries. If China wants to develop new production facilities for exports, considerable additional domestic and external funds will have to be made available. Because of a lack of data, the mission was unable to assess the volume of funds channeled to the export sector. It seems, however, that improved coordination in the area of export project financing (with the Bank of China perhaps assuming the leadership role) is needed to make the best use of existing financial resources.

2.173 Export enterprises operating under the foreign investment regulations receive another important incentive: they are allowed to import machinery and equipment without import licenses and duties, as long as the bulk of their production is exported. Such a system has been applied successfully by several developing countries to all exporters (domestic and joint ventures), and it is suggested that all Chinese exporters be given the same right. Adequate monitoring and control arrangements will prevent abuse.

2.174 Table 2.7 summarizes the principal features and characteristics of the export incentives environment described above.

(d) Non-financial incentives for export promotion

2.175 The incentive framework described above deals predominantly with financial measures and the instruments affecting firms' decisions to export. Experience in several developing countries that are successful exporters indicates, however, that other incentives are needed if a country is to exploit fully its export potential. The incentives environment needs to be complemented by non-financial incentives, frequently in the form of technical assistance and institutional support. These are of particular importance when smaller firms, first time- and indirect exporters become involved with exporting, and where new export products and/or markets are concerned. The

Table 2.7: SUMMARY OF A POSSIBLE EXPORT INCENTIVE FRAMEWORK

Incentive Measures	Necessary Conditions: Automatic	All activities for export	Administrative efficiency	Prevention of abuse	GATT accord
NEUTRAL STATUS: Basic Incentives (Production/Sales)					
o Duty-free imports	NN	NN	**	**	XX
o Indirect tax exemption	NN	NN	**	**	XX
o Access /a to foreign exchange	NN	NN	**	??	XX
o Access to working capital financing	NN	XX	**	??	XX
EXTENDED NEUTRAL STATUS: Additional Incentives (Production/Sales/Investment)					
o Duty-free imports of capital goods	NN	JV	**	??	??
o Income tax exemption	NN	JV	**	??	!!
o Additional production & sales financing	NN	JV/EB	**	**	??
o Investment financing	NN	XX	**	??	??
o Accelerated depreciation	NN	JV	**	??	!!

Notes: Keys:
XX Exist
JV Exist only for joint ventures
EB Exist only for export production bases
NN Does not exist
** Needs improvement
?? Unclear
!! Incompatible with GATT

/a Automatic access to foreign exchange could replace the current foreign exchange retention scheme.

central government has a crucial role to play in providing non-financial assistance to exporters.

2.176 In the case of China, where it is expected that a growing number of firms will become engaged in export production and sales, the provision of non-financial, technical assistance to exporters is particularly important. It most likely will have to focus on foreign trade management, a foreign trade information network, and institutional support and coordination.

2.177 Traditionally, some 12 foreign trade corporations have accounted for more than three-quarters of China's external trade. Given their almost exclusive role in conducting business with the rest of the world, they have acquired considerable knowledge over the years about the international markets in their respective lines of business, products and marketing channels. It appears that little of this knowledge is shared with the producers supplying the foreign trade corporations. Generally speaking, producers have been delinked from world markets and receive little or no information about requirements of and changes in demand.

2.178 The expected increase in autonomy and responsibility at the enterprise level will require managerial skills that are currently very limited in China. Once key business decisions (including those affecting firm's exports and imports) are made at the enterprise level, and the consequences of those decisions are borne by the enterprise, management skills become crucial. Training competent enterprise managers for firms engaging in foreign trade will be an important element in the success of China's export development strategy.

2.179 Equally important will be a foreign trade information network and the delivery of technical assistance to exporters. At the company level, information and assistance should concentrate mainly on specific markets and products (areas such as quality control, product design, packaging and marketing) for exporting firms. As the number of firms entering the export markets grows, ways should be explored as to how best to organize these firms to exchange ideas, and experiences and propose improvements in export policies, instruments and practices (similar to exporters' associations and/or chambers of commerce in other countries).

(e) Institutional arrangements for export promotion

2.180 In China, as in many other countries, a number of government agencies are involved in export promotion. Most, however, seem to be engaged in carrying out export plan targets, without necessarily following a broader strategy, and often act in an uncoordinated way. For example, to fulfill their export targets, the provinces and/or foreign trade corporations often compete for the same (limited) volume of exportable supplies. The provincial governments, however, create special incentives for exporters in their province with respect to foreign exchange retention rights. This system discourages the indirect exporters from supplying products to the final exporters in other provinces and potentially deprives China of the benefit of more and higher value added exports.

2.181 In general, the various incentives available to Chinese exporters (foreign exchange retention rights, bonuses, procurement prices, financing, and duty- and tax exemptions) are administered by various agencies (SPC, Bank of China, MOFERT, Customs, Ministry of Finance, Industrial and Commercial Bank) at the local and national levels. In several interviews the mission had with those agencies, the foreign trade corporations and producers, it became apparent that there is no central authority with an overview as to how the export promotion policy is being carried out and by which organization.

2.182 An effective export development policy for the future will require better coordination among the agencies participating in export promotion and a strong central authority responsible for the design and execution of export promotion policies. Countries that have established this type of structure have usually found it necessary to authorize a high-level body with these tasks. This body is usually supported in its work by a secretariat and/or an executing agency (e.g. a "Trade Development Council" or "Export Promotion Board"), which serves as a catalyst for inter-agency coordination, as well as for the design and implementation of the export promotion policy.

C. Concluding Remarks--Toward a More Efficient Trade Policy Environment

2.183 This annex has described the emerging trade policy environment in China and assessed its effectiveness in realizing the economic benefits from foreign trade. In light of this analysis and that of Annex 1, this last section offers some concluding observations on China's ongoing reform, which is aimed in part at building a trade policy environment that will strengthen the contribution of foreign trade to the country's modernization and development. These remarks begin by outlining a strategic framework for the trade policy reform over the long term. Based on the strategic framework, a number of policy actions are suggested that can be undertaken in the short to medium term. These suggestions are by no means comprehensive, but are believed to represent realistic transitional policies that can provide a foundation for further progress in the modernization of China's socialist economic system.

Strategic Framework for the Long Term

2.184 While the Open Door policy has resulted in a significant increase in the volume of trade, the trade policy environment may not be conducive to economically efficient trade. The reforms proposed for the import and export environment are closely related to other trade reforms and to macroeconomic reforms. Thus, they should be seen as part of a package of reforms that include reform of trade institutions (Main Report, Chapter 2), and reform in foreign exchange allocation and rate determination (Main Report, Chapters 2 and 3). Further, they would need to be coordinated and sequenced with other domestic economic reforms, including enterprise reform and price reform (Main Report, Chapter 4).

2.185 First, the current trade policy environment may lead China into an overall structure of production that is not internationally competitive: export activities may expand, but for many the economic benefits of net foreign exchange earnings may be less than the economic costs of domestic resources; even through import-substitution activities may expand, their domestic resource costs may still exceed the foreign exchange savings. Second, the policy environment may weaken China's ability to improve its international competitiveness over time: it may offer insufficient incentives for technological change, innovation, product quality improvements, and various cost saving measures in production; the productivity of workers and investments in China may deteriorate relative to those of competing countries. In the long run, the higher level and growth of national income envisioned by the Open Door Policy may be jeopardized.

2.186 While the success of foreign trade is clearly tied to the trade policy environment, an equally important factor is domestic economic conditions. Some of the key conditions are competitive markets, autonomous producers, and the mobility of domestic resources on the basis of efficient prices. Progress toward these conditions, which depends on continued domestic policy reform, is <u>necessary</u> if the full benefits of the Open Door Policy are to be realized. At the same time, the domestic policy reform by itself is not <u>sufficient</u> in bringing to bear the maximum benefits of international trade. For this, a sound trade policy is required. Thus, trade policy reform must be part of a <u>package</u> of economic reforms.

2.187 This concept of a "package" raises several long-term issues of strategic importance. They are important because they suggest that even if domestic conditions were made favorable, the present trade policy environment would not yield efficient trade with maximum benefits. (The main report discusses a parallel and consistent set of strategies and policy actions aimed at improving domestic policy and the enterprise sector and trade policy and the foreign trade sector.)

Taking Advantage of Market Forces

2.188 The modern socialist economic system envisioned by China is one in which economic decisions are made by enterprises, workers, and consumers and where the Government guides these decisions according to national objectives in a planned fashion, taking advantage of the efficieny of prices in conveying economic information. China is now in a transition toward that system, with the Government facing the difficult task of navigating the country through this initial stage without major economic imbalances. While measures based on price incentives are being introduced, they are not yet fully effective; while the role played by traditional physical and administrative measures is being transformed, they continue to influence economic decisions. As such, the Government faces a real danger that increasingly flexible but still distorted prices may begin to guide decisions of economic actors in ways that contradict national objectives and harm the welfare of the people.

2.189 Present circumstances are difficult, and it is understandable that the Government continues to rely on administrative levers to allocate foreign exchange. Nevertheless, there are limits to the ability of any administrative system to meet the objectives of efficient resource allocation and growth. The present system in which the Government attempts to allocate foreign exchange to specific enterprises for specific uses--albeit capable of improvement--can never fully succeed in meeting the objective of efficient allocation of imports. This conclusion is based neither on theory nor ideology, but simply on practicality and common sense.

2.190 In theory, it is always possible to allocate foreign exchange efficiently in a centralized manner. However, to do so requires an enormous amount of economic data of a sort that are not readily available, such as the structure of revenues and costs for every enterprise, world prices of inputs and outputs whether or not they are actually traded, and detailed and up-to-date knowledge of the economy's input-output structure. A multi-sector, multi-enterprise model of the entire economy would be needed to guide sectoral allocations. Once broad sectoral parameters are established, enterprise allocations must be set on the basis of individual cost-benefit analysis. Even in China, with its long tradition and accumulated expertise in planning, such a scheme is not realistic: it is humanly impossible even to approximate this conceptual system.

2.191 In practice, the system is heavily overworked in spite of its decentralization to provincial authorities, with scarce and valuable administrative resources carrying excessive burdens. Thousands of decisions affecting hundreds of firms must be made about which applications to approve and in what amounts. These decisions involve both technical staff and policy-makers in scores of ministries and departments in the central and provincial Governments, as well as those in China's Banking system. Moreover, the system provides significant rents to successful applicants. As long as excess demand for foreign exchange persists enterprises will be encouraged to lobby and intervene in the decision-making of authorities, a situation that will only add to the administrative burden.

2.192 Thus, the first long-term strategy of China's trade policy should be to move away from an exchange control environment that relies primarily on quantitative restrictions, and toward one that is defined by those instruments which can take advantage of market-determined signals and allocations. The advantage of using tariffs rather than quantitative restrictions to limit consumer demand and to stimulate domestic production is well-documented. The ultimate objective should be to move to a system where producers and consumers bid for imported goods in the market, and where the structure of incentives is set by economic levers such as tariffs.

Establishing Equality of Incentives

2.193 In order for individual decisions to reflect more closely the goals of efficient development, the structure of incentives at home should be aligned closely with relative international prices. The fundamental principle of China's trade policy is to conduct foreign trade on the basis of equality and mutual benefit between China and the rest of the world. One important part of that mutual benefit is higher national income and consumption for China and its trading partners. A tariff policy that would help China to realize this benefit would be to establish equality in incentives across all domestic producers.

2.194 The Government has succeeded in promoting vital export industries through selective incentives. The experiments of special economic zones, for example, have also generated positive results and lessons about promoting exports. However, these efforts have created an "air-lock" environment, in which exporters are segregated from the rest of the economy--an environment that is not necessarily conducive to generating new export products and dynamic export producers. In the long run, no country has succeeded in developing an efficient export sector where exporters have been isolated from other enterprises.

2.195 In addition to equalizing incentives for production of exports and production for the domestic market, incentives should be made equal across different activities producing for the domestic market. Existing large disparities in protection across import-substituting activities (see part A) lead resources away from areas of China's international competitiveness. Achieving equality of incentives requires a reduction in the levels of protection to import-substituting activities. The general course of action would consist of setting a timetable for replacing the quantitative restrictions with tariffs, reducing the variance in effective protection rates, and reducing the levels of effective protection to import substitutes in order to bring them into harmony with the incentives for exports. This process would include narrowing the range of tariff rates by gradually reducing the high duties on final goods and by reducing the number of tariff exemptions to as few as possible.

2.196 A long-term program of adjustments in the incentive structure will negatively affect inefficient producers. Rather than justifications for inaction, such cases call for adjustment assistance to workers and producers to raise their productivity and make them better able to compete in the new policy environment. Deferring reform of the incentive structure will simply postpone the required changes and make the adjustment all the more difficult and expensive when it takes place. Change can be gradual, but it cannot be avoided, if China's productive efficiency is to be raised.

Selective Promotion of "Infant" Activities

2.197 The strategy of a moderate and generally uniform structure of incentives does not mean that there will be no cases where selective promotion of an activity is warranted. Overall equality of incentives can usefully be supplemented by selective promotion of a limited number of activities in the economy. The objective of selective promotion should be to accelerate the rate at which the chosen activities achieve international competitiveness through higher rates of technological progress and productivity growth.

2.198 The characteristics of sound selective promotion are: (a) that it be strictly limited in scope to a few activities; (b) that the special incentives be *ex ante* limited in duration; and (c) perhaps most importantly, that the Government be prepared to cease the promotion if the desired improvements in competitiveness are not forthcoming. There is some evidence that where selective promotion of the type outlined has been attempted in conjunction with exposure to foreign competition, particularly in export markets, the rates of productivity change in both the promoted activities and in general have exceeded those of countries, with comparable levels of income and development which have not followed such policies.[1/]

Policy Actions in the Short to Medium Term

2.199 The strategic framework for the long term points to several matters that require the Government's early attention, so that the necessary changes and improvements can begin in the right direction. The suggestions made below focus on the crucial transition period facing China today. At the risk of

---

1/ See L. E. Westphal, "Empirical Justification for the Infant Industry Argument" (World Bank Staff Working Paper, No. 445, March 1981).

repetition, it is critical that the following recommended reforms be coordinated with other reforms, particularly reforms of trade institutions, discussed in the Main Report, Chapter 2.

Restructuring the System of Incentives

2.200 For China's trade policy to achieve greater equality of incentives, policy reforms are needed to generate effective exchange rates for the economy that are based on tariff protection and subsidies alone and that are more uniform across activities. These reforms will require actions on two fronts: further tariff reforms to provide a more desirable structure of effective protection; and movement to a foreign exchange allocation environment that eliminates the need for quantitative restrictions and permits the prices of imported goods to be influenced by tariffs alone.

2.201 As noted earlier, the recent tariff reform in China was a major accomplishment and achieved significant tariff reductions. The reform, however, was pursued under objectives that resulted in a tariff structure that implies a highly variable effective tariff protection. The Customs Tariff Committee recently launched a work program to adapt China's tariff codes to those specified by the International Convention of the Harmonized Commodity Description and Coding System. The new system is likely to double or triple the number of codes (from the current 2,279). Once the new codes are established, the conversion will require setting new tariff rates for a host of more specific product codes. It is suggested that the Government consider using this opportunity to achieve greater equality in the structure of effective tariff protection and greater neutrality of incentives between import substitution and export activities.

2.202 The first step in this medium-term process is for the Customs Tariff Committee to study the structure of effective protection, with the objective of:

(a) proposing alternative structures of tariff rates, to be introduced with the new tariff codes, leading to reduced levels and greater equality in effective rates across activities;

(b) proposing a phased medium-term program to continue to reduce the level and increase the equality of effective rates over time; and

(c) evaluating possible measures and their implications concerning the level and duration of any selective promotion measures.

2.203 Meanwhile, some short-term measures can be taken that would moderate the level of effective tariff protection for final goods production, help reduce the excess demand for import licenses and foreign exchange, and at the same time, increase government revenue. One measure that the Government may wish to consider is to end the current duty exemption granted for capital goods imported for "technical transformation" purposes. If total elimination of that exemption is not feasible immediately, reducing it to a partial exemption--for example, by requiring importers to pay half the relevant duty rate--could be a good starting point.

2.204 Movement away from the system of quantitative restrictions on imports would require that the duty-inclusive prices of importables rise to levels that eliminate excess import demand. The most direct mechanism by which this rise can be achieved is to continue adjustmenting the exchange rate, raising the price of importables and exportables simultaneously.

2.205 While the process of exchange rate adjustment and building the market for foreign exchange is underway, mechanisms may be needed to facilitate a transition to a market-based system of allocating foreign exchange. One mechanism is to utilize the "regulatory tariffs" discussed earlier. They can be developed into a transitional system of import surcharges that uniformly raises the cost to importers of all imports in a specified class of tariff codes. The system could contain several classes, with the surcharges for each set at a level designed to approximate the difference between the prevailing level of domestic prices and the tariff-inclusive price of imports. Once the system is in place, a progressively larger number of goods would be placed in the category of imports that is restricted by neither the plan nor the import licensing system. If import demand rose rapidly or fell precipitously, the surcharges could be adjusted.

2.206 The surcharge system would help reduce the demand for imports and thus for foreign exchange, and the government could continue to raise revenue by capturing the rents associated with access to restricted imports. One particularly important feature of the system is that it helps the government unify and reduce the "effective" exchange rates in the system gradually. It is likely that initially a number of classes of products would be necessary in order to avoid major adverse changes in the average effective rate of protection for each class, as a result of moving from quantitative restrictions to surcharges-cum- tariffs. As the reform proceeds with continued exchange rate adjustments, the surcharge levels in each class would be adjusted. The ultimate objective would be to unify and then eliminate the surcharge system altogether, so that domestic prices for importables would be set by a combination of the exchange rate and revised tariff structure. In the interim, the system would permit enterprises to improve their competitiveness and adjust to the new trade policy environment gradually at a rate set by the rate of adjustment in the surcharges.

2.207 An alternative to the import surcharge approach would be to auction the import licenses. It might also be desirable to allow exporters to offer their retained foreign exchange for sale under the auction scheme. Among the most important questions regarding an auction system are what can be imported, and who is eligible to participate. For the system to function effectively as a transitory mechanism, use of the licenses should be as unrestricted as possible. Ideally, licenses should be completely interchangeable between products, distributed to anyone, and transferable through the auction market.

The licenses would be fixed in terms of the value of the imports, so that the total value of imports could be budgeted and known in advance. Initially, the system could consist of a partial auction of "unrestricted" licenses, accompanied by a gradual widening of the coverage of such unrestricted licenses.

2.208 Under such an auction, imports of those products for which domestic demand and supply were relatively sensitive to price changes (e.g., consumer goods or inessentials) would decline proportionately more than would the imports of those goods for which price sensitivities were less (e.g., raw materials, intermediates, or capital goods).

2.209 An auction mechanism would help reduce the burden of administrative decision-making by the authorities and further narrow the gap between the supply and demand for foreign exchange. When compared with the surcharge approach, however, use of an auction to facilitate the transition has three main drawbacks: first, the level of protection given to producers becomes less explicit; second, the rate of change in that protection cannot be managed by the government; and third, the government cannot capture all the rent in the system as revenue.

2.210 The two alternative approaches described above could be implemented singly, sequentially, or even in concert, depending on circumstances. The important point is that a foreign exchange allocation system characterized by multiple effective rates can only add serious distortions to the economy. It is important, therefore, that these approaches be accompanied by the commitment and policy actions needed to narrow the gap between the official exchange rate and the effective rates implied by the level of the surcharges or the auction price. Finally, it must be emphasized that neither approach is appropriate for, nor are they intended to be, part of the foreign exchange allocation environment in the long term. The final objective of these mechanisms would be to facilitate the transition to a system in which producers and consumers bid for imports in the market, and in which the structure of incentives is set by fiscal measures.

Promoting Efficient Exports

(a) Steps toward neutrality

2.211 The framework for an export promotion policy described earlier focused on the policy environment that encourages efficient exports without introducing a major bias against other activities. Such an environment, if sustained in the medium term, should encourage the emergence of new exports and attract a growing number of producers to engage in this activity. Several of the above elements already exist or are being contemplated by the Government. However, the coverage and administration of the export incentive scheme will have to be improved considerably if the system is to achieve a neutral status for Chinese exporters. Experience in other countries has shown that it takes several years to attain this condition. The basic principles of automaticity, equal treatment of all activities generating export earnings, monitoring and control to prevent abuse, and administrative convenience are also crucial if both existing and potential exporters are to respond to the incentive scheme.

2.212 Thus, the Government may wish to consider as a medium-term objective the introduction of a system whereby the incentives would be given automatically to all enterprises participating in value added for exports. That is, any direct or indirect exporter with an export or domestic letter of credit, firm export order, or any other commercial document acceptable by the authorities and the banks should have automatic and ready access to the foreign exchange, working capital financing, and duty- and tax-free inputs necessary for export production. This status would require a change in current practices where access to incentives is not automatic, is not transparent, and is administratively cumbersome and time-consuming.

(b) Immediate steps

2.213 Achievement of a neutral status for exporters, as described above, is an undertaking that will require detailed preparation and design and perhaps several years to implement. Among the steps necessary for establishing an automatic and neutral environment for exporters are some that can be taken immediately; taking such steps would signal the Government's commitment to promoting efficient exports.

2.214 Public announcement of an export promotion policy. The Government should make its intentions regarding export promotion widely known. A medium-term export promotion program could be announced as an example of China's commitment to reforming the export incentive framework. The announcement could include a tentative calendar of steps for the coming months and years aimed at achieving a more automatic and transparent system of incentives for all activities generating valued added for exports. Institutional responsibilities for the implementation of the policy could also be spelled out, and all producers in China could be made aware of the existing incentives and expected improvements.

2.215 Access to foreign exchange. Until a market for foreign exchange were established, exporters could be entitled to automatic use of the foreign exchange needed for imports for export production. This provision could either be in the form of a "cash retention" that exporters held in their bank accounts (similar to the arrangements for joint venture operations with foreign partners), or it could guarantee exporters ready and automatic access of foreign exchange from the Bank of China. Under the latter option, a special fund could be established at the Bank of China that catered exclusively to exporters' needs for foreign exchange (up to the level of the imported content of the exports).

2.216 Access to working capital financing. Better coordination among the financial agencies providing funds to exporters is needed. Alternatively (and preferably), the authorities may wish to establish an export financing facility (an "export development fund") under the umbrella of, say, the Bank of China. This facility would offer working capital financing in local and foreign currencies for exporters' pre- and post-shipment needs, and could be complemented by an export credit insurance and guarantee facility.

2.217 Import duty and tax exemption. A system whereby all exporters enjoy automatic exemptions from import duties as well as domestic indirect taxes should be put in place immediately. The possibility of introducing a duty drawback scheme for occasional and first-time direct and indirect exporters should also be studied. Administrative arrangements enabling efficient monitoring of firms' export performance and preventing abuse of the system would be needed.

2.218 Technical assistance. Specialized centers to assist exporters in product design, quality control, packaging, and marketing should be set up, perhaps with the help of larger foreign trade corporations and appropriate ministries. In addition, the MOFERT and foreign trade corporations should strengthen the information network and improve the dissemination of information to producers. A high level body could be instrumental in coordinating all these technical assistance activities. Creation of exporters' associations, which could work together with the government, might also be encouraged.

COMMODITIES SUBJECT TO EXPORT LICENSING
(As of November 1, 1986)

No.	Item	Remarks
A.	Commodities Subject to Export Licenses Issued by the Ministry of Foreign Economic Relations and Trade (MOFERT)	
1.	Corn	Including: Mushrooms in salt water, salted and vinegared mushrooms.
2.	Canned mushrooms	
3.	Mushrooms in salt water	
4.	Cotton yarn	Licensing for these 4 textile goods applies only to Hong Kong, Macao and Japan. Cotton yarn and cotton grey cloth include blended yarn and grey cloth containing 75% cotton, not including colored cloth, yarn-dyed cloth and knitted yarn and cloth.
5.	Cotton grey cloth	
6.	Cotton polyester grey cloth	
7.	Cotton polyester yarn	
8.	Cotton	Including: Different kinds of cotton, rejects and wastes.
9.	Rabbits fur	
10.	Sheep hair	Including: Goat haircloth, furless haircloth.
11.	Crude oil	
12.	Oil products	Including: aviation gasoline, automobile gasoline, solvent gasoline, aviation kerosene, lamp kerosene, light diesel oil, regular diesel oil, heavy diesel oil, lube oil, basic lube oil, liquid paraffin, naptha, residual oil, heavy oil, liquid hydrocarbon.
13.	Tungsten and tungsten products	Tungsten products include ammonium tunstate, tungsten trioxide, tungsten powder, tungsten power carbide, cast tungsten powder carbide, tungstic acid.
14.	Coal	Including: Raw coal, screened coal, clean coal, lump coal, low-quality coal (including middlings and slurry),

	mixed coal, coal fines, coal wastes, humic acid materials, shaped coal (including coal briquets, honeycomb briquets).
15. Internal combustion engines and units for farm use	Including: Diesel engines, gasoline engines, kerosene engines, methane engines; units include generators, water pumps and gearboxes using internal combustion engines as power.
16. Leather gloves for labor protection	For those Guangdong cowhide products which are processed with supplied materials or made with the use of foreign capital, export licenses shall be issued by the Office of Guangdon Special Agent authorized by MOFERT.
17. Silks and satins	Including: Mulberry silks, tussah silks, mixed fiber silks, rayons, interweave silks, silk blends, polyester silks.
18. Silks	Including: Mulberry and tussah: cocoons, raw silks, processed silk threads, silk douppioni, spun silk, silk noil yarn, noil, noil rejects, silk rejects, cocoon silk and blended yarns containing the above-mentioned materials.
19. Pearls	Including: Fresh-water pearls, marine pearls, pearl strings, pearl necklaces, pearls for medicinal use.
20. Bleached cotton cloth	Including: Semi-bleached cloth.
21. Bleached cotton polyester cloth	Including: Semi-bleached.
22. Coverall threads	Including: Pagoda threads, which are pure cotton and cotton polyester threads.
23. White oil	
24. Genseng (Round ginseng)	Including: Red ginseng, diced red ginseng, red ginseng beards, strong-pillar ginseng, white ginseng, sun-diced ginseng, diced white ginseng, white ginseng beards, soup ginseng.

25.	Deer antlers	Including: Antlers of sika deer, red deer and white-lipped deer.
26.	Musk	
27.	Chinese angelica	Including: Chinese angelica, tongdi angelica, xiang angelica, Chinese angelica heads.
28.	Eucommia bark	
29.	Tianqi	Also named Sanqi, or root of pseudo-ginseng.
30.	Licorice root and products	Products include ointment, powder, cream and acid.
31.	Stem bark of magnolia officinalis	
32.	Queen bee jelly	Refers to fresh queen bee jelly, fresh royal jelly (including powder), which are raw material commodities, not including prepared medicines.

B. Commodities Subject to Export Licenses Issued by the MOFERT Special Commission Offices Stationed at Major Ports

33.	Peppermint compound and oil	
34.	Black moss	
35.	Cordyceps	Chinese caterpillar fungus.
36.	Milk vetch	Including: Yellow milk vetch, white milk vetch, black milk vetch and jin milk vetch.
37.	Fructus Lycii (Fruit of Chinese wolfberry)	Including: Fructus Lycii and blood Fructus Lycii.
38.	Coptis root (Chinese gold thread)	Including: Coptis root and Xilian variety of coptis root.
39.	Bulb of fritillary	Including: Sichuan, Qing, Song, Lu, Ping, Min, Xinjiang, Yunnan and Zhejian (ingot) varieties.
40.	Fresh or dried root of rehmannia	

41.	Chinese yam rhizome	
42.	Tuckahoe Poria	Including: Tuckahoe Poria in the forms of flakes, chunks, lumps.
43.	Chuanxiong (rhizome)	
44.	Luohan fruit	
45.	Chrysanthemum	Including the gong and yellow varieties.
46.	Dangshen (Root of Radix Codonopsis Pilosulae)	
47.	Pinellia (tuber)	
48.	Rhubarb	
49.	White peony root	
50.	Tuber of dwarf lilyturf	
51.	Honeysuckle flower	
52.	Ox-knee root	
53.	Tuber of Rhizoma Corydalis	
54.	Root bark of Tree Peony	
55.	Fruit of weeping forsythia	
56.	Fruit of medicinal cornel	
57.	Tuber of elevated gastrodia	
58.	Cow-bezoar	Including: artificial cow-bezoar
59.	Root of balloonflower	
60.	Large-headed atractylodes	
61.	Insulin	
62.	Eel fries	
63.	A.C. electric motors and A.C. generating-units	Including: Single-phase and three phase.

64.	Machine tools	
65.	Heparinate	Medicinal materials, not prepared medicines.
66.	Jiemeisu	Medicinal materials, not prepared medicines.
67.	Chinese ephedra	Medicinal materials, not prepared medicines.
68.	Paraffin	
69.	Cassia bark	License issued by Office of Guangzhou Special Agent.
70.	Cassia oil	License issued by Office of Guangzhou Special Agent.
71.	Ramie and textiles	Including: Raw ramie, degummed ramie, ramie slivers, ramie droppings; pure ramie yarns, threads, grey, bleached and grass cloth, and also yarns, threads, grey and bleached cloth spun with a blend of ramie and other fibers.
72.	Flax textiles	Including: Pure flax yarns, threads, grey and bleached cloth, and also yarns, threads, grey, bleached and grass cloth spun with a blend of flax and other fibers.
73.	Hu Ma (bast fiber) textiles	Including: Pure he ma yarns, threads, grey and bleached cloth, and also yarns, thread, grey, bleached and grass cloth spun with a blend of hu ma and other fibers.
74.	Hemp textiles	Including: Pure hemp yarns, threads, grey and bleached cloth, and also yarns, thread, grey bleached and grass cloth spun with a blend of hemp and other fibers.

C. Commodities Subject to Export Licenses Issued by the Commissions on Economic and Foreign Trade of the Provinces, Autonomous Regions, Municipalities Directly under the Central Government and Cities Drawing Up Their Own Plans.

75.	Sugar	Including: White granulated sugar and white fine sugar.
76.	Tung oil	

77.	Peanuts	Peanuts are purchased and marketed under centralized plans. Licenses are issued on the basis of contracts concluded and verified by the national corporation. Include raw peanuts in shells and raw shelled peanuts.
78.	Sesame	
79.	Canned water chestnuts in water	
80.	Frozen pork	Frozen pork are purchased and marketed under centralized plans. Licenses are issued on the basis of contracts concluded and verified by the national corporation.
81.	Frozen suckling pigs	License issued by the Economic and Trade Boards (Commissions) of Hunan, Guangdong and Zhejiang provinces.
82.	Garlic	Including garlic heads.
83.	Dried wecai vegetables	
84.	Fresh-water crabs	Licenses issued by the Economic and Trade Boards (Commissions) of Jiangsu, Hubei and Anhui provinces.
85.	Ham	
86.	Arabian caftans and trousers	
87.	Logs	
88.	Sawn timber	
89.	Red dates	
90.	Raw lacquer	License issued by Hubei Provincial Economic and Trade Board.
91.	Cured tobacco	Cured tobacco is purchased and marketed under centralized plans. Licenses to be issued on the basis of contracts concluded and verified by the national corporation.
92.	Plyed wood	
93.	Plate glass	

94. Reed drapery	License issued by the Tianjin Municipal Economic and Trade Commission and the Shandong Provincial Foreign Trade Bureau.
95. Reed	License issued by the Tianjin Municipal Economic and Trade Commission, the Shandong Provincial Foreign Trade Bureau, and the Heilongjiang Provincial Economic and Trade Commission.
96. Cloissone	Including: Cloissone jewelry, ornaments and articles of use. License issued by Beijing Municipal Economic and Trade Commission.
97. Stationery	Including: Writing brushes, ink slabs, calligraphy and painting paper, Xuan paper, inkstones. Licenses for Xuan paper issued by Anhui Provincial Economic & Trade Commission. License for calligraphy and painting paper issued by the Economic & Trade Boards of the exporting provinces or municipalities.
98. Drawn work	Drawn works are purchased and marketed under centralized plans. License issued on the basis of contracts concluded and verified by the national corporation. Including: Handmade embroideries: Cotton, linen, organdy and cotton polyester tablecloths, pillow cases and slips, bedspreads, handkerchiefs (cotton blended with gauze, bamboo or hair filaments), face towels, place mats, aprons, cushions, draperies and woolen needlepoint tapestry. Handmade woven and knit goods: All varieties of border trimming. Crochet garments. Except for crochet garments, all other goods mentioned above do not include silk material goods.
99. Silk garments	Embroidered garments and fabrics, silk and silk wadding garments made with

	real and artificial silk and other blend fabrics. Not including goods made of synthetic fibers.
100. Pig iron	
101. Rolled steel	Including all kinds of rolled steel, steel wires and cables.
102. Steel ingots	
103. Copper and copper products	Including: Brass, bronze, copper. Copper products include all kinds of manufactured copper, wires, threads and bare wires.
104. Aluminum and Aluminum products	Including all kinds of manufactured aluminum, wires, bare wires and steel-core wires.
105. Lead and lead products	
106. Zinc	
107. Cement	
108. Magnesium	Magnesium ingots.
109. Mercury	
110. Cobalt	
111. Bismuth	
112. Selenium	
113. Molybdenum	Including molybdenum concentrate and ammonium molybdate.
114. Sulphur iron ore	Raw ore and concentrate.
115. Coke	Including lump, crushed and power coke, not including petroleum coke.
116. Iron nails & wires	Iron nails are studs over an inch long (not including sizes of one inch or shorter).
117. Chronium ore	

	Item	Description
118.	Alloy iron	Including: Manganese iron, metallic manganese, electrolytic manganese, chromium iron (carbon chromium, middle-low carbon chromium, micro carbon chromium, vaccum chromium, nitrogen chromium. Silicon iron (silicochromium, silicomanganese, silicocalcium), molybdenum iron.
119.	Natural rubber	
120.	Soda ash	
121.	Caustic soda	Not including sodium hydroxide reagents.
122.	Polyethylene	
123.	Polypropyrene	Not including random polypropyrenes.
124.	Phosphor ore	Raw ore and concentrate.
125.	Phosphorus fertilizer	Regular calcium, calcium magnesium, heavy calcium.
126.	Sulfur	
127.	Benzene anhydride	
128.	Acetone	
129.	<u>Yuan ming</u> powder	
130.	Amino acid	
131.	Vitamin B	Medicinal materials, not prepared medicines.
132.	Tetracycline	
133.	Graphite electrode	
134.	Hand tools	Including: 1. All kinds of pliers, vises, hammers, wrenches, files, saw blades and frames; 2. Measuring tools (tape measures, straight, angular and folding rulers, clamps of various materials); 3. Tools for masons, carpenters, bricklayers and pipelayers, electric welders; 4. Other tools: Glass cutters, blacksmith shears, steel wire brushes, angle clamps.

135.	Fire extinguisher	Small fire extinguishing appliances, the outer shells are ornaments made of breakable materials such as ceramics or glass and the inside filled with fire extinguishing agents.
136.	Demolition equipment and materials for civilian use	Including: Explosives, detonators, fuses, non-electric detonating systems, detonating agents and dynamites.
137.	Rice	Rice and soybeans are purchased and marketed under central plans and licenses are issued on the basis of contracts concluded and verified by the national corporation. Rice includes glutinous rice, short-grain rice and long-grain rice. These all include unpolished, crushed and unhusked rice.
138.	Soybeans	Yellow soybeans.
139.	Rosin	
140.	Rugs	Including: Handmade and machine-made rugs, tapestries and velvet blankets (also called praying blankets) and rugs and tapestries woven with wool, silk, silk-wool interweave and chemical fibers, not including grass and hemp mats. Exports to USA excepted.
141.	Antiomny	Including: Antimonic sulfide concentrate, antimonic oxide, antimoney ingots (refined antimony, metallic antimony, antimony lumps, antimony concentrates).
142.	Tin	
143.	Calcium carbide	
144.	Frozen prawns	Including: Frozen prawns and iced fresh prawns with or without heads hauled from the ocean or bred on farms. These are purchased and marketed under central plans and licenses are issued on the basis of contracts concluded and verified by the national corporation.

145. Chestnuts	
146. Hami musk melons	Licenses issued by the Xinjiang Economic and Trade Board.
147. Oolong tea	Licenses are issued by the Economic and Trade Boards (Commissions) of Jiangxi, Fujian, Guandong and Hunan provinces and verified on the strength of foreign contracts examined and sealed by the Native Produce and Animal By-Product Corporation.
148. Soybean meal and cakes	Including: Crushed soybean cakes, tile cakes and soybean white.
149. Bristle brushes	
150. Dogbane and jute and gunny sacks	
151. Ceramics	Including: Famille rose porcelain (license issued by Jiangxi Provincial Economic & Trade Board), blue and white openwork porcelain (license issued by Jiangxi Provincial Economic & Trade Board); earthware cooking pots (license issued by the Guangdong and Guangxi Economic & Trade Boards); red stoneware (license issued by Jiangsu and Zhejiang Economic & Trade Boards); porcelain sculpture (license issued by Jiangxi Guangdong and Fujian Economic & Trade Boards (Commissions); Xinhua ceramic ware for daily use, household stoneware, heavy porcelain (license issued by the Economic & Trade Boards of the exporting provinces or municipalities).
152. Toilet paper	Licenses apply only to Hong Kong and Macao. Including large and small rolls, large and small flat paper, small facial tissues.
153. <u>Pian zi huang</u>	License issued by Fujian Provincial Economic & Trade Commission.
154. Chloromycetin	Including chloromycetin soda and unflavored chloromycetin, not including prepared medicine. License

		issued by Liaoning, Shanxi, Hubei, Wuhan, Chongqing, Jiangsu and Shanghai Economic & Trade Boards (Commissions, Bureaus).
155.	Pears	
156.	Pomelos	
157.	Pigs	Including: fresh and iced pork.
158.	Oxen	Including: fresh, iced and frozen beef.
159.	Fresh eggs	Including chicken, duck and goose eggs.
160.	Frozen goat meat	License issued by the Economic & Trade Boards (Commissions, Bureaus) of Inner Mongolia, Hebei, Hunan, Guizhou and Sichuan provinces.
161.	Peanut oil	
162.	Rapeseed oil	
163.	Rapeseed	
164.	Cottonseed oil	
165.	Live poultry	Including: Chickens, ducks and geese.
166.	Processed eggs	Including: Lime preserved eggs and salted eggs (chicken, duck and goose eggs).
167.	Pig by-products	Pig heads, trotters and tripes.
168.	Canned pork	
169.	Bean vermicelli	
170.	Sorghum	
171.	Crude & refined salt	
172.	Lichees	
173.	Jiao oranges	
174.	Watermelons	

175.	Water chestnuts	
176.	Potatoes	
177.	Chinese cabbages	
178.	Jellyfish	
179.	Peanut products	Including: Fried shelled peanuts roasted peanuts in shells or shelled, salted or dried peanuts in shells or shelled, peanut butter.
180.	Live sheep	Including: Fresh or iced fresh mutton.
181.	Live eels	
182.	Live baby pigeons	
183.	Wines and spirits	Guangdong rice wine, Maotai liquor, Shaoxing wine, Fen wine, Wuliang liquor, Luzhou liquor, Te liquor.
184.	Firecrackers and fireworks	
185.	Candles	
186.	Dried chillis	
187.	Mink fur	
188.	Anise	
189.	Fennel oil	
190.	Coffee	
191.	Walnut kernels	
192.	Black fungus	
193.	Melon seeds	Black, white and red melon seeds.
194.	Lotus seeds	
195.	Ginko fruit	
196.	Rapeseed cakes (meal)	
197.	Rapeseed (kernel) cakes	

198.	Beet meal	
199.	Bran	
200.	Dried yam	
201.	Dried cassava	
202.	Cypress bark oil	
203.	Feathers and down	Goose and duck feathers and down, washable and non-washable.
204.	Down products	Quilts, pillows, mattresses and cushions.
205.	Cotton underwear	
206.	Staple rayon underwear	
207.	Cotton bath towels	
208.	Cotton thermal underwear	
209.	Sweaters	Including sweaters made of wool, blend fabrics and acrylic.
210.	Cotton bed sheets	
211.	Woven grass products	
212.	Woven willow products	
213.	Rattan products	
214.	Bamboo products	
215.	Furniture	Including furniture made of lacquer wood, hardwood, wood, steel and steel-wood.
216.	Artificial flowers	
217.	Detergents	
218.	Corrugated paper	
219.	Pencils	
220.	Flashlights	
221.	Batteries	

222.	Battery cells	
223.	Porcelain tiles	
224.	Wall and ground tiles	
225.	Electric fans	All kinds.
226.	Wardrobes	All kinds.
227.	Steel tubing	
228.	Barite	
229.	Alumina	
230.	Wheel tires	
231.	Decanedioic acid	
232.	Rare earths	Rare earth concentrate, chlorinated rare earth, rare earth oxides, rare earth metals, rare earth alloys.
233.	Tin ore	License issued by Yunnan Provincial Economic & Trade Board.
234.	Grain and oil processing machinery	Grain mills, rice mills, hullers and oil pressers.

CHINA

CHINA'S PRIMARY COMMODITY TRADE AND THE IMPACT OF DISTORTED WORLD MARKETS

Table of Contents

CHINA

CHINA'S PRIMARY COMMODITY TRADE AND THE IMPACT OF DISTORTED WORLD MARKETS

A. China's Primary Commodity Trade: Patterns and Prospects

3.1 The future course of China's external trade depends on factors which are only partly under the control of its own government. A number of policies, not necessarily restricted to trade itself and to the exchange rate, can be used to direct the level and composition of China's external trade, but international market and price developments usually cannot be manipulated by one country, except for markets in which it can dominate demand or supply. International markets are also affected by the policies of other major trading nations, which add another element of uncertainty. Finally, the future course is dependent on past and present patterns of China's trade, which may or may not be favorable compared to the growth of world markets; changing trade patterns may be desirable but take effort and time and still may produce lesser results than was expected as world markets themselves continue to change.

3.2 Some of the main factors determining China's export prospects for primary commodities are discussed in what follows, starting with a short survey of past trends and present patterns of the country's trade in primary commodities. Next, attention is given to the issue of domestic policies, both with regard to international trade in primary products. It attempts to analyze whether these policies have conflicted in the past, and how they can be made mutually supportive in the years ahead. Next, market prospects for China's major agricultural and nonagricultural primary commodities are reviewed, taking account of possible effects on those markets traceable to the policies of other major trading countries. Finally, attention is turned to the organization of international trade in primary commodities, and changes are suggested that would give a larger role to markets and prices in determining external trade. Particular attention is given to the impact on such policies of distortions in world agricultural product markets.

Trends in China's Primary Commodity Trade

3.3 In broad terms, the composition of China's total exports has shown remarkable stability; primary commodities [1/] accounted for 50-60% of exports in all the years from the early 1960s up to the present. There has been a slight tendency for this share to become smaller (see Figure 3.1) over time, perhaps by about one-third of one percent per annum. But one should also note that the importance of oil exports after 1973 has contributed strongly to this stable share of primary commodities. Excluding oil, the share of remaining primary commodities declined from close to 60% of total exports in the early 1960s to around 25-30% in the 1980s.

1/ Defined as the sum of SITC categories 0, 1, 2, 3, 4 and 68 (food and live animals, beverages and tobacco, crude materials, mineral fuels and products, animal and vegetable oils and fats nonferrous metals).

3.4 By contrast, the composition of imports changed more dramatically over the same period. In the early 1960s, imports consisted mainly of primary commodities, but their share declined very rapidly and reached about 35% of total imports around 1970. It fluctuated around that percentage throughout the 1970s and then was reduced again from 1982 onwards, to about 15% in 1985. Cereals imports played a role in this decline (see Figure 3.2), constituting about half of total primary commodity imports in the 1960s but dwindling in importance in the most recent years. This decline, which is the result of rising domestic production in response to policy reform (see Part C), is one of the most dramatic aspects of the overall change in China's trade pattern.

3.5 The change in the composition of exports is shown in more detail in Table 3.1. The declining importance of primary commodities in total exports occurred in two separate phases: before 1975, the major commodity groups maintained their share in total exports, and the decline was concentrated in the smaller export items. Since 1975, however, the major commodities account for 80% of the total decline of the export share of (nonoil) primary commodities. In the earlier years, exports of sugar, dairy products and crude materials of animals and vegetable origin - sheep casings, medicinal herbs in particular - were more prominent, but from the mid-1970s these lagged behind. In recent years, China has become an importer of a substantial amount of sugar.

3.6 A remarkable feature of primary commodity exports, even when oil is excluded, is their rate of growth, which during the entire period was around 12-13% in value terms. As total exports were growing only slightly more rapidly before the early 1970s, but accelerated thereafter, the stable and subsequently declining share of nonoil primary commodities in total exports reflects the growing importance of manufactured goods, rather than a weakening of the export performance of nonoil primary commodities. Compared to exports of other developing countries, the rate of growth of manufactured goods exports was about the same as in the case of China, but their growth of primary goods exports was significantly slower. This holds true for all major subcategories: food, crude materials, ores and metals, and fuels.

Figure 3.1 : China: Shares of primary commodities and of petroleum in the total value of exports, 1962-1985 (in %).

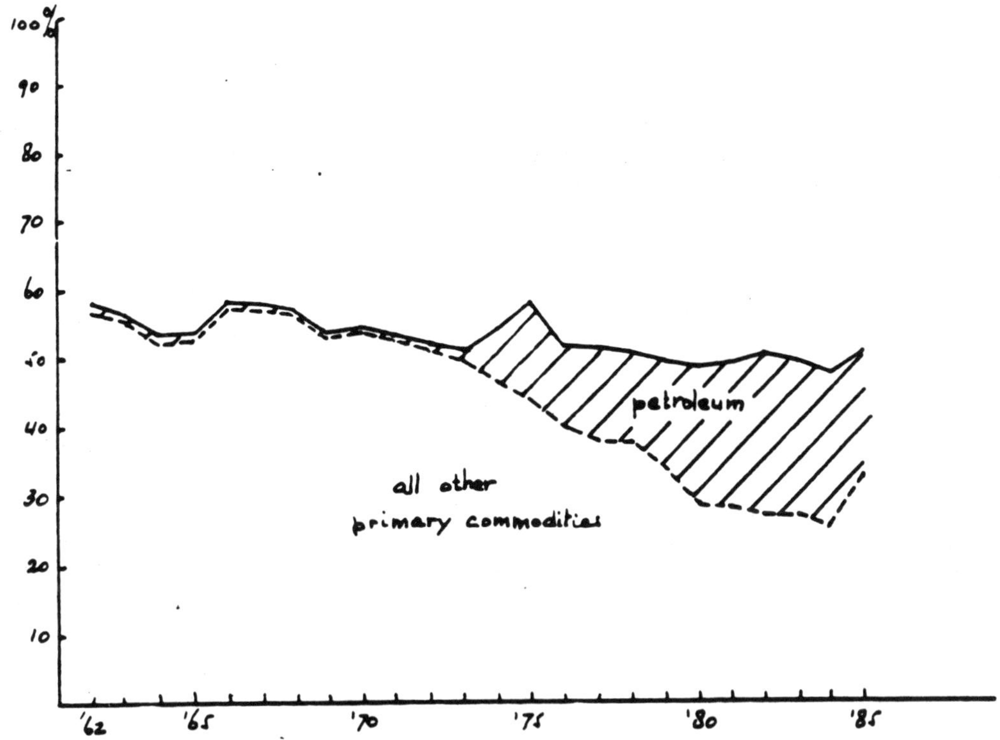

Figure 3.2 : China: Shares of primary commodities and of cereals in the total value of imports, 1962-1985 (in %).

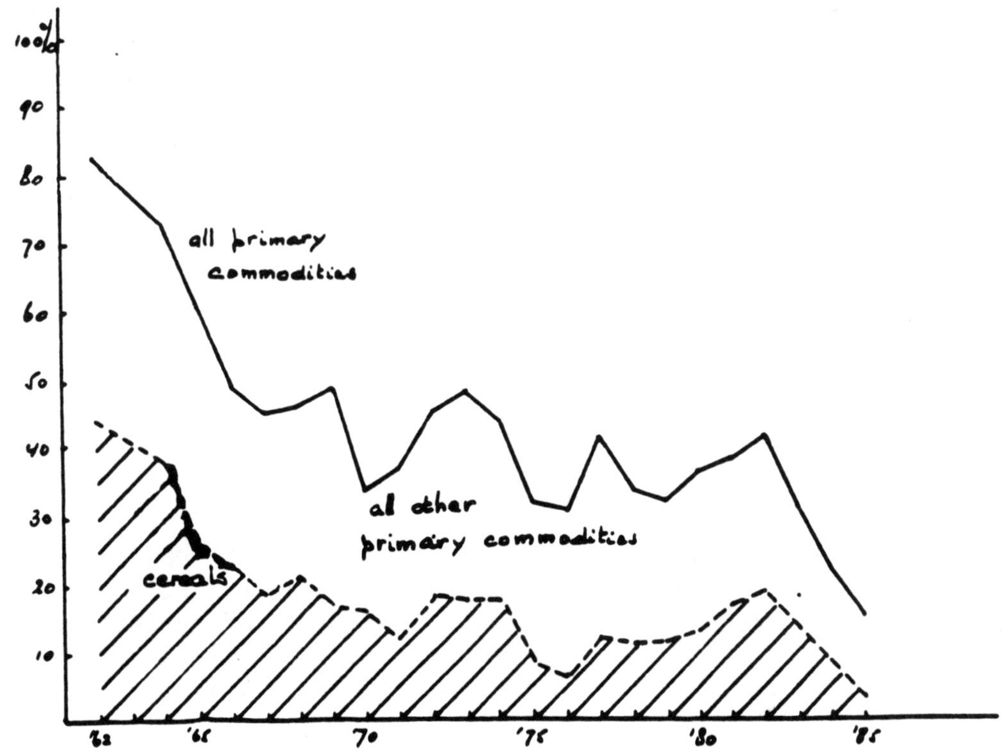

Table 3.1: CHINA: COMPOSITION OF PRIMARY COMMODITY EXPORTS, BY PERIODS 1962-1985 (IN % OF TOTAL EXPORTS)

	1962-65	1966-70	1971-75	1976-80	1981-85
Total primary commodities	55.3	56.6	54.3	50.1	49.4
of which: Petroleum and prod.	1.3	0.7	6.7	16.1	22.9
Total nonoil primary commodities	54.0	55.9	47.6	34.0	26.5
Main Commodity Groups					
Cereals and preparations	7.3	8.2	8.3	2.7	1.2
Fruits and vegetables	5.5	6.9	5.9	5.5	4.2
Oilseeds and nuts	5.1	5.0	2.5	1.1	1.7
Coffee, tea and cocoa	2.7	2.7	2.0	2.2	1.7
Live animals	4.0	3.5	3.6	2.5	1.4
Meat and preparations	1.9	3.6	3.8	2.5	1.7
Fish and preparations	2.6	3.0	3.0	2.5	1.6
Textile fibers	4.6	5.4	5.2	3.8	3.4
Subtotal /a	33.6	38.3	34.3	22.7	16.9
All other nonoil primary commodities	20.4	17.6	13.3	11.3	9.6

/a Columns may not add up to subtotal due to rounding.

3.7 The changing pattern by destination, with an increasing share of primary commodity exports going to industrial market economies and to Hong Kong, provides part of the explanation. Trade with Japan increased rapidly; exports to the USA, which in the early 1970s were virtually nonexistent, flourished; and the Hong Kong market for food, which is supplied almost exclusively by China, expanded rapidly. However, the geographical destination provides only part of the explanation. China increased its market share in a number of primary commodity markets, particularly after 1970, because of the government's intent to increase foreign exchange earnings to permit a higher level of imports. For this purpose, it pursued throughout these years a policy of managed supplies, not only for the domestic markets but also for exports. Changes in this trade regime have been implemented, particularly since 1979, but in a number of respects supply management for exports continues to characterize the present situation.

3.8 Before turning to the present organization of China's foreign trade, its motivating forces and their economic consequences, the next section briefly discusses recent developments in the supply of agricultural and other primary commodities as a result of the reforms since 1978. These have a bearing on the availability and the international competitiveness of primary commodities produced in China and thus constitute an important backdrop for evaluating the more recent export performance and prospects.

Domestic Reforms and International Primary Commodity Trade

3.9 Between 1979 and 1985, agricultural production increased by about 8% per annum, with changes in production patterns increasingly reflecting market prices and demand. The responsibility system has left decision-making regarding agricultural production mainly to farmers, who are more and more faced by free market prices or guided and negotiated prices instead of prices fixed by the government. Substantial income increases in both rural and urban areas have led to significant changes in the pattern of demand for agricultural products, in addition to shifts that came about simply because consumers could effectively express their preferences in the market.

3.10 More reliance on markets in determining output and consumption levels and allowing a higher degree of price flexibility has not progressed at an equal speed for all primary commodities. Mining of metals, minerals and fuels is largely carried out by state enterprises which, together with the manufacturing industrial and public utilities, are the subject of the urban reforms begun in late 1984. As these primary producing sectors do not supply directly to consumer markets 2/ but deliver intermediate products to other industries, they experience the effects of the reforms indirectly and more gradually. As some of these products are considered of strategic importance, and others are only produced by one or a small number of enterprises, the government has chosen to maintain its influence over prices and production levels.

3.11 Within the agricultural sector, markets have not as yet been allowed to operate equally for all commodities. In some cases, the government still exerts a substantial degree of control over prices or over the use of land for particular crops. These policies, in combination with market demand and price prospects, have together established the economic environment in which farmers make their production decisions. They led, for example, to major increases in the output of livestock and aquatic products, for which demand was strong. Better prices of cotton and vegetable oils compared to grains stimulated the former strongly, although grain production still recorded an average annual growth of 3.4% between 1979 and 1985.

3.12 Shifting patterns of supply and demand have affected the need for imports and the availability of production for exports. From being a major cotton importing country for many years, China's import needs declined in the 1980s, and from 1984 onwards a significant surplus has been exported. Exports of oilseeds and nuts, which declined during the 1970s, are again increasing substantially. The picture with respect to trade in cereals is less clear: although exports of rice and recently also maize are rising, imports have declined less than at first sight might have been expected. The different

---

2/ In 1985, the nonagricultural primary commodities (excluding fuels) represented only 12% of total primary commodities (excluding fuels).

role of the government in domestic grains markets appear to have led to fairly substantial imports to assure urban supplies in the coastal zone.

3.13 As yet, the situation does not appear fully stable; additional measures to enhance the role of markets will probably be taken, and relative prices will gradually shift further. The direction of these shifts can to some extent be foreseen, as the demand for livestock products, fish, fruits and vegetables will remain strong as long as household incomes continue to rise. The direct demand for grains to meet human consumption needs will probably rise little above present levels, except for the modest pull exerted by population growth. But, at the same time, the demand for feedgrains can be expected to increase rapidly, as the livestock sector expands. As there are physical and climatic limits to the substitution between the production of rice and of other cereals in China, a situation may arise of rice surpluses and deficits of wheat and/or maize. But rice surpluses may be a feature only during a limited number of years, while domestic demand gradually increases, and production patterns adjust further. As China's agricultural land is quite limited, it would be no surprise if the country were to become a net grain importer at higher income levels, since the same land now producing cereals can be used for higher value products that would find a ready domestic market.

3.14 Against this background, and assuming that market forces are increasingly to determine prices, the domestic prices of grain can be expected to be closely linked to international prices as China becomes a net-importing country. If domestic prices would be set higher through import levies--an issue more fully discussed below--the transition towards higher-valued outputs would be retarded, and domestic demand for livestock products would also be somewhat reduced, but it might still entail larger imports or reduced export supplies of agricultural products that give a higher return measured at world prices.

3.15 A second feature of future demand for agricultural products is the higher degree of processing that will require substantial investments in industrial capacity, for both processing and producing the required packaging. The large demand for processed agricultural commodities in the domestic market suggests, in turn, that there may also be external markets outside Hong Kong where China can offer these products competitively. Compared to the present situation, this would require major improvements, as high international standards were applied to the materials used, product quality, packaging and processing efficiency. From available data--unfortunately a small sample--the impression is that China's current competitiveness in a broad range of unprocessed agricultural products declines with increased processing.

3.16 Further progress in domestic reforms which put more reliance on markets and less on supply management through allocation planning are bound to affect the future course of exports, including those of primary commodities. Domestic demand will exercise a stronger influence over the allocation of available supplies between domestic and foreign markets and in the process, bring about domestic price changes, which, in turn will alter the relative competitiveness of Chinese products in foreign markets. Both the composition of exports and of imports will change as a consequence. The different product mix needed to meet domestic demand, including more processed products, can be expected to open up opportunities for new production capacity which is both sufficiently efficient and quality-oriented to find outlets in foreign markets.

The Organization of Primary Commodity Trade

3.17 The past and present organization of trade in China was discussed in Annex 1. This description and analysis applies equally to trade in primary commodities. For example, prior to 1979, this trade was handled by less than five FTCs. In particular, however, the practice of FTCs engaging in trade in a wide range of products of a greater or lesser profitability in order to meet overall targets is most relevant to the agricultural sector.

3.18 In the case of agricultural commodities, it appears that unprocessed products are more competitive in international markets than processed ones. Most FTCs list unprocessed goods among the ones which they can export at a profit, whereas processed products dominate the list of loss-makers. If FTCs were to pass on international prices to producers, they would pay higher prices for unprocessed commodities but lower ones for processed goods. When buying directly from farmers--as FTCs increasingly must do because of the new organization of agricultural marketing--rural incomes would be increased and an incentive provided to farmers to produce the kind and quality of products for which there are profitable external markets. This incentive is now missing. Paying lower prices for processed commodities would be an incentive to producing enterprises--many of which are under the captive control of the FTCs--to improve their efficiency and lower their costs by selling in the domestic market as well. At the same time, it would be an incentive to the FTC concerned to search for other, more efficient enterprises which may be able to produce for foreign markets.

3.19 Foreign exchange retention rights appear to favor the least deserving domestic producers of agricultural exports. Enterprises producing processed agricultural commodities receive retention rights. Farmers selling unprocessed products to FTCs in the domestic market are not provided with the right to retain any of the foreign exchange earned with their products. If retention rights are to be maintained in future, farmers should be given the same rights as processing enterprises. Agricultural sales cooperatives should be able, as is suggested for enterprises, to sell through FTCs of their own choice, possibly on an agency basis, or have the right to sell directly in foreign markets.

3.20 Future reforms in trade in agricultural commodities should be dovetailed to the strengthening of China's rural economy. The fact that agricultural processing for export is mainly organized through captive enterprises within the structure of the FTCs leads to an urban bias in locating those enterprises. It also results in a lack of cross-information flows between those enterprises and others which are limited to the domestic market but may have the potential to become exporters as well. Instead, FTCs should be instrumental in establishing rural collectives and enterprises in lines of production that promise to generate new flows of exports and to add to rural incomes.

3.21 The idea of establishing rural export bases applies the same separation of enterprises (which produce either for the domestic or the external market) from agricultural production. By instead making domestic markets more competitive and sensitive to the demands of consumers, enterprises would be forced to improve the quality of their products and the way in which they are offered. FTCs should survey the entire domestic market continuously to find products and producers able to meet international standards and assist them to enter foreign markets.

3.22 This applies to both processed and unprocessed products, but it is essential that for both the same set of rules applies. Tax incentives, retention rights to foreign exchange, and technical and organizational assistance to upgrade product quality should apply to both rural and urban activities. Where this requires the establishment of rural organizations to channel sales or to process agricultural commodities for exports, the needed technical and financial support should be forthcoming and FTCs could play a significant role in stimulating this process.

3.23 The closer integration of foreign and domestic markets that constitutes an essential recommendation of this report does not imply that there are no arguments for specific measures at the border which drive wedges between domestic and international prices. However, such border measures should be seen as exceptions rather than the rule. Specific economic arguments need to be provided which justify these measures, and three such situations are discussed in Part C.

Prospects for Primary Commodity Trade

3.24 Agricultural commodities, metals and minerals, including their semi-processed products, have played a declining role in China's exports, falling from about 54% in 1965 to about 28% in recent years (excluding petroleum). Including petroleum, the share of primary commodities has remained remarkably stable because of the increasing importance of oil exports. Exports of coal have also contributed to this stability recently. Table 3.2 shows the shifts in the export pattern of the last five years.

3.25 Better than average performance is noted for tea exports, which expanded rapidly notwithstanding an uneven development of world market prices; for cereals because of a rapid increase of maize exports to Japan; for textile fibers, where the main item is cotton which China recently started to export. Coal has also been exported in recent years, mainly the result of very rapid expansion of domestic coal production. Still, the overall trend of nonfuel primary exports as a share of total external sales is clearly downward. This should not hide, however, significant increase of those exports in recent years--as also over the longer term--well beyond the rate at which world markets expanded and notwithstanding declining prices for most of these products.

Table 3.2: SHARES OF PRIMARY COMMODITIES, BY GROUPS, IN TOTAL EXPORT OF CHINA, 1980 AND 1985 (%)

	1980	1985
Total Primary Commodities /a	49.2	50.30
Food and live animals	16.2	12.2
Of which: fruits, vegetables	(4.8)	(3.3)
fish and preparation	(2.1)	(1.4)
meat and preparation	(2.0)	(1.3)
live animals	(1.8)	(1.1)
tea, coffee, cocoa	(1.7)	(1.8)
cereals and preparation	(1.4)	(1.8)
other food and production	(2.4)	(1.5)
Crude materials excluding oil seed, ores	8.2	7.9
of which: textile fibers	(2.8)	(4.3)
others	(5.4)	(3.6)
Fuels	21.8	26.4
of which: petroleum	(20.9)	(24.5)
coal	(0.9)	(1.9)
28,66 ores and metals	1.8	1.7
22,4 oil seeds, animal, vegetable oils and fats	1.2	2.1

/a Numbers in row entries refer to SITC-codes.

3.26 As was stated earlier, China is not well-endowed with resources for agricultural production and is therefore unlikely to maintain a positive trade balance in this sector in the longer run. Domestic demand will assert itself strongly, and the rising share of livestock products in the average diet suggests that cereals imports for animal feed will tend to rise faster than remaining, but modest, cereals exports. In the process, domestic costs of all agricultural products can be expected to rise, whereas world prices are generally expected to continue their long-term decline, making exports less competitive and imports--even when restrained by border measures--more attractive.

3.27 The changes in the structure of domestic demand will also express themselves in a shift to increasingly processed agricultural commodities. The desirable integration of production for domestic markets and for exports can bring about a shift in exports as well, moving towards a larger share of processed and manufactured foods and other agricultural commodities. Presently, few of these products in China appear to have a competitive edge, but this may indicate the usually small and captive character of these industries producing for exports, rather than a general problem concerning the entire food industry. That question can be answered only by opening up the possibility to export to a much broader range of enterprises than is the case at present.

3.28 According to the most recent World Bank projections (October 1986), world consumption of nonfuel primary commodities is estimated to grow in volume terms by 2.1% per year through the end of this century. Relative prices may continue to decline in world markets by close to 1.0% per year. Even if China's exports of these commodities exceed that rate of growth significantly, particularly by shifting to higher value-added manufactures based on agricultural processing, the growth of this part of exports will nevertheless decline from the rates experienced in past years. Nor will these rates reach the desired overall rate of export growth, thus further reducing the share of nonfuel primary commodities in China's exports. Still, the contribution to overall export growth can be significant, suggesting that efforts should be made to provide the widest possible opportunities to domestic producers for participating in export trade.

B. China as a Dominant Exporter: Implications for Trade Policy

3.29 The essential thrust of much of this report has been to encourage China to reduce the extent of government intervention in trade and to put greater reliance on economic levers. It has been argued that this will encourage efficiency both in trade and in production for the domestic market, thereby increasing overall returns to China from production and trade. However, in the primary goods area, there are two circumstances in which this approach should be modified: where China is a significant exporter in world markets, either with respect to high penetration of a particular market, or in terms of its share of world trade in a particular commodity; and when China faces severe distortions in world markets, such that current world prices may not provide appropriate signals for long-term decision-making. The first situation affects China's food exports to Hong Kong and Macao, as well as China's exports of products such as silk, tungsten, and, for somewhat different reasons, certain textiles and garments. The second situation affects policy towards trade in a variety of products, but particularly sugar, dairy products and steel; this issue is discussed in part C below.

The Hong Kong and Macao Food Markets

3.30 The geographic Hong Kong and Macao and the similarity of consumer preferences as compared to China itself have made these markets very important for China. The share of China's exports destined for these markets has been remarkably stable, most years exceeding 25% of China's total exports. In recent years, Hong Kong has also become an important source for imports to China, but its trade balance has stayed strongly positive with Hong Kong. Not all Chinese exports are for consumption in Hong Kong, as a significant part is re-exported; the latter trade flow may account in recent years for about half of Chinese exports to Hong Kong. Re-exports concern in particular textiles and clothing.

3.31 Agricultural commodities, which in the 1960s were the bulk of Chinese exports to Hong Kong, have gradually become of lesser importance and recently accounted for less than a quarter of these exports, equivalent to 8% of total Chinese exports. This is important to mention, because a large part of the policy discussion in China regarding foreign trade draws its propositions and arguments from past experience concerning this particular flow of trade. In fact, not only the limited importance of this market but also its rather exceptional character suggest that generalizations based on and drawn from it are not appropriate.

3.32 The main agricultural export commodities destined for Hong Kong are live animals, fruits and vegetables, meat and preparations, fish and preparations, cereals and preparations, dairy products and eggs. Although Hongkong re-exports part of these food imports, notably to Japan and Singapore, the remaining quantities represent very large shares in total consumption. Indeed the Chinese Government has pursued policies which ensure that this market remains overwhelmingly supplied from its own hinterland.

3.33 The way in which this is done may, by itself, explain why the authorities have a rather strong focus on this market. A large number of people are employed in regulating the supplies to this market, much more than is the case for any other external trade flow. About 1,000 persons are employed in Hong Kong itself to survey the markets for all food items--particularly perishables--brought in as supplies from China and (for example in the case of oranges) from other countries. They report on the daily market situation to MOFERT, which, on the basis of this information, sends instructions down to several main shipping points regarding quantities and timing of shipments to be made. In this way, stable supplies and prices are guaranteed to Hong Kong consumers, and care is taken to maintain prices at a level which prohibits virtually any sales by other potential suppliers.

3.34 Prices in the Hong Kong market for most export products are significantly higher than for comparable products in China. As the FTCs procuring goods for the Hong Kong market pay domestic prices, this operation is profitable for most commodities, but more so for fresh and unprocessed foods than for processed ones. In some cases, however, such as eels produced in aerated ponds which require substantial investment, exports to Hong Kong can only take place at a loss. In one particular case, these losses were not absorbed by profits of the FTC on other exports, but a subsidy was provided by the government. But even in the case that exports are profitable for the FTC concerned, this may not be the case for the Chinese economy, as substantial costs of its trade organization are not charged to exporters but absorbed in the budget of MOFERT.

3.35 Again, the disadvantages of not passing on external prices to domestic producers apply in this case. The organization of trade leads to economically undesirable cross-subsidization of commodities and, in some cases, even to outright subsidies paid by the government budget. The question arises first of all whether there are economically more desirable alternatives to the present system that could achieve the same objectives more efficiently.

3.36 A possible way to open up the market to competition amongst suppliers would be to replace the present market organization by a set of export duties on trade in fresh and unprocessed agricultural products, live animals and meat. It would, when carefully set, avoid an excess of supplies to Hong Kong, as prices in that market are allowed to fluctuate only within a narrow range. The lower limit of that range would be determined by domestic prices in China's main supplying regions, increased by the necessary trade and transport costs plus the export duty. The upper limit would be the price at which other suppliers can enter the Hong Kong market.

3.37 It should be noted, however, that a discriminatory export duty exclusively on shipments to the Hong Kong market is not a practical proposal. It would be objectionable under GATT-rules, although an exception may be made because of the pending unification of Hong Kong and China within the foreseeable future. Still, in practice, it would invite exports to third countries without duty and re-exports by them to Hong Kong, which would undermine the purpose of the scheme. Export duties should thus be used on all exports of commodities which have Hong Kong as their main destination, but levied irrespective of the actual destination. That would limit the number of commodities to which an export duty could be applied; otherwise it would hurt export volumes of these commodities to other destinations, offsetting part or all of the gains obtained from dutiable exports to Hong Kong.

3.38 This said, we have to recognize that in a market such as food in Hong Kong/Macao, there can be frequent changes in the pattern of demand, whereas it is not practicable or sensible to make frequent changes in export taxes. Therefore, it seems likely that for this special market, it will be necessary to maintain some form of export licensing to accompany any export tax. An underestimation of the appropriate export tax could result in a flooding of the market, and, with inelastic demand, a decline in overall revenues for China. However, the imposition of an export tax would remove the excess profits from the hands of the FTCs, thus reducing their ability to subsidize other exports. Moreover, the tax would help to reduce the administrative burden of managing exports to these markets.

China as a Major World Market Supplier

3.39 For a few commodities, China is a major supplier to world markets but their number is small, and the total value of these exports is quite limited. In the two important commodity markets for rice and for tea, which are the most substantial from China's viewpoint, shares in the world market range between 15 and 20%. The same shares apply to some markets of lesser importance for China, for example groundnuts, sesame seeds and castor beans. China supplies about one quarter, followed by Argentina and Mexico. Silk is the main product in which China is the dominant supplier, with more than 50% of the world market in most years, and earnings exceeding 1% of total exports. In nonagricultural raw materials, China has a large share in the production and trade of several minor minerals and metals, such as tungsten, vanadium, and antimony.

3.40 In the case of products for which China has a dominant market position, the question can be raised whether the present organization of trade through FTCs should also be changed in the sense of opening up these markets to domestic competition. The answer to that question must also take account of the domestic organization of production, which varies greatly from the large number of farmers engaged in silk production to the few or even sole producing units for metals and minerals. The strategic importance of these metallic products makes it likely that their production will continue to be controlled by the central government. In that case, it seems logical to put the responsibility for exports also in the hands of those enterprises and to give them control over export functions presently performed by FTCs. Profits from these exports should accrue to these enterprises, and losses be borne by them.

3.41 In the case of silk, the situation is more complex, as both raw silk and products are exported, and producers are numerous. It would, in any case, be desirable that producers become linked to international markets and prices by abolishing the present export monopoly. This could be achieved in the case of raw silk by transferring the responsibility for exports to regionally organized farmers' cooperatives, taking over the functions of FTCs presently in charge of trade. Initially, some central guidance may be needed, to avoid over-supply to the market and lower prices, but the export of silk could be left increasingly to the producer organizations themselves, possibly with the setting of a minimum export price to prohibit excessive competition between suppliers.

3.42 Finally, China faces market constraints of one kind or another in certain commodities. In particular, there is the case of textile and garments exports, where China faces quotas imposed under national import restrictions or under the Multi-Fiber Arrangement. At current world prices, Chinese producers would be willing to supply a higher volume of exports than would be acceptable under current quotas. While these quotas can be avoided by expanding exports of individual items excluded from the arrangements, and by improving quality so as to raise value with the same volume of exports, there may be more efficient ways to organize the internal allocation of these quotas. The present arrangements severely reduce the possibilities for internal competition that would encourage efficiency improvements.

3.43 One way in which the allocation of quotas could be organized would be by auction. This is essentially the current practice for allocating textile quotas in Hong Kong, for example. The two main advantages of this approach would be greatly reduced administrative costs of allocating quotas, and capture by the government of the scarcity premium, or rent, that derives from the presence of quotas. Although not apparently a serious problem in China, in several other countries the practice of allocating quotas has also been an important source of corruption.

C. Distorted World Markets: Implications for Trade Policy

3.44 World agricultural markets are strongly influenced by national policies which that primarily domestic objectives. As a consequence, many agricultural commodities are only partly produced in countries offering the best economic opportunities, whereas another part originates in countries which can only produce those commodities behind protectionist barriers, and/or with heavy subsidies. These practices lead also to distortions in the patterns of international trade and to world prices which bear little or no relationship to the marginal costs of efficient producers.

The Determinants of Agricultural Policies

3.45 A small number of countries dominate world markets, both as importers and as exporters, and their policies matter most. The objectives of the national policies of the dominant countries determine therefore to a large extent the situation in agricultural markets, in a few cases by design but in most as a side-effect. Taking the 12 member nations of the European Communities (EC) as one unit, because of their Common Agricultural Policy (CAP), and treating the USSR and Eastern Europe also as one unit, some 20 country groups account for about 80% of world agricultural production and trade. The motivations and objectives of their agricultural policies determine, to a large extent, the patterns of world production and trade of the commodities concerned.

3.46 The patterns of production of agricultural commodities and of trade in such commodities are very different. Industrial countries account for only about one-quarter of production, but almost 60% of trade. By contrast, the selected developing countries account for almost 40% of production, but less than 15% of trade. Similarly, Eastern European countries have much lower shares in trade than in production. Even if internal trade within the European Community and between the US and Canada is excluded, the industrial countries would still be the dominant force in world agricultural trade, and therefore the following paragraphs concentrate on their agricultural policies.

3.47 Within the group of industrial market economies, a distinction needs to be made in terms of the kinds of policies with respect to their agricultural sectors they have pursued in past years. One group of countries, mainly Western Europe and Japan, have protected their agricultural sectors, whereas the others have done so to a much lesser extent. In the latter group are the US, Canada, Australia and New Zealand. To some extent, Argentina and South Africa can be put in the same class, even if their level of development is lower; they share some of the same characteristics as regards their agricultural sectors and their policies. Historically, the difference between the two groups of countries is that the former have a very long history of agricultural activity, which was the mainstay of people's livelihood for many centuries before their economies became more diversified. The second group of countries had a much more recent start, as colonies settled mainly from Europe, with abundant land resources, rapid economic diversification and with restrictions imposed on migration long before average farm sizes were reduced to those observed in Europe. The vast differences in the resources available in the two groups of countries for average farm households shown for selected countries and country groups in Table 3.4.

3.48 Agricultural employment as part of total civilian employment is relatively high in the EC and Japan as compared to the other countries, including, notably, Australia and Canada. Within the EC, there are large differences also between countries, from a low of 2.1% in the United Kingdom to 10.9% in Italy and 14.4% in Ireland. Also within those countries, some regions depend relatively heavily on employment in agriculture, for example Southern Italy, South-West and Central France and the South of the F.R. of Germany.

3.49 Farming in the more recently settled countries such as Canada and Australia gives more scope for earning incomes in agriculture without special subsidies or other support measures such as those in Western Europe or in Japan. The former have been able to generate satisfactory income levels without much government involvement and also have traditionally been able to supply both their domestic consumers and the international markets with their staple products. Even if objectives in the two groups of countries were the same, the scope for achieving those objectives is larger when farms are large, the farm population small, and the opportunities for increasing the productivity of the land are abundant.

Table 3.3: MAJOR COUNTRIES AND COUNTRY GROUPS IN WORLD AGRICULTURAL POPULATION PRODUCTION AND TRADE

	% of population mid-1983	% of agric. production aver. 1978-80	% of agric. imports 1982	% of agric. exports 1982
United States	5.06	11.10	9.55	16.97
Canada	0.54	1.39	2.01	4.33
Australia	0.33	1.15	0.52	3.11
New Zealand	0.07	0.40	0.19	1.35
European Community (EC)	6.92	9.27	35.87 /a	31.74 /a
Japan	2.57	2.92	7.95	0.68
Subtotal	15.49	26.23	56.09	58.18
CMEA-countries	8.33	16.68	11.86	5.44
China	22.00	15.22	1.94	1.98
India	15.82	7.0	0.59	1.02
Indonesia	3.36	1.76	0.57	0.52
Thailand	1.06	0.99	0.19	1.88
Pakistan	1.94	0.87	0.34	0.23
Bangladesh	2.06	0.70	0.22	0.06
Brazil	2.80	3.88	0.85	3.85
Argentina	0.64	1.41	0.11	2.29
Mexico	1.62	1.20	1.27	0.88
Turkey	1.02	1.77	0.11	1.09
Egypt	0.98	0.73	1.34	0.11
Nigeria	2.02	1.94	0.84	0.28
Kenya	0.41	0.24	0.06	0.23
Subtotal (LDCs)	55.73	37.71	8.43	14.42
Total (specified countries)	79.55	80.62	76.38	78.04

/a Including intra-EC trade.

Sources: Population data are from the World Bank's World Development Report 1985; Agricultural production is taken from the data base of the Food and Agricultural Program of the International Institute for Applied Systems Analysis (IIASA/FAP) which in turn is based on FAO's Supply Utilization Accounts (SUA); Trade data are from UNCTAD's 1985 Handbook of Trade and Development Statistics and comprise SITC sections 0, 1, 22 and 4.

Table 3.4: AGRICULTURAL LAND AND ACTIVE POPULATIONS IN SELECTED INDUSTRIAL COUNTRIES, 1980

	EC-9/a	USA	Canada	Japan	Australia
Arable and permanently cropped land (mln ha)	51.8	190.8	41.3	5.4	41.2
No. of farms (over 1 ha, in thousands)	5,671	2,428	242	4,882	179
Average farm size (in ha)	9.1	78.6	170.6	1.12	230.0
(Ibid, incl. pasture land)	(16.3)	(176.4)	(286.9)	(1.17)	(n.a.)
Agricultural employment as % of civilian employment	7.4	3.6	5.5	10.4	6.5
Agricultural value added as % of GNP	3.5	2.6	3.9	3.8	6.8

/a Excludes Greece and the recently joined members Spain and Portugal.

Source: OECD, Review of Agricultural Policies in OECD Member Countries, 1980-82, Paris, 1983.

3.50 The Western European countries--including nonmembers of the EC like Sweden; Austria and Switzerland--and Japan face a more difficult challenge in formulating agricultural policies, and, over the course of time, they have responded differently. When North American grain began to arrive in Europe in the 19th century at competitive prices, many European countries closed their borders to protect their own farmers and to avert the threat of accelerated migration to the cities when farming was no longer profitable. Over the years, numerous support measures were added through research, education, credit and substantial investments in rural infrastructure and land improvement. As a consequence, farming became more productive but never reached the stage where it could be exposed to external competition.

3.51 West European countries and Japan have attempted to increase agricultural incomes by creating a preference for domestic products in their own darkets, shielding these markets through border levies against competing products from outside. They have also provided price support for some or most domestic agricultural outputs, subsidized inputs including credit and the free provision of extension services, research, quality control services and marketing support.

3.52 Higher prices than would prevail in an open market have retarded the migration out of agriculture and have provided an incentive to produce more, regardless of competitiveness in international markets. This implies that in an open market production would be lower and imports larger, and the other industrial countries that are major agricultural exporters would contribute an even larger share to world exports of temperate zone agricultural products. Their potential markets, following from their comparative advantage, are not actually available to them, as some part of potential demand is instead being met by higher-cost domestic products produced behind protective barriers.

3.53 The situation is aggravated further when countries protecting their own producers increase their production beyond the level of domestic demand and dispose of their surpluses by subsidized sales abroad. This has been occurring with increasing frequency. Thus, countries which are relatively high-cost producers are making inroads into the markets of other, lower-cost producers. The effects are not limited to producers/exporters of temperate zone agricultural products, as in a number of cases these new supplies also compete with products from tropical and subtropical areas, such as in the case of sugar (beet vs. cane). The same is expected to occur in the coming years with regard to vegetable oils and fats.

3.54 The resolve of governments to improve relative incomes of the agricultural population is the main driving force behind the protective policies discussed briefly above. Farmers have in most countries refused to be compensated by way of income transfers, and this has put the governments in a situation where manipulation of prices remain the major instrument in addition to subsidies and free services.

3.55 Many governments have also adopted these protective policies because of a desire to be or to become self-sufficient in major agricultural commodities. Memories of war-time shortages and the perceived risks implied by dependence on foreign supplies also play a role in the setting, of agricultural policies. It is in this respect interesting to note that the EC consists of both importing and exporting member countries. The first aim was to make the importing countries switch to supplies from within the EC, but once this aim was achieved and self-sufficiency reached, the aim became to maintain or, if possible, expand the share of the EC in world export markets.

3.56 These policies of the industrial market economies have the result that world market supplies of temperate zone agricultural products tend to be abundant in normal years. In the past, two main development trends have caused demand for some of these products to rise substantially, mitigating the decline of world prices. One is the rapid increase of food imports in the developing countries, particularly grains for human consumption. The other is the entrance of the USSR into the market as a major grains importer since the early 1970s. These have, to some extent offset declining imports of Western Europe and absorbed some of the surpluses from these countries. Still, international prices for agricultural commodities have shown a relative decline. World market prices for these commodities are thus becoming more a function of the capacity and willingness of the major exporting countries to subsidize these exports, and less a reflection of the long-run marginal costs of efficient producers.

World Market Distortions: The Level of Protection

3.57 The concepts of nominal and effective protection have been discussed in Annex 2. A set of fairly detailed estimates of the extent of such protection in agriculture by the major exporters is available from a data-set constructed by the Food and Agriculture Program (FAP) of IIASA [3/] on the basis of the Supply Utilization Accounts of FAO. The latter give a detailed breakdown by countries and commodities of agricultural supplies, uses and international trade, together with price information permitting yearly estimates of nominal protection rates. The findings for 1984 are shown in Table 3.5 below.

Table 3.5: NOMINAL RATES OF PROTECTION FOR SELECTED COUNTRIES AND COMMODITY GROUPS, 1984
(in % of world market prices)

	Wheat	Feed grains	Meat	Dairy products	Industrial crops
United States	0	0	25	80	25
Australia	0	2	-11	27	-13
Canada	-5	-10	17	40	4
Argentina	-33	-37	-30	-20	-9
EC	57	60	59	39	24
Japan	53	63	65	112	87

Source: IIASA/FAP on the basis of FAO data files.

3.58 Similar estimates of nominal protection rates by Anderson and Tyers [4/] are used and presented in the World Bank's 1986 World Development Report. Broader concepts including direct and indirect transfer payments are

---

3/ International Institute for Applied Systems Analysis, Laxenburg, Austria.

4/ Tyers, Rodney and Kim Anderson: "Distortions in World Food Markets; A Quantitative Assessment," Background paper to the World Bank's World Development Report, 1986.

used in recent publications and documents of FAO [5/] and the OECD [6/] and suggest that in the industrial market economies the total support to agricultural producers is significantly larger than nominal protection rates suggest. But, irrespective of concepts and coverages, all estimates are in agreement concerning the very high level of agricultural protection in most of the industrial market economies.

Measuring the Effects of Protection

3.59 What would be the effect of the elimination or significant reduction of this protection? IIASA has recently constructed models to attempt to answer these questions by comparing results from maintaining current policies with gradual removal of protection over five years.

3.60 When OECD-countries remove border protection, the main effect is that their production of grains and livestock production is adjusted downward, and their exports decline or imports increase. This leads to significantly higher prices in the world market for meat and dairy products, but also higher returns to their production in many other countries, which in turn raises the demand for and the prices of grains. An interesting feature in the dairy market is the decline of production and exports of the EC and lower production of the US as well; dairy product markets are taken over to a very large extent by Canada, which becomes a major supplier to the US.

3.61 World market prices of agricultural commodities relative to nonagricultural prices increase on average by 9% when the OECD-countries remove border protection. Charges vary widely by commodity groups, ranging from a decline (by 2%) for nonfood agricultural products to an increase of 31% for dairy products. These price changes are shown in Table 3.6.

5/ FAO: International Agricultural Adjustment. Fifth Progress Report, November 1985, doc. C85/21.

6/ OECD: Ministrial Mandate on Agricultural Trade. Draft Report to the Council, 1986.

Table 3.6: CHANGES IN RELATIVE /a WORLD MARKET PRICES OF AGRICULTURAL PRODUCTS IN THE REFERENCE AND OECD REMOVAL OF BORDER PROTECTION SCENARIOS (%)

	Price change over 1980-2000 in the reference scenario	Additional price change in 2000 due to OECD removal of border protection
Wheat	-8	18
Rice	1	21
Coarse grains	-10	11
Bovine, ovine meat	53	17
Dairy products	37	31
Other animal products	6	-
Protein feeds	-2	13
Other food	5	5
Nonfood agricultural product	25	-2
Total Agriculture	9	9

/a Relative to nonagricultural prices.

3.62 In the reference scenario, which assumes the continuation of present policies, three groups of commodities can be distinguished on the basis of their relative price performance. Grains appear to loose ground, with prices continuing a downward long-term trend that has been observed for many decades. Very strong price increases occur, however, for meat and dairy products and almost as much for industrial crops. The remaining commodity groups show only small price changes. Once OECD border protection is removed, grains prices are considerably increased over the levels in the reference scenario and, when taken together, these price changes amount to a net real price increase which constitutes a break from past trends. Prices of meat and dairy products are increased even further, and protein feeds also join the grains in recovering ground lost in the reference scenario. Changes for the remaining commodity groups are small.

3.63 The considerable effects of removing border protection on the agricultural sector and the political strength which farmers have in most of the protecting countries cast some doubt on the feasibility of these policy changes. International pressures to reduce border protection has increased over recent years, and the financial costs of subsidies are becoming more strongly felt, together suggesting that some measures may indeed be taken. Still, this will at best be a slow process far removed from the comparatively extreme scenario used here, which removes border protection over a short five-year period. Under these circumstances of continued protection, developing countries trading agricultural products may need to take particular policy measures themselves, to avoid permitting the consequences of international distortions to affect their domestic economies in undesirable ways.

Implications for China

3.64 The above analysis makes it clear that agricultural production and price formation are not determined by comparative advantage alone, but increasingly also by the polices of the major producing and trading countries. Those policies have objectives other than economic rationality. These policies result also in a loss of world welfare, as the removal of border protection would lead to a higher world GDP. One objective of the recently initated Uruguay Round of Multilateral Trade Negotiations under the auspices of the GATT is to achieve a gradual removal of border protection and of other measures which distort agricultural production and trade incentives.

3.65 The question remains, however, what policy advice can be given to China if these international negotiations fail to produce the desired result. Distortions will, in that case, continue to exist, and, when prevailing world prices are taken as guidance in making investment allocations, resulting production and income measured at free trade prices will be less than optimal. Should China therefore take estimated free trade prices as guidance? There are considerable risks in doing so, as those prices may in fact never come about; in the meantime, China may deny itself access to cheap (subsidized) imports or face the need to subsidize exports of commodities for which it has a comparative advantage but cannot match the supply price of a subsidizing competitor. On the other hand, if actual world market prices are taken as guidance, China would have to accept a dependence on policy decisions by other countries, which may be subject to abrupt changes as a consequence of international agreements to liberalize agricultural trade or for reasons internal to that country that have nothing to do with international markets or prices.

3.66 Probably the best course to take consists of a compromise which permits the reaping of the potential benefits and avoids the potential costs and risks inherent in the present and prospective market situation for agricultural products. If China wishes to import agricultural products subsidized by major exporters, it should not deprive itself of cheap imports, but rather avoid the effects these imports can inflict on domestic production and consumption by charging import duties. These should be of an order of magnitude that reflects the difference between actual and estimated free-trade world prices. Import charges of this kind could not be considered protectionist; they would be simply a compensation measure to offset the effects of protection and/or subsidies by others. In that sense, they are countervailing duties which preclude domestic consumption from expanding and avoid disincentives to domestic agricultural producers. In addition, they transfer the subsidy provided by the exporter to the government revenues of the importing country.

3.67 One important question that remains concerns the duration of a distortion of world markets. If a distortion is brought about by some policy measure of another country, but is expected to be of a temporary nature, a countervailing border charge prevents the adjustment of domestic production and consumption which would later need to be reversed. When there are substantial investments associated with the production of the particular commodity, it is unattractive to pass on changes in world market prices, because the costs of idle capacity and subsequent new investments are high, and the process may take considerable time. Thus, when switching costs are high, the case for countervailing charges is strengthened, particularly if a situation of distortion is deemed to be only of short duration.

3.68 If distortions have gradually come into existence but have become virtually permanent features of the international market--as is the case for most of the temperate zone agricultural products--the situation may be different. Hardly any country has in the past levied countervailing charges, but instead has permitted international prices to pass through and to influence domestic production and demand. A countervailing levy for temperate agricultural products would therefore have to be added on top of the average protection which a country provides to its nonagricultural sectors in order to ensure the required protective margin to its own agricultural producers.

3.69 Countries exporting agricultural commodities which compete with subsidized exports from other countries are in a more difficult position. Particularly developing countries, even if their comparative advantage is substantial, have in that case to accept reduced profit margins on exports or may even see those profits wither away entirely. The case of sugar exports from Brazil, which is generally thought to be the most competitive producer in the world, is a demonstration of this problem, as for a number of years the world price of sugar has only permitted exports at a loss. For most countries, this situation is simply not sustainable, and if it would have to be a long-term proposition it is better not to adopt such policies at any time.

3.70 In most developing countries including China, large shifts have already taken place in the patterns of supply and demand between the agricultural and nonagricultural sectors and also within agriculture, both in response to unequal protection and to distorted world market prices. This raises doubts as to whether the issue of countervailance against the latter is a relevant issue to raise at this point. It appears that in most countries the more pertinent issue is the unequal rates of protection between sectors and the need to make protection both less severe and less discriminatory. This will require considerable effort, but promises to benefit agricultural producers substantially when achieved. Once a nondiscriminating position is reached, and, at the same time distortions, in international markets persist, the issue of countervailing charges may become relevant, but it will in most developing countries take a long time to reach that point. Still the existence of these distortions by itself makes it more urgent to address the issue concerning the relative (and mostly negative) protection given to agriculture.

3.71 In short, therefore, China will have to make judgments about the likelihood that present distortions will continue long into the future. If present subsidies by industrialized countries can be expected to be phased out in the reasonably near future, it makes sense to impose countervailing import duties and base investment decisions on long-term free trade prices. To the extent that the commodity concerned may be strategically important, this argument is reinforced. This may be true of steel imports for example. However, if distortions are likely to persist for a long time, as in sugar and vegetable oils, China would be wise to avoid countervailing duties and enjoy the benefits of developed countries' subsidies, thereby avoiding costly investment in production facilities for these commodities.

CHINA

FOREIGN DIRECT INVESTMENT: CHINA'S EXPERIENCE AND OPTIONS FOR POLICY REFORM

Table of Contents

CHINA

FOREIGN DIRECT INVESTMENT: CHINA'S EXPERIENCE AND OPTIONS FOR POLICY REFORM

4.1 In the thirty years from the establishment of the People's Republic of China in 1949 until 1979, China was essentially closed to foreign private investment. Considerable technology was imported, principally by buying machinery and turnkey plants and through technical assistance. Much progess was made in this period, but there were also many inefficiencies, and in some areas China's technology remained backward. In 1979 the Government decided to welcome foreign direct investment (FDI), and in many ways, this became the symbol of the new "open door" policy.

4.2 The Chinese authorities have rightly believed, from the beginning, that the process of attracting FDI and getting it to function in the desired ways would inevitably involve at least some amount of trial and error. They have been foresighted in their willingness to experiment and to learn from experience. Although progress has in many ways been remarkable, the Government is not satisfied with either the amount or the nature of the FDI that has so far come. In seeking to do better, some avoidable defects of policy have been discovered. This annex describes China's efforts to attract FDI and their results, and makes recommendations for policy reforms that could improve future results. This discussion is broken up into three parts: (a) a review of the role of FDI and international experience; (b) policies for and experience with FDI in China since 1979; and (c) an analysis of the current policy framework for promoting FDI and recommendations for reform.

A. The Role of Foreign Direct Investment in International Perspective

Characteristics of Foreign Direct Investment

4.3 "Investment", as used here, refers to equity or risk capital and it distinguishes FDI from loans, bonds or other forms of borrowing. The investors as a group are owners of the enterprise. They have a residual or last claim on the earnings of the enterprise: they get no returns until all other claimants, including lenders or bondholders, are paid, but they are entitled to all of whatever revenues or assets are left after those other claims are satisfied. Thus, they take the most risk of all people who provide resources to the enterprise, but will get the most rewards if the enterprise is successful.

4.4 "Direct" implies that the investor has a large enough share in the enterprise that he will exert some degree of control over its operations. Direct investment is distinguished from portfolio investment; in the latter, the investor's share is very small, and he is just the passive recipient of any profits or losses the enterprise makes.

4.5 Because private property rights, corporate law, and the organization of ownership are very different in China than in most capitalist countries, the differences between a loan and an investment, in the sense the words are used here, are not always well understood in China. In general, a loan creates a claim that is fixed in amount and usually in time as well, and that comes before the claims of investors; while an investment, as explained above, creates a claim that is not fixed in amount (or, usually, in time). An investment can earn returns only after all other claimants are satisfied, but then covers all the remaining resources of the enterprise.

4.6 Therefore, FDI involves significant risk. No return will be earned if the enterprise is unsuccessful--indeed the investment itself may be lost. This characteristic strongly motivates the investor to operate the enterprise in ways that will in fact yield returns on the investment. This motivation is one of the main reasons why many local enterprises prefer equity joint ventures to other means of acquiring foreign resources and technology. They appreciate having a partner who is committed to the success of the enterprise, rather than simply a creditor whose concern does not go beyond the repayment of a loan (which in practice is usually guaranteed by a bank or other third party anyway). A foreign partner with a significant share in the ownership of a joint venture will be interested in continuing to upgrade technology as it changes over the years after the venture is established. The partner will also be interested in providing the right technology for the venture, rather than just in selling some machinery at a profit, and will be interested in contributing to the solution of problems that the enterprise will face as it grows.

4.7 Throughout the world, almost all FDI is done by multinational companies (MNCs). There are many reasons for the existence of these companies, and among these are some fundamental economic technological characteristics. An MNC almost always has some kind of knowledge that gives it a competitive edge over other companies, and that knowledge is of a nature that can be exploited more profitably within parts of the same corporate structure than by selling it to other unrelated enterprises.

4.8 In some cases, this latter characteristic is related to the newness of the knowledge, such as how to make some recently invented product or operate some recently designed process. Companies that possess such new, highly profitable knowledge are often reluctant to sell it but may transfer it to companies in which they have an ownership interest in order to gain access to other markets or to production sites where costs are lower. A different characteristic that makes knowledge more profitable to exploit within a corporate group is that the knowledge is difficult or impossible to embody in a set of machines, plans, etc. Examples of such knowledge include skill in production layouts of complex processes, such as an automobile production, or skill in managing parts of the business in addition to the production side, such as marketing.

4.9 There is usually no need to deal with FDI, and no extra profit in doing so, when all that is required is a set of certain machines or a patented production process that is for sale. However, when other, more "disembodied" aspects of technology or management are important, then a partnership with an

MNC may be both necessary and desirable. When the problems are most difficult, most complex or longest lasting--for example, when the technology is complex or rapidly changing, or when the export markets are especially competitive--then FDI is most useful.

4.10 Foreign direct investment also has some important limitations. First and foremost, it has been concentrated, historically, in a few countries and in a few sectors. This tendency to concentrate is in part a result of the characteristics just discussed. It will almost surely persist, although the areas of concentration have changed and may change again in the future.

4.11 Most foreign investment within the last four decades has, of course, come from the industrialized countries. Perhaps less obviously, most of it has also gone to the industrialized countries; only about one-fourth of the total has gone to the developing world. Moreover, half of the total FDI that went to the Third World during 1969-76 went to only thirteen developing countries or regions; if hydrocarbons and mining investments were excluded, only seven of all the developing economies (Argentina, Brazil, Hong Kong, India, Mexico, Singapore and Spain) would show up as destinations for significant amounts of FDI during that period. However, a few smaller countries that welcomed FDI did receive amounts that were significant in relation to the sizes of their economies, such as Costa Rica, Cote d'Ivoire, and Kenya (See Tables 4.1 and 4.2).

4.12 Before the Second World War (1939-45), FDI in developing countries was concentrated mainly in mining and mineral processing, in plantation agriculture, and in infrastructure sectors such as railroads, telephone and other communications, and electric power. In the four decades since the Second World War, the sectoral focus has shifted away from infrastructure and agriculture and into manufacturing (with mining remaining a focus). Still more recently, some service activities (such as hotels, banking, insurance, leasing, etc.) have also been entered to significant degree by MNCs.

4.13 Within manufacturing, three kinds of activities account for most FDI in developing nations: (a) the manufacture of labor-intensive products of medium to high value-to-weight ratio, for export--typically electronics; (b) non-durable consumer goods, where trade marks or formulas have been important, such as pharmaceuticals and beverages for the domestic market; and (c) high technology and/or high capital cost industries, including both process industries (chemicals, metals, cement) and machinery, electrical and transportation equipment--again, initially at least, for the domestic market. Economies of scale are important in most of the activities in group (c), and in most of these activities FDI has located in countries with large markets to produce mainly for domestic consumption. (Exceptions are activities where it is important to be near inputs, such as petrochemicals.)

4.14 In the last ten years or so, a few of the most advanced developing countries have witnessed a broadening of these relatively narrow areas of attention. As the so-called "NICs"--newly-industrializing countries, such as Brazil and Spain--became internationally competitive in a wide range of manufactured products, FDI ventures in those countries have been investing and producing for export as well as for domestic markets. There are two important

Table 4.1

REGIONAL DISTRIBUTION OF PRIVATE DIRECT FOREIGN INVESTMENT FLOWS (NET, 1969-76) FROM DAC COUNTRIES TO SELECTED DEVELOPING COUNTRIES

Country	US$ Millions	Percentage of Total (excluding tax-haven countries)
Europe		
Greece	348	0.8
Spain	2,828	6.5
Turkey	97	0.2
Africa		
Algeria	328	0.8
Libya	181	0.4
Morocco	1	-
Angola	24	0.1
Zaire	354	0.8
Gabon	78	0.2
Ghana	58	0.1
Ivory Coast	38	0.1
Liberia	456	1.0
Nigeria	730	1.7
Zimbabwe	175	0.4
Zambia	113	0.3
Latin America and Caribbean		
Jamaica	-36	-0.1
Mexico	1,552	3.6
Panama	1,292	3.0
Trinidad & Tobago	19	-
West Indies	235	0.5
Argentina	782	1.8
Brazil	6,906	15.8
Chile	-412	-0.9
Colombia	227	0.5
Peru	1,112	2.5
Venezuela	-354	-0.8
Middle East		
Iran	-110	-0.3
Iraq	-61	-0.1
Kuwait	66	0.2
Saudi Arabia	106	0.2
Asia and Oceania		
India	345	0.8
Pakistan	13	-
Hong Kong	633	1.5
Indonesia	2,869	6.6
Republic of Korea	594	1.4
Malaysia	526	1.2
Philippines	567	1.3
Singapore	402	0.9
Thailand	159	0.4
Papua New Guinea	537	1.2
Sub-Total	23,778	
Tax-Haven Countries	4,638	
Other Countries	15,212	
TOTAL:	43,628	

Source: K. Billerbeck & Y. Yasugi, "Private Direct Foreign Investment in Developing Countries," World Bank Staff Working Paper No. 348, July 1979, Table SI.5, page 70.

Table 4.2

FOREIGN PRIVATE INVESTMENT IN SELECTED DEVELOPING COUNTRIES AND REGIONS

1979

Country	FDI/GDP
Singapore	19%
Malaysia	15%
Peru	15%
Hong Kong [a/]	15%
Indonesia	11%
Kenya	9%
Costa Rica	8%
Taiwan[a/]	8%
Venezuela	7%
Chile	7%
Brazil	7%
Ghana	6%
Israel	6%
Côte d'Ivoire	6%
Philippines	6%
Argentina	5%
Colombia	5%
Mexico	5%
Pakistan	4%
South Korea	3%
Morocco	2%
India	2%
Thailand	2%
Nigeria	1%
Egypt	1%
Algeria	1%
Turkey	1%
China[b/]	1%
Yugoslavia	0%

Sources: United Nations Center for Transnational Corporations, Transnational Corporations in World Development, 1983, except for:

a/ Balasubramangam, V.N., "Incentives and Disincentives for Foreign Direct Investment in Less Developed Countries," Weltwirschaftlisches Archiv; data for 1978.

b/ Mission estimates for 1985.

aspects of this phenomenon. First, a very wide range of manufacturing activities, set up in middle-income developing countries to serve the domestic market, has after many years proved able to export when given appropriate incentives. Second, MNCs, that years ago were not at all interested in exporting from their developing country plants, have adopted a truly multinational view and are now exporting some products from and importing other products to virtually every country in which they have ventures. Obviously, these two aspects are complementary, simultaneous parts of the same process. FDI companies that produce for the domestic market are now the same ones that produce for export. This is a profound change of the role of FDI in development, with important implications for Chinese efforts to derive maximum benefit in the long run from FDI.

4.15 Another characteristic of FDI that must be taken into account is that it responds to opportunities for profit, and that in almost all cases it compares alternative uses of its financial resources and of its management time when deciding whether or not to pursue a project in a particular country. If a country does not look promising the MNC management will not spend much time on it.

4.16 Because FDI involves a capital flow into the host country, it is sometimes seen as an alternative to other forms of capital inflows, such as foreign aid or foreign borrowing. This view is correct, as far as it goes, but is not the complete story. First, because the additional capital associated with FDI is committed to a particular investment in productive facilities, like any such investment it requires complementary expenditure on infrastructure services, education, etc. Second, as has already been discussed, FDI almost always brings more than just financial resources with it. It usually involves (a) the transfer of some production technology; (b) some management and organizational know-how that includes the production process and such other aspects of the business as organization, accounting, marketing, etc.; and (c) export marketing channels or other aspects of access to export markets. For all these reasons, FDI is only in small measure an alternative to increased foreign borrowing or to increased domestic saving.

Country Strategies for Foreign Direct Investment

4.17 Individual developing countries have adopted different approaches to FDI. Leaving aside for the moment the special cases of mineral extraction activities, and of small, poor countries that are not particularly attractive to most other types of FDI, it seems that there have been three basically different kinds of experiences during the last forty years: (a) Some of the middle-income developing countries have been generally open to FDI. Brazil is the archetype of the successful, open country; Argentina, Mexico and the Philippines have been somewhat less open but still fit this category; (b) Other countries have been more defensive and have limited FDI either moderately (India, Turkey until recently) or severely (South Korea until recently; Japan is an example from earlier times); and (c) Finally, a few countries that were potential recipients of FDI and sought to attract it have failed to create an appropriate policy framework (notably, Egypt and Yugoslavia).

Countries Open to Foreign Direct Investment

4.18 Brazil has been more open to FDI than almost any of the developing countries, and only a few small Asian economies such as Hong Kong and Singapore are more open. Brazil's large market makes it very attractive for FDI, and its generally welcoming treatment has combined with this attraction to give it the largest stock of FDI of any developing country--about US$30 billion, equivalent to about 12 percent of GDP. This is now almost all in manufacturing, where FDI ventures account for perhaps one-third of all production in that sector. Even though FDI is concentrated to some extent in some manufacturing subsectors such as automobiles, chemicals, and tobacco, it accounts for at least 10 percent of production in 17 of Brazil's 21 manufacturing subsectors.

4.19 The Brazilian constitution guarantees FDI equal treatment with domestic investment. FDI is welcomed in almost all parts of manufacturing. In addition to general openness to FDI in almost all manufacturing activities, Brazil has from time to time mounted special efforts to attract FDI in specific activities where it was judged to be most useful, such as automobiles, shipbuilding, capital goods and chemicals. In each of these sectoral programs high level officials negotiated a comprehensive program with MNCs, establishing a set of conditions which satisfied the government as to the amount and nature of the investments, local procurement, etc , and satisfied the MNCs as to protection, availability of imported inputs, financing, etc. What the government wanted from FDI were technology and the capital inflow. Exports did develop later, not in response to FDI regulations, but as a result of changes in the macroeconomic framework, and the changing business practices of many MNCs.

4.20 Since the late 1960s/early 1970s, there have been two major changes in Brazil's approach to FDI. First, drastic policy changes altered the incentive structure facing the entire manufacturing sector; and export sales were made much more profitable. FDI ventures, as well as purely Brazilian companies, responded by increasing exports in what was referred to in the 1970s as the Brazilian miracle. Since the debt crisis of 1982, Brazil's industrial base, which was built up over a century, and the exporting experience of over a decade, permitted Brazil to earn the enormous trade surpluses that have enabled it to service its very large debt. All FDI ventures in manufacturing were estimated to have a surplus of exports over imports of 3.4% of their total sales in 1977; since then, the surplus has surely increased. The second change in Brazil's approach has been to move to a less permissive stance toward new FDI ventures. There is greater pressure to form joint ventures with local private firms and/or with parastatals, instead of wholly owned subsidiaries, and the import of technology has been made more difficult in order to protect existing firms (including FDI ventures) that develop technology in Brazil. The temporary reservation of the mini and microcomputer sectors for Brazilian firms is the most extreme example of this latter change.

4.21 Brazil has got what it wanted from FDI. MNCs provided the technology and much of the capital to develop priority sectors, and in its competition with, purchases from, and interchange of labor with other firms in

Brazil, FDI helped to diffuse advanced technology and good management practices throughout the economy. When incentives were changed to promote manufactured exports, FDI ventures responded well. FDI has been an important part, although by no means the whole story, of Brazil's transformation into a modern industrial economy that today can export such products as aircraft, armaments, a wide range of machinery and equipment, telecommunications systems, and a variety of automobile parts including tires and complete engines. This success is due to the combination of a natural attractiveness to FDI with policies that treated FDI as a positive-sum game. Brazil insisted on the few major aspects of performance it wanted most from foreign investors, but then granted them other things that they needed in order to be successful, and so new foreign investors continued to be attracted as the years passed.

Countries with Defensive Strategies

4.22 South Korea and India furnish examples of a less welcoming, more defensive approach to FDI. These countries have systematically restricted the role of FDI in their economies and have rigorously screened FDI proposals and controlled the companies whose entry was permitted. To some extent these decisions represent reactions against past colonialism and a desire to avoid foreign economic domination in the future. Protection for domestically owned enterprises against competition from local partners of MNCs was desired, and foreigners were to be kept from reaping benefits that included subsidized credit and protected local markets.

4.23 In South Korea, FDI was limited until the 1980s to joint ventures in a narrow list of sectors. It was excluded from activities that competed with Korean firms in export markets or for local inputs. Ownership shares of foreigners in joint ventures were limited to 50 percent, except in enterprises that exported 100% of their output or had a particularly difficult and valued technology. India has similarly reserved many industrial sectors from any FDI at all and has further restricted joint ventures with more than 40% foreign ownership to a narrower list of specified industries. As can be seen in Table 4.2, neither India nor South Korea attracted much FDI. Even though each of them had many inherent attractions, their policies restricted FDI to far below its potential.

4.24 South Korea has, of course, accomplished a remarkable record of growth and development without much help from FDI. During the 1980s, however the Government has begun to liberalize some of the restrictions on foreign investment. FDI inflows have responded, bringing not only more capital but also some leading edge technology to Korea in automobiles and some electronics products, for example. India also has recently begun to relax some of its restrictions.

Countries with Inappropriate Policy Frameworks

4.25 Egypt and Yugoslavia furnish examples of yet a third kind of experience with FDI. Both countries had more or less socialist regimes and were closed to FDI. Then, Yugoslavia in the late 1960s and Egypt in the early 1970s decided to open their economies to FDI and, in fact, passed many laws and regulations designed to encourage it. Both were countries with good-size domestic markets, and hence potentially attractive to FDI, especially of the import-substituting type. This would have fit in well with the desire of the countries to use FDI to import advanced technology to modernize their economies and make them more efficient.

4.26 However, they both involved themselves in a contradictory situation not unlike China's. Their overall policy framework discriminated against exports (except, in Egypt, of tourist services), but they imposed some version of an enterprise-level foreign exchange balance requirement on FDI ventures. This and other major problems have kept the level of FDI very low in both countries (see Table 4.2), except for some recent inflows of foreign capital into banking and real estate in Egypt, induced partially by the chaotic conditions in Lebanon. Yugoslavia has modified the foreign exchange balance requirement, going back and forth between a more liberal and a more rigid policy several times in the last twenty years, without being able to settle on a system that permitted reasonable access of FDI ventures to foreign exchange. Egypt suspended the requirement after only a few years. but other problems have persisted. Both countries would still welcome more FDI but have been unable to create conditions that would make their inherent attractiveness effective.

4.27 These and other examples lead to the conclusion that a successful approach to FDI, regardless of the particular objectives sought, requires internal consistency among a country's objectives, its possibilities and its policies. Singapore and Brazil, for example, were each successful in using very different kinds of FDI to pursue very different paths of development. They were successful because they adopted objectives and implemented policies that were consistent with their inherent possibilities. South Korea did well without much FDI, again adopting policies and objectives that coincided with its potential. Egypt and Yugoslavia implemented policies that were not consistent with their possibilities and more or less failed in their efforts to attract FDI.

B. Foreign Direct Investment in China Since 1979

The Different Forms of Foreign Direct Investment in China

4.28 The door was opened to FDI in 1979, with the adoption of the Law on Joint Ventures Using Chinese and Foreign Investment, still the law that regulates equity joint ventures. Most countries permit several different kinds of cooperation between foreign and local enterprises. In the West, some of these activities are thought of as FDI, and others are not. Confusion sometimes arises, however, because China often lumps many of these activities together when preparing statistics. Six different kinds of arrangements can be identified that, taken together, comprise what is often referred to as FDI in China. These are as follows:

(i) Wholly foreign-owned ventures: This category, as is obvious and clear from its name, a corporate entity which is completely owned by foreigners, established and operating in China.

(ii) Equity joint ventures: Sometimes called simply joint ventures, this is a corporate entity owned partly by foreigners and partly by Chinese, established and operating in China. This form of FDI is the only one regulated by the Chinese Law on Joint Ventures Using Chinese and Foreign Investment, and the operational definition of an equity joint venture in China is an enterprise established under that law.

These two forms together, are the only ones that are unequivocally FDI in the normal international usage of the term. The third and fourth forms may also be considered to be FDI in normal usage, at least in some cases.

(iii) Contractual joint ventures: Sometimes called cooperative ventures or cooperative joint ventures, these are joint undertakings between one or more foreign entities and one or more Chinese entities. Their nature is potentially very flexible, being, in fact, whatever the contracting parties agree. They may involve the creation of a corporate entity (like an equity joint venture), but often do not. Profits and losses may be allocated in any way specified in the contract, often without attempting to put precise valuations on the different contributions of the individual parties. In many ways, contractual joint ventures are often similar to equity joint ventures. In both forms, the foreigners usually contribute some or all of the machinery and/or other technology and are responsible for exports if any; the Chinese usually contribute land, buildings, and most of the raw materials; and both sides cooperate in some way in management. Some activities under this rubric are normal joint ventures in all but name, set up in a legally different form to avoid some of the requirements of the equity joint venture law. Others involve much less close relations between the foreign and local partners and are more like forms (v) and (vi), to be described below.

(iv) Joint development: Sometimes called cooperative development, this form is used for foreign-Chinese cooperation in exploiting natural resources--most commonly for offshore oil. The essence of this form is that the various parties' returns are in the form of specified shares of the physical output of the enterprise. Typically, the Chinese parties use their share for domestic purposes, while the foreign parties are required to sell their share abroad. Joint development enterprises are regulated by a separate set of laws and regulations.

The next two forms to be described would not be thought of as FDI in the usual western use of the concept. They do not involve a sharing of risks and profits, and the foreign partner usually has no voice in the management of the enterprise. However, the value of machinery imported under them is counted as FDI by the Chinese authorities.

(v) Compensation trade: The essence of this form is that the purchase of machinery from abroad, by a local enterprise, is financed in whole or in part by goods produced after the purchase. In direct compensation trade, the goods are produced by the enterprise, while in indirect compensation trade, the goods are produced by a different Chinese enterprise and purchased by the one which imported the machinery. This activity is, typically, simply a way to finance the importation of machinery by future payments of goods--a form of counter-trade. In some cases, the maker of the machinery may supply some management assistance or other soft technology as well, but this is not usually a major feature of the arrangement.

(vi) Processing and assembling: In these arrangements, the foreign parties provide some or all inputs to a product, and sometimes some machinery and other know-how; the Chinese enterprise uses the inputs to make the product, which it then returns to the foreigner, who pays a fee for the service. The foreign parties may provide some machinery and/or technical assistance as well.

4.29 Each of these six activities, whether normally thought of as FDI or not, shares many of the important characteristics of FDI (albeit sometimes only in small or very small degree). They usually involve at least some technology transfer (often including at least some management skills), and they usually involve a transfer of at least some additional investable resources to China, even if only for a few years. The potential benefits of the various forms of FDI are summarized in Table 4.3.

4.30 Two additional activities bear mentioning here. First is foreign borrowing, which is often lumped with FDI as foreign capital absorbed by China. Second is the leasing of equipment from foreigners, which is another way to get some elements of both technology transfer and investable resource transfer. Leasing is in fact similar to compensation trade; the main difference is that compensation trade, in effect, guarantees the exports to provide the foreign exchange to pay for the imported equipment, while leasing does not. This difference looms large in Chinese eyes, because of the strong concern for foreign exchange and the approach of allocating it administratively by enterprise rather than through markets.

Table 4.3: POTENTIAL BENEFITS OF SOME FORMS OF USING FOREIGN CAPITAL

Form	Benefit				
	Advanced machinery	Management training,etc.	Export channels	Foreign capital	Automatic FX balance
Wholly foreign or equity JV	yes	yes	yes	yes	no
Contractual JV	yes	weak	yes	some	no
Compensation trade	weak	no	some	weak	yes
Processing agreements	no	no	yes	weak	yes
Leasing	yes	no	no	weak	no

4.31 The availability of these varied forms of absorbing foreign capital is, in general, good for China, because it gives enterprises great flexibility in choosing the best way for them to associate with foreign companies. While equity joint ventures potentially offer a wider range of benefits than do the other forms, they are also more difficult to negotiate and may be more complex to operate. In many cases the particular needs of a given enterprise can be well satisfied with a simpler form of cooperation, and it is wise to permit such simpler forms. In particular, the contractual joint venture has been so popular in large part because of the lack of legal restrictions on its structure. It may be that some additional laws and regulations are needed for these ventures--indeed, in some areas a clearer definition might encourage more investment--but care should be taken to avoid unnecessary restrictions that could "kill the goose that lays the golden egg."

China's Objectives for Foreign Direct Investment

4.32 The dominant reason for, and objective of, China's opening to FDI was and continues to be transfer of technology to China, in order to modernize the economy and make it more efficient. The previous approach to importing technology--i.e. importing turnkey plants or buying particular product or process technology--had led to many inefficiencies. While it seems clear that some of those problems were not inherent in the approach--rather they were caused by poor planning and implementation--it became more and more clear that (a) there was more to modernization and efficiency than just specific technological processes, and (b) at least in some cases, the most cost-effective way to get technology was by forming a continuing relationship with the foreign supplier of the technology, in which the supplier also had an interest in a profitable outcome. Thus, the equity joint venture was introduced.

4.33 Other objectives have also been important in shaping China's dealings with FDI. The economic reforms begun in the late 1970s attached increased importance to increasing exports. FDI ventures were seen as a way to do this, both through producing products of exportable quality and price, and because of skill or access in marketing such products overseas. Furthermore, some soft aspects of technology, including management skills, were recognized as being needed and available from abroad, especially if the foreigners had a stake in the outcome of the enterprise.

4.34 Unlike most other developing countries, China does not seem to value very much the capital itself that is associated with FDI. Statistically, during the late 1960s and early 1970s, FDI accounted for about one-fourth of all net capital flows from the OECD to developing countries--an amount sufficient to finance approximately 5% of total investment in the developing world. Many other developing countries have prized FDI for this function--it complements domestic savings and foreign borrowing, increasing the total resources available to the country to finance investment. China, however, tends to view the capital inflow associated with FDI as temporary, to be serviced while in China and to be returned in full in the future, much like a loan. (Under Chinese law, foreign equity joint ventures are established for fixed, limited periods, although the law allows for indefinite extensions if all parties agree.) Indeed, far from regarding the capital inflows associated with FDI as a good thing, many officials in China attach more importance to the possibility that some FDI ventures may use more foreign exchange than they generate, thus creating a drain on China's own foreign exchange resources.

4.35 China has made FDI easiest, and given it the strongest incentives, in four Special Economic Zones (SEZs) and fourteen coastal cities. The SEZs are also located on the coast, and in general these are all places where a large share of FDI would have been likely to locate in any event. Many of the coastal cities are major industrial and commercial centers, while two of the four SEZs are close to Hong Kong, and all four are in regions from which most overseas Chinese originated (which means they speak the same dialects).

4.36 The SEZs appear to have been created for several reasons. They were clearly designed to function as export platforms and to attract investment from overseas Chinese. (Ventures in SEZs need special permission to sell any part of their production within the rest of China.) It seems, in addition, that Chinese policy makers regard the SEZs as places to experiment with FDI in relative isolation from the rest of the economy, to facilitate the differential treatment that FDI requires in a nonmarket economy and to be able to contain unforeseen bad effects that might occur.

China's Experience with Foreign Direct Investment, 1979-85

4.37 China has made significant strides in attracting FDI in the seven short years since 1979. One of the less advanced aspects of this history, however, is the collection and reporting of statistics describing it. The data are fragmented and not always internally consistent. We rely here mostly on the recent work by Chen, [1] which seems to be as comprehensive and up-to-date as anything available in China or abroad. As Chen cautions his readers, however, the estimates may be inexact.

The Volume of Investment

4.38 Some of the data presented by Chen are reproduced as Tables 4.4 through 4.7. Considering first all of the first six forms listed above (of which the latter two are not truly FDI): by the end of 1985 over 7000 agreements had been signed and approved, for a total foreign investment of US$16.2 billion. Of this, only US$4.6 billion had actually been invested. Excluding compensation trade, and processing and assembling, which in most countries would not be counted as investment, and also the small number (but large amount) of joint oil production agreements, the totals for wholly foreign owned ventures, equity joint ventures and contractual joint ventures were 4,742 project agreements signed and approved, for US$8.5 billion, of which only US$2.4 billion had by end-1985 actually been invested.[2]

4.39 To put these numbers in perspective, US$8.5 billion would have been about 3 percent of China's GDP, while US$2.4 billion was about 0.8%. Compare the percentages shown in Table 4.2. Brazil, whose economy is about two-thirds as large as China, but which has pursued a strategy of capitalist development and welcoming of FDI for most of the twentieth century, might be used to give a very approximate idea of how much FDI China might ultimately attract; Brazil has a stock of FDI estimated at something above US$30 billion, or about 12 percent of its GDP. (This estimate corrects for some underestimation bias in the official estimates reported in Table 4.2.)

4.40 Statistics of FDI cited from here on will refer only to equity, contractual, and wholly owned ventures unless otherwise labelled.

4.41 The number of new ventures approved each year increased through 1985, when over 2800--more than half the cumulative total through that time--were signed. In 1986, however, the number of new approvals fell. In the first six months, approvals were down 20 percent from the same period in 1986, and, for the first nine months as a whole, the drop was 42 percent. Now, it is obvious that the figures cannot grow forever. There will be short periods of lesser activity, perhaps for accidental reasons or reasons having nothing to do with China. And probably at some point the inflows of FDI will level off on a longer-term basis. But most observers believe that the decline in

---

1/ Chen, Nai-Ruenn, "Foreign Investment in China: Current Trends," US Department of Commerce, March 1986.

2/ The definitions of contractual joint ventures, compensation trade and processing and assembling agreements are not sharp enough to classify every activity definitively. Thus, which FDI projects to include in the data for contractual joint ventures is to some extent a question of judgment and interpretation.

Table 4.4

Annual Foreign Investment in China by Type

	1979	1980	1981	1982	1983	1984	1985
1. Equity joint ventures							
a. Number of agreements	6	20	28	29	107	741	1,300
b. Foreign investment pledged ($million)	8	63	28	29	188	1,060	
c. Foreign investment realized ($million)					74		
2. Cooperative ventures							
a. Number of agreements		320	70	402	331	1,089	1,500
b. Foreign contribution pledged ($million)		500	1,300	926	504		
c. Foreign contribution realized ($million)					238		
3. Wholly foreign-owned ventures							
a. Number of agreements					15	26	46
b. Foreign Investment pledged ($million)					4	99	
4. Joint oil development							
a. Number of agreements	8	4	0	1	18	0	4
b. Foreign contribution pledged ($ million)	110	1,112	0	170	1,031	0	
c. Foreign contribution realized (%million)	110				296	520	
5. Compensation Trade							
a. Number of agreements	--417---		173	282	183	311	
b. Value of equipment to be supplied by foreign companies ($million)	--381---		79	265	107	160	
c. Value of equipment actually supplied by foreign companies ($million)					150		
6. Total (including processing assembling arrangements)							
a. Foreign contribution pledged ($million)						2,650	5,850
b. Foreign contribution realized ($million)						1,254	1,570

Note: In this and the following tables, blank space indicates that figures are not available or are not applicable.

Source: "Foreign Investment in China: Current Trends" by Nai-Ruenn Chen, March 1986, Office of the PRC and Hong Kong, US Department of Commerce, International Trade Administration.

Table 4.5

Cumulative Foreign Investment in China by Type

	1979-82	1979-83	1979-84	June 1979-85	September 1979-85	December 1979-1985
1. Equity joint ventures						
a. Number of agreements	83	190	931	1,618	1,897	2,231
b. Foreign investment pledged ($million)	141	315	1, 00	2,380		
c. Foreign investment realized ($million)	103	177				
2. Cooperative ventures						
a. Number of agreements	792	1,123	2,212	3,030	3,408	3,712
b. Foreign contribution pledged ($million)	2,726	3,230		5,580		
c. Foreign contribution realized ($million)		530	768			
3. Wholly foreign-owned ventures						
a. Number of agreements	33	48	74	94	109	120
b. Foreign investment pledged ($million)	367	371	470	492		
c. Foreign investment realized ($million)	40					
4. Joint oil development						
a. Number of agreements	13	31	31	31	31	35
b. Foreign contribution pledged ($million)	1,392	2,420	2,420	2,420		
c. Foreign contribution realized ($million)	486	782	1,302			
5. Compensation Trade						
a. Number of agreements	872	998	1,371		1,585	
b. Value of equipment to be supplied by foreign companies ($million)	725	930	992			
c. Value of equipment actually supplied by foreign companies ($million)	413	563				
6. Processing and assembling arrangements						
a. Number of agreements	1,600					
b. Value of equipment actually supplied by foreign companies ($million)	197					
7. Total "foreign direct investment" in China						
(1) Number of agreements					7,030	
(2) Foreign contribution pledged ($million)	4,958	7,700	10,350		14,700	16,200
(3) Foreign contribution realized ($million)		1,776	3,030			4,600

Source: "Foreign Investment in China: Current Trends" by Nai-Ruenn Chen, March 1986, Office of the PRC and Hong Kong, US Department of Commerce, International Trade Administration.

Table 4.6

Cumulative Investment in China by U.S., Japanese and West European Firms

	As of December 1984			As of September 1985
	Total	USA	Japan	Western Europe
1. Equity Joint Ventures in China				
a. Number of agreements	931	62	57	51
b. Foreign investment pledged ($ mill.)	1,400	134	120	260
2. Cooperative Ventures				
a. Number of agreements	2,212	19		
b. Foreign contribution pledged ($ mill.)		170	95	11
3. Wholly Foreign-Owned Ventures				
a. Number of agreements	74	3		1
b. Foreign investment pledged ($ mill.)	470		15	
4. Joint Oil Development				
a. Number of agreements	31	18	5	
b. Foreign contribution pledged ($ mill.)	2,400	679	810	600
5. Compensation Trade				
a. Number of agreements	1,371			
b. Value of equipment to be supplied by foreign companies ($ mill.)			160	
6. Total "foreign direct investment" in China				
(1) Number of agreements 1/	4,619			
(2) Foreign contribution pledged ($ mill.)	10,000	1,030	1,200	1,080
(3) Foreign contribution realized ($ mill.)		1,776	3,030	4,600

1/ Not including processing and assembling arrangements.

Source: "Foreign Investment in China: Current Trends" by Nai-Ruenn Chen, March 1986, Office of the PRC and Hong Kong, U.S. Department of Commerce, International Trade Administration.

Table 4.7

Number of International Equity Joint Ventures in China by Size of Foreign Investment

US$ Million	Cumulative through 1984
Below 0.25	311
0.25 - 0.5	177
0.5 - 1.0	127
1.0 - 2.0	111
2.0 - 3.0	40
3.0 - 4.0	15
4.0 - 5.0	14
5.0 - 6.0	3
6.0 - 7.0	8
7.0 - 8.0	5
8.0 - 9.0	2
9.0 - 10.0	3
Above 10.0	25
Unknown	90
Total	931

Source: "Foreign Investment in China: Current Trends", by Nai-Ruenn Chen, March 1986, Office of the PRC and Hong Kong, U.S. Department of Commerce, International Trade Administration.

1986 was not a random occurrence, but rather resulted from a growing disenchantment with opportunities in China as perceived by potential investors. Of the various negative factors behind these perceptions, difficulties caused by the foreign exchange balance requirement were perhaps the most important single one, especially for advanced technology equity joint ventures (see paras. 4.84-4.88).

Sources and Destinations of Investment

4.42 Hong Kong dominates all other countries and regions as the source of FDI, according to the statistics. (An unknown part of foreign investors that legally are Hong Kong firms are in fact owned and controlled by firms in other foreign countries or, in some cases, by enterprises of the Peoples Republic itself.) As of June 1985, fully 85 percent of the total value of FDI came from Hong Kong. Japan accounted for another 5 percent, the USA for 4 percent, and all other countries combined had only 6 percent. (Even if joint petroleum ventures are included, Hong Kong still would account for 66.5 percent of the total, and there were no joint petroleum ventures from Hong Kong.) Hong Kong's share in the number of contracts is even higher, as they tend to be smaller than those from other nations.

4.43 Although precise breakdowns are not available, over 3500 of the 4700-odd agreements signed and approved, accounting for over US$5 billion of the US$8,5 billion planned FDI, were contractual joint ventures with Hong Kong firms. An overwhelming number of these were located in Guangdong--over 90 percent as of the end of 1982. Of course, some concentration of foreign investors among Hong Kong and/or other overseas Chinese is perfectly natural and appropriate. And the contractual joint venture form, as noted earlier, has the considerable advantage of minimal legal restrictions on the mode of cooperation. But, while these ventures contributed to employment, income and exports for China and also may be facilitating the eventual political joining of Hong Kong to the Peoples Republic, most of them have done little to advance the goal of modernization of the Chinese economy. In fact, in at least a few of these ventures, the Hong Kong partner is a company set up by an enterprise on the mainland, for the purpose of avoiding some of the restrictions placed on Chinese enterprises with regard to direct exports and imports, retention of foreign exchange earned by exports, travel abroad, etc.

4.44 Most FDI projects in China are small, considering the size of the country. The average planned foreign investment per project is US$1.8 million (which is about half of the total project cost); the averages by type are US$1.5 million for equity joint ventures, US$1.8 million for contractual joint ventures and US$5.2 million for wholly foreign owned ventures.[3/] Considering equity joint ventures as of the end of 1984, 37 percent had FDI of less than US$250,000, another 36 percent were also under US$1 million, and another 21 percent were under US$5 million. Only 5 percent were over US$5 million.

3/ The average size of contractual joint ventures is distorted by the inclusion of a few recent agreements for very large projects. The typical enterprise in this form is considerably smaller.

4.45 Among equity joint ventures, at the end of 1984, 60 percent were in manufacturing. Only 6 percent were in agriculture; 34 percent were in services.

4.46 The SEZs and the coastal cities have been hosts to the lion's share of FDI. As of the end of 1984, Shenzhen SEZ alone was the site for 216 actual and planned equity joint ventures out of the total of 931 for the entire nation. The three other SEZs accounted for another 100 projects, so the share of all four SEZs was 34 percent of all actual and planned equity joint ventures. Considering all six forms counted in China as FDI, by 1985 Shenzhen alone accounted for 4400--more than half--of the total of something over 7000 agreements. 4/

C. Policy Analysis and Recommendations

4.47 Until 1979 Chinese officials had limited contacts with western capitalist economies or institutions, and tended to view foreign private investment as exploitative and coercive. During the last eight years, however, the Government has approached FDI in a pragmatic and experimental manner. As has already been suggested, there are basically three types of economic opportunity that attract FDI to most developing countries: (a) rich natural resources, where FDI produces at least in part for export; (b) low input costs, including low taxes and little governmental regulation, which attract FDI to manufacture labor-intensive goods of moderate to high value-to-weight ratios, mainly for export; and (c) a large domestic market, for which FDI produces a wide variety of goods, mainly for sale in that market. Each of these three kinds of FDI have different needs and respond to different aspects of the economic and political environment.

4.48 The exploitation of natural resources--in the case of China, mostly petroleum and coal--is a highly specialized topic that will not be analyzed here. It does seem, however, that China is attracting significant foreign investment in this area. In the remainder of this section, policies relevant to export-oriented manufacturing to FDI with at least some significant domestic market orientation will be dealt with in turn. First, however, some comments may be made about a few aspects of the environment that affect all FDI.

4/ These four SEZs were established in places that, while near ports, Hong Kong, etc., were themselves quite undeveloped. Much basic infrastructure has therefore had to be constructed, and in fact a good part of it is being constructed by FDI. Indeed this private infrastructure construction is one reason for the large share of China's total FDI being located in the SEZs.

Policies of General Effect

4.49 Aspects of the policy environment that affect all FDI include: (a) general macroeconomic policies, especially the exchange rate; (b) the procedures for promoting, screening and approving FDI projects; (c) interference with the management and operation of ongoing projects; (d) exploitative vs. collaborative behavior of domestic partners and of governmental authorities; and (e) access local sources of finance.

The Exchange Rate

4.50 As analyzed elsewhere in this report (see main report, chapter 3), the RMB is currently valued above the exchange rate that would prevail if there were no barriers, taxes, or subsidies on Chinese imports or exports. This means that exports are less profitable than they would be if trade were freer and, combined with other policies, has the result that Chinese economic policy discriminates against exports. This fact, together with the shortage of foreign exchange that such policies create, has serious implications for FDI ventures--or indeed for any enterprises that are responsible for their own profits and losses. Export-oriented enterprises see higher costs and lower profits than they otherwise would, and, as a result, fewer of them are created. Other FDI enterprises, faced also with the rationing of foreign exchange, find it even more difficult to export enough of their production to satisfy the foreign exchange balance requirement. Fewer of these are established, and, of those that are, many export only the minimum necessary amount, because they do so at a loss, whereas in a freer trade environment some would find exporting profitable and would undertake it more willingly and with greater success.

4.51 Another negative effect of the overvaluation of the RMB is the devaluation risk that may be associated with foreign equity investment. Potential investors may perceive that if the ongoing economic reforms are successfully pursued to their logical end, the reduction of trade restrictions and export subsidies may well require a significant compensating devaluation of the currency. This would reduce the foreign currency value of equity investments in China. Concern about such a future might cause potential investors to reduce the value of their equity investment, or even to delay investment.

Screening and Approval Procedures

4.52 The difficulties that many potential foreign investors have encountered in China in negotiating not only with potential partners but also with the Government have been serious enough to generate a host of publications about how to deal with them. All of those publications put a lot of emphasis on the need to exercise patience.

4.53 One pervasive characteristic of the environment for setting up a joint venture is the complexity and the many changes over time of the rules, procedures, incentive structure, etc. Box 4.1 illustrates the long list of institutions that are involved in screening and approval. Table 4.8 describes the complex and widely varying incentive structure. As these exhibits show, ventures of different sizes are subject to approval by municipal, provincial, or central authority. Different ministries (or their municipal or provincial equivalents) enter the picture, depending on the sector of the proposed venture. Each Special Economic Zone has its own set of procedures and incentives. Municipal and provincial governments frequently issue new rules and permit new incentives, which of course differ from place to place. Moreover, these are often not collected in any one published document, and in some cases are not published at all--some incentives may be available on request but not publicized, and even some regulations may be unpublished.

4.54 In the initial stages of investigating how a project should be structured, what its market would be, and what are the qualifications of possible Chinese partners, many potential foreign investors have had problems in getting timely access to these important facts. As to the screening and approval process, considerable progress has been made in delegating authority to approve FDI ventures below certain size limits to provincial and municipal authorities--although these lower level authorities may also require difficult and lengthy negotiations. Sometimes, they are much more rigorous in their negotiations than the central government would desire. In SEZs, approval procedures are generally speedier than elsewhere in China. In the 22 articles of October 11, 1986, Article 17 is devoted to a call for improved efficiency and prompt response to foreign investors and FDI enterprises by all levels of government, and specifically requires a decision on approval or disapproval of new FDI enterprises within three months.

4.55 Export-oriented investment responds to different incentives than investment aimed at the domestic market. For the latter. reasonable access to that market is the main incentive; investors usually ask for high protection and these demands must be moderated. (Proper incentives to investment generally, including issues about protection, are discussed elsewhere in this report.) Income tax exemptions and other small incentives that may marginally increase after-tax profits have little or no influence on investment decisions of domestic-market oriented ventures, and thus in most cases are needless giveaways from the government to the investors. Export-oriented investment, on the other hand, requires conditions for competing with other countries, such as highly cost-effective labor, free access to inputs at world market prices, excellent infrastructure, etc. For competitive reasons, income tax exemptions may be useful in attracting such investment but will not make up for deficiencies in other areas. In a country such as China, it may make sense to concentrate a package of fiscal and other incentives for export-oriented firms on certain geographic areas that have the transportation, labor, and infrastructure needed by such firms. However, it is important that a "free trade environment," discussed elsewhere in this report, be available throughout the country for any firm that wishes to export.

4.56 The whole area of incentives, screening and approval procedures, a sore point with foreign investors in many countries, merits more effort in China to eliminate unproductive delays and the proliferation of different agencies that must be dealt with. While the decentralization of approval powers to provincial and municipal governments is a good thing, and probably unavoidable in so vast a country, more stability over time and more assurance that local authorities _practice_ the general principles and laws adopted by the central government would also be useful. Several developing countries, including some of China's neighbors and competitors for FDI, have done good jobs on these points.

Box 4.1 GOVERNMENT ORGANIZATIONS INVOLVED IN INVESTMENT APPROVAL

The following is a list of many of the organizations directly or indirectly involved in the approval of foreign investment projects and a brief description of the role they play. Their participation may vary with the size and complexity of the project.

State Council: Approves large projects requiring total investment of Y100 million or more.

State Planning Commission (SPC)/Local Planning Commissions (LPC): Approves project proposals and feasibility studies; involvement depends on project size.

State Economic Commission: May be involved in reviewing project proposals; oversees implementation of State plans.

Ministry of Foreign Economic Relations and Trade (MOFERT)/Local Foreign Economic Relations and Trade Commissions (FERTC): Responsible for final approval of all investment contracts; may examine and approve project proposals and feasibility studies in some localities; may be involved in partner selection and negotiation.

China International Engineering Consulting Corporation (CIECC): Appraises technical renovation projects and reviews joint capital construction projects at SPC request; can provide consulting services for feasibility study preparation.

Central Industrial Ministries (or Ministerial Corporations)/Local Industry Bureaus or Corporate Branches: Oversee development of the industry; allocate funds; supervise factories; approve preliminary feasibility reports for proposed projects; may be directly involved in negotiations; may take equity position; or, as parent entity. become joint venture partner.

Ministry of Finance (MOF). General Tax Bureau manages State tax revenues and handles joint venture tax issues; the Accounting and Management Department oversees joint venture accounting practices.

Ministry of Labor and Personnel/Local Labor Management Bureaus: Administer overall labor and wage aspects of enterprises; approve labor contracts; review employee dismissal; may supply labor to joint ventures.

Box 4.1 (continued)

<u>State Bureau of Supplies and Materials/Local Goods Regulator Department:</u> Organize and direct allotment, supply, and management of goods controlled by the State; undertake storage and transportation of materials.

<u>State Administration of Commodity Prices/Local Pricing Bureaus:</u> Determine domestic prices for import and export goods; prices of JV products sold domestically may be subject to review and approval.

<u>State Administration of Industry and Commerce (SAIC)/Local Bureaus of Industry and Commerce:</u> Protect legal business operations; issue business licenses; register all businesses including equity joint ventures contractual joint ventures, wholly foreign.owned enterprises, and foreign company offices; also register trademarks.

<u>General Administration of Customs Local Custom Branches:</u> Supervise and control import and export activities; levy customs and other tariffs; approve applications for customs tariff reduction or exemption.

<u>State Administration of Exchange Controls (SAEC)/Local Exchange Control Branches.</u> Administer foreign currency income and expenditure of all economic entities, including JVs and wholly foreign-owned enterprises. SAEC approvel needed before joint ventures or wholly foreign-owned enterprises can set up accounts with and/or borrow funds from foreign banks.

<u>Audit Office:</u> The Foreign Investment Audit Bureau supervises income and expenditures of JVs, foreign businesses, and State firms using foreign investment.

<u>State Council Special Economic Zone Office:</u> Approves investment incentives offered in SEZs as well as the zones' development plans.

<u>Local Land Management Department:</u> Approves use of site by JVs if land is not contributed as part of equity; regulates land-use fees.

<u>Local Bureaus of Electricity Use and Planning:</u> Approves power allocation for enterprises with high energy consumption.

<u>Bank of China (BOC)/BOC Trust Consultancy Company (BOCTCC)/Local Branches of BOC and Subsidiaries of BOCTCC:</u> Not directly involved in project approval but provide financial support to Chinese entity or joint venture through loans or taking equity positions.

Source: The China Business Review/May-June 1986.

Independence of Management

4.57 Chinese regulations and other actions have restricted the ability of FDI managers to implement and achieve the good management practices and efficient operations that are among the major benefits which FDI can bring. Among the major grievances have been limitations on the ability to select workers, to reward them for good performance or punish them for bad performance, and to fire them if necessary. These restrictions have included limitations on determination of the organization of productive processes and of the size and composition of the work force. Other, more subtle modes of interference occur when the Chinese managers or workers in joint venture enterprises respond to the dictates of political officials (both inside and outside the enterprise), rather than to the appropriate official of the enterprise, on matters relating purely or mainly to the operations of the enterprise. Here again, the government has recognized that it is necessary to increase the independence of enterprise management--indeed this is being done throughout the economy, not only in FDI ventures--and in Articles 12 and 15 of the October 11, 1986 provisions have guaranteed considerable freedom to managers in exporting and in internal organizational matters, including hiring, firing and setting wages.

Exploitative vs Collaborative Behavior

4.58 Recently many articles have appeared in the international press about problems that FDI ventures have encountered in doing business in China. World Bank and IFC staff have investigated some of these cases. The great majority of the problems are the result of one or both of two problematical aspects of the Chinese environment: the requirement that each enterprise earn all the foreign exchange it needs (see paras. 4.84-4.88), and the habit of some Chinese partners and many government officials of continually trying to extract the most short-run benefit, or minimize their own short-run costs, in dealing with foreign investors.

4.59 Chinese partners in joint ventures have become known for continuing to demand additional concessions from their foreign partners after agreements have been reached. Government officials use occasions when enterprises need help because of unforeseen problems (sometimes caused by government policy) to extract additional concessions from the joint venture or from the foreign partner. This deliberate practice was explained by one governmental official who explained that he greeted protests from the investors, when faced with new demands, with the suggestion that they should adopt the attitude, "You never know how much you can do until you try."

4.60 Some foreign investors may also be to blame for getting their joint ventures into problems that they could have predicted (or perhaps in some cases even did predict). Especially after long and difficult negotiations, some foreign investors may end up agreeing to conditions that are likely to lead to problems, thinking that it may end up being easier to solve the problems after they appear. The history of FDI in China so far suggests that more reasonable and more forthright negotiation by all parties would be desirable.

Table 4.8

Overview of Investment Incentives

Location/Investment Approval Ceilings	Enterprise Income Tax (EIT)	Industrial & Commercial Consolidated Tax (ICCT)	Land Use Fees	Additional Information/ Target Sectors
Nationwide Provinces, autonomous regions, and open cities generally have local approval ceilings of $5 million unless otherwise noted. The inland cities of Chongqing, Harbin, Jinan, Shenyang, Wuhan, and Xian may also approve projects valued up to $5 million independent of the provinces in which they are located.	New JV contracts for 10 years or more: - tax exempt for first 2 profit-making years - 50% tax reduction for subsequent 3 profit-making years JVs with long-term capital recovery, or in underdeveloped, remote areas, or engaged in low-profit operations such as farming, forestry, animal husbandry, and deep-pit coal mining: - 15-30% tax reduction for 10-year period after expiration of exemption and reduction, with approval from the Ministry of Finance - 40% refund on tax paid on income reinvested in China for 5 or more years by a foreign JV participant Wholly Foreign-Owned Enterprises: - tax exempt in first profit-making year - 50% tax reduction for subsequent 2 years - 15-30% tax reduction extension for 10-year period after expiration of exemptions and reductions, with approval from the Ministry of Finance Local EIT: Projects may be reduced or exempt at discretion of local authorities	On Imports Exemption from raw materials, parts, components, and packing materials imported by foreign partner for processing or assembly into complete production or for making export goods Exempt with approval of tax authority: - equipment/materials imported as part of investment	Preferential treatment at discretion of local authorities, usually provided for cultural, educational, scientific, or public welfare enterprises. For other sectors, see individual listings	Special concessions for harbor construction projects: - income tax rate 15% - exempt from tax during first profit-making year - 50% reduction next 5 years (may be extended for enterprises in financial difficulty) Exempt from 10% profit remittance tax Guarantee of docking fees high enough to help generate projected incomes
Special Economic Zones (SEZs) Shantou, Shenzhen, Xiamen, Zhuhai Heavy Industry: Y 50 million Light Industry Y 30 million Nonindustrial: (e.g. hotels) Y 100 million	For foreign investments of $5 million or more in: Service trades: - tax exempt for first profit-making year - 50% reduction for following 2 years High technology: - tax exempt for up to 5 years For Xiamen SEZ: Contracts of 10 years or more involving upgrading of export oriented enterprises: - exempt for first 4 profit-making years - 50% reduction next 5 profit-making years Low profit enterprises in SEZ Xiamen - reduced or exempt	On Imports: With approval, the following are exempt: - machinery, equipment, components, parts, raw and semi-finished materials, fuel, and automobiles for use in construction and production in SEZ - foodstuffs and tableware for use in hotels, catering trade, tourism, and food industries - machinery, equipment, and accessories imported for offshore oil exploitation 50% reduction on wines, liquors, tobacco, and daily necessities other than those restricted for import by MOFERT On Exports: Products produced in SEZ are exempt (Note: goods purchased from inland but exported via SEZs are subject to applicable export duties) On Domestic Sales in SEZs: 50% reduction on items such as mineral oil, liquors, and cigarettes produced in SEZs Local government may approve reduction or exemption on certain products On Domestic Sales in the Interior: All items transported to and sold in the interior of China are taxed according to rate set by tax law	For Shenzhen SEZ: projects involving advanced technology may be exempted from local land-use fees For Xiamen SEZ: contracts of 10 years or more involving upgrading of export-oriented enterprises, exempt during construction period and first 5 years of operation	Exempt from 10% profit remittance tax 50% depreciation on machinery and equipment during first year of use Customs Duties: Incentives offered are similar to ICCT import guidelines Shantou SEZ: petrochemicals, electronics, textiles, plastics, toys, building materials, metal products, agriculture, tourism, real estate, electricity, transportation Xiamen SEZ: electronics, microcomputers, precision machinery, instruments and meters, building materials, fine chemicals, textiles, food processing, tourism, transportation, communications Zhuhai SEZ: building materials, electronics, daily-use chemicals, food, machinery, petroleum

Location/Investment Approval Ceilings	Enterprise Income Tax (EIT)	Industrial & Commercial Consolidated Tax (ICCT)	Land Use Fees	Additional Information/ Target Sectors
14 Coastal Cities and Hainan Island Shanghai and Tianjin ($30 million); Dalian and Guangzhou ($10 million); Hainan Island ($5 million). In April 1986 the central government rescinded the approval ceiling of $5 million for the rest of the original 14 cities -- Qinhuangdao, Yantai, Qingdao, Lianyungang, Nantong, Ningbo, Wenzhou, Fuzhou, Zhanjiang, and Beihai -- although some of these cities still claim this right. Foreign investment in these 10 cities must now be officially approved by their respective provincial governments	For most industries, 20% reduction of regular rate for specified period 15% tax rate may be granted to: - technology-intensive enterprises - enterprises involving $30 million foreign investment - projects in energy development (excluding oil), transportation, port construction (criteria for approval varies with each city)	On Imports: Production equipment, business facilities, and building materials imported as part of investment, as well as vehicles to be used by enterprise are all exempt Raw materials, spare parts, components or packing materials imported for producing export products are all exempt. (Will be taxed if goods are sold domestically.) On Exports: With the exception of a small number of products controlled by the State, all other export products are exempt On Domestic Sales: Products sold in China are taxed according to rate set by tax law		Customs Duties: Import of production equipment, building materials, raw materials, parts and fittings, components, motor vehicles, and articles for office use are exempt
Economic and Technological Development Zones (ETDZs) in 14 Coastal Cities	15% tax rate For investments in transportation, energy, and telecommunications, less than 15% Fuzhou ETDZ: low-profit enterprises may be granted reduction or exemption of income tax Local EIT: Reduction or exemption may be approved by local government Qingdao ETDZ: exempt for first 2 profit-making years; 50% reduction for next 3 years Tianjin ETDZ: exempt until 1990		Ningbo ETDZ: reduction in land-use fees Guangzhou ETDZ: foreign firms providing badly needed technology will be exempt from land-use fees.	All ETDZs exempt from 10% profit remittance tax Products made by JVs, that use 70% domestic raw materials, and are badly needed in China, may be sold wholly or partly on China's domestic market Guangzhou ETDZ: Overseas Chinese from HK, Macau, and Taiwan: - granted extended tax exemption or reduction if they reinvest share of profits in China - if investment is in advanced technologies, investor may sell products on China's domestic market during first 2 years
Beijing ($10 million)				Food processing, electronics, textiles, building materials, machinery, metallurgy, chemicals, agriculture, animal husbandry
Fujian ($10 million)	Exempt for high advanced technology		50% reduction in land use fees for overseas Chinese	Infrastructure (including harbors, railways, power stations, and highways), mining, home appliances, microcomputers, precision instruments, chemicals, engineering, building materials, textiles, food processing, aquatic products
Gansu ($5 million)	Exempt for highly advanced technology		- Fees may be waived during construction period for certain projects. - Reduced by at least 50% based on national average.	Water conservancy, textiles, leather, pharmaceuticals, timber, metallurgy, tourism
Guangdong ($10 million) Guangzhou: $10 million Hainan: $5 million	For investments in low-profit industries or for enterprises in underdeveloped areas, after first 5 years of exemption and reduction, may be granted tax reduction of 15-30% for following 10 years Investments in the province's mountainous countries granted additional preferential treatment	2 year exemption for certain products approved for sale in China (excluding sugar, cigarettes, wristwatches, spirits, TVs, and cassette recorders)		Exempt from 10% profit remittance tax Energy, communications, transportation, food processing, textiles, building materials, ceramics, mining, offshore oil, petrochemicals, electronics, microcomputers, agriculture, animal husbandry, fish farming
Guangxi ($5 million)	JVs in underdeveloped, remote areas exempt from enterprise income tax during first 5 years For investments producing advanced internationally competitive products: - exempt for 2 years - 50% reduction for next 4 years Local EIT: JVs in underdeveloped, remote areas exempt Exempt if annual income less than Y 1 million		Production of internationally competitive products exempt from provisional urban real estate tax for 7 years, 50% reduction for following 3 years Hi-tech JVs exempt from land-use fee	Quick depreciation of fixed assets for JVs in underdeveloped areas Telecommunications, shipping, hydroelectric power, food processing, household electrical appliances, chemicals, minerals, machinery

Location/Investment Approval Ceilings	Enterprise Income Tax (EIT)	Industrial & Commercial Consolidated Tax (ICCT)	Land Use Fees	Additional Information/ Target Sectors
Guizhou ($5 million)			Low-profit enterprises exempt for 1-3 years from provisional urban real estate tax	Energy (coal and hydropower), transportation, building materials, metallurgy, machinery and electronics, textiles, agriculture, tourism
Hebei ($5 million)	Low-profit enterprises pay reduced rate or are exempt during first 5 years			Exempt from 10% profit remittance tax Food processing, textiles, building materials, electronics, chemicals, tourism, animal husbandry
Heilongjiang ($5 million) Harbin: $5 million			Average land use fees less than in neighboring provinces and cities Prior to 1987: - 3 year exemption on land use feeds - 70-90% reduction of on-site development fees	Minerals, agriculture, timber, coal mining, petroleum processing, heavy machinery, precision instruments and meters, livestock breeding, poultry farming, pharmaceuticals, sugar-refining, paper-making
Hunan ($5 million)	Low-profit enterprises exempt for first 5 years Local EIT: JVs having difficulty paying taxes exempt for first 5 years		Lower land use fees for investments in advanced technology industries	Food packaging, textiles, electronics, machine building, metullurgy, chemicals, construction materials, transportation, electric power, posts and telecommunications
Jiangxi ($5 million)	For new JVs of 10 years or more: - tax exempt in first 2 profit-making years - reduction for next 6 years For investments of $10 million or more, or investments in advanced technology industries, or for long-term projects (i.e., energy exploration and harbor development): enterprise income tax rate reduced to 15-24% Additional 10-15 year period of 30% reductions for investments in agriculture and animal husbandry. Local EIT: Exempt for investment of $10 million or more, or investments in advanced technology industries, or for long-term projects	Reduction or exemption of ICCT on certain products approved for sale in China	Exempt or reduced on approval Investments in animal husbandry and agriculture exempt from land use fees for 5 years	Animal husbandry, aquaculture and food processing, building materials (including cement, glass, and gypsum), minerals, porcelain, chemicals, transportation, electronics (including computers), communications, leather tanning, plastics, textiles, power plants
Liaoning ($10 million) Dalian: $10 million Shenyang: $5 million			Shenyang City: foreign investments greater than $2 million or total investment of more than $6 million, producing 70% of their products for export are eligible for significant reductions of land use fees, and for a 50% reduction in site development fees	Machine-building, electronics, petrochemicals, building materials, metallurgy, light industry, textiles, transportation, communications, nuclear power
Nei Mongol ($5 million)			Land use fees 30-50% less than in coastal cities.	Machine-building, metallurgy, energy, electronics, chemicals, textiles, leather, food processing, packaging, animal husbandry, porcelain, railroad consruction, building materials
Ningxia ($5 million)	JVs with contracts of 10 years or more: - tax exempt for first 5 profit-making years - 20-40% tax reduction for following 10-15 years			Food, light industry, textiles, electronics, machine-building

Location/Investment Approval Ceilings	Enterprise Income Tax (EIT)	Industrial & Commercial Consolidated Tax (ICCT)	Land Use Fees	Additional Information/ Target Sectors
Qinghai ($5 million)	Xining City: - enterprises importing capital technology exempt for 3-5 years			Nonferrous metallurgy, animal husbandry, leather processing and tanning, food processing, light industry, textiles, machinery, plastics
Shaanxi ($5 million) Xian: $5 million	JVs involved in agriculture and forestry or located in towns and villages: - exempt from income tax in the first 5 years of operation - 15-30% reduction in following 10 years			Export goods, produced in this inland province will receive free transportation Machine-building, textiles, electronics, light industry, mining, tourism
Shanxi ($5 million)	5-10 year tax holiday for the following types of enterprises: - those with low profit activities in the agriculture, forestry, and animal husbandry sectors - those in underdeveloped mountainous areas or other remote regions - those involving investment of more than $3 million or hi-tech projects that have a long lead time to recoup investment Local EIT: Exempt for 5 years	Exempt, upon approval, from taxes on export products	Enterprises in undeveloped or remote areas or those in coal and chemical industries eligible for preferential land use rates Hi-tech projects and non-profit-making ventures exempt from land use fees All projects exempt from property tax for 1-3 years The following may be exempt from property tax for 3-5 years: low-profit investments, projects in remote or mountainous regions, projects involving investment of more than $3 million, high-tech projects requiring significant lead time	Overseas Chinese investors, applicable for further preferential treatment Raw materials, fuel, and electricity sold at local market prices (usually lower than in coastal regions) to enterprises involving foreign investment. Up to 10% discount if paid in foreign exchange Coal mining, glass, ceramics, gas, light industry, chemical fibers, construction materials, food processing, animal husbandry, tourism
Xinjiang ($5 million)	Foreign partners' reinvesting profits in area for 5 years or more can claim 50% reimbursement of income tax already paid on reinvested sum Local EIT: exempt for 5 years 50% reduction for enterprises with annual profits less than $1 million	Export products (excluding products restricted by State) are exempt	Enterprises engaged in agriculture, animal husbandry, and irrigation can enjoy lower rate or exemption of land use fees average for area is Y 1-30/m^2/yr 50% reduction in property tax for 5 years	Textiles, papermaking, electronics, detergent making, fur processing
Yunnan ($5 million)	15-30% reduction of income tax from the 6th to 10th profit-making years for JVs and cooperative enterprises with terms of 10 years or more For agriculture and forestry projects as well as enterprises outside of Kunming area, enterprise income tax reduced by 30%		Enterprises with contract periods of 10 years or more eligible for preferential land use fees at the rate of Y 2-30/m^2/yr	Energy development, transportation, nonferrous metals, forestry (including timber processing and development of natural spices), agriculture, animal husbandry, machine building, electronics, textiles, pharmaceuticals, building materials, tourism
Zhejiang ($5 million)	15% tax rate for production of import substitutes or advanced technology products on approval		Enterprises with advanced technology or in tourism are eligible for unspecified preferential land use fees	Exempt from 10% profit remittance tax Carpet-making, marble, tourism

Source: The China Business Review, May-June 1986.

4.61 Of course, it is normal and legitimate for each party in a business transaction to seek to maximize his own gains. Foreign investors are presumably doing this, and it is not recommended that the government act any differently. The problem is that some officials are focussing too much on the short-run gain to be extracted for their enterprise or agency, at the moment, to the detriment of the country's long-run gain from FDI as a whole. This conflict arises for two reasons. First, treating the particular investor or enterprise harshly can result in its closing, failing to expand, or otherwise operating in such a way that benefits are reduced not only to it but also to the Chinese economy; second, such practice may keep, and in fact probably has kept, other investors away or caused them to invest less.

4.62 Many Chinese partners and many officials do not act in this short-sighted way, and some high officials are concerned about this problem. There have been reports in the press of official exhortations to be more reasonable and more far-sighted. In examining the experience of other countries with FDI, it is clear that the successful countries treated the process as a positive sum game--they approached FDI as an activity that could and should leave all parties better off than they were before. They treated the foreign investors as potential long-term allies in the development of the country. To insure a positive contribution, they regulated FDI; they directed it to where they wanted it; they prohibited it from some activities and gave it incentives to engage in others. But they did this in ways that helped the FDI enterprises to prosper, and thus they attracted more reinvestment of profits from existing enterprises and more new investment from others. At least some government officials agree that China should aim at maximizing long-term benefits from all potential foreign investors, not just immediate benefits from those already there. Of course, the implementation of such a policy may be more difficult than its adoption, but the potential rewards are worth considerable effort.

Local Sources of Finance

4.63 It is normal practice in most countries to finance a certain part of a company's needs with debt. The appropriate debt/equity ratio varies with the riskiness of the venture, the expected variability in its cash flows, and other factors, but in most cases investors find it unnecessarily expensive to finance companies completely with equity. In China, some progress has been made in providing institutions and channels through which FDI ventures can borrow, both in RMB and in foreign currency, but much still remains to be done.

4.64 One related problem is the legal ceiling placed on the debt/equity ratio of each foreign joint venture, which depends only on the size of the company. (Small companies must be financed 100% with equity, medium-sized can have some debt, etc.) These restrictions make little sense from the point of view of the enterprise or of the investor. From the Chinese point of view, the restrictions may be motivated simply by a desire to limit the amount of foreign debt that is lent or guaranteed by agencies of the government. If so, the development of a well functioning system of independent financial intermediaries would reduce this concern and allow more sensible financial structures tailored to the needs of the individual enterprise.

4.65 There are two other related problems with the current state of affairs regarding financing. One is a problem for the enterprises: it may be difficult for them to borrow what they need. The other is a problem for China: almost every existing source of loans or loan guarantees in effect involves the Chinese State, ultimately, as the lender or the guarantor. This fact may be in part responsible for the government's mixed feelings about FDI as a source of capital. What is needed is the creation and strengthening of institutions and channels that (a) can lend to FDI enterprises, and that (b) are not subsidized by the State and are responsible for their own profits and losses. This latter feature depends on the success of the economic reform of the financial sector and has ramifications that go beyond the provision of loans to FDI enterprises. The plans for financial sector reform appear to be aiming in the right directions to address these problems.

4.66 Debt financing and/or guarantees are currently available from the Bank of China (which lent US$240 million to more than 220 FDI ventures in 1985) and other government banks such as the Construction, Agriculture, and Industry and Commerce Banks, the China Investment Bank, and the China Development and Investment Corporation. Less official sources include CITIC and the provincial and municipal ITICs. Local branches of offshore banks are also permitted to furnish these services.

4.67 A major impediment to the effective functioning of local financing of enterprises in China is the absence of a legal structure that would permit effective granting of collateral through mortgages, regulate bankruptcies, etc. Development of such laws and supporting institutions will, of course, take time and is an integral and important part of the entire economic reform now in process in China. They are necessary for the greater and more efficient functioning of FDI as well.

Policies for Export-Oriented Foreign Direct Investment

4.68 To attract FDI that is focussed on producing manufactured goods primarily for exports, any country must compete with other countries that are also trying to attract the same investments. For some products the competition is regional (e.g., East Asia), and for some it is world-wide, but the competition is explicit and it is very keen. By and large, the three most important characteristics that investors look for are: (a) low cost, productive and disciplined labor; (b) good transportation and communication facilities; and (c) relative freedom from government interference, including the right to import inputs and to export freely, the right to repatriate profits, the right to obtain local financing, etc. Other attractive characteristics are low costs for other inputs such as land, utilities, etc.; political stability; and low taxes.

4.69 Geographically, China's location in the Far East places it in direct competition for this kind of investment with the world's star performers. China has been having trouble meeting this competition; with the notable exception of overseas Chinese, located mainly in Hong Kong, most potential foreign investors have not found China to be as attractive as its competitors with respect to the characteristics mentioned above.

4.70 The most successful performers in terms of attracting FDI have mostly been small economies, without rich natural resources. Because of these characteristics, they do not have available to them the options of trying to develop through import substitution, or of raising incomes through the export of natural resource-based products. Their markets are not large enough to support the production of most goods for which economies of scale are important. Therefore, if they are to develop, they have no choice but to specialize in the export of products in which they can compete internationally, and to use the earnings of these exports to pay for the importation of everything else.

4.71 Potential foreign investors in export-oriented ventures find that labor in China is neither as cheap as they had expected nor highly productive. Foreign investors have also encountered high rents for factory sites, and deficiencies in communication and transport systems. They have encountered bureaucratic difficulties in doing business.

4.72 Recognizing these problems, the government has been taking steps to solve them. Progress has been made on each of the problems mentioned. Most recently, the 22 Articles of 11 October, 1986 promise better treatment in regard to surcharges on wages, site rentals, utility supplies and charges, taxes, and freedom to manage enterprises without interference, including the freedom to hire, fire, and set wages independently. Additional regulations issued on 1 December, 1986 provide for importation of inputs without the need for licenses or the payment of duties or other taxes. An inter-ministerial committee (the State Council's Foreign Investment Leading Group) has been set up, in part to ensure the following of the letter and the spirit of these regulations by local authorities. Moreover, as different localities are issuing the more detailed regulations to implement these provisions, there are signs of competition among the localities which should help to assure an improved climate for FDI enterprises. Thus, although the implementation of these new rules and their effects on FDI remain to be seen, there is reason to be optimistic about a significant increase in China's competitive position in the market for export-oriented FDI.

Policies for Other Forms of Foreign Direct Investment

4.73 As already noted, the overwhelming attraction of China for most potential foreign investors is its domestic market. Before discussing the policy environment for such investment, it is well to review a few facts about it.

4.74 First, enterprises that are established with domestic sales as their primary goal may also export. As discussed earlier, this usually takes some time, and it also takes the proper incentive structure. The time is necessary for the enterprise to get established, train the work force, sometimes to achieve an efficient scale of operations, find or help create sources of high quality and competitively priced inputs, and, in general, build up the quality of product and get the costs of production down to where it can compete in international markets. High-tech activities tend to take the longest time.

Even when costs are reduced, and quality has been achieved, more time is often needed to penetrate and create product acceptance in foreign markets. Appropriate incentives, which are also crucial, are discussed in detail elsewhere in this report (see main report Chapter 2, and Annex 2).

4.75 In fact, in most countries the typical exporter of manufactured goods (except a narrow range of those intensive in either unskilled labor or particular raw materials) started by producing for the domestic market. This is true in today's developed countries and also in the so-called "newly-industrialized" countries such as Brazil, Mexico and Spain. China appears to be similar in potential to those countries, and in the long run a strategy that will produce a diversified range of manufactured exports from China almost certainly will have to be based on efficient production of most of those same goods for the local market. It should be stressed, however, that efficient import substitution can be just as good for China's balance of payments as exports; i.e. saving foreign exchange is as valuable as earning additional foreign exchange.

4.76 Third, most FDI that is aimed at tend to export markets will not bring much advanced technology. Rather, it will tend to be intensive in unskilled labor and/or raw material inputs. Most technology-intensive activities will only come to China if they can sell a significant part of their production locally.

4.77 Finally, the potential for technology transfer from FDI is by no means limited to the joint venture itself. Contacts with other enterprises can diffuse technology and good management practices throughout the economy. Such contacts should be encouraged; FDI enterprises should be encouraged (but not forced without regard to price and quality) to purchase inputs from local sources, to sell products to local users, and to compete with Chinese enterprises.

4.78 In sum, FDI is to make its full potential contribution to the modernization and technological transformation of the economy, a significant part of it must be able to profit from domestic market sales. This activity can be just as beneficial to China's balance of payments as purely export-oriented ventures. Moreover, such FDI ventures, if they are to be fully exploited as agents of modernization, must not be isolated geographically or otherwise, but rather should be fully integrated into the local economy.

4.79 The transfer of advanced technology available from FDI enterprises that produce mainly or even wholly for the domestic market is now explicitly recognized. The regulations of 11 October specifically provide for better treatment of such enterprises. However, experience suggests that the Chinese concept of useful "advanced technology" being applied may be too narrow. At times, there is excessive focus on "hardware" machinery and equipment, or the plans, patents, or process description for making such equipment. As noted elsewhere in this report, good management, labor training, efficient organization of production and of all other functions of the enterprise as well--the so-called "soft" aspects that increase efficiency--are just as important and indeed may be essential if the advanced machinery is to repay its cost.

4.80 In spite of the progress that has occurred, the actual environment for FDI aimed at the domestic market is still not very attractive. The single biggest reason for this is the foreign exchange balance requirement. The government has realized that its general objective that each FDI enterprise balance its own foreign exchange must be modified in many cases and it has agreed to provide enterprises with ways to earn foreign exchange through domestic sales. It has made further accommodations, on a case-by-case basis, for enterprises that needed more foreign exchange than had been planned. A set of 14 articles promulgated in January 1986 set out some principles for accommodating enterprises which cannot easily earn their own foreign exchange. But the idea that it is strongly desirable that every enterprise earn all of its foreign exchange needs still reigns, and this full balance is still the expected norm for FDI ventures, with cases to the contrary being considered as both exceptional and undesirable. Perhaps in part because of this attitude, the implementation of the ad hoc modifications often falls short of what is needed. A regular supply of foreign exchange, in sufficient quantity, over a sufficiently long period of time, is often not available.

4.81 Thus, the foreign exchange balance requirement, even with the many ad hoc adjustments that have been made, is still deterring potential investors from coming to China and is causing unnecessary difficulties for some FDI ventures that are already there. There are only two other countries that allow FDI but impose a balancing requirement for foreign exchange (Egypt and Yugoslavia). The requirement has worked very badly in both countries, having been abandoned in Egypt and frequently modified, without success, in Yugoslavia.

4.82 Ultimately, the best way to solve this problem is to have an efficient market in foreign exchange. FDI ventures (as well as local enterprises responsible for their own profits and losses) could then trade foreign exchange at a price at which the economy as a whole balanced its foreign exchange sources and uses, and allocated foreign exchange to those people and enterprises who would use it most productively. The options for China for moving in this direction are discussed elsewhere in this report (see main report, Chapter 3).

4.83 Immediate steps that merit consideration to reduce the unnecessary costs of the foreign exchange allocation system to FDI, especially its negative effects on potential new investors in China, include: (a) developing a more regular, reasonable and longer-term system of allocating foreign exchange to FDI enterprises that need and deserve it; and (b) permitting all FDI enterprises to buy and sell foreign exchange freely among themselves, or from other enterprises having surplus foreign exchange retention rights. It must be stressed that this solution would be a second-best solution to the wider foreign exchange market options discussed in Chapter 3 of the main report, and would be subject to the problems of multiple exchange rates mentioned there.

4.84 Within the last few months, legal markets for foreign exchange conversion of RMB have been developing in China, and Article 14 of the provisions of October 11 apparently allows for some sort of market. However, at the time of this writing, it is not clear how such markets will be permitted to function, or indeed even if they can function well in an environment of very scarce foreign exchange. Reform of the system of foreign exchange allocation is a complex matter, especially in the midst of an ongoing reform of so many aspects of the industrial and financial sectors. However, the importance of the problem for FDI adds to the urgency of finding a solution.

CHINA

EXTERNAL BORROWING AND DEBT MANAGEMENT

Table of Contents

CHINA

EXTERNAL BORROWING AND DEBT MANAGEMENT

5.1 Access to external commercial funds since the 1970s has given developing countries a new flexibility of macroeconomic management. This access helped to promote growth in developing countries by systematically raising investment levels beyond what would have been possible with their own domestic savings resources. But the leverage of debt works both ways. Such an increase in investment, if used efficiently, promotes growth. But if wasted on inefficient projects, the accumulation of debt with no corresponding growth in the domestic economy carries with it high costs and will make the country vulnerable to external financial pressures.

5.2 The basic questions facing a country in its use of foreign finance will be (a) deciding the appropriate opportunity and purpose to borrow, i.e, for investment or for consumption; and (b) determining an appropriate volume of borrowing at a given time (i.e., the rate of debt accumulation). Each of these are decisions involving a series of economic judgments. Another set of issues relates to (c) the actual borrowing program with respect to currency, maturity profile, and sourcing composition. This latter involves a series of financial calculations and judgments: What currency should be borrowed? What market should be tapped? When is it appropriate to go to market? What are the most appropriate instruments? Finally, (d) how the borrowing of all parties is to be coordinated in a manner that is optimal for the country as a whole.

5.3 This annex seeks to provide guidelines for borrowing strategy, given both economic and financial considerations. Section A proposes a series of guidelines for foreign borrowing and describes China's borrowing in international perspective. China's debt and its various characteristics are analyzed and compared to the debt characteristics of other countries at the same and higher levels of income. The structure and composition of China's debt is also described. Section B outlines China's present borrowing strategy and approach, and Section C describes some issues raised by China's current approach to debt management and explores options.

A. China's Foreign Borrowing in International Perspective

Reasons for Borrowing: Use of Debt in a Growth Strategy

5.4 The motivation for foreign borrowing is to make more rapid economic growth possible. This is consistent with the observation that in the early stages of development, when a developing country's domestic savings and capital stock are low, returns to investment are high. Given this capital scarcity, the increased investment that foreign borrowing makes possible will, if wisely targeted, increase growth. Borrowing is thus seen as a potent developmental tool in support of economic growth.[1] Use of this tool, however, if it is to be a successful instrument supporting growth, must fit into a strategy of debt-supported growth which is sustainable in the long run. This requires good project selection and, in the long run, that the country generate an excess of savings over investment (or exports over imports), in order to repay the debt. At the macroeconomic level, the key element is a consistent medium-term plan which includes the balance of payments and makes explicit the choice between foreign and domestic resources to finance growth. The appropriate degree of reliance on domestic or foreign resources will depend on whether the amount of debt implied by the foreign resource inflow is sustainable by the country in the long run. Maintaining a sustainable growth of debt for a given set of economic objectives depends on maintaining appropriate domestic as well as external economic policies.

Domestic Policies

5.5 Maintaining a high level of domestic savings is a crucial element of successful borrowing. Instruments for achieving this are monetary and fiscal policies which maintain macroeconomic balance and encourage savings and an efficient allocation of resources, especially of investment resources. Interest rates that are positive in real terms are important for promoting household savings and ensuring that enterprise investment decisions are guided by the cost of capital. A government contribution to savings (defined as a positive balance of government revenue over current expenditure) also helps reduce overall reliance on foreign savings. In many countries, large government fiscal deficits have both directly reduced total savings and have contributed indirectly (e.g., through high inflation) to reduced household and enterprise saving and investment.

5.6 Since infrastructure and other public sector investment is usually a large share of total investment, ensuring its productivity is an essential aspect of effective debt management. Adequate project evaluation to ensure efficient investment, budgetary controls to ensure an appropriate contribution of government to savings, and proper macroeconomic management are each crucial domestic aspects of debt management policy.

1/ Foreign resources can be used to supplement domestic resources, to increase investment and thereby output growth. The national income identity usefully demonstrates this role of domestic and foreign resources:

(1) $Y = C + I + G + (X - M)$

(2) $I = (Y - C - G) + (M - X)$; or

(3) Investment = domestic savings + foreign savings

Where Y stands for national income, C for private consumption, G for government expenditure, I for investment, X for exports, and M for imports.

External Policies

5.7 The higher the rate of growth of exports, the higher the level of imports consistent with a sustainable debt path. Chapter II of the Main Report outlines the importance of an appropriate trade strategy for the promotion of exports and highlights the fact that protection of domestic industry and an overvalued exchange rate are important sources of anti-export bias. An overvalued exchange rate which makes imports look cheap, and makes debt service appear less costly in terms of domestic resources. This is true a fortiori, if potential borrower see further real appreciation as a possibility in the future. As a result, it has in many countries been a source of overborrowing and debt-service problems.

Country Differences in the Debt/Growth Strategy and Debt Indicators

5.8 Over time, different countries have chosen different growth paths using different trade strategies and combinations of domestic savings and borrowing. Many Asian economies have taken a strongly outward-oriented approach to trade and a conservative approach to borrowing, keeping debt levels very low and relying on domestic savings to finance growth. South Korea, by contrast, pursued growth through heavy emphasis on exports and intensive use of borrowing. As a result, Korea's debt has grown rapidly, but its rapid export growth has kept the debt burden manageable.

5.9 While it is difficult to generalize, many middle-income countries, especially those in Latin America, pursued inward-looking trade strategies, but borrowed heavily to finance growth. Over time, domestic savings declined, partly due to fiscal and monetary policies which discouraged private savings and resulted in negative government saving, and partly due to external economic policies, including overvalued exchange rates, which led to a flow of private capital abroad. Foreign resources came to substitute in part for domestic savings to maintain the same level of investment. While the foreign resource inflow permitted growth to be maintained in the initial years, the inflow could not be sustained, and the eventual result was a lower overall investment and growth rate with higher indebtedness.

5.10 A more inward orientation, and conservative use of debt characterized India, until it liberalized its trade regime in the 1980s. China, until recently, followed a similarly conservative growth path, with limited emphasis on trade, limited use of foreign borrowing, and reliance on domestic savings to finance growth. These different approaches are reflected in a country's accumulation of debt and other debt indicators discussed below.

5.11 The debt/GDP ratio relates a country's debt volume to its economic productive capacity. Essentially, it compares the stock of debt to the flow of national income from which the debt is to be serviced. China's debt-to-GDP ratio is low in comparison to that of other countries (Table 5.1). In 1980, debt in relation to GDP was only 1.9%, rising to 7.7% in 1985.[2/]

5.12 A second way to look at debt is in relation to a country's exports. Exports provide the actual foreign exchange resources to meet future obligations. It also indicates how many years' exports would be required to repay a country's debt in its entirety. In general, the more open an economy, and the higher the proportion of exports in GDP, the more "liquid" will a country be with respect to meeting external obligations, and the higher the absolute volume of debt sustainable. It has often been held that at debt/export ratios approaching 150%, debt servicing difficulties are inevitable. However, there are countries such as Korea, which have sustained ratios close to this level without debt difficulties.

Table 5.1: EXTERNAL BORROWING-SELECTED COUNTRIES, 1984
(%)

	Medium and long term debt/GDP	Total debt/GDP	Total debt/exports
Argentina	40	58	449
Brazil	46	56	348
India	15	16	184
Korea	33	57	141
China (1985)	4	8	80

Sources: Debt: OECD 1985 Survey; GDP: World Development Report, 1986; China: staff estimates.

5.13 Table 5.1 shows that a high ratio of debt to GDP is not always related to a high debt/export ratio.[3/] A country such as Korea has a high ratio of debt in relation to GDP, and yet low debt in relation to exports, since the economy is open and export-oriented. Likewise, a low debt/GDP ratio can coexist with a high debt/exports ratio, as in the case of India.

2/ Officially reported figures do not fully reflect actual debt volumes. A recent national debt survey, carried out in September 1986, sought to address the reporting deficiency. However, these figures differ from creditor statistics (OECD), which are higher than the debt survey figures. Using creditor estimates, the figure is 7.7%, while Chinese Debt Survey data would show 6%.

3/ The comparisons are based on OECD debt statistics, using creditor data. These are usually more comprehensive than debtor statistics. See Box 5.1 for a description of their differences.

Debt Service Ratios

5.14 A third indicator of creditworthiness is the debt service ratio, relating interest and amortization payments to the foreign exchange earned through exports of goods and services. For creditors, the ratio provides an indication of the ease with which the borrower will be able to meet payment obligations. For the debtor, the ratio indicates the proportion of foreign exchange earnings pledged to repaying debt and not available for imports and enhancement of growth. Traditionally, debt service levels above the 12-15% range were thought to threaten developing countries import capacity. This level is modest by today's standards. However, if debt-service ratios are significantly higher, debt servicing difficulties are likely to occur. China's debt-service ratio is lower than that of most other countries. However, the proportion of China's debt service that is concessional is very small. While most countries at China's income level have relied heavily on official lenders, as a newcomer to concessional windows, it is not likely that China will ever benefit, to the degree that other low-income countries have, from official or concessional funds. Therefore, the debt service "cushion" available to other developing countries, is not available to China.

Table 5.2: DEBT SERVICE RATIOS - BY TYPE OF CREDITOR, 1984

	Debt service as % of exports of goods and services	% concessional debt service	% noncessional debt service
Argentina	46.8	1.4	98.6
Brazil	53.3	0.5	99.5
India	12.7	42.7	57.3
Korea	21.6	3.2	96.7
China (1985)	6.8	1.5	98.5

Source and Notes: As for Table 5.1. China: concessional and non-concessional debt service: OECD Survey 1985.

5.15 In sum, China's debt volume, debt ratios and servicing obligations are low for a country at its level of development. Its recent history as a capital exporter and conservative stance provide much of the explanation. However, as important as the actual volume may be, the structure and composition of a country's borrowing can be of equal significance, and in this respect China is unusual, with the bulk of its borrowing from commercial rather than official sources and a relatively large share of its debt is short-term.

Box 5.1. DEBT REPORTING STATISTICS

Debt statistics can be collected from either creditor or borrower sources. There are three major credit-reporting systems, and one debtor-reporting system. They vary in their coverage, reporting network and classification. Thus, it is necessary to pool data from these different sources, to obtain a full estimate of debt from different markets.

The Organization for Economic Cooperation and Development (OECD) debt statistics are the most comprehensive source of creditor-reported statistics on external debt. These data are published annually and are generally available only with a lag. OECD 1984 statistics showed China's external debt at \$12.4 billion with bank borrowing of \$5.2 billion, other commercial borrowing at \$5.2 billion, and official lending of approximately \$1.9 billion; 1985 figures are not yet available.

The Bank for International Settlement (BIS) reporting system is also based on creditor-reported quarterly data from banks in 25 reporting areas worldwide. As such, its reporting net is slightly smaller than that of OECD. End-1984 statistics for bank borrowing was \$4.2 billion, which, together with other estimates of commercial borrowing (of \$5.2 billion) and official lending, gives a total debt of \$11.3 billion.

Finally, the International Monetary Fund's International Banking Statistics (IBS) relies on creditor-reported statistics collected in 32 banking centers worldwide, and also integrates debtor-reported figures on interbank debt. As of 1984, it reported China's bank debt at \$5.0 billion, which, together with estimates of other commercial borrowing (nonbank borrowing) of \$5.2 billion and official lending, gives a total debt of \$12.2 billion.

The World Bank's reporting system is a debtor-based reporting system; its figures are collected from member countries. Coverage includes public and publicly guaranteed debt. Where reporting countries' debt monitoring is weak, the Bank's figures may differ substantially from those in the creditor-reporting system. Short-term debt is not always reflected in the Bank's system, and debt of nonpublic borrowers (private-sector debt) is not always included in the statistics.

Borrowing In a Risky Environment

5.16 The external environment has become more difficult in recent years. Unprecedented changes in exchange and interest rates have affected the terms of developing country borrowing. Developing countries borrowing at variable rates in the 1970s, when interest rates were low or negative in real terms, found by 1981 that their interest costs had as much as tripled as the result of higher interest rates in major industrial countries. Currency fluctuations associated with this interest rate volatility further increased the effective costs of borrowing. Finally, fluctuations in commodity prices and lower economic growth in industrial countries affected developing country exports. This heightened risk must be integrated into borrowing strategy.

5.17 A second change in the external environment is that the terms on which resources are available to developing countries have become harder. The availability of concessional resources has declined, and blend of resources has become harder. In addition, the average terms on commercial borrowing are harder, as interest rates are again positive in real terms. The "grant element" embodied in resource flows to developing countries has fallen from 32% in 1970 to 7% in 1985 (see Box 5.2). Together, these imply a higher average cost of borrowing and the heightened need, therefore, to ensure that the funds are productively deployed.

5.18 The third major change has been that since the late 1970s, a major part of developing country borrowing has financed adjustment rather than only investment. When countries' incomes were reduced by terms of trade changes, many borrowed to smooth consumption levels along the adjustment path. What was difficult to predict was the prolonged and perhaps permanent change in the international environment, and the fact that the world economy would not soon return to its earlier configuration of prices and interest rates. As a result, countries which borrowed in anticipation of such a return to "normalcy", and which expected to repay their borrowing with the proceeds of higher export earnings, were unable to do so.

Box 5.2: GRANT ELEMENT

The "grant element" of a loan seeks to measure the concessionality of aid funds extended at a given set of terms as compared to grant terms. The benefit of a loan is a product of five factors, i.e., a loan's interest rate, maturity, grace period, volume, and the relevant discount rate. The concept of grant element attempts to compare different loan terms by discounting interest and amortization payments at a common interest rate, usually 10%, and expressing the discounted present value of the loan payments as a proportion of the face value of the loan.

The grant element of a loan is greater the longer its maturity and grace period and the lower its interest rate. For example, the grant element of IDA funds--the concessional lending arm of the World Bank--is about 77%, while the grant element of IBRD funds, calculated in this way, would be 22%. A concessional loan is defined as having a grant element of 25% or more. By this definition, IDA loans are concessional.

The grant element of loans to developing countries has fallen in the past decade, a result of the changing composition of LDC debt, the harsher terms on which even official development assistance resources are available, and the declining availability of such resources. Resources were available to LDCs with an average grant element of 32% in 1970; this had fallen to only 7.4% by 1985.

Changing Grant Element Over Time
(%)

1970	1975	1980	1985
31.9	21.0	8.6	7.4

Source: World Bank, World Debt Tables.

Microeconomic Aspects of External Debt Management

5.19 These factors make the choice of a strategy of growth, trade and borrowing a more complex affair than in the past. The external environment makes it difficult to make predictions about exports, interest rates or exchange rates. Thus, while the overall volume of borrowing and its use in the economy continue to be very important, the more micro-oriented aspects of foreign borrowing, such as managing risk and uncertainty are also crucial. Taking into account the uncertainty in the economic environment requires managing (i) the composition of debt; (ii) the maturity structure of debt; (iii) the vulnerability of the debt structure to interest rate changes; and (iv) the currency composition of borrowings.

Borrowing Sources

5.20 Managing the source of borrowing is now one of the most important aspects of a sound borrowing strategy. Until recently, developing countries were limited to borrowing from official and concessional sources and had only limited access to commercial bank lending or bond markets. This has changed since the 1970s, as access to commercial funds and capital markets grew. Most countries attempt to tap the largest possible volume of concessional resources; other official resources may not be explicitly concessional, but if their grant element is positive, their terms and conditions will be better than those available in commercial markets.[4/] Most countries also make some use of commercial borrowings for projects not eligible or attractive to official financiers, and because of the flexibility that commercial funds offer: i.e., their rapid disbursement, quick availability and fungibility of use.

Maturity Structure of Debt

5.21 The maturity structure is an important variable in present-day debt management. Until the mid-1970s, trade credit from suppliers was generally the only short-term borrowing available, and its volume was limited. This has now changed, and the management of the maturity structure is an important consideration for all countries. Since short-term debt must be rolled over at frequent intervals, it exposes the borrower to liquidity risk, the risk that when the debt matures the borrower will not be able to obtain new funds. Liquidity risk exists even for the strongest borrowers, who under normal conditions have steady access to the markets, and even borrowers such as the World Bank are very mindful of liquidity risk. Lenders' views about developing countries as a whole, or countries in a particular region, can be affected by problems in only a particular country in the group--a phenomenon known as "contagion."

4/ There are exceptions to this, especially when bilateral sources are "tied" to imports from the country providing the credit. If the goods being financed are overpriced, the borrowing country does not gain much by the lower interest rates. Careful evaluation of the effective cost of the borrowing is thus crucial.

5.22 A balanced maturity structure means that the volume of short-term debt and maturing long-term debt is such that "bunching" of repayments is avoided. This ensures that a country can service its debt smoothly. Many countries also try to maintain reserves to cover a certain proportion of their short-term debt, so that, in the event of a liquidity problem, the country is able to meet its debt obligations and still be able to import goods. Finally, a balanced maturity structure, with a modest level of short-term debt, helps reduce interest rate risk by reducing the proportion of total debt that is subject to repricing in a given period.[5/] In LDCs which had to reschedule their debt, the level of short-term debt was much higher (equivalent to more than five months' imports) than in nonrescheduling countries (where it was equivalent to less than two and one-half months' imports).

5.23 Table 5.3 shows two indicators of the maturity structure of borrowing for selected countries. The first is the volume of short-term debt in relation to total debt, a reflection of possible "bunching" problems. The second is its magnitude in relation to imports. If a country chooses to finance all imports using trade credit, (and assuming the maturity of such credits averages three months) at any one time the country's short-term debt outstanding will be equal to about three months' worth of imports. If some imports are financed with concessional or other funds, then short-term debt equal to three to four months of the trade-financed imports would be expected.

Table 5.3: MATURITY STRUCTURE OF DEBT, 1984 /a

	Short-term debt (%)	Short-term debt/months' imports
Argentina	30.9	13.2
Brazil	18.2	7.6
India	9.4	1.7
Korea	42.9	6.9
China	51.1	2.9

/a As percent of total debt outstanding excluding IMF credit.

Sources: Debt: OECD 1985 Survey; Imports: World Debt Tables, 1985/86.

5/ As countries increasingly borrow at variable rates, with rates on long-term borrowing also adjusted at six-monthly or other intervals, it is no longer sufficient to control only short-term debt.

Interest-rate Sensitivity of Debt

5.24 Interest rate risk is the risk that the interest costs on a country's debt will rise above the levels originally contracted, possibly to a level which makes continued debt servicing impossible. Vulnerability to interest rate risk depends on the overall volume of short-term debt and the proportion of long-term debt which is at variable rates. Minimizing interest rate vulnerability implies maximizing the proportion of total borrowings at fixed rates. Managing it requires ongoing evaluation of the debt service stream under a range of different assumptions about interest rates. In "normal" times, interest rates on short-term loans have usually been lower than long-term fixed interest rates. Thus, there is a trade-off between interest costs and interest rate risk (see Box 5.3).

5.25 However, in the past decade it has not been cheaper to borrow at floating rates than at fixed rates. As interest rates on developing countries' floating-rate liabilities rose to almost 20%, fixed rates would have been the better alternative. Predicting the future, however, is always difficult. In making a borrowing decision, countries need to look at the rates likely to apply to a floating-rate borrowing over time and to compare these with a fixed-rate borrowing. Since locking in high fixed rates can also be costly (e.g. in the recent falling interest rate environment), countries may also explore ways to avoid this risk. For example, fixed-rate bonds can be issued with "call" provisions, enabling the borrower to buy in or "call" the bond before maturity, and bank loans can be contracted with "prepayment rights," enabling the borrower to pay off the loan before its term. Such options have a price and add to the interest cost of borrowing, and a borrower would need to evaluate this higher cost against the potential cost savings from prepayment.

Managing Currency Risk

5.26 Currency risk arises from exchange rate variability and refers to the possibility that the cost of debt service, vis-a-vis the local currency or an alternative currency, rises unexpectedly. In the past, developing countries had access only to a few currencies, primarily the US dollar. As a result, many countries have been affected by the rapid and large movements in currency fluctuations in recent years. Because LDC borrowing was concentrated in US dollars, the effective cost of LDC borrowing increased dramatically during 1982-85, when the US dollar appreciated substantially and unexpectedly against other currencies. It has declined more recently, with the rapid depreciation of the US dollar. (The effective cost of loans denominated in Japanese yen have, of course, moved in the opposite direction.)

5.27 Managing currency risk is a complex process. Essentially there are three strategies available: one is a simple diversification of borrowing sources, perhaps the most straightforward approach; a second strategy is to seek to minimize the absolute cost of debt service by choosing currencies with the lowest absolute interest cost; a third is to minimize the variability of debt service by choosing currencies whose value is related to domestic variables. A diversification strategy essentially relies on the probability that, over the long run, speculation on relative currency values is usually

Box 5.3: BREAK-EVEN REFINANCING RATE FOR SHORT-TERM BORROWING

Many countries are faced with the choice of borrowing either short term or long term. As short-term debt must be rolled over at frequent intervals, it exposes the borrowing country to interest rate risk--the risk that when the loan comes due, the interest rate on the refinancing will be higher than on the maturing funds. Although in a typical financial environment, short-term rates are below long-term rates (the yield curve is "positively" sloped), the ultimate cost of a series of short-term borrowings may be higher than the cost of a longer-term borrowing which carries a higher initial interest rate. For short-term borrowing to be less expensive than long-term, the borrower must be able to refinance successive short-term loans at rates such that the total cost over full the life of the borrowing is less than or equal to the cost of longer-term funds.

The "break-even refinancing interest rate" is the maximum interest rate(s) at which a series of short-term borrowings can be rolled over, while not exceeding (over the life of the longer-term funds) the interest cost of a fixed-rate borrowing. For example, if a country has the choice of borrowing two-year funds at 10%, or borrowing short-term funds for one year at 9%, and then refinancing for the second year, the break-even refinancing rate can be calculated to be 11.1%.[1] At any refinancing rate higher than this, it would be cheaper to borrow the longer-term funds costing 10%. The following table shows how this break-even refinancing concept plays itself out over the longer run.

Year	Scenario I	Scenario II	Scenario III
1	7.5	7.5	7.5
2	8.0	8	8.0
3	8.0	9	8.0
4	8.0	10	6.0
5	9.0	11	6.0
Floating rate cost	8.0	9.0	7.16
Cost (Saving) over 8% fixed rate	0	1% Cost	0.84% Saving

In Scenario I, interest rates rise slowly 10.9%, but over the 5-year period, the borrower breaks even with the cost of a fixed rate borrowing. In Scenario II, although it is cheaper than a fixed rate borrowing at the outset, the rapid rise of interest rates wipe out any initial savings. In Scenario III, it would be cheaper to have borrowed at floating rates.

1/ $\$100 = \frac{\$9}{(1+r)} + \frac{11.1}{(1+r)^2} + \frac{\$100}{(1+r)^2}$ where r = 10%, the fixed two-year rate.

not profitable, and on the assumption that interest rate differentials tend, over time, to be offset by changes in currency values so that the effective borrowing cost of all currencies turns out to be roughly the same. Strategies which seek to minimize the cost of borrowing would mean borrowing the currency which is expected to be least costly, based on predictions of interest rates and exchange rates. This would be a "speculative" strategy, and, to the extent that interest rate parity holds, it will be very difficult to gain over the long run. Finally, "hedging" strategies would involve minimizing the real cost of variability of debt service arising from currency fluctuations. One way to do this would be to borrow in a currency whose movement is related to changes in the price of the country's major export.

5.28 The cost to developing countries arising from the concentration of their borrowing portfolio serves to highlight the importance of focusing on the effective cost of borrowing and not simply on the nominal cost. The effective cost incorporates both the interest cost and the increase in the cost of borrowing due to appreciation of the borrowed currency (or reduction in the case of depreciation) and translates this into an annualized effective interest rate. One way to evaluate the likely effective cost of borrowing is to calculate the exchange rate implied by the interest rate differentials on two loans. For example, if the five-year Yen interest rate is 5%, while the dollar interest rate for a five-year maturity is 7%, interest parity would imply an appreciation of the Yen. The implied appreciation can be compared to the borrower's own judgment of exchange rate movements. Choosing which currency to borrow is thus a matter of judgment (See Box 5.4).

Managing the Borrowing Process

5.29 In order to manage the borrowing process in an orderly way and achieve the desired outcomes with respect to the volume and composition of debt along the lines just described, it is usually necessary to have a system of reporting and explicit controls managed by a governmental body. Of course, the most important management levers are fiscal, monetary and exchange rate policies that effectively control aggregate demand and the balance of payments. However, even where policy and price signals are appropriate, individual borrowing units will make their borrowing decisions on the basis of a financial analysis, but the full costs of borrowing--including the nonfinancial and social costs to the economy--may significantly exceed the financial costs to an individual borrower.

5.30 In the simplest case, a country's borrowing will be subject to creditor-imposed limits, and the cost of borrowing for all borrowers rises as additional amounts are borrowed by any one borrower, and as market saturation is approached. Since this cost is not paid by the borrower himself, it is not integrated into the individual borrower's financial calculus, and borrowing may take place which increases costs for others. Some countries have attempted to shift this cost back to the borrower by imposing a tax on interest payments.

5.31 Second, in many countries the distinctions between sovereign borrowings of the government and other borrowings for which the government is not formally responsible have been blurred by requirements that governments guarantee such debt. Clearly, if the government is to become liable for nonsovereign debt, it must be in a position to control it (see Box 5.5).

Box 5.4: EXCHANGE RATE VOLATILITY AND THE EFFECTIVE COST OF BORROWING

The effective, or exchange rate adjusted, cost of borrowing is often very different from the nominal, or interest cost of borrowing. Currency appreciation can double the effective cost of servicing debt, and what appeared to be a low interest rate may turn out to be a high one.

For example, take the case of the two 5-year borrowings described in the text: Yen (at 5%), and dollars (at 7%). Interest parity theory predicts an appreciation of the low-interest rate currency, the Yen. Specifically, it would suggest an annual appreciation of the Yen of 2% (7% less 5%) or a 10% appreciation of the Yen over five years. At an exchange rate of ¥ 150 = $1, the implied future appreciation would be 10% of 150, or 15. The implied future exchange rate is therefore ¥ 135=$1.

If the yen indeed appreciated to ¥ 135, all of the interest savings would be wiped out and the effective cost of the yen borrowing would be 7%--the same as for the dollar borrowing. If it appreciates beyond ¥ 135, the yen borrowing would be more costly than the dollar borrowing.

Formalizing this, the formula for the "break-even exchange rate" in its simplest form is:

Break-even yen exchange rate = $ER_{Y} - [(i\$ - iy) \times N \times ER_{y}]$ or

Today's yen rate - [interest rate differential (%) x # of years x today's yen rate].

Deciding which currency to borrow means a judgment as to whether the yen appreciation will be greater (or less than) implied by interest parity.

Box 5.5: SOVEREIGN vs NONSOVEREIGN DEBT

Sovereign external debt is traditionally defined as that debt in foreign currency owed by a government or its agents to nonresidents. Since the debt is that of the government, which is liable regardless of circumstance, commercial risk--the possibility that the project may fail and the borrower cannot pay--is not an issue. Nonsovereign debt is an external obligation of a nongovernmental borrower (a "private," as distinct from "public," debtor). In lending to private borrowers, the creditor has both the "commercial risk" of the project or borrower being unprofitable and the "transfer risk" that, even if the project goes well and generates profits in local currency, the government may not make foreign exchange available to repay the debt.

This distinction is becoming blurred in two ways. First, the line between government and a governmental unit which has borrowed in its own name is becoming a thin one. While the borrower may in fact be independent and have borrowed without recourse to a guarantee from the government, as a practical matter, the government may have to become involved, should any difficulty arise. The consequences of not doing so would be reluctance on the part of creditors to make new funds available to the country or to increase significantly the cost of new funds.

In yet another development, the role of the banking system has come under scrutiny. Increasingly, developing country banks, through their foreign branches, have become active in deposit taking. Because external debt is defined on a "residency" basis--that is, only debt owned by residents to nonresidents would be counted as external debt--such deposits have not traditionally been included in the definition of a country's debt. (For example, in the case of China, the BOC in London is not a resident of China.) Strictly speaking, of course, it would be incorrect to include them. However were there to be difficulties in any of these banks, the domestic bank headquarters would almost assuredly have to step in to make good on their obligations. Following this, if difficulties remained, the government authorities would be compelled to assist their bank. Thus, while such deposits are formally not a country's sovereign debt, the authorities will want to keep close watch over their volume and integrate such deposits into internal estimates of debt. And, in the case of a country such as China, since BOC is a national bank, such debt may also be included in "sovereign" debt.

Increasingly, governments are also being asked to look after true private-sector debt. Thus, the government may be pressured into making good on private-sector debts in order to protect its own borrowing capacity or access. This has happened even where the inability of the private borrower to repay was the result of strictly commercial lending misjudgments. In the case of Chile, for example, the government took over the liabilities of private sector borrowers, where it had no role in authorizing, approving, evaluating or sanctioning them in any way. The consequence of not doing so would have been to undermine an urgently needed agreement with creditors to reschedule debt.

5.32 Individual borrowers will presumably not borrow unless they are confident that they can repay. However, borrowers often incorporate some assumption about the future price of foreign exchange into their evaluation of the costs of a borrowing transaction. In many cases, these expectations have underestimated the actual extent of the local currency exchange rate depreciation. The result has been that borrowers were unable to meet the now increased local currency cost of their debt, and the government has been forced to step in.

5.33 Consequently, most countries, including many industrial countries, impose controls on foreign borrowing. These controls almost always cover the foreign borrowing by the government and its agencies. Some governments are also controlling the foreign borrowing of nonsovereign or private enterprises. In many countries, the banking system has become a major source of indebtedness through its interbank deposit-taking and borrowing activities abroad. These deposits are not sovereign debt (unless the bank in question is a government-owned bank) but are part of the country's overall indebtedness. Finally, the government's controls may attempt to cover short-term debt or cover only longer-term debt with maturities above one year.

5.34 The nature and actual mechanisms of control vary widely. The controls can be loose, requiring only prior registration by the borrower with the registration authority, or they can be very strict, with approval and scrutiny by the government of every borrowing. Such approval may extend to scrutiny of a borrowing's maturity, interest rate and currency. Mechanisms of control range from a system of authorization requirements to the use of taxes and surcharges on interest paid abroad to increase the effective cost of borrowing. Different approaches and their relevance to China are discussed in Section C below.

5.35 In general, the more decentralized the system of controls, the more important is a well-designed system of _ex post_ monitoring and reporting. The government may not feel that it needs to control each and every borrowing by individual (nonsovereign) borrowing units. However, it is crucial that the authorities have a sound information base about the indebtedness of the country as a whole and that they know the future cash-flow stream implied by the current stock of all foreign (sovereign and nonsovereign) liabilities of the country in order to manage the external sector. To the extent that the government opts for fewer controls over borrowing by nonsovereign units, the more important macroeconomic management becomes.

B. China's External Borrowing

Borrowing Trends

5.36 Limited borrowing was undertaken by China in the 1950s to build up its industrial base. Since 1980, China's debt has grown rapidly (Table 5.4). The total volume of debt in 1980, $5.4 billion, amounted to less than 1.9% of GDP. By 1984, the last year in which China experienced a balance-of-payments surplus and reserve accumulation, debt outstanding had risen to $13.0 billion or 4.5% of GDP. This changed considerably in 1985 and 1986. Based on the government's own estimates, total debt outstanding at end-1985

Table 5.4: OUTSTANDING EXTERNAL DEBT, 1980-86 /a
(in million of US dollars)

	1980	1981	1982	1983	1984	1985 Official estimate	1985 Creditor estimate
	Estimates						
Foreign governments /c	446	926	1,479	2,216	2,727	3,634	3,634
International institutions	-	47	97	568	593	1,185	1,185
Foreign banks:	3,754	2,620	1,870	4,489	4,520	8,130	9,589
Buyers' credits	(142)	(343)	(638)	(666)	(540)	(549)	(549)
Bank of China foreign branches	(3,612)	(2,277)	(1,232)	(1,290)	(1,382)	(2,680)	(2,680)
Loans	(..)	(..)	(..)	(...)	(286)	(4,879)	(4,879)
Foreign banks in China	(..)	(..)	(..)	(-)	(2)	(22)	(22)
Other	(-)	(-)	(-)	(2,533)	(2,310)/d	(...)	(1,459)/d,/e
Bond issues	-	-	40	60	62	1,000	1,000
Suppliers' credit and advanced export receipts /f	1,038	1,108	1,590	1,592	1,600	1,736	1,736
Other trade credits	-	-	-	687/g	2,039/g	...	2,100/g,/e
Leasing companies & parent companies of foreign enterprises	-	-	-	...	38	140	140
Other (including IMF)	195	1,085	982	-	508/h	...	500/h,/e
Total	5,433	5,785	6,058	9,608	12,085	15,825	19,884
Memorandum items							
Medium- and long-term debt	5,433	5,785	6,058	5,624/i	6,485/i	9,046	10,834
Short-term debt	-	-	43	3,984/i	5,600/i	6,419	9,007/j
of which: foreign banks	(-)	(-)	(-)	(2,057)/i	(2,600)/i	(3,737)	(6,407)/j
Total debt as percent of GDP	1.9	2.2	2.3	3.5	4.5	6.0	7.5
Short-term debt:							
as percent of total	-	-	6.6	41.5	46.3	...	45.4
as percent of reserves	-	-	-	24.9	31.5	...	68.2

/a Includes known medium- and long-term debt and short-term debt. Short-term nonbank trade credits that are not guaranteed by Export Credit Agencies are not included.

/b Consistent with balance of payments projections.

/c Includes some trade credits provided by Export Credit Agencies.

/d Equal to the difference between China's debt to foreign banks as identified in creditor data and its debt to foreign banks as identified in official (SAEC) statistics.

/e Estimated.

/f Suppliers' credits are referred to as "deferred payments" in official statistics.

/g Derived as the difference between official development assistance plus nonbank trade credit guaranteed by Export Credit Agencies in creditor statistics; and loans from foreign governments plus deferred payments in official statistics.

/h Equal to the difference between external debt based on creditor statistics and external debt based on official statistics.

/i Based on creditor statistics.

/j Based on creditor statistics; for trade creditor statistics, and official (SAEC) statistics for foreign bank debt.

Sources: State Administration of Exchange Control (SAEC); OECD Statistics on External Indebtedness, Paris 1985; BIS International Banking Statistics, First Quarter 1986, Basle, July 1986; and IMF estimates.

was $15.8 billion, or 5.7% of GDP. This figure appears to underestimate the actual debt volume, as it may not have captured the full balance of liabilities to leasing companies, borrowings by joint ventures, and the borrowing by Chinese-owned companies located overseas. Estimates, based on information derived from creditor sources, place China's external borrowings at $19.3 billion, or 7.0% of GDP, for 1985. With the 1986 current account deficit of some $7.4 billion being financed primarily by foreign borrowing of $5.6 billion, China's debt rose to a level of $24.9 billion by end-1986, equivalent to some 9.2% of GDP.

5.37 Maturity Structure. In 1985, the maturity structure of China's borrowing became less favorable than in the past. Medium- and long-term debt outstanding at end-1985 was estimated by the authorities to be $9.4 billion out of a total of $15.8 billion, or 60% of the total. Short-term debt was $6.4 billion or about 40% of the total. Creditor estimates suggest it may have been slightly higher, some $10.4 billion, or about 54% of a larger total of $19.3 billion. One implication of China's large short-term debt is that its future gross borrowing requirement will be very large. Over and above any net new borrowings required (plus the refinancing of maturing long-term loans), a significant share of China's market access will be taken up simply to roll over short-term debt. However, the Chinese authorities made efforts to improve this structure in 1986, replacing short-term with medium-term debts. By end-1986, it is estimated that short-term debt had fallen to $5.4 billion, or only 21.7% of the total.

5.38 Borrowing Units. There are three major groups of borrowers: (a) official borrowing windows for the government; (b) financial institutions with some government sponsorship; and (c) "independent" borrowing units, such as joint ventures and Chinese enterprises. Each is responsible for handling all borrowing from a specific source of funds and for undertaking the appropriate borrowing program:

5.39 Official Windows. There are five official government borrowing windows, each with authority and responsibility for a subportion of China's overall borrowing program:

(a) MOFERT is responsible for all concessional and other bilateral borrowings from aid agencies, and loans, frame agreements and/or guarantees from export credit agencies. MOFERT is also generally responsible for arranging trade credit to the FTCs under its jurisdiction, including nonguaranteed suppliers credits to such FTCs;

(b) the Ministry of Finance is the agency responsible for all borrowings from the World Bank among multilateral institutions;

(c) the People's Bank is responsible for borrowings from the Asian Development Bank, which China recently joined, and is responsible for borrowings from the IMF. PBC is also responsible for authorizing the borrowing of those individual borrowing units under its jurisdiction which have recently been granted foreign borrowing rights, and it also borrows from foreign governments;

(d) the Ministry of Agriculture is responsible for all borrowings from UNDP/IFAD; and

(e) The Bank of China is responsible for undertaking commercial borrowing on behalf of the Government of China. In addition, BOC may undertake certain borrowings for its own operations. Finally, the BOC is the administrator of the "energy loans" received from Japan.

China's borrowing through each of these windows is generally thought to represent sovereign debt, inasmuch as the borrowing is that of the government itself.

5.40 By far the most important of these official borrowers has been the Bank of China (Table 5.5). It taps a number of market sources, including the bilateral financing it arranges on behalf of borrowers in China, borrowing from commercial banks, and deposit-taking activities in financial markets abroad. Bilateral financing agreements account for about 20% of BOC's total borrowing, commercial borrowing for 40%, and deposit-taking for 28%. Bond issues make up less than 6% of its overall borrowing due to limited market access. In addition, the Bank of China's branches abroad take deposits in the Euromarkets and other interbank markets. Such deposit-taking by overseas branches, which amounted to $6.3 billion at end-1985, is not included in official debt statistics. The central government (through the Ministry of Finance, MOFERT and MAAF) is China's next-largest official borrower. The Central Government receives most of its funds from official sources. The government undertakes virtually no commercial borrowings nor has it independently tapped bond markets.

5.41 The process of borrowing has become substantially decentralized since China's opening to the commercial markets since 1980. At present, there are, in addition to the ministerial units and government agencies outlined above, eight other entities authorized to borrow abroad independently in their own name. These are three national-level financial institutions (Bank of Communications, CITIC, and China Investment Bank); two provinces (Fujian and Guangdong) and three municipalities (Shanghai, Tianjin, Dalian). The borrowing windows in the latter cases are the financial institutions owned and operated by these government units, mostly provincial international trust and investment companies (ITICs). The ITICs now account for almost $1 billion, or some 6%, of China's total debt.

5.42 In addition to the five ITICs affiliated with provinces having the authority to borrow abroad, Chinese authorities are experimenting on an ad hoc basis with authorizing foreign borrowing by other ITICs which do not have "general rights" to borrow abroad. Ad hoc, one-time authorizations to contact foreign banks have been granted to a number of such ITICs, with a view to testing their market access and increasing the potential number of borrowers. The actual amounts involved have been very small, however, some $5-10 million per ITIC, and the total number of institutions also small. Provincial governments have undertaken little borrowing on their own and account for less than 0.2% of China's total debt, all of it borrowed from commercial banks.

Table 5.5: SUMMARY EXTENAL DEBT, 1985
(US$'000)

Financing sources: / Borrowing units	Total	International financial institutions: Bilateral	International financial institutions: Multilateral	Foreign banks and other financial institutions	Buyers' credit	Foreign banks in China	Bond issues	Deferred payment and borrowing from exporters	Private deposits from overseas in BOC-HQ	International financial leasing	Foreign enterprises (parent companies)
Central government	3,989,368.2	1,717,188.3	867,440.0	67,399.3	-	-	-	1,337,340.0	-	-	-
Provincial governments	31,733.3	-	-	31,733.3	-	-	-	-	-	-	-
People's Bank	317,299.2	-	317,299.2	-	-	-	-	-	-	-	-
Other domestic financial institutions /b	934,867.6	-	-	440,105.0	1,962.5	9,190.0	458,481.0	-	10,249.4	6,879.1	-
Bank of China	9,457,766.8	1,917,200.1	-	3,781,040.0	547,710.7	-	541,800.0	-	2,670,010.0/a	-	-
Leasing companies	58,728.1	-	-	47,789.1	-	4,224.0	-	-	-	6,715.0	-
Joint-venture companies	296,210.9	-	-	212,127.8	-	4,043.2	-	48,629.3	-	22,558.1	16,852.5
Cooperative enterprises	116,450.5	-	-	57,036.3	-	256.0	-	7,058.3	-	597.7	51,502.2
Other domestic enterprises	625,683.4	-	-	233,943.9	-	4,427.4	-	351,351.0	-	6,574.4	29,386.7
Total	15,826,188.2	3,634,394.4	1,184,739.8	4,879,174.7	549,673.2	22,141.4	1,000,281.0	1,736,378.6	2,680,259.4	43,324.3	97,790.0
Memo Item											
Overseas branches of BOC	6,308,000.0	-	-	2,395,080.0	-	-	-	-	3,913,000.0	-	-

/a Deposits from Hong Kong and Macau.

/b CITIC, ITICs and BOC in Shenzhen.

Source: State Administration for Exchange Control, People's Bank of China.

5.43 Under certain circumstances, enterprises--Chinese enterprises and joint ventures--are also permitted to borrow directly abroad. Such borrowing usually takes two forms. The first is trade credit from banks and suppliers, which has been arranged outside the usual channels of MOFERT. The second is direct borrowing for project finance. Chinese domestic enterprises do most of their foreign exchange borrowing through the foreign-loan windows of the BOC. However, a small number do borrow abroad directly, and the volume of such borrowing accounts for about 4% of China's total reported external debt. There are two primary borrowing sources of such enterprises: commercial banks and suppliers. Most of their commercial bank borrowing would be guaranteed by BOC, while the suppliers credits would be guaranteed by an OECD export credit agency. Borrowing by Chinese-foreign joint ventures now accounts for just under 2% of China's external debt. Special regulations are in force which govern borrowing by joint ventures and are described in the following section. Joint ventures borrow almost exclusively from commercial banks, usually with a guarantee from the BOC or another Chinese guarantor.

The Planning Process for Borrowing

5.44 Currently, all foreign borrowing by China is classified either as "plan" or "nonplan" borrowing. Plan borrowing finances projects and activities at both the central and provincial level that are approved under five-year and annual Plans. Nonplan borrowing finances projects and activities outside of the five-year and annual Plans.

5.45 Borrowing within the Plan. Plan borrowing includes the following major borrowing units: the central government borrowing through MOF, MAAF, MOFERT and enterprises under control of MOFERT; borrowing by CITIC and other ITICs to finance plan projects; borrowing by BOC from foreign commercial banks to finance plan projects; and borrowing by provincial governments (either directly or through BOC) for large projects included in provincial governments' annual plans. Plan borrowing, in practice, covers all borrowing from international organizations and foreign governments, some suppliers' credits (including those guaranteed by export credit agencies in creditor countries), most syndicated loans from foreign commercial banks, and bond issues abroad by CITIC and other ITICs.

5.46 Borrowing outside the Plan. Borrowing outside the Plan includes borrowing by BOC for purposes other than projects included in the annual plan. In practice, such borrowing includes interbank borrowing by BOC, foreign-exchange deposits held in BOC headquarters and abroad, foreign exchange deposit taking by other financial institutions, short-term trade credits, borrowing by joint venture companies and 100% foreign-owned companies, borrowing by Chinese enterprises either directly or through foreign partners of joint venture companies, all borrowing at the provincial level to finance small projects, lease financing, and borrowing from offshore Chinese enterprises (mainly in Hong Kong).

5.47 The development of the borrowing plan takes place in a series of steps. First, PBC recommends to the State Council the maximum amount of external borrowing that should be undertaken for a specified future period. This role is consistent with its responsibilities as the Central Bank of

China, including its responsibility for overall balance-of-payments management.[6/] The breakdown between official and nonofficial sources is part of this recommendation and is based on medium-term balance-of-payments and debt service projections. Second, the State Council, on the basis of PBC's recommendation and in consultation with the State Planning Commission (and other relevant departments), approves the overall debt limit as well as its split between official and nonofficial sources. Within this limit, the Planning Commission develops a program for Plan borrowing, based on project proposals submitted to it by the project executing agencies such as MOF, MOFERT, their branches, foreign trade corporations, and provincial governments.

Debt Reporting

5.48 Prior to 1986, borrowing within the Plan was approved by the State Council on advice of SPC, but no central institution was specifically charged with the authority for reporting or controlling Plan foreign borrowing to ensure that it remained within approved limits. Individual borrowers kept records of disbursements, principal repayments, and interest payments. These data were reported to the SAEC, but only with a lag and for the purpose of compiling balance-of-payments statistics.

5.49 Borrowing outside the Plan, which was relatively unimportant until 1984, was not subject to direct central control, although special regulations affected some types of such borrowing. For example, joint-venture companies and 100% foreign-owned companies were permitted to borrow abroad without SPC or SAEC approval but were required to balance their foreign exchange receipts and payments. The foreign exchange balance requirement was intended to ensure that any debt service on foreign borrowing undertaken by these companies would not become a drain on official foreign exchange reserves. The procedures in place prior to April 1986 meant, therefore, that concessional and official financing was subject to central control, while much commercial financing was not.

5.50 Following the large increase in external debt in 1985, the Chinese authorities decided to subject all external borrowing to centralized reporting and control, so as to ensure that the total volume of debt and its composition did not result in future debt-servicing difficulties. As a first step, in April 1986, the State Council appointed the SAEC as the sole agency responsible for monitoring and controlling China's external borrowing. A number of steps have been taken since April 1986. Reporting channels were established for all borrowing units. Borrowing units are now required to report all transactions related to external borrowing.

6/ According to the Provisional Foreign Exchange Regulations issued in 1980-81 and still in force, the PBC has powers to: implement monetary policy; manage the monetary and securities markets; issue currency; control credit; supervise overseas borrowing; set rates of interest and foreign exchange rates; control foreign exchange; manage China's foreign reserves; control short-, medium-, and long-term foreign borrowing. The BOC manages China's foreign reserves on behalf of PBC.

5.51 Debt statistics reported to SAEC basically have the same coverage as data that previously was reported to SAEC for balance-of-payments statistical reporting purposes. However, the reporting is now required on a more timely basis. Moreover, it is intended that borrowing units should provide SAEC with disaggregated information (i.e., foreign loan contracts and related documents) to permit the SAEC to calculate and project debt service directly. This should facilitate greater accuracy in data collection and projections. At the branch level, moreover, the debt reporting system now covers a number of borrowing units which previously did not report their external borrowing for balance-of-payments statistical purposes, which did not report it as external debt, or which reported data that was not comprehensive.

Authorization Procedures

5.52 The actual contracting and disbursement of Plan loans is, in principle, subject to scrutiny on a loan-by-loan basis. Even where borrowing has been "approved" by the State Council, all borrowing operations are subject to prior approval by SAEC. Exceptions are made only for BOC and CITIC, which may borrow up to specified limits without obtaining prior approval, but with all borrowing to be reported, ex post. Their bond issues abroad, however, continue to be subject to prior approval by SAEC. For the other ITICs and provincial governments, each individual loan within the quota must be preauthorized by the SAEC on a case-by-case basis. SAEC reserves the right to scrutinize financial aspects of the transaction. Finally, in addition to these controls, the People's Bank has placed limits on the net foreign liabilities of the BOC and other financial institutions. In using any foreign borrowing authority delegated to them by SAEC, these institutions must also ensure that these limits are met.

5.53 For borrowing outside the Plan, procedures are somewhat different. Under certain circumstances, Chinese enterprises may borrow directly. To do so, the borrowing entity must submit a request to SAEC for the borrowing, accompanied by approval documentation from its supervising ministry or bureau and documentation from the local planning authorities. Such documentation is to include the terms of the borrowing, including a schedule of drawdowns and repayments. In addition, if a guarantee of the BOC is required by foreign bank lenders, this letter of guarantee must also be submitted to SAEC. SAEC reviews these filings and the terms of the proposed borrowing. Where the foreign bank lender does not require a guarantee of a major Chinese guarantor (BOC, CITIC, CIB), enforcement of these authorization requirements is difficult. To the extent that suppliers or banks are willing to lend without the comfort of a guarantee, it is possible that substantial unauthorized borrowing may take place and is not reported.

5.54 Joint ventures have general authorization to borrow as required to support their production activities. MOFERT, as the supervisory body for all aspects relating to foreign investment, is responsible for monitoring such borrowing activity and reporting it to SAEC, but no approval is required for the actual borrowing. Thus, statistics on joint-venture borrowing reflect their activity only with a lag and may also reflect only partial information. Hitherto, substantial borrowing by joint ventures has not been reported.

5.55 Enterprises based in Hong Kong have been established by a number of Chinese provinces to undertake agency and representation services on behalf of the province. Until recently, the approval for the establishment of such enterprises was obtained from the local provincial FERT. Since mid-1986, the approval of MOFERT itself is required. The business license of these representation agencies is issued by Hong Kong, and the enterprises, though wholly Chinese-owned, are incorporated in Hong Kong. Such representative agencies are permitted under their articles of incorporation to borrow and lend, and their borrowing activity is typically on behalf of the province which has established them, with the proceeds of foreign borrowings onlent to domestic Chinese enterprises located within the province. In other cases, the agency may lend to a joint venture in the province or to the provincial ITIC, which would onlend to enterprises in the province.

5.56 These Hong Kong windows have not in the past been closely controlled, because they represent a very new vehicle for the use of foreign funds, and because the borrowing of such representative agencies in itself is not borrowing by Chinese residents. Such borrowing, moreover, would not be classified as China's debt, defined on the standard residency basis. However, such entities have the financial support of their provincial backers, and provincial authorities have been known to assist these agencies in meeting obligations. To the extent that this does occur, the borrowing of these agencies does represent a potential cash drain on China and should therefore be included in reporting and any estimates of overall liabilities and projections of interest service.

Guarantees, Potential Liabilities and Other Obligations

5.57 In addition to direct borrowing undertaken to finance projects, China has indirect or potential liabilities, which have arisen out of its growing participation in international markets. These are, firstly, guarantees, or "contingent liabilities," now issued by a wide variety of Chinese institutions; secondly, loans by a variety of nongovernment borrowers, which appear to have sovereign characteristics, and which could become China's sovereign obligation; and lastly, obligations under leases and other contractual arrangements. The most important of these are probably guarantees.

Guarantees

5.58 The most important guarantor has always been the Bank of China, which has provided guarantees for a variety of Chinese borrowers including provinces, Chinese enterprises, joint venture and foreign enterprises. In addition, provincial governments are also important guarantors of the borrowings of enterprises in their jurisdiction. The foreign exchange guarantees of provincial authorities are issued by the provincial planning commission,[7/] which is the body responsible for allocating the sources and uses of foreign exchange in the province. Finally, guarantees are also issued by Chinese financial institutions such as the ITICs. Foreign banks in China also issue guarantees, mostly on behalf of joint ventures. Guarantees of foreign banks are not contingent obligations of China.

5.59 Foreign lenders to China have a strong preference for lending backed by a guarantee. Among the reasons cited is the absence of a "mortgage law" defining property rights and title to collateral, which would give lenders some rights in the event of default. Essentially, banks see a guarantee as a substitute for access to collateral, and a more effective mortgage law would significantly reduce the burden on major guarantors (and on China) of incurring unnecessary obligations in support of what is essentially not sovereign debt. Foreign banks prefer the strongest possible guarantor, usually seen to be the Bank of China. CITIC and certain other financial institutions may also be acceptable. For certain types of transaction, guarantees of some provincial governments' planning commissions may also be acceptable, as are the guarantees of an ITIC of the province.

5.60 As a result of these foreign banks' lending requirements, there has also been a demand by Chinese borrowers for a more decentralized guarantee authority, so that access to foreign funding can be available to a wider range of Chinese borrowers. A decentralized authority was also seen as helping to broaden the role of the ITICs in channeling foreign capital. As a result of these considerations, in 1984, guarantee authority was given to China's national investment banks, most ITIC's, and foreign bank branches. This was further broadened in 1985 to include other financial institutions and some Chinese banks. At present, some 68 financial institutions, in addition to provinces and the central government, can issue guarantees.

5.61 One consequence of this decentralization of authority has been increased guarantee activity and a lack of control over the growth of contingent liabilities outstanding. As a part of the planning process for debt management, measures were developed to improve the regulation of guarantees which support foreign borrowing. SAEC has now formalized criteria for determining the eligibility of institutions to provide guarantees for foreign currency borrowing. This process gave rise to the approval of the 68 financial institutions mentioned. SAEC has indicated that these entities have been scrutinized for their ability to honor commitments, and that limits have been placed on the total volume of guarantees outstanding. These limits, promulgated in February 1987, have been set in relation to an entity's own foreign exchange holdings (for non-financial enterprises) and for financial enterprises, so that loans and guarantees together do not exceed 20 times an entity's foreign exchange.

7/ Guarantees of local currency borrowings are guaranteed by the provincial bureau of finance.

5.62 The total volume of guarantees issued by these entities is not known, but there are indications that it is large in absolute terms, in relation to the resources of the guarantors, and in relation to other demands on the guarantors' foreign exchange. Thus, it is not clear that the guarantee truly insures foreign exchange availability. The guarantee does, however, appear to provide assurances that the obligations under the guarantee has been registered with the foreign exchange plan at either the central or local level of government. Finally, the borrowing underlying the guarantee must be approved by SAEC under the procedures established in April 1986 for borrowing by Chinese enterprises. A guarantee from a Chinese financial institution thus indicates that the institution has access to foreign exchange and is a viable institution and signifies the belief of SAEC and the Planning Commission that the guarantor is capable, and that its cash flow should be sufficient to pay off the borrowers' obligation if need be.

Potential Liabilities: The Sovereign/Nonsovereign Debt Issue

5.63 China's increasingly decentralized approach to foreign borrowing, and the independent accessing of markets by individual enterprises, has led the authorities to begin to emphasize the distinction between debt that is official, or sovereign debt, and debt that is owed by Chinese borrowers, who borrow on the strength of their own name. China's sovereign debt, in its narrowest definition, includes the borrowing of official central government agencies (MOF, MOFERT, MAAF) and the People's Bank and the Bank of China.

5.64 However, a broader definition, and one which would have more practical significance, would include a variety of other borrowers. The near sovereign nature of the borrowing of Chinese financial institutions is clear, and, in the view of most creditors, it is almost certainly perceived as sovereign borrowing. The three "national-level" financial institutions (Bank of Communications, CIB, CITIC), which are permitted to borrow "in their own name," do so with the explicit support of the Chinese government. CITIC, for example, is described as being an entity "directly under the sponsorship of the State Council," and CIB is described as being "under the sponsorship of the State Council." The provincial ITICs have no such explicit central government support. However, as entities wholly owned by provincial governments in a unitary governmental system, the implicit nature of the support--and the likelihood that ITICs' borrowings represent government liabilities--is evident. The debt of Chinese enterprises that borrow directly is also potentially sovereign debt. As described earlier, the bulk of their borrowing is undertaken in the form of suppliers' credits, and foreign suppliers providing such credits typically require a guarantee from the Bank of China.

5.65 Most of these institutions' credibility, whether as borrowers or as guarantors, derives from their association with the government. Thus, as a practical matter, the government could be required to address the problem and to meet their obligations, if the foreign party could not reach agreement with the guarantor at the local level, in order to protect its own credit standing. While this might not always result in the authorities making good on ITICs or provincial guarantees, in practice, the pressure on them to do so will be heavy, especially if the foreign lender is important to China.

Other Obligations: Compensation Trade, Leasing, etc.

5.66 China has made substantial efforts to attract foreign direct investment in recent years under the guidance of MOFERT, the government agency responsible for all aspects of direct investment. MOFERT licenses direct investment in a number of different forms. These are (a) equity joint venture; (b) cooperative joint ventures; (c) compensation trade; (d) processing ventures; (e) leasing; and (f) exploration ventures. As outlined in Annex 4, not all of these represent equity inflows in the traditional sense. Of the six types of direct investment, four of them--compensation trade, contractual ventures, processing and assembly, and leasing--are more akin to debt than to equity. Conceptually, these types of foreign direct investment represent claims on export earnings much in the way debt service does.

5.67 A number of important points are worth emphasizing in regard to these financing arrangements. The first is that, under present arrangements, they enable an enterprise to bypass standard banking channels in obtaining financing. As such, they also bypass the standard reporting and authorization channels for debt, since direct investment is monitored by MOFERT. Secondly, most of these arrangements are substantially like borrowing, in that a contractual future stream of payments has been agreed. These payments may be in cash (lease payments) or in kind (compensation trade). The cash payments under a lease are no different from cash interest payments on debt; in-kind payments are a pledge of exports and therefore reduce the country's import and debt-service capacity. Finally, the nature of the arrangements suggests that they may be a fairly expensive way of borrowing. The foreign partner may increase the price of the machinery, offer machinery that is difficult to price, or lower the price of exported goods in repayment in a way that is difficult to verify.

China's Approach to the Capital Markets: A Summary

5.68 China's borrowing decisions have become decentralized. One consequence of decentralization has been some difficulty in controlling borrowers' access to markets and limiting the overall amounts borrowed. The Chinese authorities have already recognized the need to control total borrowing, and once the total has been determined, the need to allocate this overall ceiling among the entities permitted to borrow. A second result of the decentralization has been that decisions as to when, where and what to borrow have been generally uncoordinated. Thus, China's outstanding liability portfolio is to some extent the result of the aggregation of individual borrowers' choices, and its composition does not reflect a borrowing strategy. Finally, the decentralization has led to certain inefficiencies in borrowing. As Table 5.6 shows, there are substantial pricing distinctions among the different borrowing units. Such pricing distinctions are, in theory, unjustified since, for all practical purposes, all such borrowings effectively represent the sovereign obligation of China.

Table 5.6: DIVERSITY OF BORROWING SPREADS ON FLOATING RATE BORROWINGS SELECTED CHINESE BORROWERS, 1986

Borrower	Date signed	Maturity (years)	Spread
BOC	04/86	5	0.1875
BOC	04/86	10	0.3125
Shanghai Hotel	01/86	10	0.625
Jinghua Building	06/86	10	0.625
Guilin Hotel	08/86	8	0.875
Hopewell Power China Ltd.	04/86	10	1.375
Indar Travel Service	03/86	10	0.625
Lum Chang Guangzhou	07/86	6	0.875

Source: World Bank, Debtor Reporting System.

5.69 The financial costs of this uncoordinated approach are high, perhaps as much as 0.5% p.a., or $50 million per year (0.5% on an estimated $10 billion of debt owed by "nonsovereign"/second-tier borrowers). This should be compared with the potential benefits of a decentralized approach, such as contact with markets, increased borrower sophistication, or improved production efficiency through more rapid access to foreign funds. These benefits, of course, could also be obtained by a more decentralized and competitive foreign exchange lending system; all borrowers need not have access directly to foreign markets.

C. Issues and Options

5.70 Although China's external debt and debt service are still relatively small in relation to a number of other developing countries, they have risen rapidly in recent years, and the composition of the debt is not optimal. A high proportion of China's debt has been contracted at variable interest rates, making it vulnerable to sharp changes in world interest rates. There is thus a need to control not only the overall volume of debt but also to improve its structure to ensure that foreign borrowing does not result in future debt servicing problems. While this report is not intended to specify the exact limits on the level of external borrowing that would be sustainable, the medium-term balance of payments scenarios in Chapter III of the Main Report illustrate the need to limit foreign borrowing to achieve a viable medium-term balance of payments.

5.71 In addition, the particular issues of concern in China relate to the number and types of institutions permitted to borrow abroad and to guarantee foreign borrowing by other borrowing units. The implications of this proliferation of institutions for China's borrowing costs and risks, for the growth of contingent liabilities, and for the blurring of the distinction between "sovereign" and "nonsovereign" debt are also major issues of debt management which China will have to address.

5.72 External debt management for China consists of essentially five aspects:

(a) determining the permissible volume of foreign borrowing in the immediate period ahead and the next several years, in order to ensure that the country is protected from external economic shocks and does not encounter debt servicing difficulties;

(b) determining the appropriate type of borrowing (in terms of maturity structure, currency, interest rate characteristics) and the appropriate approach to the markets;

(c) ensuring that limits on external borrowing are met through appropriate approval procedures and close monitoring of external debt to ensure that external debt policy is implemented as intended. (An essential prerequisite for the formulation of an appropriate external borrowing strategy is the availability of accurate data on outstanding debt and debt service payments);

(d) controlling contingent liabilities and debt-like flows; and

(e) clarifying the ultimate responsibility for borrowing by "nonsovereign" borrowers.

Planning the Volume of Foreign Borrowing

5.73 The fundamental objective of debt management is to ensure that debt obligations can be fully serviced in the future without creating undue pressure on the balance of payments. In its broadest sense, it is related to macroeconomic management and the guidance of the balance of payments is through a changing external environment. More narrowly, it means setting limits on the aggregate amounts of external borrowing consistent with the medium-term BOP outlook. The formulation of such limitations cannot be based on indicators of external indebtedness at present, or external debt in the past. Rather, it is necessary to examine the future implications of alternative limits for the overall balance of payments. This means examining trends in debt service in relation to the level of reserves and in relation to export receipts, and examining the amount of gross borrowing relative to the availability of credit.[8/]

5.74 This examination should be performed in the context of a medium-term balance-of-payments analysis. This analysis involves making alternative

---

8/ This borrowing requirement is the sum of the current account deficit, principal repayments on medium- and long-term debt and outstanding short-term debt, less capital inflows from official creditors.

projections for five or more years into the future. Various assumptions about important variables such as the target rate of economic growth and domestic investment, export and import prices, the demand for China's exports in importing countries, exchange rates, and interest rates should be incorporated. Close attention should be paid to the ratio of current account deficit to GNP and the ratio of imports to GNP.

5.75 Each balance-of-payments projection should contain debt service payments, total amount of external debt, its maturity structure and the composition by creditors. This debt profile should be assessed in the light of the principles enumerated in Section A. In particular, close attention should be paid to the evolution of the following indicators over the next five-year period: (a) the ratio of outstanding debt to GNP; (b) the ratio of short-term debt to total debt; and (c) debt service ratio.

5.76 On the basis of the examination of various alternative projections and external borrowing strategies, one can identify a broad magnitude of foreign borrowing consistent with the objective of minimizing the risk of encountering payments difficulties. Once the limits on external borrowing are determined, macroeconomic policies should be adjusted, so that the balance of payments is kept consistent with such limitations.

Market Approach and Portfolio Composition

5.77 Having determined the overall level of borrowing and its composition in line with the above principles, borrowing must be planned to ensure that the cost of borrowing is minimized, and that interest rate risk, liquidity risk and exchange rate risks of borrowing are kept within reasonable limits. In the case of China, these objectives could met more easily if foreign borrowing were planned in a more integrated fashion than is currently the case.

5.78 Coordinated borrowing by all Chinese institutions is also recommended in order to improve China's approach to international markets. A coordinated approach is necessary to ensure that the currency composition and the maturity structure are consistent with the overall debt strategy and that overall cost of borrowing is not driven up by a bunching of borrowing, or by allowing institutions with lower credit standings to enter international markets. The extension of borrowing rights to other institutions in China's current circumstances would further complicate debt management without providing any obvious advantages and would in all likelihood increase the cost of borrowing. Indeed, the broad range of present borrowers has already implied substantial costs.

Controlling External Borrowing

5.79 Once the volume and approach to the market have been determined, ensuring that limits are adhered to and composition is met is essential. For this, approval and control procedures are required. In addition to the Bank of China, there are eight institutions which have prior right to borrow abroad, subject to SAEC approval. Some of these institutions have argued that they should be able to borrow without SAEC approval. In addition, a number of financial institutions that are not currently permitted to borrow abroad have argued that borrowing rights should be extended to them. It is recommended that SAEC approval continue to be required for all borrowing abroad by financial institutions and that borrowing rights are only very gradually extended to other institutions. It may be desirable to limit access to foreign markets by other borrowers and financial institutions, especially those that have a lower credit standing in international markets, to rationalize overall borrowing costs.

Debt Reporting

5.80 A fundamental prerequisite for managing debt is an accurate data base on debt outstanding and future debt service payments. The SAEC has greatly improved the coverage of China's external debt data base since it was given its new responsibilities in April 1986. Further improvements in a number of areas, however, would greatly enhance the ability of SAEC to control and monitor external debt. Despite the improved coverage of official statistics, there is still a gap between these data and those obtained from creditor sources. Steps must be taken to ensure that data obtained through the national debt survey is updated on a continuous basis. Data collected should meet the requirements of all users (including users responsible for reporting China's debt to the World Bank, IMF, and other creditors) and avoid duplication in data collection.[9/]

5.81 It is also necessary to collect timely data on contingent liabilities as well as the actual foreign liabilities of the Government of China (issues of controlling such liabilities are discussed below). Debt covered by these guarantees, if such guarantees are official guarantees, constitutes sovereign debt of China. It is therefore necessary to fully incorporate such contingent liabilities into external borrowing plans. The growth of contingent liabilities (implicit or explicit) could also be reduced by reducing the number of institutions permitted to provide guarantees.

5.82 Data should also be collected for debt-type flows such as compensation trade, leasing, contractual joint ventures, etc. Likewise, accurate reporting is required of the potential liabilities arising from the "quasi-sovereign" nature of deposit-taking by BOC's foreign branches, borrowing by Chinese-owned enterprises incorporated abroad, in particular enterprises based in Hong Kong that appear to have been established partly to circumvent foreign borrowing regulations.

Defining Sovereign Debt and Official Guarantees

5.83 There is substantial confusion over what is China's sovereign debt, and what rests on the creditworthiness of the borrower alone. Sovereign liabilities include, potentially, all borrowing and guarantees by Chinese borrowers and obligations of joint ventures and borrowing by overseas Chinese

---

9/ A number of technical suggestions in this area have been made to the government by the IMF and will not be discussed in this Annex.

enterprises. Creditors' behavior suggests that they consider the bulk of China's external debt to be sovereign. The Chinese authorities argue that this is not so, and that even the BOC borrowing on behalf of the government is only an organ of the state, not the state itself. As a practical matter, however, it appears that most debt in the event of difficulties, would come to be sovereign if China places a high premium on is future credit standing. Thus, BOC's borrowing must be considered sovereign debt; in addition, any borrowing by the other national-level financial institutions permitted to borrow abroad (CIB, CITIC) is also fairly clearly sovereign borrowing. The same is true of the debt of provinces, their ITICs, and all other national-level banks.

5.84 There is also a danger that borrowing by joint ventures or counter-trade practices could be construed as liabilities of China, and lead to an unplanned increase or an inappropriate composition of debt. It is therefore recommended that all such borrowing require prior registration with SAEC. Approval could be given on a fairly automatic basis, so as not to discourage investment by joint ventures; however, SAEC should have authority to investigate and delay for a specified time period any borrowing by joint ventures over a certain amount. At the same time, it should be clarified that joint venture debt is not sovereign debt.

5.85 The case of the Chinese trade and financial corporations incorporated in Hong Kong is somewhat more complex. However, it appears that the Government of China is likely to be ultimately responsible for such debt. To clarify and emphasize their nonsovereign nature, these corporations could be treated as foreign corporations, and the nonsovereign nature of their borrowing made clear, so that these are known not to be guaranteed implicitly--or explicitly by the government. Alternatively, if the government wishes to continue to offer implicit guarantees, such debt should be included in SAEC's debt program.

5.86 If the distinction between sovereign and nonsovereign debt remains fuzzy, the question of guarantees is even more so. It is not clear if the guarantees are sovereign guarantees and the debts guaranteed by all these institutions therefore are intended to constitute sovereign debt. In any case, these guarantees are probably construed by creditors as implicit government guarantees and thus associated borrowing is de facto sovereign debt. There is, therefore, an urgent need to clarify the distinction between sovereign and nonsovereign debt and to distinguish fully between sovereign debt and guarantees and nonsovereign debt and guarantees.